Power to the People

Power to the People

Constitutionalism in the Age of Populism

MARK TUSHNET AND BOJAN BUGARIČ

OXFORD
UNIVERSITY PRESS

OXFORD
UNIVERSITY PRESS

Oxford University Press is a department of the University of Oxford. It furthers the University's objective of excellence in research, scholarship, and education by publishing worldwide. Oxford is a registered trade mark of Oxford University Press in the UK and certain other countries.

Published in the United States of America by Oxford University Press
198 Madison Avenue, New York, NY 10016, United States of America.

Library of Congress Cataloging-in-Publication Data
Names: Tushnet, Mark V., 1945- author. | Bugarič, Bojan, author.
Title: Power to the people : Constitutionalism in the Age of Populism /
Mark Tushnet and Bojan Bugaric.
Description: New York : Oxford University Press, 2021. | Includes index.
Identifiers: LCCN 2021016751 | ISBN 9780197606711 (hardback) |
ISBN 9780197606735 (epub) | ISBN 9780197606728 (updf) |
ISBN 9780197606742 (digital-online)
Subjects: LCSH: Constitutional law—Political aspects. | Populism.
Classification: LCC K3171 . T89 2021 | DDC 342—dc23
LC record available at https://lccn.loc.gov/2021016751

DOI: 10.1093/oso/9780197606711.001.0001

Note to Readers
This publication is designed to provide accurate and authoritative information in regard to the subject matter covered. It is based upon sources believed to be accurate and reliable and is intended to be current as of the time it was written. It is sold with the understanding that the publisher is not engaged in rendering legal, accounting, or other professional services. If legal advice or other expert assistance is required, the services of a competent professional person should be sought. Also, to confirm that the information has not been affected or changed by recent developments, traditional legal research techniques should be used, including checking primary sources where appropriate.

(Based on the Declaration of Principles jointly adopted by a Committee of the American Bar Association and a Committee of Publishers and Associations.)

You may order this or any other Oxford University Press publication
by visiting the Oxford University Press website at www.oup.com.

Table of Contents

Note on Sources

The final stages of manuscript preparation occurred while we continued to be unable to retrieve physical copies of material that we have cited and quoted. We verified as many of the citations and quotations as possible through online resources, but more than a handful were inaccessible to us (and some online materials lacked pagination, making it impossible for us to verify the page numbers for quoted material). As a result, we are sure that some inaccuracies in citations and quotations remain, and we apologize to any readers who are unable to locate cited material because of those inaccuracies.

Introduction

Around the world we see self-described populist leaders dismantling their nation's constitutions. The names are familiar: Viktor Orbán, Narendra Modi, Hugo Chávez, Rafael Correa, Evo Morales, Jarosław Kaczyński. And then there are politicians who appear to be trying out for the role: Donald Trump, Boris Johnson. These men lie at different points on the traditional left/right spectrum. That has led to a widespread view that populism *as such* is inconsistent with constitutionalism.

This book examines that view closely, though in reasonably short form. To preview our conclusion: some versions of populism are of course inconsistent with some versions of constitutionalism. Once we examine various populisms, though, we find that the relation between populism tout court and constitutionalism is far more complex than the common view has it.

Another conclusion: populism comes in conservative and progressive variants. If you're a conservative, you're going to think that conservative populism sits easily with constitutionalism while progressive populism is anti-constitutional. And—with the politics reversed—the same goes for progressives: you're going to think that progressive populism actually promotes constitutionalism properly understood but conservative populism undermines constitutionalism. If you're a centrist, you're going to think that both kinds of populism are anti-constitutional because they each go too far, though in different directions.

Of course, sometimes conservative and progressive populists slide into authoritarianism. When they do, they are best described, in Douglas Johnson's phrase, as authoritarians masquerading as populists.[1] We think that people ought to talk about these political disagreements without dressing them in fancy conceptual arguments about populism "as such" and constitutionalism "as such."

To support these conclusions, we adopt several argumentative strategies. The most general description of our approach is "comparative and sociolegal." Legal analysis informed by constitutional and political theory (roughly, the domain of lawyers) directs us to look as carefully as we can at what constitutions say and

---

[1] Douglas A. Johnson, "In Defence of Democratic Populism," in HUMAN RIGHTS IN A TIME OF POPULISM: CHALLENGES AND RESPONSES (Gerald L. Neuman ed. 2020), at p. 192 (Johnson uses the phrase in the article's abstract).

Power to the People. Mark Tushnet and Bojan Bugarič, Oxford University Press. © Mark Tushnet and Bojan Bugarič 2021. DOI: 10.1093/oso/9780197606711.003.0001

how they are and can be interpreted. Analysis of the ways in which different constitutional structures provide incentives to political actors (again roughly, the domain of some political scientists) is also important. Those modes of analysis must be supplemented with equally careful attention to the historical and political contexts in which populisms rise and fall. Taken together, these ways of looking at populisms place our study where we believe comparative constitutional studies should be.[2]

We devote several chapters to identifying various candidates for definitions of the central terms "constitutionalism" and "populism." The candidates you choose, we argue, decisively affect your conclusions about the relation between them. In Chapter 1 we argue that the candidate for "constitutionalism" that best facilitates understanding is a thin one. We sometimes call this a least-common-denominator definition: its components are elements that nearly everyone committed to a normative idea of constitutionalism would agree on, and it doesn't include elements that some people sincerely committed to such an idea wouldn't think essential to the project of constitutionalism.

Chapter 2 turns to "populism." We explain that a definition that identifies necessary and sufficient conditions or the like isn't really available. Rather, we find themes in variants of populism, not all of which appear in every variant. And yet, every variant contains enough of these themes to make it at least coherent to try to understand what people generally describe as populism. After these definitional chapters, we relate thin constitutionalism to the themes we've identified in populism. To restate our conclusion: sometimes particular themes manifested in a variant of populism are inconsistent with one or another component of thin constitutionalism, and sometimes they aren't.

We regard ourselves as progressives and are sympathetic to many aspects of progressive populist programs. Those sympathies come out most directly in the concluding chapter, the title of which we've used in the book's title, on pro-constitutional populist reforms. Even so, we try to present conservative populist programs in a sympathetic light as well—while sometimes criticizing them on the merits rather than because they are populist.

Part Two provides two kinds of case studies. Several chapters examine how populism manifests itself in specific nations, while others focus on specific institutional aspects of populisms, such as how they treat the courts and how they exercise executive power. These chapters exhibit our strategy: we do our best to explain how a supporter of a specific variant of populism might fairly regard that variant as consistent with thin constitutionalism, and then ask how well those

---

[2] For the term "comparative constitutional studies," *see* Ran Hirschl, *From Comparative Constitutional Law to Comparative Constitutional Studies,* 11 INTERNATIONAL JOURNAL OF CONSTITUTIONAL LAW 1 (2013).

explanations hold up (some better than others, we argue). And, again to preview an important theme: sometimes populists, having won reasonably free and fair elections, face intense opposition from those from whom they have wrenched a modicum of political power; they reasonably seek to overcome that opposition by putting in place new institutions that are themselves consistent with thin constitutionalism though of course different from the constitution in place when the populists won their elections.

These rhetorical strategies produce a "disaggregated" analysis of populism and its relation to even thin constitutionalism. We take up themes one by one and argue that each theme can and does come in some versions that are consistent with constitutionalism and some that aren't. Picking populism and constitutionalism apart might be a mistake, though. Perhaps if you look at the way in which different themes are packaged in each variant of populism, you'll find that nearly every package contains enough anti-constitutional versions of themes that we should treat the package as a whole as inconsistent with thin constitutionalism even if we can find some themes in the package that are consistent with constitutionalism. We discuss this issue specifically in Chapter 5, dealing with what political sociologist Kim Lane Scheppele astutely called the Frankenstate, an anti-constitutional monster assembled from body parts that function reasonably well when put together in a normal state. While modifying and we think improving Scheppele's formulation, we argue that Frankenstates involve interactions among constitutional innovations that populists put in place, and that only some combinations of innovations produce a Frankenstate.

As we note in Chapter 2, there's an enormous scholarly literature on populism.[3] We subscribe to several services that notify us of recent scholarly publications about populism, and just about every day we're told that a new paper about populism is available. We've read a lot of the literature, and we don't think we've missed any fundamentally important work. What's clear, though, is that we're not offering any particular analytic point as our distinctive contribution. Every point we make has been made by someone somewhere before. What we've done is assemble observations scattered in prior work to create a core argument about the relation between populism and constitutionalism. The assemblage of arguments is distinctive even if every element in it isn't.[4]

---

[3] There's also an enormous literature on constitutionalism, of course, but, we think, rather little on least-common-denominator or "thin" versions of constitutionalism. Hans Kelsen, interestingly, provides an early twentieth-century example of thin constitutionalism that comes close to our version. *See* Hans Kelsen, "On the Essence and Value of Democracy," in WEIMAR: A JURISPRUDENCE OF CRISIS 84–109 (Arthur Jacobson & Bernhard Schlink eds. 2002), 84–109 (originally published as Vom Wesen und der Wert der Demokratie (Tubingen, Mohr, 1929)).

[4] The analogy to the idea of a Frankenstate hasn't escaped us.

Several years ago, Paris Aslanidis published an article, "Avoiding Bias in the Study of Populism."[5] Among the forms of bias Aslanidis identified was a regional one: specialists in European politics looked at the forms of populism they observed in Europe and offered generalizations about populism as such; specialists in Latin American politics based their generalizations about populism on what they saw in "their" region. The prominence of discussions of populism in academic circles has produced a related development. Studies that once might have been described differently are rebranded as studies of populism. So, for example, we found an article on "Islam and Populism in the Middle East" that a decade or two ago would have had the title "Political Islam in the Middle East."[6]

These are examples of what is more formally described as a "selection effect." The conclusions you draw about populism and constitutionalism depend upon the populisms you include in your study. Populism is a worldwide phenomenon, and avoiding selection bias entirely is probably impossible. We've tried to base our arguments upon a reasonably large set of examples, but we don't have the complete universe of contemporary populisms in view. We don't discuss populisms in Africa, for example. Still, we think that our "sample" is large enough to support our skeptical conclusion that generalizations about the relationship between populism and constitutionalism are hazardous. Perhaps a wider study would show that our examples of populisms that are consistent with thin constitutionalism are exceptions, swamped by the far greater number of populisms that aren't. We doubt it, but we're open to argument.

We think of selection bias as an obvious and well-known problem in the sociology of knowledge. We conclude this Introduction with another problem in the sociology of knowledge specific to study of populism and constitutionalism. The field of comparative constitutional law has a strong cosmopolitan tilt. And that is important at the moment because, as we discuss in Chapter 2, the populism that has become a focal point for scholarship in the field has a strong *anti*-cosmopolitan tilt. Scholars of comparative constitutional law associate with other cosmopolitans, most notably the cosmopolitans from nations where cosmopolitanism is disdained. Put bluntly, our friends are under attack, and that affects the way we think about the topic. Not surprisingly, we tend to think that a populism that does that has to be normatively unattractive—and, because the norms in our field are about constitutionalism, we'll tend to think that populism is

[5] 2 CHINESE POLITICAL SCIENCE REVIEW 266 (2017).

[6] Vedi R. Hadiz, *Islam and Populism in the Middle East*, 26 COMPARATIVE POLITICS NEWSLETTER 45 (Fall 2016). Hadiz drew on his book ISLAMIC POPULISM IN INDONESIA AND THE MIDDLE EAST (2016). Jan Zielonka & Jacques Rupnik, *From Revolution to "Counter-Revolution": Democracy in Central and Eastern Europe 30 Years On*, 72 EUROPE-ASIA STUDIES 1073 (2020), offer an astute analysis of democratic decline in that region, which makes it clear that not all of the decline is fairly attributed to populists, even though the authors use the term a bit indiscriminately.

anti-constitutional. The preceding sentences have used the words "we" and "us" because the authors of this book do feel the pull of these concerns. We hope that our awareness of them allows us to think about the issues in a way less distorted by our personal friendships and the like.

Political scientists are less susceptible to this problem because their methods bring them into contact with populism's supporters as well as its critics. They can bring less normative baggage than constitutional lawyers to the first step, understanding populism. Political scientists, though, tend to have a less sophisticated understanding of constitutionalism than lawyers do. So, when they take the next step of connecting populism to constitutionalism, they make mistakes resulting from oversimplification.[7]

Finally, we reject the view, prominent in studies of comparative constitutional law and democratization, that a single well-defined set of institutions and norms is required for successful democracies to operate. We believe that such a "one-size-fits-all" model offers a theoretically and historically flawed version of "institutional fetishism." Just as there are varieties of capitalism, there are varieties of democracy and liberal constitutionalism. Representative democracy, judicial review, the civil service, and indeed most of the institutions associated with well-governed democracies can assume many different forms. At the highest level of generality, we can talk about institutions that any democracy based on the rule of law must have such as an independent judiciary or accountable government. Make the discussion even a bit more concrete, and we find many different forms of such institutional structures. Our study of the relationship between constitutionalism and populism shows that populist "confrontations" with constitutionalism are often nothing more—or less—than attempts to find appropriate institutions, consistent with commitments to constitutionalism, that allow populists to deal with the political challenges they face.

---

[7] We discuss these difficulties in Chapter 2.

PART ONE
THE FRAMEWORK

1

What Is Constitutionalism?

I. Defining Constitutionalism

What is constitutionalism? The only sensible follow-up is this: why do you want to know? Scores of books have been written offering scores of descriptions of constitutionalism: descriptions of the real world of constitutions and prescriptions for the authors' "best" account of constitutionalism as a system of values. Each author has in mind some purpose for which she is providing the description. As should be clear already, our purpose is to provide some leverage on the analysis of contemporary populism.

That purpose sets some important guidelines for our answer to the question posed in the chapter's title. Because we are interested in contemporary populism, we are interested in contemporary constitutionalism. We aren't going to spend time on describing "Athenian" constitutionalism, or "medieval" constitutionalism, although for other purposes examining those and many other forms of constitutionalism would be quite valuable.

More important, we aren't going to discuss constitutionalism as what philosophers call a "regulative ideal"—a reasonably comprehensive set of values that we could use as a benchmark against which we could measure actual constitutional performance. Consider a relatively simple question: Are laws against hate speech consistent with constitutionalism as a regulative ideal? On some accounts, clearly no—such laws violate ideals of freedom of expression. On other accounts, clearly yes—such laws are required to ensure that everyone can participate in civic life on an equal basis. Proponents of each view will of course provide elaborate arguments rooted in stories about individual autonomy, democratic self-governance, and the like to justify their particular view of constitutionalism as a regulative ideal. Precisely because each view is reasonable—as are many others—we think it unhelpful to rely on "regulative ideal" versions of constitutionalism in our inquiry into the relation between contemporary constitutionalism and contemporary populism.

Of course, we do need some benchmark—some rough idea of what we mean by "constitutionalism"—if we are to make any progress toward our goal. The "regulative ideal" approach to the question relies upon what we call a "thick" account of constitutionalism. Thick accounts build a fair amount of detail into the story. A thick account might for example provide answers to questions about the

Power to the People. Mark Tushnet and Bojan Bugarič, Oxford University Press. © Mark Tushnet and Bojan Bugarič 2021. DOI: 10.1093/oso/9780197606711.003.0002

kinds of political demonstrations that must be permitted—where the "must be" means "constitutionalism requires that they be permitted." We could provide other examples, but the point should already be clear: thick accounts are detailed, though perhaps not to the level of resolving questions about hate speech regulation or other quite specific matters. Thick accounts can operate at a quite granular level, as "regulative ideal" accounts as we describe them do, or at a middle level of abstraction.[1]

The thicker the account, the more readily will we be able to identify tensions between constitutionalism and populism. Yet, the thicker the account, the more readily will we be able also to identify tensions between constitutionalism and any real-world political practices. Consider a relatively simple mid-level abstraction: contemporary constitutionalism, it might be said, requires that eligibility to vote must be close to universal. Every jurisdiction that we know of excludes children from the franchise. What about exclusion of long-term residents, lawfully present, who aren't citizens of the jurisdiction? Exclusion of those convicted of serious crimes while they are imprisoned? For some period afterward? Should we regard the rather large number of nations with one or more of those practices as falling short of the requirements of contemporary constitutionalism? Perhaps we should. Yet doing so may well dilute the sting of assertions that *other* shortfalls are more serious.

We pursue a different strategy here. We offer a relatively thin account of contemporary constitutionalism. Its principles are stated at a reasonably high level of abstraction: the judiciary must be reasonably independent of political control, methods of determining popular support for policy choices must be reasonably reliable, and a few more.[2] Many different systems, some of them populist, satisfy the requirements of a thin constitutionalism.[3]

---

[1] We think it worth noting that the linkage between constitutionalism and some version of liberalism, and in particular with democracy, developed in the early modern period, well after the concepts of constitutionalism and democracy came on the scene. In a sense, then, our "thin" constitutionalism can be treated as a branch of a tree of which thicker versions are other branches.

[2] For a similarly thin definition of constitutionalism, *see* Wojciech Sadurski, *Constitutional Democracy in the Time of Elected Authoritarians*, 18 INTERNATIONAL JOURNAL OF CONSTITUTIONAL LAW 324 (2020), at p. 328 (listing "free, fair, and regular elections," "civil and political rights, in particular those which are instrumental to unconstrained political communication necessary for a democratic electoral choice," "separation or dispersion of powers," and "the rule of law . . . [including] constitutional rules which [the government] cannot change at will whenever political expediency so demands"). Sadurski's exposition of these principles, though brief, suggests that he would give them somewhat more content that we would. *See also* JEREMY WALDRON, POLITICAL POLITICAL THEORY (2016), ch. 2 ("Constitutionalism: A Skeptical View"); TOM GINSBURG & AZIZ Z. HUQ, HOW TO SAVE A CONSTITUTIONAL DEMOCRACY (2018), at p.10: "Our definition aims to be as minimalist as possible without simply equating democracy with elections alone."

[3] Paul Blokker, *Populist Understandings of the Law: A Conservative Backlash?*, 13 PARTICIPAZIONE É CONFLITTO 1433 (2020), offers a sociolegal account of what he calls "embedded constitutional democracy," in which the idea of constitutional democracy takes different forms depending upon the socio-historical context. Perhaps our "thin constitutionalism" can be understood as our attempt to dis-embed the idea of constitutionalism as much as possible, to take account of all the variations that

We don't contend that thin constitutionalism is the most attractive version of constitutionalism. For us it is mostly a heuristic device that allows us to lay out the complex connections between populism and constitutionalism more clearly than relying on a thicker idea would. We do think that it captures something like a least common denominator of constitutionalism: Whatever else you think constitutionalism requires, you'll agree that it requires at least thin constitutionalism. What's more, thicken the account even a bit and we're going to find reasonable disagreement: you say that constitutionalism requires this specific thing, but I can point you to constitutional systems that seem to me to do just fine without it.

We worry that too much of the discussion of the relation between constitutionalism and contemporary populisms is unproductive between participants in the discussion have thick versions of constitutionalism in mind—and too often those thick accounts either are undefended or conflict with other thick accounts being put forth, in which case the participants are talking past each other. Our hope is that the idea of thin constitutionalism can provide a common ground for discussion. It can do so in the negative sense that we should all agree that a populist government that fails to satisfy thin constitutionalism's requirements is indeed anti-constitutional. And, for us more important, the idea of thin constitutionalism can help clarify some of the criticisms offered of some contemporary populisms, in which the language of constitutionalism is used as a vehicle for expressing substantive disagreement with the regime's policies. The idea of thin constitutionalism brings out the essentially political—rather than constitutional—nature of objections to specific populisms.

Before identifying what thin constitutional requires, though, we must note one problem associated with thin accounts. As we have suggested, thick accounts make it too easy to find fault with actual practices. Thin accounts, though, may make it too difficult to do so. The reason is straightforward. Each high-level abstraction can be brought to ground through a large number of what we call "specifications," each of which is reasonable on its own but many of which are inconsistent with others.[4]

Again, the hate speech example is useful. Thin accounts of constitutionalism may require free expression and civic equality. Hate speech laws might be inconsistent with free expression (on some views) but required by civic equality (on some other views). We think that this disagreement is an entirely reasonable

actually occur. (Complete dis-embedding is impossible without abandoning "constitutionalism" as an analytic category.)

[4] Specifications can be understood as the way in which reasonable disagreements about constitutional meaning manifest themselves. For a discussion of such reasonable disagreements, *see* JEREMY WALDRON, LAW AND DISAGREEMENT (1999).

one—which implies that having laws against hate speech and prohibiting them as unconstitutional are both consistent with constitutionalism on a thin understanding.

As we will show in our discussion of populism and in our case studies, reasonable alternative specifications of abstract principles are everywhere. Much of the asserted tension between constitutionalism and populism occurs because populist regimes adopt a specification that critics don't like even though it is, in principle, a reasonable specification. As we argue in what follows, we believe that sometimes the specifications *as they operate in particular circumstances* are troublesome, but the circumstances, not the specifications, should be the focus of concern.

II. The Elements of Thin Constitutionalism

Thin constitutionalism today has four elements.

- *Majority rule*: Policy over a wide range of issues is determined by the preferences of a popular majority today.
- *Entrenchment*: Some policies can't be changed by a simple majority of today's voters. These policies involve both rights and structures for making decisions (including structures for determining what unentrenched policies a contemporary majority prefers).
- *Judicial independence*: Judges who resolve disputes over the application of policies in individual cases should be independent of direct political control (that is, shouldn't be responsive to politicians themselves chosen by the people), but should be directly accountable to "the law" and indirectly accountable to the people.
- *Politicians and political parties*. Office-holders and office-seekers—politicians—organized in parties seek popular support for the programs the politicians propose.

These elements seem simple enough, but when we examine each in detail, real complexities emerge. And the elements interact in complicated ways.[5]

---

[5] A cautionary note: we always have to keep in mind that we are discussing *thin* constitutionalism. Real-world constitutions narrow the range of policies subject to choice by popular majorities by entrenching some policies and having an extensive list of entrenched rights and structures. For example, the current constitution of Brazil entrenches a balanced-budget requirement, that of Germany commits the nation to social welfare policies, some nations give constitutional status to their central banks, and others create ombuds offices with protections akin to those given judges. Some or all of these might be good ideas, but none, we think, are required by a thin understanding of contemporary constitutionalism.

A. Majority Rule

Contemporary governments can address an enormous number of issues: tax policy, environmental degradation, the scope of privacy rights against the government and against private companies, and much more. They needn't take up any particular policy at any moment, of course, but when they do address a policy issue, thin constitutionalism requires that the policies in place be chosen by contemporary majorities. More precisely, it requires that a majority vote taken today determines what the policy shall be going forward, no matter what some past majority has chosen—and only until voters in the future choose a different policy.[6] Today's electorate might not put existing environmental policy up to a vote, accepting for the moment the policy choices made by their predecessors, but that too is a choice made by today's voters.[7]

As we will see, the range of policy choice open to majority rule is wide but not unlimited because some policies are entrenched against contemporary majority choice. More important for the moment, the principle of majority rule has to be implemented by real-world institutions. How do we know what policies contemporary majorities want?

Thin constitutionalism requires only that majority preferences be reliably determined—unless the procedures for determining those preferences are themselves entrenched.[8] The first question, though, is, "majority of whom?" The quick answer seems simple enough: a majority of adult citizens.[9] Thin constitutionalism allows for some narrowly defined groups of adult citizens to be excluded from the count: citizens living abroad for an extended period and, more controversially, for some time persons convicted of some crimes. Contemporary populisms tend not to challenge the "adult citizen" requirement, so we don't focus more attention on it.

More important, *every* actual mechanism for finding out what policies today's majority prefers is imperfect. We'll examine several mechanisms in a moment, but take elections as the simplest example. Not everyone will vote in every election (put another way, compulsory voting, while perhaps a good idea, isn't required by thin constitutionalism—or, indeed, by contemporary constitutionalism itself). And we can be pretty confident that in any nation voting rates will

---

[6] In British constitutional theory A.V. Dicey made this the centerpiece of his definition of parliamentary supremacy. Recent controversies over the existence of "constitutional" statutes in the United Kingdom have revived interest in this definition. We discuss some of these controversies in Chapter 6, on Brexit.

[7] Thin constitutionalism is thus not intrinsically unstable—does not put all policy choices up for grabs at every moment—because voters (and political leaders) decide which policies to reconsider.

[8] This is the first place where we see how the elements of thin constitutionalism interact.

[9] Again, specific national constitutions might include *more* people in the group whose preferences count—in some places, for example, young people, in others long-term resident noncitizens. Excluding such groups is consistent with thin constitutionalism, though.

fall into patterns. The most widespread one is probably that the well-educated and well-to-do vote at higher rates than the less well-educated and the less well-to-do. Thin constitutionalism—in contrast to constitutionalism as a regulative ideal—accepts these patterns of effective limitations on voting (or other ways of determining preferences). It requires only that policy choices result from some reasonably reliable mechanism for determining those preferences. And contemporary populists don't defend their policy choices on the ground that they reflect "true" majority preferences in the face of patterned effective limitations on determining preferences, so again we put this issue aside.

To summarize: thin constitutionalism requires that when the nation's people can make policy choices—which is to say, when they choose policies on subjects not constitutionally entrenched against majority decision—the choices should match the preferences of a majority of the nation's adult citizens as revealed by mechanisms that are reasonably reliable tools for determining what those preferences are. The tools don't have to be perfect—they only have to be good enough.

There are a large number of (imperfect) mechanisms for determining the majority's preferences. Thin constitutionalism allows the use of pretty much any mechanism that produces reasonably reliable measures of those preferences. The simplest, of course, is reasonably free and fair elections. We know, of course, that elections can measure majority preferences imperfectly. The simplest case is probably the most common: political parties compete in elections by offering platforms that address many subjects. A party or coalition can win a majority because voters prefer its platform as a whole to the platform the losing party offers. That doesn't mean, though, that a majority prefers every item in the winning party's platform over the corresponding item in the losing party's platform. A stylized example drawn from the U.S. experience: a conservative party wins on a platform promising tax cuts and substantially less environmental regulation. The party could win an election focused on the tax issue because a majority might really like the idea of tax cuts and only mildly oppose reducing environmental regulation. Or another example: an unexpected policy issue—for example, how to respond to a novel pandemic—arises during a government's term in office; the majority that supported its election couldn't have had preferences about the policy response to the novel issue, and so the government's actions might or might not reflect majority preferences.

That's why thin constitutionalism allows for the use of other mechanisms for determining a contemporary majority's preferences. Referendums can supplement elections, for example. And again, we know that referendums are imperfect mechanisms, mostly because they typically offer voters a simple "yes/no" choice on policies about which the voters might well have more nuanced views. (We present a case study of the Brexit referendum later to illustrate this problem.)

Innovations in the technology of democracy now offer additional mechanisms for determining (reasonably reliably) the majority's views. We discuss some of these innovations in the final part of this book. They include deliberative polling, delegating policymaking power to a randomly selected group of people rather than to elected representatives, and participatory budgeting built from the ground up. Thin constitutionalism allows for the use of any of these mechanisms so long as they are reasonably well-designed to provide a reasonably reliable measure of majority preferences. And, once again, perfection isn't required: the measure of reasonableness should probably be, roughly, whether the chosen mechanism is at least as good as reasonably free and fair elections are as a method of determining majority preferences.

This brief discussion opens up some of the complexities associated with the idea of majority rule as a basic principle of thin constitutionalism. If reasonably free and fair elections provide the benchmark for determining whether some other mechanism for determining majority preferences is good enough, what makes an election reasonably free and fair? And, what does thin constitutionalism have to say about cases where two ways of determining majority preferences seem to conflict (or where one mechanism is entrenched and others prohibited)? This is perhaps the most difficult issue, because its answer depends upon an answer to the deeper question: Is majority rule a substantive or a procedural requirement of thin constitutionalism?

- *Free and fair elections.* For elections to be reasonably free, candidates and parties have to be able to present a full range of policy options to the public: of course, that the current government should be replaced, but also that taxes should go up or down, that public services should be expanded or privatized, and so on through the list of all matters on which policy can be made. Reasonably free and fair elections, that is, require freedom of political expression.

  We don't want to offer a full theory of free expression here.[10] Any such account, though, has to begin with the observation that freedom of expression always competes with other important values—social stability, personal privacy, civic equality, and much more. Thin constitutionalism requires only that the balance struck between political expression and those competing values be reasonable. And that, we think, is going to vary with social and political circumstances. Some restrictions on political expression in highly polarized nations with a history of civic violence might be reasonable even when the same restrictions elsewhere would be unreasonable. New

---

[10] For the views of one of us, *see* MARK TUSHNET, ADVANCED INTRODUCTION TO FREEDOM OF EXPRESSION (2018).

information technologies might alter the balance among the concerns for autonomy, public understanding, and other considerations underlying the general account of free expression.

For elections to be reasonably fair, voters have to be able to cast their votes as they wish, and the votes that they cast have to be counted. Thin constitutionalism prohibits physical intimidation of voters and fraudulent vote counting. Subtler forms of coercion, such as an implicit threat that someone who votes the "wrong" way will lose her job, are also inconsistent with thin constitutionalism, although detecting such coercion might be so difficult as to make this criterion unusable in practice.

- *Substance and procedure in majority rule.* Consider a nation whose constitution says that all lawmaking power resides in the legislature, and doesn't authorize referendums. A social movement agitates for a referendum on some issue, saying that the legislature's position on the issue doesn't reflect what today's majority wants. Of course, the movement can put pressure on the legislature in all sorts of ways, including organizing a "referendum" on the issue.[11] But is the procedure set out in the constitution the *only* way to determine majority preferences that have legally binding effects?

  Or go back to our example of a conservative political party elected on a platform of tax cuts and deregulation. Suppose high-quality opinion polls regularly show high levels of support for maintaining or even tightening environmental regulations. The presidentially controlled environmental regulatory agency authorizes an increase in the amount of air pollution a factory can emit. Can a citizens' group get a court order barring the deregulation on the ground that the opinion polls provide a better measure of a majority's preferences than does the president's campaign platform?

  These are fancy ways of asking whether majority rule is a substantive principle or a procedural one. On the substantive view, the majority's preferences govern once we know what they are, no matter how we gain that knowledge—by elections, referendums, opinion polls, or any other source. On the procedural view, the only ways that count for determining the majority's preferences are the mechanisms set out in the constitution—which could but need not include the full list of mechanisms for determining a majority's preferences.[12] So, to go back to our examples, if the nation's constitution bars referendums, no purported referendum creates binding law no matter how overwhelming the majority is, and the factory can increase the amount of pollution it spews into the air.

---

[11] Proponents of Catalan independence organized a public "consultation"—really, a referendum without binding legal effect—on the issue. The Spanish courts held the consultation unlawful and the central government has prosecuted those who organized the consultation for (in effect) sedition.

[12] Our point here has to be qualified by our discussion in the next section of this chapter of how entrenched provisions—including those for determining majority preferences—can be modified.

We can imagine a political theory in which the substantive view prevails. But, we think, constitutionalism no matter how thin has some irreducible procedural core.[13] One specific payoff is important in terms of the history of populisms. An elected president can't use decrees beyond those authorized by the Constitution to impose what the president contends are the views of today's majority in the face of legislative resistance. That payoff is less important today, where populist presidents usually have support from the legislature.[14]

There's a broader payoff, though. Thin constitutionalism means that political leaders speaking for a majority have to use the institutions in place to advance their policies, or change those institutions according to rules for changing them. Where the constitution in place entrenches some policy or procedure for adopting policies, thin constitutionalism means that the constitution has to be amended to replace that policy or procedure. As we will show, critics of populism sometimes contend that populist enthusiasm for constitutional amendments shows why there's a tension between populism and constitutionalism. But, as long as populists use the constitution's amendment rules to change the constitution, they are acting in a manner consistent with thin constitutionalism.[15]

A final point: the word "reasonable" is doing a lot of work in our explanation of thin constitutionalism. It's quite difficult to offer anything more specific, and people will often disagree about whether some policy choice is reasonable. Note, though, one important feature: all the choices we've discussed—that is, all the choices subject to the test of reasonableness—are themselves produced by the institutions of majority rule. The question then is whether those imperfect institutions have operated well enough to produce something we can fairly call a reasonable though of course contestable choice.

We suggest two perspectives on that question. The first is for observers or critics of the system. We think they should imagine that the choice had been made by a government whose motives they didn't suspect, and ask themselves

---

[13] From different traditions, the work of Lon Fuller in jurisprudence and Joseph Schumpeter and Robert Dahl in political science converge on this conclusion. See LON FULLER, THE MORALITY OF LAW (1964); JOSEPH SCHUMPETER, CAPITALISM, SOCIALISM, AND DEMOCRACY (1942); ROBERT DAHL, DILEMMAS OF PLURALIST DEMOCRACY (1982).

[14] Venezuela since around 2015 might be thought a counterexample, but as we argue in our case study of Venezuela, though Hugo Chávez, who died in 2013, was a populist leader, his successor Nicolas Máduro is a straightforward authoritarian.

[15] We note here, and discuss in more detail in Chapter 4's case study of Hungary, that the *substance* of constitutional amendments adopted even in regular form can be inconsistent with thin constitutionalism when they undermine the ability of current policy to reflect current majority views by making it exceedingly difficult to displace a government whose policies no longer reflect those preferred by the majority. This is a different problem from the one discussed in the text, that populist enthusiasm for amending constitutions is itself an indication of an anti-constitutional mindset.

whether they would regard the choice as a reasonable one. The second is an institutional perspective: should courts assessing the choice find it outside the range of reasonable options a democratic majority should have available? We take that question up later in this chapter.

B. Entrenchment

Thin constitutionalism, we have argued, requires that some things—specifically, some principles of free expression and civic equality (in connection with free and fair elections) and some procedures for determining majority preferences—be "entrenched." The idea of entrenchment is intuitive: entrenched provisions can't be changed by the procedures used to enact and repeal ordinary laws—the laws on which majority rule prevails.

Thin constitutionalism—indeed, we think, any sensible view of constitutionalism—does not assume that whatever happens to be entrenched in a constitution is good. A constitution might protect individual privacy "too much," in the sense that it shields from public view facts that voters would find relevant to their choice of representatives. Or, it might protect privacy too little, allowing the press to degrade targets of sensationalistic stories with little or no public benefit. A constitution might make it too difficult to expand social welfare provisions by requiring a balanced budget, or too easy to do so by guaranteeing a long list of social welfare rights.

As we've noted, proposing to "de-entrench" some existing constitutional provision shifts the subject from a list of policies that can be changed only by some supermajority to the list of policies that can be changed by majority rule. Doing so isn't in itself anti-constitutional. What matters is whether the substance of the entrenched provision matters so much that it has to be protected from change by current majorities (and subsequent change if the majority's preferences change).

The rules dealing with financing election campaigns in the United States provide a useful example. As interpreted by the U.S. Supreme Court, principles of freedom of expression severely restrict legislatures' power to develop rules restricting contributions to and expenditures by political candidates and parties. Critics of those decisions have proposed a constitutional amendment that would authorize legislatures to adopt "reasonable" regulations of campaign finance. Would "amending the First Amendment" in this way be anti-constitutional?[16]

---

[16] The example isn't quite what we need, because the proposal can be characterized as an amendment aimed at correcting the Supreme Court's misinterpretation of the First Amendment and restoring the amendment's proper interpretation. To clean up the example, imagine that the constitution entrenches a specific set of rules about campaign finance, which a current majority comes to believe, reasonably, no longer fits the nation's conditions.

Other well-functioning constitutional democracies have quite different systems of financing political campaigns, including systems of complete public financing with private contributions and expenditures prohibited and systems that limit private contributions and expenditures. Perhaps there are reasons specific to the United States to be concerned that legislatures wouldn't adopt similar systems, or that such systems would operate badly in the United States even if they operate reasonably well elsewhere. But, we think, arguments about such a proposal should be conducted at that level of detail, not at the level of concern about "constitutionalism."

An important form of entrenchment occurs when legislation must pass through what political scientists call "veto gates." A veto gate exists at each point in a multistage policymaking process where approval by some person or body is required before a proposal moves to the next stage. A legislative committee can be a veto gate; so can a lower house, or an upper house, or the president—or a constitutional court. The more veto gates there are, the greater the chance that actual majority preferences won't be reflected in binding law. Veto gates block the adoption of *new* policies, which means that they induce a bias in favor of the status quo, even in the face of majority preferences as revealed outside the legislative process, for example in opinion polls. Another metaphor is that some constitutional provisions are speed bumps, slowing down movement toward a policy's implementation without definitively blocking the policy.[17] From one point of view, speed bumps offer a chance for additional deliberation about the policy's wisdom; from another, slowing progress toward implementation gives opponents more time to build support for repealing the policy.

Ordinary majorities can't change entrenched provisions they believe to be bad ones, or eliminate an entrenched veto gate when some piece of legislation fails to get through it or an entrenched speed bump that's slowed down implementation dramatically. But thin constitutionalism does allow amendments to entrenched provisions by supermajorities. Many amendment rules exist: requiring two-thirds or three-quarters approval rather than a simple majority, requiring approval by a referendum, requiring approval by two successive parliaments with an intervening election.[18]

---

[17] For the term "speed bumps," *see* Tom Ginsburg, Aziz Z. Huq, & Mila Versteeg, *The Coming Demise of Liberal Constitutionalism*, 85 UNIVERSITY OF CHICAGO LAW REVIEW 239 (2018), at p. 253 ("At best, constitutional design features serve as speed bumps to slow the agglomeration and abuse of political power; they cannot save us from our worst selves completely.").

[18] We've used examples of written constitutions with entrenched provisions and written amendment rules. Entrenchment occurs even where the constitution is unwritten and sometimes in the interstices of written constitutions. Entrenchment where the constitution is unwritten comes in the form of settled practices and strong norms protecting them against change. These norms mean that a politician who wants to change the entrenched rules ordinarily has to build up a great deal of support for change, more than she needs to secure changes in ordinary policy. Or, where the politician manages to implement a change in norms without supermajority support, the changed norm won't "stick" when the politician leaves the scene.

Amendments become sensible when experience reveals that the constitution's authors made a mistake.[19] When nationally organized political parties came onto the scene, the initial U.S. system for choosing a president and vice president led to a constitutional crisis. After the crisis was resolved, the Constitution was amended to prevent its recurrence. Amendments make sense when accumulated experience leads to a better understanding of what mechanisms promote good governance. As Thomas Jefferson memorably put it in 1816:

> Some men look at constitutions with sanctimonious reverence, and deem them like the ark of the covenant, too sacred to be touched. They ascribe to the men of the preceding age a wisdom more than human, and suppose what they did to be beyond amendment. I knew that age well; I belonged to it, and labored with it. It deserved well of its country. It was very like the present, but without the experience of the present; and forty years of experience in government is worth a century of book-reading; and this they would say themselves, were they to rise from the dead.[20]

Finally, technological developments can make new techniques of governance available.

A further point about entrenchments and their alteration by amendments according to prescribed rules: some constitutions contain, or have been interpreted to contain, provisions that simply can't be amended at all within the rules the constitution sets out (so-called "eternity" provisions). The German Basic Law, for example, says that it can't be amended to eliminate its protection of "human dignity" or the nature of the state as "social and federal" under the rule of law. The Indian Supreme Court has held that amendments to the constitution's basic structure—which includes commitments to federalism, secularism, and judicial independence—are unconstitutional.

Amendment rules and eternity provisions themselves might be badly designed—or so today's people might think. An easy case: suppose the amendment rule requires approval by three-quarters of the people, but 70 percent believe that that rule is too stringent. A harder case for many: suppose secularism is protected by an eternity clause but three-quarters of the people think that their country would be better off with a modest religious establishment. An even more difficult case: the constitution's structure as a federal republic is protected by an eternity clause but a substantial majority comes to believe that economic change,

---

[19] At the U.S. constitutional convention George Mason said that an amendment procedure was needed because the new constitution "will certainly be defective." Similar observations were made during the French constitutional convention a few years later.

[20] Thomas Jefferson to Samuel Kercheval, July 12, 1816, available at https://founders.archives.gov/?q=Ancestor%3ATSJN-03-10-02-0128&s=1511311111&r=2, archived at https://perma.cc/97S5-NXM3.

changes in social conditions, and advances in the technologies of governance now make a fully centralized government better than a federal one.[21]

Does thin constitutionalism address eternity clauses or amendment rules that from the point of view of today's supermajority are overly stringent? The standard answer, we think, is that if you don't like the constitution you have, if only because of its amendment rules or eternity clauses, you can scrap it—technically, replace rather than amend it.[22] Some constitutions, though, say that they can be amended by some supermajority rule but replaced only through some even more stringent process.[23] And then the obvious question: What if people think that the replacement rule is too stringent?

Here we want to truncate our presentation. Today's populists all seem reasonably happy to use existing amendment rules to implement the changes they favor, as to both substantive rights and procedures for enacting laws (including changes in judicial power, which some populists have come to see as the most significant veto gate in their systems).[24] For that reason we would say today's populists seem mostly happy to comply with thin constitutionalism's requirement, if it be one, that the constitution can be amended only by adhering to the amendment rules as they happen to be.[25]

What about amendments adopted pursuant to existing amendment rules that change the amendment rules themselves? As with other amendments, such amendments might be problematic if, for example, they increase the difficulty of amending provisions that make it difficult to displace a government in power. Other amendments to the amendment rules might not be troublesome in thin constitutional terms. Once again, we think that the focus should be on the substance of the amendments and their actual effect in the circumstances at hand rather on the fact of amendment itself, even the amendment of amendment rules.

We feel some obligation, though, to say something about the largely theoretical question about getting rid of bad eternity clauses or overly stringent

---

[21] Some but not all of these difficulties can be handled by creative constitutional interpretation—finding that some substantial move toward centralization actually is consistent with federalism properly understood, or finding that some public recognition of a religion is consistent with secularism properly understood.

[22] Sometimes the terminology is "substitution" rather than "replacement," but the underlying idea is the same.

[23] See Rosalind Dixon & David Landau, Tiered Constitutional Design, 86 GEORGE WASHINGTON LAW REVIEW 438 (2018).

[24] They have sometimes pressed the definition of "amendment" and "replacement," with critics contending that what populists have described as an "amendment" is actually a "replacement" that didn't go through the more stringent processes for replacements. We provide a few examples in our case studies, but our general view is that here too a standard of reasonableness applies: Is it reasonable to treat a change as a (mere) amendment rather than as a replacement?

[25] A possible counterexample is provided by the 1999 constitutional revision in Venezuela, which expressly departed from the requirements in the constitution-in-place for replacing the constitution. The case is complicated by the fact that the (non-populist dominated) high court held that departing from the constitution's requirements was lawful. For a more complete discussion, see Chapter 3.

amendment rules.[26] We think that they can be done away with through what has to be understood as a revolutionary transformation of the constitutional order, one that expressly breaks the bounds of the existing constitution.[27] Relative to the existing constitution, revolutionary transformations are extralegal.[28]

C. A Short Note on Why Thin Constitutionalism Isn't about Limiting Government Power

By now readers may be impatient at our failure to say anything about what they might think at constitutionalism's heart: constitutionalism, on one common view, is about limiting government power, to protect the natural liberties people have and want. The well-regarded Stanford Encyclopedia of Philosophy's first sentence on constitutionalism is this: "Constitutionalism is the idea, . . . that government can and should be legally limited in its powers."[29]

We don't include an expansive idea of limited power in our conception of thin constitutionalism. Of course, whatever happens to be entrenched operates as a temporary limitation on government power. And equally of course "rule of law" requirements that *are* within our conception of thin constitutionalism are themselves limitations on government power. Thin constitutionalism places some limits on pure majoritarianism, but "limiting government power" isn't the ultimate goal of constitutionalism, as some formulations occasionally suggest. The reason: we limit government power to protect liberty. Sometimes, though, exercising power protects liberty. The most obvious cases involve the use of national power to control abuses of power by petty local tyrants who corruptly abuse their public positions to put people under their thumb. These cases are easy even if we define "liberty" as something that can be threatened only by public power. That's

---

[26] The question is not entirely theoretical. The U.S. Constitution provides that each state, no matter what its population, shall have equal representation in the upper house (currently, two senators per state), and that no amendment can change the principle of equal representation. Many in the United States, though almost certainly not a supermajority, believe that that "eternity" provision is a bad one. And courts are sometimes protected by an eternity clause or, more often, by a judicially created "basic structure" doctrine.

[27] For clarity's sake we note that a prominent recent work, BRUCE ACKERMAN, REVOLUTIONARY CONSTITUTIONALISM (2020), employs a notion of revolutionary constitutionalism that is, we think, quite a bit different from the one so thinly outlined here. Exploring our disagreements would blur our focus on our primary effort to discuss populism and constitutionalism.

[28] The scholarly literature on this point divides between those who argue that revolutionary transformations are not constrained by law in any sense, and those who contend that such transformations are bound by some (rather thin) specifications of fundamental human rights. We take no position on this dispute.

[29] Wil Waluchow, "Constitutionalism," THE STANFORD ENCYCLOPEDIA OF PHILOSOPHY (Spring 2018 ed., Edward N. Zalta ed.), available at https://plato.stanford.edu/archives/spr2018/entries/constitutionalism/.

one conceivable definition, but not the only one—and so not a definition that should be built into the idea of constitutionalism.

Suppose we care about human liberty because it's a good thing for people to have. Specifically, liberty is good because it lets people choose the kind of life they want to live, free from domination. Private power can limit people's choices, sometimes more dramatically than public power does: think of a state that barely is able to keep civic peace, and large employers who offer jobs on the condition that their workers do pretty much whatever the employer wants pretty much all of the time. Or compare the everyday intrusions on privacy emanating from government (traffic cameras, perhaps) with the intrusions on privacy built into the algorithms of our social media giants. Exercising public power against private power can protect individual liberty understood in this way.[30]

Our conclusion is that the idea that constitutionalism is about limiting public power is one possible version of constitutionalism, but it's not one that everyone committed to constitutionalism does (or, in our view, should) accept—and so isn't part of thin constitutionalism.[31]

D. Judicial Independence

Thin constitutionalism as described to this point requires only that policies across a broad range be made according to the preferences of a contemporary majority as determined by reasonably reliable mechanisms, some but not all of which are entrenched in the Constitution, and that entrenched policies be changed only according to the rules regulating constitutional amendments. Thin constitutionalism also deals with how we enforce and apply the law under the heading of "separation of powers."

The "veto gate" concept gives us some insight into the way thin constitutionalism deals with the separation of powers. The concentration of power in a single institution, we've all learned, is the very definition of tyranny. The body that makes the law shouldn't implement it, and the body that enforces the law shouldn't interpret it. Separation of powers protects our liberty. And, the folk wisdom that two heads are better than one implies that separation of powers

---

[30] Here are two relevant quotations from classic liberal writers: Montesquieu—liberty means that "the government must be such that one citizen cannot fear another citizen"; Locke—"The Injury and the Crime is equal whether committed by the wearer of a Crown, or some petty Villain." Both are quoted in Steven Kautz, "On Liberal Constitutionalism," in THE SUPREME COURT AND THE IDEA OF CONSTITUTIONALISM (Steven Kautz et al. eds. 2011), at p. 32.

[31] MARTIN LOUGHLIN, THE FOUNDATIONS OF PUBLIC LAW (2010), provides a good account of the long history of republican and "political" constitutionalism, ideas that don't rest on principles of negative liberty.

often improves the quality of legislation by getting several institutions to agree before a law becomes effective.

Everyone knows that two heads are better than one, but also that too many cooks spoil the broth. A system with too many veto gates and speed bumps can produce an overall body of law that is worse than one with fewer—at least if you're not a committed libertarian who thinks that more law is always worse than less law.[32] Policymaking at the national level in the United States has been stymied by "gridlock" resulting from having too many veto gates. We don't think anyone has produced a decent theory telling us how many veto gates and speed bumps are optimal. We're reasonably confident, though, that there's no general argument against reducing the number of veto gates and speed bumps from whatever it happens to be in any constitutional system. Eliminating them all, of course, means consolidating power in a single person, typically an authoritarian dictator—and that's clearly inconsistent with thin constitutionalism. Beyond that there's little general to say. Sometimes going from seven veto gates to five won't be a problem; sometimes it might be.

Thin constitutionalism requires only that there be some separation of powers, but not much beyond that—with one important qualification: thin constitutionalism clearly requires that laws be interpreted and applied by courts that are independent of the legislature and the executive government.

After policies are adopted, they have to be applied. And application will sometimes be controversial. The legislature adopts a law saying that factories that emit pollution use the "best available technology" to minimize their emissions. A factory faces a fine for using something less than the best available technology; its owners say that there's actually nothing better to deal with the precise pollutant the factory emits. Thin constitutionalism requires that courts ultimately be available to resolve this dispute.

We write "ultimately" because thin constitutionalism doesn't require that the dispute be immediately sent to a court for final resolution, or even that a preliminary resolution be made by a court, or even that the court refuse to give deference to a preliminary resolution made outside the courts. Thin constitutionalism requires only that a court be available to take a look at the dispute and ensure that the outcome conforms to the anti-pollution law the legislature enacted.

How deep does that look have to be? Clearly, a law can be applied to a person only when doing so is consistent with a reasonable interpretation of the law. So, the courts have to interpret the law. Does thin constitutionalism require more than that? Most contemporary constitutions—but not all—allow the courts to

---

[32] More precisely, by preserving the status quo a larger set of veto gates and speed bumps leaves a wider range of policies to be determined by the choices made by private parties regulated by private rather than public law.

hold statutes unconstitutional or "disapply" them in specific cases.[33] Almost all allow the courts to hold executive actions unlawful when the actions aren't authorized by either the constitution (when the executive uses "decrees" to exercise its prerogative powers), or by statutes (when the executive uses a different category of "decrees," the term used in civil law systems, "secondary legislation," the term used in the United Kingdom, or "regulations," the term used in the United States). And almost all tell the courts to interpret statutes to be consistent with the constitution where doing so is within the broad bounds of reasonable interpretation.

We note, though, that even where constitutional review is authorized it is not comprehensive—courts won't hear some constitutional claims because, for example, the challenger wouldn't benefit from winning on the constitutional issue or, more important, because the constitution commits the substantive constitutional question to resolution by the political branches (this is known as the "political questions" doctrine). And some constitutions allow legislatures using ordinary majority rules to "override" judicial decisions finding a statute unconstitutional.

We're agnostic on whether thin constitutionalism requires some form of constitutional review by the courts. That some constitutional systems that almost everyone would treat as "constitutionalist" get by without robust constitutional review suggests that it doesn't.[34] But, even if it does, we think the existence in decent constitutional systems of an "override" power and the political questions doctrine make it clear that quite thin constitutional review is enough. Context matters, of course: There's some reason to believe that long-established democracies can get by with rather weak forms of constitutional review, and some evidence, albeit quite spotty, that on occasion robust review can protect what law professor Samuel Issacharoff calls fragile democracies from shattering.[35] That the evidence isn't tremendously strong cautions against including robust review as a requirement of thin constitutionalism.

For thin constitutionalism the courts' domain, then, is statutory interpretation and to some modest degree review of statutes and executive actions for consistency with the constitution. Within that domain, how are courts to behave?

---

[33] Jan-Werner Müller shows how after 1945 "a highly constrained form of democracy" emerged as a response to the totalitarian excesses of the 1930s and 1940s. Key parts of this "post-war constitutional settlement" were powerful constitutional courts. JAN-WERNER MÜLLER, CONTESTING DEMOCRACY: POLITICAL IDEAS IN TWENTIETH CENTURY EUROPE (2011), at pp. 128–40.

[34] In designing his proposed constitutional court, Hans Kelsen didn't include a provision for review of claims that legislation violated individual rights. The post-war paradigm of constitutional law does require such review, and we think it reasonable to conclude that contemporary constitutionalism does so as well. But, as we argue in the text, that requirement can be satisfied in ways compatible with populism's commitment to majority rule.

[35] SAMUEL ISSACHAROFF, FRAGILE DEMOCRACIES: CONTESTED POWER IN THE ERA OF CONSTITUTIONAL COURTS (2015). See also CARLES BOIX, CONSTITUTIONS AND DEMOCRATIC BREAKDOWNS (2005);

The standard answer is that constitutionalism, no matter how thin, requires that courts be independent, but that's pretty clearly an incomplete answer. The standard example of lack of judicial independence is "telephone justice": before deciding a case, a judge calls a politician and ask what result the politician wants.[36] Beyond that, though, the idea of judicial independence gets complicated, because we want judges to be accountable—to something—as well as independent. Accountability matters because a completely independent judge could enforce the law based on his biases against one of the parties or on her idiosyncratic views about what good public policy requires (by relying on a distorted interpretation of a clear statute, for example).

Spelling out what accountability means turns out to be surprisingly difficult. One dimension seems simple enough: judges should be held accountable to "the law." Their decisions should rest entirely on reasons drawn from the legal system itself. That's one reason telephone justice is bad: it leads judges to make decisions based on "politics" in a narrow sense, and no legal system worthy of the name (or at least no legal system that satisfies thin constitutionalism's requirements) includes such reasons within the set of permissible ones.

The complications come in when we try to move beyond that. Some legal systems allow judges to refer openly to policy considerations when they interpret statutes, for example, while others insist that judges rely entirely upon the statute's text (itself a complicated proposition). Some legal systems allow judges to refer to unwritten principles of fundamental human rights when they assess a statute's constitutionality; others insist that judges rely only on the written text.

Put generally: what counts as a decision according to law varies from one legal culture to another. In our view, thin constitutionalism requires that judges justify their decisions by adverting to the kinds of reasons their legal culture treats as legal. We write "adverting to" deliberately. We think it a mistake to say that thin constitutionalism requires that decisions "be" consistent with the law because, as always, there's going to be reasonable disagreement about what the law actually requires. Critics of a decision might say that the judge is only pretending to rely on reasons made available in the law, and sometimes that's going to be correct— but distinguishing between pretense and reasonable disagreement is almost always going to be an exercise in political rather than legal analysis.

That accountability to the law directs us to examine what kinds of reasons the legal culture recognizes leads us to a second dimension of accountability. The legal culture is necessarily an elite culture, which creates a tension between judicial independence (understood to require accountability to law) and majority rule.[37] Thin constitutionalism resolves the tension by requiring some sort of

---

[36] Or the politician calls the judge to tell her how to rule.

[37] In the field of constitutional law, Alexander Bickel's term "the countermajoritarian difficulty" captures this concern.

accountability to the public, typically through the mechanisms for appointing and removing judges. Here too contemporary constitutionalism recognizes many possibilities. In Australia and Canada judges on high courts are appointed by the prime minister acting alone, though subject to rather strong cultural norms; in the United States they are nominated by the chief executive and confirmed by the upper legislative house; in states within the United States, judges are elected;[38] in most nations judges are chosen by a judicial selection committee composed of a mix of politicians and representatives of civil society.[39]

In light of this variety, we think it impossible to say more than that thin constitutionalism permits (and may require) some reasonable form of judicial accountability to the public. Typically questions about judicial independence and accountability don't arise until politicians propose to change the form of judicial appointment or removal. Sometimes critics describe such changes as threats to judicial independence even if they are on their face a shift from one reasonable version of accountability through appointment to another, which itself would have been fine had it been in place all along.[40] Such criticisms introduce a more general issue for thin constitutionalism—the problem of what we call retrogression—to which we now turn.

E. Two Related Problems— Specification and Retrogression

We suggested earlier that criticism of constitutional developments that invoke notions of constitutionalism that are thicker than the thin constitutionalism we've described are quite likely to be problematic. Here we elaborate that suggestion, with the goal of showing that the problems lie in what are ultimately disagreements with the policies aided by the constitutional developments: criticism that takes the form of concerns about constitutionalism conceals the underlying concern, which is with the substantive policies the criticized government is pursuing.

We've already introduced some of the examples we'll use to develop this argument. Suppose the critic has a moderately thick notion of constitutionalism that includes ideas about freedom of expression, equality, individual autonomy, judicial independence, personal privacy, limits on executive power, and so on through the list of everything that's contained in most modern constitutions.

---

[38] For a case study of judicial elections in Bolivia, see Chapter 8.

[39] Removal mechanisms include impeachment and, more important, term limits and age limits on sitting judges.

[40] Our case studies of the judicial appointment process in India and Israel in Chapter 8 examine this question.

Almost always these ideas will be expressed in general terms. The U.S. Constitution says that "Congress shall make no law . . . abridging the freedom of speech"; the German Basic Law says, "Every person shall have the right freely to express and disseminate his opinions in speech, writing and pictures and to inform himself without hindrance from generally accessible sources." The U.S. Constitution says, "No state shall . . . deny to any person . . . the equal protection of the laws." The German Basic Law says, "All persons shall be equal before the law."

These provisions are typical in the level of generality with which they state the governing principles. In specific cases or in connection with specific pieces of legislation, though, the general principles can be brought to ground in many different ways. To take the most obvious example, essentially every statute treats some people differently from others and the principle of "equality before the law" has to take that obvious fact into account. Consider a problem the Japanese constitutional court faced. We know that the principle of equality before the law allows the government to punish murderers more severely than robbers. A statute imposed greater punishment on people who killed one of their parents than on those who killed strangers. Is that statute consistent with equality before the law? (The court held that it wasn't.) What about a ban on video game and pool parlors near schools but not farther away? The South Korean constitutional court upheld a ban on billiard parlors near elementary and high schools but didn't let the government ban them near kindergartens and universities.[41]

Or, to return to earlier examples, the principle of free speech can be specified in ways that make hate speech regulation permissible or unconstitutional: For the first, specify the principle as "no discrimination on the basis of content"; for the second, specify it as "restrictions on expression must be proportional to the harm caused by the regulated expression." Judicial independence can be protected by vetting judges through a judicial appointment commission or by insisting that the legislature and executive agree on judicial appointments.

Of course, you can define constitutionalism as requiring one or another of these specifications down through the entire list. If you do, though, we're going to end up with hundreds of competing definitions. And almost all of them are going to be reasonable ways of specifying the general principles of constitutionalism. That means that thickly specified constitutionalisms—and the plural is important—can't be the basis for critical evaluation of constitutional developments. Or at least it can't be such a basis when the developments shift a nation's constitutional order from one reasonable specification to another. Only

---

[41] See Shingori Matsui, *Why Is the Japanese Supreme Court So Conservative?*, 88 WASHINGTON UNIVERSITY LAW REVIEW 1375 (2011), at pp. 1388–89; Yoon Jin Shin, "Proportionality in South Korea: Contextualizing the Cosmopolitan Rights Grammar," in PROPORTIONALITY IN ASIA (Po Jen Yap ed. 2020), at pp. 90–91.

our thin constitutionalism supports criticisms that reach beyond parochial views of what constitutionalism requires.

That's the general argument—a system consisting of reasonable specifications of foundational constitutional principles can't be criticized as anti-constitutional except under quite specific circumstances (circumstances that we explore in our case study of Hungary as a "Frankenstate"). But our statement has itself been quite abstract. We make it more specific with some examples.

- *Free expression: libeling public officials.* Public officials have to expect that someone sometime will criticize them quite severely for what they've done either in their public roles or in their private lives. That criticism can harm their reputations. When the criticism is unfair—for example, when it rests on a factually false premise—a legal system might reasonably give the public official a remedy for the harm to reputation. That's what the law of libel does.

  We'll assume, we think accurately, that contemporary constitutionalism bars nations from adopting the classical common law rules of libel law: strict liability for publishing reputation-damaging falsehoods, a presumption that false statements do harm reputation, the burden of proving truthfulness on the publisher. Even with those elements ruled out, many possibilities remain. The United States gives false statements about public officials a high degree of protection: the official loses unless she can show that the falsehoods were published by someone who either knew that they were false or acted with "reckless disregard" of their truth or falsity. Elsewhere public officials can win if they show that the publisher failed to comply with professional standards for verifying factual statements before publishing them. In yet other nations the officials can win if they prove that the statements were false and provide evidence that the statements did indeed harm their reputations.

  Now consider a government that proposes to change the libel rules currently operating—say, from the stringent U.S. rule to the somewhat less speech protective "journalistic standards" one. Is this intrinsically a "retrogression"—an erosion of constitutionalism?

  Here are two arguments why it isn't. First, the government might provide reasons for the change, pointing for example to changes in the media environment that have generated a much larger number of scurrilous and false allegations about public officials that had been the case when the highly speech-protective rule was adopted (with the effect, perhaps, of making it more difficult to attract people to public service). If that's a reasonable argument, we think it difficult to describe the change as a retrogression; it's just a change. Second, and more straightforward, if the "journalistic standards" rule had been in place from the beginning, we wouldn't worry that the nation was somehow falling short of constitutionalism. Changing from one reasonable specification of freedom of speech to another is, again, just a change.

Suppose, though, that we're confident that the government's proposal is motivated by a desire to punish its critics. Within broad limits, shouldn't the answer be that it depends upon whether the critics are right or wrong—not in their factual assertions, but in their core criticisms? If the government's pursuing good policies, scurrilous and false allegations against it are bad in part because they impede its ability to carry out those policies. And if the government's pursuing bad policies, we want to minimize the risks critics face, including risks of liability under libel law.

- *Judicial independence: packing the courts.* Suppose a progressive government takes office with an ambitious program—a "Green New Deal" or an innovative tax program to soak the rich. The principle of majority rule tells us that the government should be given a fair shot to implement its program. The government's legal advisers look at the veto gates the government's program has to get through. They identify three: a crucial committee in the lower house that's likely to have jurisdiction over key aspects of the government's program; a practice—the filibuster—in the upper house that in effect allows a minority to block the program; and the nine-person constitutional court whose current majority seems likely to obstruct the government's ability to implement its program. The advisers make three proposals: send the legislation to some other committee by changing the lower house's rules, eliminate the filibuster, and add two judges to the constitutional court. The advisers note that the constitution expressly gives each legislative house the power to determine its own rules and that nothing in the Constitution entrenches the number "nine" as the court's size. Before enacting the rest of its program, the government implements all three recommendations and packs the court by adding two members. Is this "court-packing" anti-constitutional?[42]

The same arguments we've deployed earlier work here as well. Changing the legislature's rules as the constitution permits can't plausibly be described as anti-constitutional. The same goes for changing the court's size. An eleven-member constitutional court is well within contemporary parameters, and no one would blink if the court had had eleven members all along. Each of the three actions removes a different veto gate. The only reason to allow the removal of the first two but worry about removing the third would be some sort of quasi-religious veneration for the courts.

---

[42] The problem gets more complicated if the court's size is constitutionally entrenched. All is well if the government's majority is large enough to secure a constitutional amendment. If it isn't, the question we discussed earlier—what to when the amendment rule in place is too stringent—arises.

Maybe that sort of veneration is a good thing (though we doubt it), but we're reasonably confident that constitutionalism doesn't require it.

F. Politicians and Political Parties

We've already relied on the final component of thin constitutionalism—the important role that politicians and political parties play, especially but not exclusively when majority preferences are determined by elections.[43] Politicians and their parties present political agendas to the public, and voters choose among the parties on the basis of the agendas they offer.

The other components of thin constitutionalism are almost entirely normative, identifying the "oughts" that define thin constitutionalism. This component has some normative content but is primarily descriptive: under contemporary circumstances reliably determining what a majority prefers is as a matter of fact greatly facilitated by politicians and political parties.

The focus here is on why voters (as a shorthand for "the public") support a politician or a political party, not on the politicians. A politician might quite cynically offer a political agenda to the public not because she believes that implementing it would be good for the country but simply because she thinks it's an agenda that a majority will support, and she wants to be elected (and re-elected) simply because she like to exercise power (or thinks that she'll benefit financially more from being elected than from anything else she might do). The politician's motivation doesn't matter, from the point of view of thin constitutionalism; the agenda the voters favor does.

One important qualification: consider a cynical politician who simply wants to exercise power. He wins by offering an agenda a majority favors (with the imperfections we've noted earlier about how party platforms only imperfectly reflect majority preferences). Then he proposes constitutional changes, using the existing amendment rules, that actually facilitate the implementation of that agenda. By removing some veto gates or speed bumps, the changes make it easier for the politician to accomplish anything and, at some point, the politician's underlying motivation to retain power comes to the fore. He implements a program that increases his power but actually doesn't have majority support, but with the veto gates and speed bumps destroyed, there's almost no way other than domestic turbulence to stop the now autocratic leader from hanging on to power.

---

[43] Politicians and political parties can propose referendums and other mechanisms for determining majority preferences outside of elections, and can take positions on referendums and the like. Our exposition is eased by focusing solely on elections, but our general points apply to politicians' role in every preference-determining mechanism.

This is indeed a problem for thin constitutionalism. But, as we'll argue in detail later, it's a problem associated with majority rule, not populism. The problem arises from the possibility that a proto-authoritarian can win an election by presenting a platform that a perhaps temporary majority prefers to the alternatives on offer. And the most obvious remedy, we think, is to hold elections rather frequently as a way of making it more likely that the government's agenda continues to have majority support.[44]

We might want to thicken constitutionalism to prevent this outcome. Some of our case studies suggest, though, that sometimes elections are enough to prevent proto-authoritarians from entrenching themselves. And, as important, thickening constitutionalism to prevent this outcome necessarily limits the ability of contemporary majorities to get what they want—it limits majority rule. At the level of constitutional theory and design, the relevant questions are the following: How great is the risk that a proto-authoritarian will win enough elections to become a true authoritarian ruler? How important are the policies that will be blocked by the thicker constitutional provisions used to prevent that outcome? And how likely is it that those policies would be adopted in a thin constitutional system? Our most general argument is that those questions can't be answered simply by saying that the politicians we worry about (today) happen sometimes to present themselves as populists, but have to be addressed by looking in detail at specific national conditions. Or, in an oversimplified tag line: we should worry about proto-authoritarian politicians, not populist politicians.

III. Constitutionalism, Norms, and Guardrails

The constitutionalism we've been discussing so far, thin or thick, is all about institutions—elections, courts, and more. For some time now, though, it's been clear that there's more to constitutionalism than institutions. Constitutionalism, again whether thin or thick, can be sustained only if there's something like a pro-constitutional culture behind it, a commitment by most of a nation's people to the idea of constitutionalism itself. And, we've come to understand, a pro-constitutional culture is sustained by norms and guardrails, to use terms popularized by political scientists Steven Levitsky and Daniel Ziblatt.[45]

Norms and guardrails are political practices that guide the behavior of politicians and ordinary citizens. For Levitsky and Ziblatt, the most important thing is that you treat the people you disagree with about politics as wrong but

---

[44] Of course, if the opposition doesn't offer an attractive alternative, as our case study of Venezuela suggests, elections aren't going to help.
[45] STEVEN LEVITSKY & DANIEL ZIBLATT, HOW DEMOCRACIES DIE (2018).

not your enemies. They have misguided views about what's good for the country, but they're working with you in the common political endeavor of making the country better. That's the most general one, but it gets worked out in more particular practices: You can protest when the legislature adopts policies you disagree with but you can't threaten the people you oppose with violence; you can go to court to find out whether they've done something unconstitutional, but you have to accept defeat when the courts rule against you—continuing the fight through ordinary political means.

Of course, we agree that a pro-constitutional culture, norms, and guardrails are important, yet as lawyers with some feeling for political science we have to be modest about what we can usefully say.

Where does a pro-constitutional culture come from? The classic answer is, "The family, education, religion, and some forms of economic organization." Responding to social developments, we (and others) would add "civil society" broadly understood and certain types of political parties (those in which membership requires active engagement within the party) to the list.[46] Lawyers can't contribute much to a discussion of how those institutions promote a pro-constitutional culture. We can of course say things about the ways in which constitutions can insulate the institutions from outside intrusion, thereby giving them space to be pro-constitutional. Yet, when they have that space, they can be anti-constitutional as well, and lawyers have nothing to say about how, for example, a family should be organized so as to make it likely that its members will be pro- rather than anti-constitutional. (We can't resist moving outside our disciplinary lane a bit, though, to observe that in our view the world of the twenty-first century places enormous pressures on the institutions traditionally thought to foster a pro-constitutional culture. Our discussion at the book's conclusion of some pro-democratic methods of populist governance might be construed as describing new institutions that can perform the pro-constitutional function that these traditional ones no longer can.)

When we move from culture to norms and guardrails, we think a legal perspective can be helpful, though the legal story we tell is a bit depressing. The problem starts with the observation, obvious as soon as it's stated, that norms aren't written down (if they were, they'd be what we've called institutions). That generates quite a few difficulties. We describe them here in an abstract form; our

---

[46] A word about two items on the list: some classical political theorists supported what's known as the "*doux commerce*" theory, according to which the ordinary face-to-face interactions between traders induced mutual tolerance of disagreements (after all, traders had to bargain with each other). Agrarian theorists argued to the same effect about how the daily activity of farming and selling what one raised created communities of mutual tolerance. And not all political parties have pro-constitutional effects. For an argument that elite-dominated conservative parties have sometimes facilitated the displacement of democracy by autocracy, *see* DANIEL ZIBLATT, CONSERVATIVE PARTIES AND THE BIRTH OF DEMOCRACY IN EUROPE (2017).

discussion in Chapter 8 of judicial reform proposals in the United States gives the arguments concrete content, and Chapter 10 examines the arguments in detail. Here we preview the arguments we make there.

When we look at some specific political practice or some series of political actions, we can't be sure that there's a norm or guardrail in place at all—or, perhaps more precisely, when some people do something that other people disagree with, the claim that the former group are trashing a norm or guardrail can become just another version of the underlying political disagreement: "You say that there's a norm that we're violating, but you're wrong: this particular thing we're doing operates in a norm-free domain where you can act pro-constitutionally simply by exercising whatever political power you happen to have."

Even when people can agree that there's a norm in the premises, they can—and will—disagree about what the norm is and so they will disagree about whether one side is breaching a norm. The reason is obvious: by definition norms aren't written down; they're content is inferred from practices people have engaged in in the past (recent or remote).

As lawyers familiar with the common law tradition, we do know something about inferring content from practices. Legal rules in a common law system aren't written down in canonical texts. They are inferred from decisions made by judges in the recent or remote past. We figure out what the rules are by standard methods of common law reasoning: We describe a prior case as resting upon a principle broader than the narrowest one necessary to justify the result, and then apply that principle to the problem we're facing; we say that a court's statement of a broad principle to explain its result was dictum and that the case should be read in light of the specific facts at hand; we draw analogies for the present case from decisions dealing with similar but slightly different facts; and much more.

Arguing about what norms are in place, and about whether something controversial violates a norm, is just like that. The effect is to reproduce the basic disagreement about policy in the discussion of norms and their purported violation.

A pro-constitutional culture, norms, and guardrails might well be centrally important to sustaining constitutionalism, and such a culture can be nurtured in many institutions, though whether it actually is nurtured depends a lot on how those institutions are structured. As lawyers our contribution must be limited: some skepticism about whether we get any purchase on the relation between constitutionalism and populism by focusing on norms and guardrails. Thin constitutionalism might be enough to sustain democracy, and more democracy might lead ordinary people to commit themselves even more deeply to democracy, a possibility we hint at in Chapter 12. We aren't completely agnostic about the ability of the institutions that legal scholars tend to pay most attention to, to sustain a pro-constitutional culture, but we don't want to exaggerate the contributions we can make with the distinctive tools that lawyers can deploy and use.

IV. Thin Constitutionalism's Attractions

Consider a person who supports a political agenda. She is committed to democracy, which means that she wants to see that program implemented, but only if she can persuade a majority of her co-citizens to support it as well. She also is committed to principles of constitutionalism. We believe that no matter what her political agenda, she would be satisfied with the principles of thin constitutionalism—majority rule, amendable entrenched provisions (with the possibility of replacing the existing constitution if she garners sufficient support from others), an independent judiciary. And—this is the central point—she might not be satisfied with anything thicker because her political agenda might be inconsistent with anything thicker. Eternity clauses are the most obvious example, but so would be thick conceptions of free expression, individual autonomy and privacy, and civic equality.

Here's another way of making this point. Spell out what you think constitutionalism requires, and ask yourself whether someone with a substantially different political agenda from yours would be unreasonable were she to reject the constraints on policy choices that version imposes. We believe that only thin constitutionalism fills the bill—that only anti-democrats can reasonably reject its principles.[47]

The payoff for the purposes of this book is simple and clear. we should examine each version of contemporary populism to see whether it is consistent with thin constitutionalism. Asking for more, in constitutional terms, from any specific version of populism is to conceal disagreement with that populism's program. It puts a constitutional mask over political disagreement. When that occurs, as we argue in the following chapters, we believe that scholarly honesty requires that we insist that the mask be taken off. And, though we are less certain about this, we hope that unmasking the politics underneath the nominally "constitutional" criticism will enhance the political effectiveness of the critics' positions.

---

[47] This defense of thin constitutionalism resembles well-known arguments in political theory—the idea associated with John Rawls that we try to figure out the principles of justice we would choose behind a veil of ignorance, and the related but somewhat different idea that principles of justice have the characteristic that no one could reasonably reject them. We should be clear that we are not *relying* upon those arguments to justify thin constitutionalism, only pointing out the similarity between them and our argument.

2

What Is Populism?

I. The Conventional View and Our Alternative: An Introduction

As we've noted, we write against a background of popular and academic publications arguing that populism is by definition antithetical to constitutionalism.[1] By attacking the core elements of constitutional democracy, such as independent courts, free media, civil rights, and fair electoral rules, populism by necessity degenerates into one or another form of anti-liberal and authoritarian order.[2] Populist leaders set up an opposition between the people and their enemies and take advantage of opportunities made available by new media to dominate political discourse. Or so it is said.

We argue that such an approach is both historically inaccurate and normatively mistaken. Even confining ourselves to relatively recent history, we can find examples of forms of populism that didn't degenerate into authoritarianism and that actually promoted democracy. The U.S. New Deal, for example, strengthened democracy by thickening a social safety net that enabled working people to participate actively in their own governance. At a major campaign rally in 1936, Franklin Delano Roosevelt said:

> We had to struggle with the old enemies of peace—business and financial monopoly, speculation, reckless banking, class antagonism, sectionalism, war profiteering. They had begun to consider the Government of the United States as a mere appendage to their own affairs. We know now that Government by organized money is just as dangerous as Government by organized mob. Never before in all our history have these forces been so united against one candidate

---

[1] *See generally* Cristóbal Rovira Kaltwasser, "Populism vs. Constitutionalism: Comparative Perspectives on Contemporary Western Europe, Latin America, and the United States," in THE FOUNDATION FOR LAW, JUSTICE, AND SOCIETY POLICY BRIEF (Oxford 2013), at pp. 2–3, available at https://ora.ox.ac.uk/objects/uuid:0b3a92d0-401b-4af8-a4bd-89afb98e7454; JAN-WERNER MÜLLER, WHAT IS POPULISM? (2016); WILLIAM GALSTON, ANTI-PLURALISM: THE POPULIST THREAT TO LIBERAL DEMOCRACY (2018); YASCHA MOUNK, THE PEOPLE VS. DEMOCRACY: WHY OUR FREEDOM IS IN DANGER AND HOW TO SAVE IT (2018); Stefan Rummens, "Populism as a Threat to Liberal Democracy," in THE OXFORD HANDBOOK OF POPULISM (Cristóbal Rovira Kaltwasser, Paul Taggart, Paulina Ochoa Espejo, & Pierre Ostiguy eds. 2017), at p. 554.

[2] Takis S. Pappas, *Populists in Power*, JOURNAL OF DEMOCRACY 30:2 (2019), at p. 70.

Power to the People. Mark Tushnet and Bojan Bugaric, Oxford University Press. © Mark Tushnet and Bojan Bugaric" 2021. DOI: 10.1093/oso/9780197606711.003.0003

as they stand today. They are unanimous in their hate for me—and I welcome their hatred. I should like to have it said of my first Administration that in it the forces of selfishness and of lust for power met their match. I should like to have it said of my second Administration that in it these forces met their master.[3]

Roosevelt innovated in the use of the new radio medium by giving thirty "fireside chats" to reach into households around the country. Yet no one seriously contends today that Roosevelt was a threat to democracy—though we must note that his opponents, such as the businesspeople who supported the American Liberty League, said exactly that. Perhaps FDR was a populist, in which case populism doesn't always foreshadow authoritarianism. Or perhaps FDR wasn't a populist, in which case at least some of the elements of "populism" are actually common tropes in ordinary politics.

The current populist map offers examples of such democratic populists, who seek to protect and defend democracy by making it more responsive, equitable, and inclusive. This category includes Spain's Podemos Party and the Indignados Movement, Syriza in Greece, the Left Party in Germany, the Socialist Party in the Netherlands, Five Star Movement in Italy, Bernie Sanders in the United States, and (more controversially) Evo Morales in Bolivia and Rafael Correa in Ecuador.[4]

To understand the relation between populism and constitutionalism we must distinguish among varieties of populism, each of which has different political consequences. As our critique of major works on populism shows, populism always coexists with a variety of different "host" ideologies: agrarian populism, socioeconomic populism, ethno-nationalist populism, reactionary populism, authoritarian populism, progressive populism (and more).[5] The host ideologies significantly affect, perhaps even determine, how populism affects democracy and constitutionalism.[6] Elisabeth Ivarstflaten observes: "Some extremists

[3] Franklin D. Roosevelt, "Campaign Address at Madison Square Garden, New York City," Oct. 31, 1936, in PUBLIC PAPERS AND ADDRESSES OF FRANKLIN D. ROOSEVELT, VOL. 5: THE PEOPLE APPROVE 1936, at pp. 568–69 (1938). We note that the important recent work, JORGE TAMAMES, FOR THE PEOPLE: LEFT POPULISM IN SPAIN AND THE US (2020), uses this quotation to the same effect.

[4] PIPPA NORRIS & RONALD INGLEHART, CULTURAL BACKLASH: TRUMP, BREXIT AND AUTHORITARIAN POPULISM (2019), at p. 11.

[5] MARGARET CANOVAN, POPULISM (1981); Noam Gidron & Bart Bonikowski, "Varieties of Populism: Literature Review and Research Agenda," Weatherhead Center for International Affairs, Harvard University, Working Paper Series no.13-0004 2013, available at https://scholar.harvard.edu/gidron/publications/varieties-populism-literature-review-and-research-agenda, archived at https://perma.cc/7DBS-HSMT; Cas Mudde & Cristóbal Rovira Kaltwasser, "Populism," in THE OXFORD HANDBOOK OF POLITICAL IDEOLOGIES (Michael Freeden, Lyman Tower Sargent, & Marc Stears eds. 2013), at pp. 493, 495–98.

[6] Robert H. Dix, Populism: Authoritarian and Democratic, 20 (2) LATIN AMERICAN RESEARCH REVIEW 29 (1985); Margaret Canovan, Trust the People! Populism and the Two Faces of Democracy, 47 POLITICAL STUDIES 2 (1999). Perhaps the only "ideology" that can't be associated with populism is an ideology of centrism, the view that policies should always be some compromise among all the possibilities offered by any significant political force.

are also populists, some populists are also extremists; but not all populists are extremist, and not all extremists are populists." Substitute any other noun for "extremists" and you have our perspective.[7]

Empirical studies of effects of populism on constitutional democracy show a mixed picture: populism has both negative and positive consequences for democracy. Sometimes authoritarian populism leads to democratic backsliding and breakdown, and sometimes democratic populism fosters democratization.[8] Once we couple populist discourse with different host ideologies, the relationship between populism and constitutional democracy is quite complicated. We don't deny that sometimes conservative and progressive populists slide into authoritarianism. When they do, they are best described, to quote Douglas Johnson again, as authoritarians masquerading as populists.[9]

The next section develops our critique of generalized accounts of populism. We argue that scholars should direct their attention to the questions posed by specific actions taken by individual populist governments rather than make generalized claims about populism and constitutionalism as such. Most general accounts of populism treat populism as a style of politics or form of political discourse devoid of any particular ideology. Coupling populism with different host ideologies shows that populist parties and leaders have quite different conceptions of the people, goals, and relations to liberal democracy. As political theorist Camila Vergara asks, "why should we lump together under the same label such radically different political projects?"[10] We then offer a "map" of different "actually existing populisms" and examine how different populist ideologies and ideals translate into constitutional law. The conclusion—mundane as it might seem—is that sometimes populist governments act in anti-constitutional ways, and sometimes they do not.

---

[7] Elisabeth Ivarsflaten, "Siren Songs: Reflections on Contemporary Populism in Europe's Old Democracies," in SYMPOSIUM: POPULISM IN COMPARATIVE PERSPECTIVE (Matt Golder & Sona Golder eds.), CP: NEWSLETTER OF THE COMPARATIVE POLITICS ORGANIZED SECTION OF THE AMERICAN POLITICAL SCIENCE ASSOCIATION 26:2 (2016), at p. 51.

[8] As Hawkins and Kaltwasser put it, "despite the fact that there are good reasons for worrying about the rise of populism, scholars are probably putting too much emphasis on the downsides and thus not considering potential positive effects of populist forces." Kirk A. Hawkins & Cristóbal Rovira Kaltwasser, What the (Ideational) Study of Populism Can Teach Us, and What It Can't, 23 SWISS POLITICAL SCIENCE REVIEW 526 (2017), at p. 531.

[9] Douglas A. Johnson, "In Defense of Democratic Populism," in HUMAN RIGHTS IN A TIME OF POPULISM: CHALLENGES AND RESPONSES 192 (Gerald L. Neuman ed. 2020).

[10] Camila Vergara, Populism as Plebeian Politics: Inequality, Domination, and Popular Empowerment, 28 JOURNAL OF POLITICAL PHILOSOPHY 222 (2020), at p. 222.

II. Is Populism (Always) Antithetical to Constitutionalism? On the Importance of Definitions and Their Implications

A. Populism as Anti-Liberalism: Is There a Single Formula to Define Populism?

Handbooks, research guides, and companions to populism abound. Authors use the term to refer to a large number of political movements, and no agreed-upon definition has yet emerged. The most widely used approach to populism in contemporary academic literature is the "ideational" approach. It treats populism "as an ideology, as a set of ideas or as a worldview."[11] Political scientist Cas Mudde's version is the most commonly used. According to Mudde, populism is "a thin-centered ideology" that "considers society to be ultimately separated into two homogeneous and antagonistic groups, 'the pure people' versus 'the corrupt elite,' and which argues that politics should be an expression of the *volonté générale* (general will) of the people."[12] Similarly, Jan-Werner Müller, another widely cited political scientist, defines populism as "a way of perceiving the political world that sets a morally pure and fully united—but . . . ultimately fictional-people against elites who are deemed corrupt or in some way morally inferior."[13] As Benjamin Moffitt correctly notices, both Mudde and Müller highlight two core features of populism: "(a) the divide between 'the people' and 'the elite' and (b) the homogeneity, unification and moral 'purity' of 'the people.'"[14]

Mudde and Müller contend that populism, as they understand it, is a threat to liberal democracy. For both, populism's essential trait is a rejection of pluralism: "Populism holds that nothing should constrain 'the will of the (pure) people' and fundamentally rejects the notions of pluralism and, therefore, minority rights as well as the 'institutional guarantees' that should protect them."[15]

Treating populism as inherently anti-liberal and anti-pluralist is in some tension with another element of the ideational approach to populism, the argument that populism is "thin centered," able "to cohabit with other, more comprehensive ideologies."[16] The implication of the thin-centered nature of populism is that it "does not stand alone as an ideology but is rather always combined with other ideologies."[17] As Paul Taggart puts it, populism is chameleon-like, ever adapting

---

[11] BENJAMIN MOFFITT, POPULISM (2020), at p. 12.
[12] Cas Mudde, *The Populist Zeitgeist*, 39 GOVERNMENT & OPPOSITION 541 (2004), at pp. 544, 543.
[13] MÜLLER, note 1 above, at p. 17.
[14] MOFFITT, note 11 above, at p. 13.
[15] CAS MUDDE & CRISTÓBAL ROVIRA KALTWASSER, POPULISM: A VERY SHORT INTRODUCTION (2017), at p. 81.
[16] Ben Stanley, *The Thin Ideology of Populism*, 13 JOURNAL OF POLITICAL IDEOLOGIES 95 (2008), at p. 100.
[17] MOFFITT, note 11 above, at p. 13.

to the colors of its environment.[18] As a thin-centered ideology, populism shares characteristics of other thin-centered ideologies such as nationalism, feminism, and green politics rather than being a thick ideology like liberalism, socialism, or fascism. To fully understand the logic of the different populisms, we have to approach them as socially and historically contingent categories. Political scientist Anna Grzymala-Busse argues that we should recognize that populism takes a variety of guises rather than analyzing populism per se.[19]

Yet, despite the widespread agreement that populism can assume many forms, many political scientists and legal scholars tend to reduce populism to a set of generic elements such as anti-pluralism, the people's homogeneity and exclusivity, nationalism, a strong single leader, impatience with institutions, direct popular rule, and vilification of minorities.[20] According to this literature, populism "fundamentally opposes the essence of constitutionalism," and, is "the mirror-image opposite, and a major foe, of contemporary liberal democracy."[21]

Professor Müller's formulation is probably the most widely cited. He argues that populism is not only anti-elitist but also anti-pluralist: Populists claim that "they, and they alone, represent the people."[22] In their worldview, there are no opponents, only traitors. The opposition leaders are delegitimized through being cast as not caring about ordinary citizens, but only about their narrow self-interest as an "elite." By denying any legitimate role in policy-making to this elite, populism rejects pluralism—or at least rejects what we might call "comprehensive" pluralism, in which all claims have to be taken into account as policy is made.

The second element of the "inner logic of populism" is the noninstitutionalized notion of the people: "For them, 'the people themselves' is a fictional entity outside existing democratic procedures, a homogeneous and morally unified body whose alleged will can be played off against actual election results in democracy."[23] What populists actually assert is "that there is a singular and morally privileged understanding or will that has not been manifest through the formal structures of democratic choice."[24]

---

[18] Paul Taggart, Populism (2000), at p. 4.

[19] Anna Grzymala-Busse, *Global Populisms and Their Impact*, 76 Slavic Review S3 (2017).

[20] In addition to the sources cited in note 1, *see* Gabor Halmai, *Is There Such a Thing as Populist Constitutionalism? The Case of Hungary*, 11 (3) Fudan Journal of the Humanities & Social Sciences 323 (2018).

[21] Cas Mudde, "Are Populists Friends or Foes of Constitutionalism," The Foundation for Law, Justice, and Society Policy Brief (Oxford 2013), at p. 4, available at https://ora.ox.ac.uk/objects/uuid:fc657de0-ab0c-4911-8d2b-646101599b65, archived at https://perma.cc/6EVA-4V3M; Pappas, note 2 above, at p.70.

[22] Müller, note 1 above, at p. 8.

[23] *Id.* at p. 20.

[24] Aziz Z. Huq, *The People Against the Constitution*, 116 Michigan Law Review 1123 (2018), at p. 1133.

This leads us to a third element said to be characteristic of populism, the role of the "leader," often said to be charismatic. The populist leader does what the people want, but populist leaders are said to believe that they have some sort of privileged access to knowledge about what the people want, independent of any institutional mechanisms (such as regular elections) that only imperfectly reveal the people's wishes. The formal structures of liberal democracy have to be put aside if they prevent the populist leader from implementing what he or she concludes the people want. Populist leaders distrust all the traditional institutions of liberal democracy that stand between them and the wishes of the people. As a result, many populist parties openly flout the rule of law and explicitly reject the values of liberal democracy, because those institutions impose procedural hurdles to doing what the people want. A corollary of this element is the strong personalization of power, reflected in the fact that leaders like Orbán and Kaczyński have managed to concentrate almost unlimited political power in their hands.

Müller's definition of populism has many followers in the constitutional law literature. Hungarian constitutional scholar Gábor Halmai, for example, contends that populist constitutionalism is an oxymoron: there can be populist constitutions, but there cannot be populist constitutionalism, because the values of populism are antithetical to the values of constitutionalism.[25] Italian law professor Cesare Pinelli has argued that while populists are unlikely to question representative democracy, "They attack non-majoritarian institutions on the ground of their lack of democratic legitimacy."[26]

Paul Blokker, a political sociologist, advances a more tentative definition of populism, in large part because he expressly includes left- and right-wing versions within his purview. For him, in populist constitutionalism, "the actual engagement of (different groups of) citizens in society is substituted for by the idea of a united people, represented by the populist leader. The main culprit is identified in corrupt elite rule . . .," which, he notes earlier, is "detrimental to the common good." Further, populism "tend[s] to deny a strong separation of politics and law and endorse[s] a stronger link between constitutions and the people." Populists criticize "the idea of the law as *non-political and neutral*" and "what is perceived of as a strong separation between law, on the one hand, and politics and morality on the other. . . ." With others, Blokker describes this attitude as "instrumentalism." This makes populists "critical about the strong and independent nature of apex courts, the role and form of judicial review, and the extensive and entrenched nature of individual rights." It "tend[s] to suffer from an exclusionary

---

[25] Halmai, note 20 above.
[26] Cesare Pinelli, *The Populist Challenge to Constitutional Democracy*, 7 EUROPEAN CONSTITUTIONAL LAW REVIEW 5 (2016), at p. 15.

tendency, which results from the quest for an authentic people, and in practice risk[s] sliding into either authoritarian or 'leaderist'-plebiscitarian modes. . . ."[27] Finally, Blokker asserts that "majoritarianism" is a characteristic feature of populism, and that populism involves "a political appeal to the people, and a claim to legitimacy that rests on the democratic ideology of popular sovereignty and majority rule."[28]

As this last quotation suggests, we believe that much of what Blokker described as characteristic of populism is more accurately described as characteristic of democratic politics and of law itself. Take a relatively simple example, the rhetorical opposition populists are said to draw between the people and the elites. Social scientists Bart Bonikowski and Noam Gidron looked at almost 2,500 speeches by U.S. presidential candidates between 1952 and 1996—the "pre-populist era," we'd say—and found that that rhetoric was quite common.[29] By this account, more or less every U.S. presidential candidate since 1952 has been a populist, which strikes us as more than implausible. Casting yourself as the candidate of the people against the elites isn't distinctively populist.[30]

On a deeper level, consider populist views of the role of law in governance. We can imagine a view of politics as founded on natural law or something similar, but most democratic theorists, we believe, agree that democracy ultimately "rests on" some version of an "ideology of popular sovereignty." Similarly with majoritarianism: a well-known result in social/public choice theory shows that majoritarianism is the only voting rule that generates stable policies (as long as preferences are stable).[31] And there is a jurisprudential defense of an instrumentalist view of law rooted not only in Carl Schmitt's work, to which Blokker alludes,[32] but also in the American Legal Realist tradition and its descendant

---

[27] Paul Blokker, *Populism as Constitutional Project,* 17 INTERNATIONAL JOURNAL OF CONSTITUTIONAL LAW 535 (2019), at pp. 540, 549, 552, 537 n. 4. We emphasize that "leaderism" is for Blokker only a tendency. We suspect that only specialists in Spanish and Greek politics could name off the top of their heads the leaders of Podemos and Syriza, often described as populist parties in those nations. Though Blokker does not associate "leaderism" with charismatic leaders, the association is often made. *See, e.g.,* Jane Mansbridge & Stephen Macedo, *Populism and Democratic Theory,* 15 ANNUAL REVIEW OF LAW & SOCIAL SCIENCE 59 (2019), at p. 60 (describing as a "non-core" characteristic of populism "a single leader embodying the people."). We note that not all populist leaders are fairly described as charismatic, Jarosław Kacyński being the most obvious.

[28] Blokker, note 27 above, at p. 541, quoting Margaret Canovan, "Taking Politics to the People: Populism as the Ideology of Democracy," in DEMOCRACIES AND THE POPULIST CHALLENGE (Yves Mény & Yves Surel eds. 2002), p. 25.

[29] Bart Bonikowski & Noam Gidron, *The Populist Style in American Politics: Presidential Campaign Discourse, 1952–1996,* 94 SOCIAL FORCES 1593 (2015).

[30] Similarly, Danielle Resnick points out that some leaders of military coups in Africa used "people power and anti-elite rhetoric" to justify their actions. Danielle Resnick, "Two Generations of African Populism: Applying a Cumulative Conceptual Approach," in SYMPOSIUM: POPULISM IN COMPARATIVE PERSPECTIVE (Matt Golder & Sona Golder eds.), CP: NEWSLETTER OF THE COMPARATIVE POLITICS ORGANIZED SECTION OF THE AMERICAN POLITICAL SCIENCE ASSOCIATION 26:2 (2016), at p. 65. Here too we think that associating the rhetoric with populism is misleading.

[31] This is May's Theorem.

[32] Blokker, note 27 above, at p. 549.

Critical Legal Studies. The Realists and their successors argued that *in the end* though not necessarily proximately law was always instrumental. *Avant la lettre*, they were critical of aggressive forms of constitutional review and skeptical about claims that general guarantees of individual rights generated specific outcomes in controversial cases.[33] We think it worth entertaining the view that populists have a better understanding of law *as such*, that is, as ultimately instrumental, then their critics.[34] As with Mudde and Kaltwasser, for Blokker what appears to single out populism from other forms of political activity by ordinary people, then, is a principled anti-pluralism.

Conceptualized in this way, populism does indeed conflict with liberalism's commitment to pluralism, openness, and protection of individual rights. Moreover, after Müller moves from the analysis of populism's inner logic to an examination of what populists actually do when in power, populism becomes almost indistinguishable from authoritarianism and dictatorship. Müller's catalogue is depressing: The hallmarks of populism in power are colonization of the state, mass clientelism and mass corruption, and the systematic repression of civil society.[35]

Most of Müller's claims seem reasonably accurate with respect to the central focus of his story, the particular type of populism that has evolved in East Central Europe. Authoritarian populists in Hungary and Poland have successfully institutionalized, through legal reforms, a new version of a semi-authoritarian regime, halfway between "diminished democracy" and "competitive authoritarianism."[36] Following similar scripts, which counsel sustained attacks on rule of law institutions, civil rights and freedoms, the media, and electoral rules, leaders

---

[33] For a discussion of what we call the specification problem, see Chapter 3. Elsewhere Blokker writes that conservative populists "justify their legal actions by taking issue with legalistic or *liberal* understandings of law and constitutionalism. . . ." Paul Blokker, *Populist Counter-Constitutionalism, Conservatism, and Legal Fundamentalism*, 15 EUROPEAN CONSTITUTIONAL LAW REVIEW 519 (2019), at p. 531. The alternatives he describes are different, in our view: The (instrumental) critique of legalism is jurisprudential, the anti-liberal critique is political (and of course conservative). Similarly with his undifferentiated list in his description of the idea, criticized by conservative populists, "of a neutral, universalist, individualist, and secularist understanding of law." *Id.* at p. 533.

[34] Paul Blokker, *Populist Understandings of the Law: A Conservative Backlash?*, 13 PARTICIAZIONE É CONFLITTO 1433 (2020), at pp. 1442, 1443, 1445, 1446, describes right-wing populist critiques of liberal conceptions of law as abstract and "incapable of interacting with 'thick' or 'real' community life," as a threat to national identity, as "a partisan minority ideology," and as "instruments of particular groups of society." We think it would be valuable to supplement this with a similar account of left-wing populist critiques of liberal conceptions of law, which we would associate with American Legal Realism and Critical Legal Studies. Our tentative view is that such a confrontation would cast doubt on the idea that we can sensibly think about "the law as such," and (therefore) on the idea that populists challenge the ideal of the rule of law as such.

[35] MÜLLER, note 1 above, at pp. 29–31.

[36] David Collier & Steven Levitsky, *Democracy with Adjectives: Conceptual Innovation in Comparative Research*, 49 WORLD POLITICS 430 (1997); STEVEN LEVITSKY & LUCIAN A. WAY, COMPETITIVE AUTHORITARIANISM: HYBRID REGIMES AFTER THE COLD WAR (2010).

in both nations dismantled almost all the key cornerstones of constitutional democracy in Hungary and Poland in a relatively short period of time.[37]

Yet, while Müller's definition relatively accurately captures the "inner logic" of one particular type of populism, authoritarian populism, it leaves out many other possible types of populism, which do not necessarily share the same characteristics. Though Müller puts anti-pluralism at the center of his analysis, his presentation, in contrast, *could* be understood to refer to nearly all forms of political activity by "ordinary" people unified for political purposes only in a project aimed at displacing existing ruling elites with political leaders more attuned to the interests of the people—interests that could in principle vary depending on which groups of ordinary people are most immediately affected by specific policies. The corruption and moral inferiority that Müller sees in populism's description of ruling elites could, again in principle, be a way of characterizing their failure to take the interests of (a possibly pluralist) "ordinary" population adequately into account. Criticizing the reductionist nature of such accounts of populism, legal theorist Neil Walker argues that "a simple equation of populism with authoritarianism is unduly reductive." According to Walker, populist constitutionalism occupies "a space between authoritarian and popular versions of constitutionalism, overlapping both but not reducible to either." He nevertheless concludes that populist moment contains "an authoritarian impulse."[38] Here we disagree and argue that it is impossible to give such attributes to populism in general.

One problem with Müller's analysis, and of those who follow his lead, is "selection bias." He looks at Hungary and Poland in detail and glances at some other nations, and says that his sample is representative of a generic populism. We believe that expanding the sample to include other nations—Greece and the Syriza Party; Spain and the Podemos movement; and, importantly, a number of Latin American examples—complicates the story rather dramatically. Of course scholars are entitled to define their subjects as they wish. Our concern is that selection bias has led to mistaken generalizations: seeing some things in the sample, authors say that those things characterize populism as such, without asking whether those things occur in other populisms—and, again importantly, whether they occur in non-populist politics.[39]

---

[37] Grzegorz Ekiert, "How to Deal with Poland and Hungary," Occasional Paper 13, Center for European Studies, Harvard University (Aug. 17, 2017), available at https://www.socialeurope.eu/book/op-deal-poland-hungary, archived at https://perma.cc/97UR-CC2Z.

[38] Neil Walker, *Populism and Constitutional Tension*, 17 INTERNATIONAL JOURNAL OF CONSTITUTIONAL LAW 515 (2019), at pp. 515, 525, 528.

[39] The selection bias has attracted some attention. Thomas Frank critiques Müller for describing populism as such based upon a sample that includes only racist and authoritarian demagogues. THOMAS FRANK, THE PEOPLE, NO: A BRIEF HISTORY OF ANTI-POPULISM (2020), at p. 35. Marco D'Eramo and Daniel Steinmetz-Jenkins criticize Müller's definition of populism for including a figure like Bernie Sanders from the ranks of the populists while failing to discuss the ways in which Sanders and his supporters lack many of the characteristics that Müller contends define populism.

B. Populism: From a Single Formula to "Varieties of Populism"

Theories that define populism in a singular generic form fail to analyze the impact of host ideologies on the legal and constitutional consequences of various populist forces.[40] When we examine the relationship between populism and constitutional democracy, each version of populism must be considered together with its host ideology.

Margaret Canovan, a political theorist, was one of the first scholars of populism who argued that populism comes both in democratic and authoritarian forms. As Camila Vergara summarizes Canovan's view, populism is "born out of crisis as a cure for the failures of traditional forms of representation," and that sometimes populism was a "corrective to the excesses of pragmatism."[41] For Canovan, populism is a democratizing phenomenon aimed at perfecting democratic representativeness, renewing the political system from within. Similarly, for Hannah Arendt, "these episodes of collective self-assertion are invariably fleeting and stand in tension with the need for a more stable constitution of collective freedom, embodied in the rule of law, and representative institutions."[42]

To label these movements "populist" in a pejorative sense is to misunderstand this inherent instability of the democratic project. As James Miller argues, populist "outbursts are essential to the continued vitality, and viability, of modern democracy—even as (and precisely because) they challenge the status quo, destructive though that challenge may be."[43]

Marco D'Eramo, *They, the People*, 103 NEW LEFT REVIEW 129 (Jan.–Feb. 2017); Daniel Steinmetz-Jenkins, *The Logic of Populism*, 64 (2) DISSENT 186 (2017).

Because we focus on contemporary populism, we confine to this footnote Frank's additional observations about past populist movements. Frank lists several historical figures associated with progressive and democratic populism in the United States: Andrew Jackson, the Populist Party, and FDR. Frank also reminds us of an alternative definition of populism, offered by historian Lawrence Goodwyn; in the opening statement of his book, Goodwyn argues that "[t]his book is about the flowering of the largest democratic mass movement in American history. It is also necessarily a book about democracy itself." LAWRENCE GOODWYN, THE POPULIST MOMENT: A SHORT HISTORY OF THE AGRARIAN REVOLT IN AMERICA (1978), at p. vii. For Goodwyn, populism represented "a vision of democratic participation that was actually more advanced than what we settle for today. Far from being a threat to democracy, Populism was democracy's zenith."

[40] As Camila Vergara argues, note 10 above, at p. 222, these theories have contributed to a "totalitarian turn" in the conception of populism toward an identitarian, xenophobic, and oligarchic form of politics clothed in populist rhetoric.

[41] Vergara, note 10 above, at p. 229.

[42] JAMES MILLER, CAN DEMOCRACY WORK? A SHORT HISTORY OF A RADICAL IDEA FROM ANCIENT ATHENS TO OUR WORLD (2018), at p. 11.

[43] *Id.* As Vergara argues, "this normative dimension of populism, as a 'corrective' was gradually lost within the theoretical discussion especially after the 'discursive turn' in the interpretation of the concept in the late 2000s," Vergara, note 10 above, at p. 230. In our view, it was lost in part as well because of the selection bias we have described.

In another important recent study of populism, political scientists Pippa Norris and Ronald Inglehart argue that populism comes in authoritarian and libertarian versions. What primarily distinguishes authoritarian from libertarian populism is the embrace of the authoritarian values such as security, conformity, and obedience, which lead to "prioritizing collective security for the group at the expense of liberal autonomy of the individual." Libertarian populist parties typically "use populist discourse railing against corruption, mainstream parties, and multinational corporations, . . . blended with the endorsement of socially liberal attitudes, progressive social policies and participatory styles of political engagement."[44] Podemos, Syriza, the Five Star Movement, and Bernie Sanders are examples of democratic, liberal, socially inclusive forms of populism.[45] The examples demonstrate that authoritarianism and anti-pluralism do not define every movement that goes under the label "populist."[46]

In another work that seeks to avoid selection bias, political scientists Jane Mansbridge and Stephen Macedo argue that there is a "common conceptual core" of populism, which fits all cases of populism, both Left and Right, those in the United States, Europe, and elsewhere. Their minimal common core defines populism as "the people" in a moral battle against "the elites." This minimum core definition precludes neither progressive nor conservative nor authoritarian forms of populism. Furthermore, they argue, the core can be good for democracy, because the core elements can "benefit democracy by taking democratic politics back to its normative roots in the wants and needs of ordinary citizens and challenging, on egalitarian and justice grounds, elite political, economic, and cultural domination."[47] We see their position related to populism's asserted anti-pluralism in this way: "The people" may be internally differentiated, including for example "farmers" and "workers" as the U.S. Populist Party did in the late nineteenth century. They are united, though, in opposition to "elites," who are not simply another interest group in the pluralist universe.[48]

---

[44]   NORRIS & INGLEHART, note 4 above, at pp. 7, 11.

[45]   The list is not meant to suggest that this form of populism is an exclusive domain of the political left. But it is empirically less likely to find democratic populism among radical right-wing parties.

[46]   For a similar argument, see Bart Bonikowski, *Ethno-nationalist Populism and the Mobilization of Collective Resentment*, 68 (S1) BRITISH JOURNAL OF SOCIOLOGY S181 (2017), at p. S190 (pointing out that "populism has also been employed by mainstream politicians who operate within the constraints of democratic institutions. And even when populist movements have radical origins, the resulting political outcomes can be benign with respect to democratic stability.").

[47]   Mansbridge & Macedo, note 27 above, at p. 60.

[48]   *See also* Gilles Ivaldi, Maria Elisabetta Lanzone, & Dwayne Woods, *Varieties of Populism Across a Left-Right Spectrum: The Case of the Front National, the Northern League, Podemos and Five Star Movement*, 23 SWISS POLITICAL SCIENCE REVIEW 354 (2017), at p. 355 (concluding that "all four parties converge . . . on their conception of the elite as a separate 'caste,' . . . [but] differ . . . in their conception of the 'true' people that they presumably represent . . ."). The authors also observe that "the idealized people are systematically defined as an inclusive entity that transcends *existing attachments* . . ." (emphasis added). *Id.* at p. 370. That formulation suggests that populists

Mansbridge and Macedo warn that the moral antagonism inherent in populism's core elements might undermine "the democratic commitment to treating all members of the polity, including members of the elite, with respect... [and] the capacity of democracy for negotiation and compromise."[49] They emphasize, though, that this moral antagonism doesn't place the core elements at odds with constitutionalism. Instead, they identify some dangerous characteristics that are associated, in different degrees, with different populisms. Some of these characteristics are strongly suggested but not entailed: the idea of a homogeneous people, the idea of an exclusive people, greater direct popular rule, and nationalism. Others frequently accompany populisms, but are merely contingently correlated with it: a strong leader embodying the people, vilification of minority groups, and impatience with deliberation.

For Mansbridge and Macedo, populism and constitutionalism come into conflict only when some of the elements from the other groups of characteristics accompany populism's core elements. This two-pronged definition of populism better fits the complexity and multiplicity of forms that populism can assume. It allows us to see a multifaceted nature of populism, which sometimes comes in democratic form, and sometimes in authoritarian or illiberal forms.[50]

The combination of populism and constitutionalism "sounds odd especially to a European ear," but populist constitutionalism is a well-established tradition in the United States.[51] As law professors Joseph Fishkin and William Forbath argue, many U.S. populist movements contributed to creating an "anti-oligarchy" concept of constitutionalism, which sought to empower and protect the democratic nature of the American constitution.[52] In the same way, Bruce Ackerman has argued that the key founding moments of American constitutionalism are best defined as the episodes of democratic populist constitutionalism. In his most recent book, Ackerman extends his analysis to several historical cases of revolutionary constitutionalism around the world and shows that populism can be compatible with constitutionalism.[53]

---

acknowledge "existing attachments," which is to say some form of pluralism, and—perhaps—that it can be reflected in policy choices other than those directed at the elite caste.

[49] Mansbridge & Macedo, note 27 above, at p. 60.

[50] Mirroring the minimalist core definition of populism by Mansbridge and Macedo, David Fontana puts forward an argument for "unbundling" the antiestablishment and democratic part of populism from the authoritarian and xenophobic version. David Fontana, *Unbundling Populism*, 65 UCLA LAW REVIEW 1482 (2018).

[51] Lucia Corso, *What Does Populism Have to do with Constitutional Law? Discussing Populist Constitutionalism and Its Assumptions*, 3 (2) RIVISTA DI FILOSOFIA DEL DIRRITO 443 (2004), at p. 444.

[52] Joey Fishkin & William Forbath, *The Anti-Oligarchy Constitution*, 94 BOSTON UNIVERSITY LAW REVIEW 669 (2014).

[53] BRUCE A. ACKERMAN, WE THE PEOPLE: FOUNDATIONS (1991); BRUCE A. ACKERMAN, REVOLUTIONARY CONSTITUTIONS: CHARISMATIC LEADERSHIP AND THE RULE OF LAW (2019).

These dissenting views about populism and constitutionalism support Professor Robert Howse's observation that "[t]he populist label is a form of 'othering' that eschews serious engagement with those who see more promise than peril in today's disruptive politics," and that it is often attached to give "a pejorative cast on democratic politics of any sort that challenges elitist liberal democracy. . . ." He also observes that "[t]he answer, 'That's just . . . how we define populism' . . . seem[s] thoroughly question-begging." He distinguishes the policies of good (economic) populism from bad (political) populism. The policies of good populism, according to Howse, will be consistent with inclusion and pluralism. They would include New Deal-like initiatives that tax and regulate the wealthy, and large businesses, but all the while allowing them to participate and continue to thrive in the polity.[54] For Howse, Sanders's version of democratic populism seeks to work *within* the legal constraints of constitutional democracy.

C. Is Populism a Threat to or Corrective for Constitutional Democracy?

What do empirical studies show about populism, in its many versions, and constitutionalism? While the populist surge has become global, our knowledge about its political and legal implications remains anecdotal and muddled.

Quantitative studies are helpful in combating what psychologists call the "availability" heuristic, which in our context means attributing to all populisms the characteristics of the examples that come most readily to mind. To begin, then, we offer the classification developed by political scientist Mattia Zulianello, who looked at sixty-six populist parties in thirty-three European nations. He identified forty-five right-wing populist parties, eleven left-wing ones, and, interestingly, ten that he described as "valence" parties, which "compete by focusing on . . . issues such as the fight against corruption, increased transparency, democratic reform and moral integrity, while emphasizing anti-establishment motives."[55] In other contexts, we think that these last parties would be called parties seeking good government. Zullianello's analysis shows, at least, that populism comes in a variety of flavors, and suggests the possibility that not all populisms pursue a single set of policies, including policies about constitutional reform.

---

[54] Robert Howse, *Epilogue: In Defense of Disruptive Democracy—A Critique of Anti-populism*, 17 INTERNATIONAL JOURNAL OF CONSTITUTIONAL LAW 641 (2019), at pp. 642, 645.

[55] Mattia Zulianello, *Varieties of Populist Parties and Party Systems in Europe: From State-of-the-Art to the Application of a Novel Classification Scheme to 66 Parties in 33 Countries*, 55 GOVERNMENT & OPPOSITION 327 (2020), at p. 329.

Examining the effects of populism in power, two systematic quantitative studies come to roughly similar conclusions. The first study used data on nineteen Latin American states from 1982 to 2012, and found that populist governments erode institutional and legal constraints on executive power.[56] So did an analysis of the impact of populist rule on liberal democracy in Europe and the Americas.[57] Both studies found that four essential elements of liberal democracy came under populist attack.

- Populists systematically evade and override checks and balances on the executive branch, like legislatures, courts, electoral agencies, central banks, and ombudsmen. Houle and Kenny found that after four years of populist rule, courts have 34 percent less independence than they would have under a typical democratic government.
- Populists don't like criticism from the media, which they see as controlled by elites who seek to subvert the popular will, and they frequently threaten or restrict media outlets.
- The studies found that two terms of populist rule resulted in a 9 percent decrease in the standard index of civil liberties.
- The final element of liberal democracy to suffer under populist rule is the quality of elections. Populists both change and violate these rules for their own political advantage.

This isn't encouraging, even if one acknowledges that the underlying quantitative measures might be imperfect: The effects are large enough that small defects in measurement are unlikely to distort the conclusions enough to make things look a lot worse than they really are.

A more recent study, analyzing data from thirty European countries between 1990 and 2012, suggests that we must look at populism and its "host" ideology. The study tests distinct effects of left-wing and right-wing populism on democratic quality. Its major findings are that right-wing populism has a stronger negative effect on minority rights than left-wing populism, and that there is no conclusive evidence that both types of populism have the same effect on the checks and balances.[58]

[56] Christian Houle & Paul D. Kenny, *The Political and Economic Consequences of Populist Rule in Latin America*, 53 GOVERNMENT & OPPOSITION 256 (2018).

[57] Nathaniel Allred, Kirk A. Hawkins, & Saskia Ruth, "The Impact of Populism on Democracy, in ALACIP Congress, 2015, cited in Saskia P. Ruth-Lovell, David Doyle & Kirk A. Hawkins, "Consequences of Populism, for The Guardian's *The New Populism* Project," Mar. 6, 2019, available at https://populism.byu.edu/App_Data/Publications/TP_Consequences_Memo.pdf, archived at https://perma.cc/ZD8W-7VLL.

[58] Robert A. Huber & Christian H. Schimpf, *On the Distinct Effects of Left-Wing and Right-Wing Populism on Democratic Quality*, 5 POLITICS & GOVERNANCE 146 (2017). Similarly, Mudde and Kaltwasser argue that "empirical research based on the ideational approach allows [us] to analyze

As our case studies later show, these quantitative studies—which don't suffer from selection bias nearly as much as more anecdotal accounts to—illuminate the Hungarian and Polish cases.

Australian political scientist Benjamin Moffitt argues that a number of contemporary cases of populist radical right parties from Northern Europe complicate this characterization of populism. "Rather than being directly opposed to liberalism, these parties selectively reconfigure traditionally liberal defences of discriminated against groups—such as homosexuals or women—in their own image, positing these groups as part of 'the people' who must be protected, and presenting themselves as defenders of liberty, free speech and 'Enlightenment values.'" One of the early examples of this approach was the Dutch right-wing populist Pim Fortuyn. Fortuyn combined an anti-Islam, anti-migration, and anti-EU platform with a relatively strong social-liberal position on gender, sexuality, and the like. A similar approach is present in the discourse of Geert Wilders, currently the most popular Dutch right-wing populist. Wilders and similar right-wing populists in Western Europe position themselves as liberal defenders of LGBTQ rights, gender equality, freedom of speech, secularism, and other important liberal values. Although Moffitt agrees that such a move toward what he calls "liberal illiberalism" is often driven by the opportunistic populist agenda to put a more acceptable face on otherwise illiberal politics, he also emphasizes that it is "misguided to portray populism as the direct opposite of liberalism."[59]

Drawing a comparison with nationalist populism in East Central Europe, political theorist Rogers Brubaker shows how ethno-nationalism in Northern and Western Europe has shifted from nationalism to "civilizationism." This shift has been driven by the notion of a civilizational threat from Islam and has given rise to identitarian "Christianism," which internalizes liberalism, secularism, philosemitism, gender equality, gay rights, and free speech as "an identity marker of the Christian West vis-à-vis a putatively intrinsically illiberal Islam." At least in this respect, Western European populists do not necessarily oppose liberal constitutionalism. In East Central Europe, in contrast, ethno-nationalism remains fundamentally nationalist and deeply illiberal. There nationalist populisms externalize liberalism, "construing it as a non-national and even anti-national

the conditions under which populist forces can have a positive or a negative impact on real existing democracies as well as during different phases of (de)democratization." Cas Mudde & Cristóbal Rovira Kaltwasser, *Studying Populism in Comparative Perspective: Reflections on the Contemporary and Future Research Agenda*, 51 COMPARATIVE POLITICAL STUDIES 1667 (2018), at p. 1671.

[59] Benjamin Moffitt, *Liberal Illiberalism? The Reshaping of the Contemporary Populist Radical Right in Northern Europe*, 5 POLITICS & GOVERNANCE 112 (2017), at pp. 112, 118. There are important precedents for this liberal illiberalism, Moffitt argues. The examples include "centrist populism," "new/centrist populism," and "liberal populism." *See id.* at p.114. *See also* Christopher Bickerton & Carlo Invernizzi Accetti, "'Techno-populism' as a New Party Family: The Case of the Five Star Movement and Podemos," 10 CONTEMPORARY ITALIAN POLITICS 132 (2018).

project that subordinates the interests of the nation to foreign capital, on the one hand, and to foreign models of multiculturalism, Roma rights, LGBT rights, and refugee protection, on the other hand."[60] These two different types of populism present different challenges for constitutionalism in Europe. While authoritarian populism in Hungary and Poland has already undermined many key features of constitutional democracy, the populists in Western Europe at the moment pose a lesser threat to constitutionalism and the rule of law.

The Italian populist coalition between the League and the Five Star movement, which was in power for only fourteen months between 2018 and 2019, is a good example of the complexity and ambiguity of this different kind of populism. The coalition government undermined none of the key pillars of Italian constitutionalism, or at least did so no more than any other government had. As Matteo Bonelli reports, "[T]here has simply been no structural undermining of institutional safeguards and democratic and rule of law institutions."[61] Moreover, as Lucia Corso argues, the Italian case clearly defies the characterization of populism as inherently opposed to liberal constitutionalism. As she shows, the Five Star Movement and, to a lesser extent, the League, seem largely to support the rule of law.[62] The most recent constitutional referendum about the reduction of the size of the Italian parliament, proposed by the populist cabinet when still in power, can hardly be described as opposing constitutionalism or the rule of law.[63]

Nor did the Austrian populist coalition, in power from 2017 to 2019, attack such key pillars of liberal constitutionalism as the independent judiciary or the legislative branch of government. Both the Italian and Austrian populist governments were in power only briefly, and all we can say is that those populist governments didn't immediately go after liberal constitutionalism, much less our "thin" constitutionalism. Still, their behavior is a mark against the argument that populism is always and everywhere anti-constitutional. In both countries, more radical, right-wing populists (the League and FPÖ) were *forced* to share their power with their slightly more moderate populist coalition partners. True, these populists did challenge many of the unwritten norms that provided the

---

[60] Rogers Brubaker, *Between Nationalism and Civilizationalism: The European Populist Moment in Comparative Perspective*, 40 ETHNIC & RACIAL STUDIES 1191 (2017), at p. 1208.

[61] Matteo Bonelli, "The Italian Paradox: Is There Such a Thing as Too Strong Constitutional Safeguards?," in POPULISM AND DEMOCRACY (Sascha Hardt, Aalt Willem Heringa, & Hoai-Thu Nguyen eds. 2020), at p. 239.

[62] Lucia Corso, *When Anti-Politics Becomes Political: What Can the Italian Five Star Movement Tell Us about the Relationship Between Populism and Legalism*, 15 EUROPEAN CONSTITUTIONAL LAW REVIEW 462 (2019).

[63] A constitutional referendum about the reduction of the size of the Italian parliament was held in September 2020. Voters were asked if they approved a constitutional law that would amend the Italian constitution in various aspects, most notably by reducing the number of MPs in the Parliament from 630 to 400 in the Chamber of Deputies and from 315 to 200 in the Senate. The referendum proposal was approved, with 69.96 percent voting in favor. The key argument was that the move would reduce costs and slash privileges for lawmakers.

institutional glue making the legal institutions work. But, as we'll argue in the next chapter, challenging such norms isn't always anti-constitutional—because the norms might be, or might have become, unnecessary or, worse, positively harmful to promoting the public good.

What is the empirical record for a democratic or left-liberal version of populism? Moffitt argues that left-wing populists "often extend their conception of 'the people' to include various minority groups, which on the face of things seems to be in line with pluralism and liberalism." Using the examples of Syriza in Greece, Podemos in Spain, Jean-Luc Melenchon's La France Insoumise, Raffael Correa in Ecuador, and Evo Morales in Bolivia, some of which we deal with in our own case studies later in this book, he shows that left-wing populists "have put forward characterisations of 'the people' that cannot seriously be considered either 'pure' or 'homogenous.' "[64] Spain's Indignados "tried to develop a definition of the 'people' that was inclusive to most marginalized minorities—including ethnic, religious and sexual."[65] According to Moffitt, the majority of left-wing populists in Europe and North America cannot be seriously accused of authoritarianism.[66]

As Norris and Inglehart argue, though left-wing populism is less common than its right-wing counterpart today, support for left-wing populisms has grown in recent years in Europe and the United States.[67] Though Müller asserts that the Greek left-wing populist party Syriza has tried "to undermine the independence of courts and free media,"[68] he offers little evidence in support: anecdotal evidence of a few attempts by Syriza politicians to criticize unfavorable judgments of the courts and to influence the media, but surely those institutions can't be immune from *criticism*; the issue must be "Are such criticisms warranted?"[69] Syriza's political rhetoric develops an "inclusionary populism," "reclaiming 'the people' from extreme right-wing associations and reactivating its potential not as an enemy but rather as an ally of democracy in times of economic and political crisis."[70] Another study argues that Podemos in Spain represents "a clear radical left-libertarian universalistic profile advocating minority rights, gender equality and civic liberties, pledging also to fight discriminations."[71]

---

[64] MOFFITT, note 11 above, at pp. 71–72, 84.

[65] Mudde & Kaltwasser, note 15 above, at p. 48.

[66] MOFFITT, note 9 above, at pp. 107–8.

[67] NORRIS & INGLEHART, note 4 above.

[68] Jan-Werner Müller, "What's Left of the Populist Left?," Project Syndicate. Feb. 21, 2019, available at https://www.project-syndicate.org/commentary/populist-left-wrong-political-strategy-by-jan-werner-mueller-2019-02?barrier=accesspaylog, archived at https://perma.cc/QA4C-SXKH.

[69] In Chapter 8 we develop an additional argument, that every true constitutional system must figure out how to combine judicial independence with judicial accountability to law, and that the latter requirement can (though it need not) include some degree of accountability to ordinary political institutions.

[70] Yannis Stavrakakis & Giorgios Katsambekis, *Left-Wing Populism in the European Periphery: The Case of SYRIZA*, 19 JOURNAL OF POLITICAL IDEOLOGIES 119 (2014), at p. 135.

[71] Ivaldi, Lanzone & Woods, note 48 above, at p. 364.

These examples of democratic, liberal, socially inclusive forms of populism clearly show that authoritarianism and anti-pluralism are not necessarily the key elements of populism. We agree that *some* populist movements have the characteristics described by Müller, Mudde and Kaltwasser, Walker, and Blokker. Once we examine various populism*s*, though, we find that the relation between populism tout court and constitutionalism is far more complex than the common view has it, and that ultimately whoever tries to evaluate that relation will have to build an assessment of the political merits of different populist agendas into that evaluate. We recurrently refer to that necessary feature of the evaluation as "the merits," making it clear, we hope, that controversial political judgments, explicit or implicit, pervade every analyst's view.[72] We turn in the next chapter to examining that relation in more detail.

---

[72] For an example, *see* Johnson, note 9 above, at p. 208 ("Sometimes a social movement targeting elites is necessary to crack through a strongly entrenched and self-reinforcing status quo.").

3

Populism and Constitutionalism

In Chapter 2 we argued that the word "populism" doesn't refer to a general theory of politics. If we're right, we can't do with "populism" what we did with "constitutionalism"—offer something like a least-common-denominator version that every populist would agree with. As we pointed out there, a least-common-denominator version of populism reduces it to its "core" elements, but doing so makes the term applicable to every political contest in which someone frames the issues as "the people versus the elites." Everything else depends upon specifying particulars. Still, there's something to the idea that we can talk about "populism" as a general phenomenon while acknowledging that in the real political world, we face only different varieties of populism.

We capture this idea by saying that populism is associated with a number of themes, combined differently in specific populisms. Some populisms emphasize one theme more than others, other populisms don't implicate some individual themes, and yet of course all populisms resemble the others—but most also resemble many forms of "ordinary" or non-populist politics.

The remainder of this chapter examines the relation between populist themes and thin constitutionalism. Our strategy is to separate out the themes we find in various populisms and address the relation between each and thin constitutionalism. We show how each theme can sometimes be inconsistent with constitutionalism, sometimes consistent with it. And we regularly point out that not all political leaders and movements conventionally called populist articulate the themes we are discussing and—as our earlier reference to Franklin Delano Roosevelt hinted—that some political leaders and movements conventionally *not* labeled populist articulate the themes.

We emphasize that each theme *can be* consistent with thin constitutionalism. We agree that each theme can be articulated and, more important, implemented in ways that are inconsistent with even thin constitutionalism: Proto-authoritarians can invoke each theme to advance their authoritarian political agendas. When they do the proper object of concern and criticism should be the agendas and not the use of the populist themes.

The case studies of "bad" populisms we present in Chapter 4 develop that point in detail. We offer a preview here, using thin constitutionalism's twin

Power to the People. Mark Tushnet and Bojan Bugarič, Oxford University Press. © Mark Tushnet and Bojan Bugarič 2021. DOI: 10.1093/oso/9780197606711.003.0004

requirements of judicial independence and accountability to law as our example. Consider three actions Poland's PiS (Prawo i Sprawiedliwość—Law and Justice) government took bearing on judicial independence. It created a new body to "manage" and discipline judges. This was a direct attack on judicial independence because the new body was completely under the government's control and applied standards that singled out for discipline judges who weren't enthusiastic enough about PiS programs. It also reduced the mandatory retirement age for judges. The effect was to force into retirement many judges who, the government believed, might have habits of thinking or be committed to ways of legal analysis that would incline them to impede the government's programs. This wasn't a direct attack on judicial independence, but it was an indirect way of reducing the judges' accountability to law. And, finally, it installed a judge whose views were completely in line with the government's as head of the constitutional court when the term of the sitting chief justice ended. As we will argue in more detail, this last action shouldn't be seen as implicating questions of judicial independence in any interesting way.

Governments in Hungary and Turkey similarly took actions that were inconsistent with thin constitutionalism. Although we argue in this Chapter that not all populist governments do the same, we don't want to leave the impression that populism in general is consistent with thin constitutionalism because, as we argued in Chapter 2, there really is no such thing as populism in general. We also have a more limited point. Not everything a bad populist government does is inconsistent with constitutionalism, and it weakens political arguments against such governments to focus too much on actions that when analyzed carefully—the installation of a new chief justice in Poland, for example—aren't constitutionally problematic.

We begin by discussing three themes that, though closely related, are often identified as separate components of populism: that populists represent a *pure* "people" against corrupt elites, that populists represent a *unified* "people" and are for that reason anti-pluralist in principle, and that populists deny the legitimacy of opposition to their programs. We then turn to the role of "leader-ism" in populism, with special attention to the idea that populist movements are often fueled by the personal charisma of individual leaders. We follow by taking up what is perhaps the most important connection between populisms and thin constitutionalism, the claim that populists are impatient with all institutions that obstruct the adoption and implementation of their programs; this is said to set them against constitutionalism understood as something that at least temporarily stops and certainly slows down majoritarian policy-making. A brief concluding section discusses a grander form of the claim about anti-institutionalism, this one operating at a rather deep jurisprudential level.

I. The "People" against the Elites

Populists say that they represent the "true" people of the nation, and that their opponents represent—and are—an elite that looks out only for its own well-being without any concern for anyone else: so the story goes. And the story is clearly true of rhetoric commonly used by most populist parties and their leaders. But, as usual, the story needs to be examined more closely to understand what's going on when populists campaign and govern.

We begin by clearing away some underbrush dealing with campaign rhetoric generally and then with political theory at quite a high level. Then we turn to our central points: elites sometimes do indeed govern in their own self-interest and do badly by the nation as a whole, and they sometimes do indeed weaponize the constitution to preserve their positions, making it sensible for populists to change the constitutions that block their political success.

At the lowest level, political campaigning consists of saying, "Vote for us, and don't vote for them." In this quite ordinary sense, "we-they" thinking is built into politics. "We're looking out for your interests, they aren't" is a somewhat more pointed version of ordinary political rhetoric. If you want a more formal state-ment: political campaigning has a positive and a negative side. Maybe populists do more negative campaigning than non-populists, thereby creating a pervasive "us against them" atmosphere.[1] That's an empirical claim, and there's not a lot in the scholarship dealing with populism to support it—but maybe it's correct.

Another version of the "us against them" argument is this: of course political rhetoric involves a lot of that kind of rhetoric, but who is the "them" that's the target? Non-populist versions target the *party* or parties on the other side, while perhaps populists distinctively or disproportionately target social, economic, or religious classes on the other side: in India, the Bharatiya Janata Party (BJP) sends the message, "Vote for us because we're on your side, and our opponents are secular elites and Muslims." The "vote for us" part is ordinary political rhet-oric; identifying the other side as a social and religious group might be distinc-tively populist.

Here the problem is that sometimes describing the opposing party in terms of the social groups it represents is accurate (or at least accurate enough for purposes of ordinary politics). When the BJP says that the Congress Party, its historic opponent, represents the interests of a secular Western-oriented elite (and is willing to accept support from Muslims), it's just describing the Congress Party reasonably well. Contrast that with the United States. Suppose we think of

---

[1] More precisely, we'd want to know the ratio between positive and negative campaigning by populists and non-populists.

the movement led by Donald Trump as at least a proto-populist movement.[2] Its supporters might describe the Democratic Party as dominated by secular, cosmopolitan elitists, but they'd be wrong—the Democratic Party is a messy coalition *containing* those groups but also containing a bunch of other groups so that the Democratic Party can't accurately be described as a "them" identified as a social or other class.

So, on the level of rhetoric, we're left with some empirical questions: How much do populist parties differ from other parties in their use of "us versus them" rhetoric? How often do populist parties identify the "them" as a social or other group? And, how often is that identification accurate? This isn't a book of empirical studies, but we're reasonably confident that the answers are going to vary quite a bit from one populist movement to another.

Now we shift to a dramatically higher level of abstract political theory.[3] Scholars of populism see Carl Schmitt's political theory expressed in populist "we-they" rhetoric. Schmitt was a conservative German constitutional theorist who provided arguments on behalf of the Nazi Party in some important cases, and was a member of the Nazi Party until he was sidelined basically for being too smart. According to Schmitt, anyone who took his or her politics seriously had to see the world as divided between "friends" and "enemies." If you didn't think that you had to defeat your enemies as decisively as you would want to in a war, you weren't serious about your own politics. U.S. Supreme Court Justice Oliver Wendell Holmes described this point of view: "If you have no doubt of your premises or your power and want a certain result with all your heart you naturally express your wishes in law and sweep away all opposition. To allow opposition . . . seems to indicate . . . that you doubt either your power or your premises."[4] Holmes went on to say that the "theory" of the U.S. Constitution—what we have come to know as liberal constitutionalism—rejected this Schmittian perspective.[5]

---

[2] We actually do think that, but the example works even if Trumpism isn't quite populist under standard definitions because we're concerned with the characteristics of the target of its rhetoric.

[3] We confine to this note a discussion of another general theory of party politics, associated with the economist Joseph Schumpeter and the earlier sociologist Robert Michels. According to this theory, democratic politics always involves a circulation of elites, never the replacement of elite government by popular government. The reason is that democratic government requires political parties and that political parties are inevitably organized as hierarchies with a political elite at the top of each party. We take no position on the accuracy of this general theory, but observe only that even if true it doesn't mean that populist parties are inevitably elitist parties in the sense of speaking for a social or other class-based elite: The elites with which the theory is concerned are all internal to the political parties.

[4] Abrams v. United States, 250 U.S. 616, 630 (1919) (Holmes, J., dissenting).

[5] Schmitt's approach to politics was attractive to Nazis not only because of the "friend-enemy" distinction but because of his views about leadership. A nation's leader spoke for it, and his positions were endorsed by public "acclamation"—the kind of leader-ism that we discuss later in this chapter.

Some populist parties and leaders are undoubtedly closet Schmittians. But, as we've just argued, we would move far too quickly were we to say that every leader who described politics in "us versus them" terms was at heart a Schmittian (and so a proto-Nazi). We think that invoking Schmitt in a general account of populism blurs too many lines to be helpful.

With those matters out of the way, we can address what we think are the real issues about populist opposition to elites.

Political elites representing social or other classes do indeed sometimes screw up—or, less pejoratively, in exercising their power elites advance policies that impose costs on those to whom populists appeal without bearing similar costs themselves. Sometimes they do so believing in good faith that the policies they pursue are good for the nation as a whole; sometimes that good-faith belief comes with an awareness that the policies have the attractive side effect of providing special benefits to the elites or at least exempting themselves from burdens other carry; and sometimes they pursue policies that they know aren't especially good for the nation but are good for themselves. Populists— but not only populists—can win elections by identifying these kinds of policy misadventures.

Consider a common story told about European left-wing populist movements like Podemos and Syriza.[6] The story begins with neoliberalism and continues with a narrative about the adoption—or in Greece the imposition—of policies of economic austerity to respond to the domestic effects of the worldwide economic crisis of the early 2000s.[7] According to this story, neoliberal policies shrank the social safety net purportedly as means of enhancing productivity and promoting economic growth in the long run; neoliberals promised that the benefits of growth would be widely shared, and would be enough to replace and even enhance the reduced public social-safety-net benefits. As things turned out, the story continues, even when neoliberal policies did lead to increases in national wealth, the increases went mostly to the elites who supported neoliberal policies; few were distributed to those who had lost the benefits previously provided by the social safety net. Populist movements arose in response to the "bait and switch" tactics of neoliberals.

A similar story is told about austerity as a response to the financial crisis. What policies might lead a nation out of the crisis? Two options were on the table

---

[6] We provide some details about these movements in our case studies in Chapter 7.

[7] For an example, *see* Jorge Tamames, For the People: Left Populism in Spain and the US (2020). We aren't political scientists or economists and can't stand behind this story on our own authority. We acknowledge that it rings true to us, but even if it turns out to be mistaken, the story's central feature—populism as a response to elite policies that disadvantage those to whom populists appeal—is what's important for our argument.

(again, according to the story): large-scale debt-financed public expenditures or austerity. The former would provide some immediate infusions of money into the economy, including direct payments to many ordinary citizens, but— according to its opponents—risked catastrophe in the future when the debt came due. The latter would inflict immediate pain, including increasing already high unemployment, but would produce a more stable recovery. Given these options, elites favored austerity. Maybe they were right on the policy level, but they were insulated from austerity's immediate costs, and ordinary people not only were hurt in the short run but failed to get what they might have under the alternative policy.[8] No surprise, then, that a political movement targeting "them" on behalf of "us" gained traction.

We could go on, but conclude by identifying two common failures by political elites that populists have focused on.

- *Corruption.* Cultures of corruption are found around the world. Politicians abuse their positions to extract money for themselves and their friends. Populists—but again not only populists—win votes by pointing out corruption at the highest levels. It sometimes turns out that once in office they too succumb to temptation, but we think it a mistake to read the outcomes back into the initial political successes: Luis Ignacio de Silva (Lula) in Brazil might have corruptly accepted some benefits from construction companies when he was president, but no one has yet found evidence that Lula was corrupt over the decades he campaigned for the office (and similarly with Evo Morales in Bolivia and Rafael Correa in Ecuador, though there we have allegations but rather little evidence of post-election corruption).

  Populists who campaign on anticorruption platforms, where they have real evidence of real corruption, are doing what good politicians do— pointing out policy failures by the people in power who they want to throw out of office. Populists who invent corruption to campaign against are another matter. So, again, we need to look at specific examples of populist charges against "corrupt elites" rather than taking populist rhetoric about such elites as counting against populism as a political movement.

---

[8] In 2013, even the IMF admitted that austerity was wrong (in a paper by Olivier Blanchard, its chief economist. Olivier Blanchard & Daniel Leigh, "Growth Forecast Errors and Fiscal Multipliers," https://www.imf.org/external/pubs/ft/wp/2013/wp1301.pdf. Austerity remained the official policy in the EU until recently. In 2012, it was constitutionalized in the EU treaty (a balanced budget rule and a constitutional debt brake). For more general critique of austerity, *see* MARK BLYTH, AUSTERITY: THE HISTORY OF A DANGEROUS IDEA (2013).

- *Exclusion.* Corruption is one form of exclusion—corrupt elites take for themselves the benefits of public office and economic growth that could be distributed to the general public. Inequality is another.[9] Some populist movements focus on civic exclusion—a reluctance by political elites to allow full participation by some segments of the public in civic life. Sometimes the exclusion is on quite a large scale, as when the voice of indigenous people in Bolivia was simply disregarded when policy was made. Sometimes the exclusion is smaller but significant, as when some religious citizens find themselves hampered in gaining public recognition of their commitments by rules designed to accommodate religious pluralism within a modern nation.

    Sometimes (that word again) these exclusions are defensible within a thin constitutionalist framework, sometimes they aren't. Bolivian populism seems to us a movement toward civic inclusion that's entirely compatible with thin constitutionalism. Similarly with some (but not all) policies associated with the BJP's effort to enhance or, as they would put it, recognize the role of Hinduism in Indian civic culture. Some populist movements go too far by converting efforts at civic inclusion into policies that effectively exclude some groups, some don't. Particulars matter, and when something goes wrong, it's the wrongness, not the populism, that we should focus on.

Political elites use the levers of power embedded in the constitution to defend and preserve their positions both before they lose elections to populists and, importantly, afterward. Nothing wrong with that of course, but it does reverse the narrative: here it's "them—the populists—versus us, the elites." And, when people who have lost elections hang on to power by hunkering down in institutions they still control, it's neither surprising nor anti-constitutional for their opponents to try to figure out ways to consolidate their victory.

We provide one quick example, and then a more extended one.

- *Traditional and new media.* Sometimes populists win elections over the opposition of traditional elites who control many standard press outlets. How can a populist government get its message out without distortion (as it sees things)? By exploiting other media. FDR's fireside chats and the interminable weekly television speeches by Hugo Chávez are examples. In Brazil prior to his election Jair Bolsonaro exploited the existing vulnerabilities of WhatsApp to distribute misleading information to his supporters. As that

---

[9] For a discussion of populism and inequality, *see* Rosalind Dixon & Julie Suk, *Liberal Constitutionalism and Economic Inequality*, 85 UNIVERSITY OF CHICAGO LAW REVIEW 368 (2018), at pp. 372–73.

example shows, not all of these workarounds are attractive, but they aren't anti-constitutional. In contrast, other ways of getting the message across can be inconsistent with thin constitutionalism, particularly direct press censorship and elimination of competition for government-controlled television stations.[10]

Our second example involves constitutional courts. One characteristic of today's populist governments is sometimes noted but its significance underemphasized: they all take office after a reasonably free and fair election.[11] Taking office, they typically find that other constitutional institutions are staffed by people appointed under prior governments. Perhaps the most important such institution is the constitutional court. How will the existing constitutional court respond to the new configuration of power?

Sometimes constitutional courts accede, using theories of constitutional interpretation that tell them to do so. Venezuela provides an extremely interesting example. After winning election in 1999 Hugo Chávez proposed to replace the existing constitution with a new "Bolivarian" one. The existing constitution had provisions laying out procedures for amending and replacing the constitution, but Chávez bypassed them.[12] He organized a national referendum to create a constituent assembly authorized to draft a new constitution, and then held elections for that assembly. The major parties opposed to Chávez refused to participate in both the referendum and the ensuing elections. As a result, the referendum passed, and Chávez's supporters won a narrow majority of the total vote for the constituent assembly but held 125 of the assembly's 131 seats. The assembly on its own motion converted itself to an interim legislature and began to promulgate ordinary laws.

---

[10] Sometimes governments—but not only populist ones—use their power to place public notices in newspapers as a tool to encourage newspapers to report on them favorably. And sometimes governments—again not only populist ones—encourage rich political allies to take over newspapers and other media outlets with the same purpose. Whether the former practice is inconsistent with thin constitutionalism is, we think, a quite difficult question, the answer to which turns on how effective the practice is in stifling opposition. The latter practice, though quite unattractive, seems to us clearly consistent with thin constitutionalism—and we suspect that it would take a rather thick version of liberal constitutionalism to come up with a doctrine explaining why the practice should be unconstitutional. WILLIAM DOBSON, THE DICTATOR'S LEARNING CURVE: INSIDE THE GLOBAL BATTLE FOR DEMOCRACY (2012), provides examples of how authoritarians use these techniques of media control short of direct press censorship to stifle opposition.

[11] Viktor Orbán's victory in 2010 might require a modest modification of this assertion. The election was free and fair. Orbán's party won the election with just short of 53 percent of the votes. Hungary's election laws, mirroring other such laws in nations with proportional representation systems (Hungary has a "mixed" system), gave the winning party a bonus. (The idea behind doing so is that it promotes stability when coalition governments are formed.) The bonus's effect in Hungary was to give Orbán a majority large enough to amend the constitution on its own.

[12] The provisions for altering the constitution distinguished between limited amendment and broader changes, imposed a supermajority requirement in the legislature for a general reform, and, important to Chávez, required that all changes be initiated by the legislature. Constitution of Venezuela, arts. 245–48 (1961).

Not surprisingly, the opposition went to the existing constitutional court—with members appointed before Chávez's victory—arguing that Chávez couldn't convene a constituent assembly. The constitutional court disagreed, relying on a quite strong and controversial account of the "constituent power." For present purposes the key point is that Chávez got his way when an existing institution that he had no say in staffing *didn't* act as a veto gate.[13]

Sometimes, though, constitutional courts staffed by members appointed before the populist victory *are* veto gates or speed bumps. A prominent scholarly account describes this in terms directly relevant to our argument. The Canadian political scientist and constitutional scholar Ran Hirschl calls the process "hegemonic self-preservation."[14] Using several case studies, Hirschl begins by observing that constitutional courts in India, Israel, and elsewhere were created by cosmopolitan and secular elites within those nations. When the courts were created and for many years thereafter those elites dominated electoral politics as well. And, through the operation of the ordinary rules for appointment members of the constitutional court, those same elites staffed that court.

Constitutional courts staffed in that way collaborated with their compadres in the legislature and executive government, which typically meant exercising the power of constitutional review with a light hand. But, according to Hirschl, things changed when the elites began to see the first signs of their impending loss of power. Entrenched in the constitutional court, they began to ratchet up constitutional review, anticipating the need, as they saw it, for someone to preserve the cosmopolitan and secular values they genuinely believed were embedded in the constitution.

Hirschl wrote before the wave of populism hit around the world, and so didn't address populism directly. His story, though, is a compelling one and we think it easily fits into ours. Note that "hegemonic self-preservation" works only for a while. Eventually, the ordinary processes of judicial appointments, which produced elite domination of the institutions, will allow for the new populist government to gain control of the court. "Eventually," though, can be a long time, particularly where the very process of judicial appointment is complex and includes substantial representation from the elites who are in the process of being displaced. And populist governments might reasonably worry that they don't have that much time available to get enough things done to prove to their supporters that they deserve to stay in office.

---

[13] For a discussion of the Venezuelan court's decisions on the constituent power, *see* David Landau, *Abusive Constitutionalism*, 47 UNIVERSITY OF CALIFORNIA AT DAVIS LAW REVIEW 189 (2013), at pp. 204–5.

[14] RAN HIRSCHL, TOWARDS JURISTOCRACY: THE ORIGINS AND CONSEQUENCES OF THE NEW CONSTITUTIONALISM (2007).

What to do? Clearly, change the composition of the constitutional court. Sometimes that can happen without much difficulty, either through attrition or by using existing appointment methods. Sometimes it takes institutional change: alter the way constitutional court judges are appointed, expand or shrink the constitutional court's size, change its jurisdiction to insulate policies from review by that court, and sometimes even create a new court staffed by the new government's appointees to do the work the prior constitutional court did.[15]

The political logic we've laid out is quite clear. What of its constitutional logic? The changes do eliminate or weaken an existing veto gate or speed bump. Yet, as we argued in Chapter 1, the status quo number or force of veto gates and speed bumps isn't baked into thin constitutionalism. Whether changing the number is anti-constitutional depends upon what's getting through the veto gate or over the speed bumps afterward—that is, it depends upon the merits of the populist program.[16] And assessment of those merits inevitably requires open political judgments not cast in the seemingly neutral language of constitutionalism as such.

II. Anti-Pluralism

The idea that populists are anti-pluralist in principle is more than a bit fuzzy because pluralism itself comes in many forms: interest-group pluralism, for example, is an account of the ways in which political decision-making is structured around attempts by groups defined with reference to their mostly material interests to advance those interests; ethical pluralism asserts that we have many basic values that aren't ranked in some hierarchy but that have to be advanced by accommodation and compromise. The critique of populism as anti-pluralist seems to us an ill-defined blend of different kinds of pluralism.

We have to begin with our usual disclaimer: of course there *are* anti-pluralist forms of populism no matter how one defines "pluralism." But, equally, there are forms that aren't. The easiest examples involve interest-group pluralism. Historically some populist movements have expressly been pluralist in that sense; they accurately described themselves as alliances of farmers and labor. Some contemporary populisms clearly appeal to farmers and small business owners. Many populist political agendas include proposals that appeal to discrete segments of the nation's population—pluralist in the interest-group sense.

---

[15] For a valuable survey of these techniques, *see* David Kosar & Katarina Sipulova, *How to Fight Court-Packing?*, 6 CONSTITUTIONAL STUDIES 133 (2020).
[16] We discuss some cases in Chapter 8.

And, just to drive the point home, the constitution adopted when Evo Morales was Bolivia's president describes the nation as "plurinational."

Another version of the "anti-pluralist" claim is that populists describe their nation as a single entity, a unified "people" organized around some important central political values and propositions. On one level this is obviously true—but true of constitutionalism generally rather than of populism. The Preamble to the U.S. Constitution begins, "We the People of the United States," but no one seriously thinks that its adopters were populists, nor that the U.S. Constitution is a populist constitution in any meaningful sense.

Populists claim that the policies they advance promote the interests of their nation's people—but so does every other politician. And, like other politicians, populists agree that political values sometimes conflict. Take the circumstances of populist politics in Bolivia and Ecuador. To simplify the story without overly distorting it: Morales and Correa—and their supporters, we have to emphasize—had three goals. They wanted economic growth, which meant addressing the concerns of foreign investors; they wanted to distribute more equitably both existing resources and the additions to national wealth that economic growth would bring; and they wanted to protect the traditional values associated with indigenous peoples and to preserve indigenous communities as much as possible. These goals were in some tension. Most obviously, the quickest route to economic growth and better material conditions for the nation's poor lay through the exploitation of natural resources located in areas occupied by indigenous people. Every policy these populist parties pursued had to be a compromise. And, notably, though Morales and Correa remained quite popular, their political support faded over time because their policies necessarily compromised the values their movements were committed to.[17]

Further, consider this sentence from a report in the *New York Times*: "While . . . [the] Law and Justice Party [PiS] has long been the dominant force in the United Right coalition [in Poland], it depends on the support of two junior conservative partners to stay in power: the Agreement and United Poland parties." The story deals with a conflict among the coalition partners that "almost brought down the government."[18] The dispute—over regulating mink farms—seems trivial to us, but what matters for present purposes is that PiS had to work out compromises with its coalition partners to stay in power.

But, those who say that populism is anti-pluralist might respond, these examples involve compromises *within* a populist coalition. Pluralism in politics,

---

[17] That the social bases for Latin American populist governments are heterogenous and complex—and so require compromises to be struck within the governing party (and are not always successfully struck)—is a theme running through the essays collected in LATIN AMERICA'S RADICAL LEFT: CHALLENGES AND COMPLEXITIES OF POLITICAL POWER IN THE TWENTY-FIRST CENTURY (Steve Ellner ed. 2014).

[18] Marc Santora, *Why Is the Polish Government Teetering? Just Follow the Minks*, NEW YORK TIMES, Oct. 8, 2020, p. A11.

they might say, requires compromises with your opponents. We'll discuss a broader version of that claim in this chapter's next section, but for now we limit our answer to the simple: not always.

Consider the problem we just described facing PiS. And suppose—it's hardly impossible—that the United Poland Party starts making increasingly difficult demands as a condition of staying in the coalition. PiS might compromise with United Poland. Its leaders might also start looking around for replacement partners, which would lead it to propose compromises with parties currently outside the government. And, from the other side of the fence, savvy opposition leaders can look for points at which *they* can come up with policies that would fracture the populist coalition.

Bolivia offers an example that complicates the story. We start with a central feature of Bolivian populism, one about which no compromise was possible. That feature is what classical liberals would describe as the transformation of subjects into citizens: For centuries the nation's indigenous peoples were the subjects of politics whose interests governing elites took into account only out of their own self-interest—and to the extent only of that self-interest. They didn't treat indigenous peoples as autonomous political actors. A compromise on the principle that indigenous peoples should be citizens not subjects was properly unimaginable for Bolivia's populists.[19] That doesn't mean that Morales's Movement Toward Socialism wasn't open to compromise on other issues—and indeed its policies on a range of economic issues worked out compromises to accommodate competing values.

The example illustrates a general point. Political parties, including populist ones, have agendas that contain policies at the core of the parties' commitments and policies that, while important to the party, are less important. We don't think that there's anything anti-pluralist happening when a party, even a populist party, refuses to compromise on core policies—and uses its majority to push through those policies unaltered over strenuous opposition.

Again, we can imagine responses. One is straightforward political disagreement. The core policy you're shoving through, opponents can assert, is a bad one. And, of course, sometimes the opponents will be correct. Some populist parties take a politically unattractive ethnonationalism as a core policy and enact it in quite rigorous form. The problem here, though, is the policy, not the populism or the refusal to compromise.[20]

---

[19] To be a bit snarky, try to design a compromise on this issue: count each indigenous person as three-fifths of a citizen; provide twice as much representation per capita for non-indigenous peoples; severely gerrymander representation in the national legislature.

[20] There's a related response: This policy shouldn't be as central to your program as it is. And, as a peripheral policy it would be one that you should be willing to compromise on. Again, this is basically a political disagreement about the policy's importance, not a criticism of populist unwillingness to compromise.

Another response might be that the policy, though good or at least reasonable, is too complicated for us to be confident that the populist party's proposal is the best, or even a pretty good, way of actually implementing the policy. Here we use an example from U.S. politics, which isn't really an example about populism but does illustrate the response: Suppose your program has universal health-care as a core commitment, and your party has come up with a plan it regards as suitable. Maybe it could be improved by tweaking it a bit or changing it substantially. If you're unwilling to compromise you might end up with a worse outcome than you could have had. That's true in principle, but it's not difficult to see why proponents of the policy might be skeptical when these seemingly technical suggestions come from people who haven't demonstrated any real interest in the policy. The U.S. experience with Obamacare is suggestive: Democrats spent months trying to accommodate Republican objections to their initial plan, only to discover that the people they were dealing with really didn't want any program to be enacted and used the time wasted in bargaining to build opposition to the Democrats' plan.

The events that followed are instructive as well. After discovering that negotiations with Republicans were futile, congressional Democrats—and only they—voted in favor of Obamacare. They had the votes to do so, and then were met with the Republican talking point that for the first time a majority party had enacted a major social program without support from the opposition. We don't think it fair to describe this process as one in which Democrats used their majority to ram a program through without considering what their opponents thought. We don't contend that the Democratic Party that enacted Obamacare was a populist party, but we do think that the Obamacare example suggests some caution about asserting that a majority party, whether populist or not, doesn't care about what its opponents think.

We've argued that a refusal to compromise on central aspects of your program isn't always a bad political practice (and have hinted that it's not truly distinctive about populist parties). Maybe the problem is different. Maybe refusal to compromise on central aspects can be acceptable, but good-faith politics in a constitutional system requires a willingness to compromise on less important aspects—and maybe populists refuse to compromise about anything. If they did, maybe it would be accurate to describe them as anti-pluralist in principle. The claim that populists don't compromise about anything is an empirical one, and frankly we're skeptical. Narendra Modi's BJP in India, even with a dominant political position, has had to scale back some of its proposals about who counts as a citizen in the face of opposition, for example. But, skepticism aside, this version of the claim that populists are anti-pluralist requires empirical support that, as far as we know, hasn't been provided yet.

And, as we discuss in the next section, compromise involves concessions by both sides. Sometimes the people who have lost to populists don't regard those who have defeated them in reasonably free and fair elections as people worth bargaining with, even on policies that aren't central to the populists' programs. So, even if we did see populist parties refusing to bargain across the entire range of policies, we'd still have to ask whether they had tried and failed to find someone on the other side to talk with, or refused to reach out altogether.

III. The Role of Opposition

Political movements in constitutional cultures generally have to treat their opponents as people who disagree with them in good faith about what policies would be good for the country—a loyal opposition. Populism's critics say that populism's anti-pluralism comes down to a broad claim that *any* opposition to any policy advanced by a populist government is similarly illegitimate—that the "us versus them" thinking associated with populism leads populists to deny that their opponents are loyal.

For a few decades in the middle of the last century the U.S. House of Representatives had a committee on "unamerican activities," and the country had a Subversive Activities Control Board.[21] Liberal constitutionalists were uncomfortable with these practices because they embodied a judgment that some forms of opposition to the existing government were disloyal and not merely mistaken. As populism's critics see things, populism's content is the same: If you don't agree with us, you're not really a true Hungarian or Indian. And if you're not a true Hungarian or Indian, you must be something else—a rootless cosmopolitan or an enemy of the people.

Those phrases have an ugly history. The first comes with a great deal of anti-Semitic baggage, the second with a history of abuse in Stalinist Russia. And some populisms are properly charged with always seeing opposition as disloyal. Viktor Orbán often describes his opponents as un-Hungarian, and was willing to accept political support from the anti-Semitic Jobbik Party. Narendra Modi leads a political party that treats India's Muslim citizens as less-than-truly Indian.[22]

But, as we have repeatedly argued, not all populists do this sort of thing. It's hard to see in the programs of Podemos, Syriza, and Bernie Sanders anything

[21] The SACB never accomplished anything other than self-promoting publicity, having been rendered completely ineffective by court decisions.

[22] In late 2019, the Modi government modified India's naturalization laws to give preferential treatment to non-Muslim (that is, Hindu) refugees from neighboring states while maintaining the existing procedures for Muslim refugees. There have been credible allegations as well that in compiling its citizenship registry, the government requires more to show that a Muslim resident is a citizen than it does for Hindu residents.

that treats their opponents as acting outside the bounds of reasonable disagreement. What we do see is a kind of "diagnostic" rhetoric about the sources of opposition. Sometimes populists argue along these lines: our policies are clearly good for the country as a whole. Why do our opponents disagree with our quite reasonable policy proposals? Because unlike us, they aren't trying to make the nation better. They're out to protect their own interests or, worse, the interests of foreigners who want to dominate our country.

Sometimes—not always—that diagnosis is within the bounds of ordinary political disagreement, as when Southern European populists saw the European financial institutions—outsiders in nearly every sense—insist upon austerity programs. The populist argument against neoliberal policies saw those policies as the product of a "Washington consensus" (sometimes, in Southern Europe, a "Berlin" consensus), that is, an agreement about policy options shared among elites from many countries. Brexit's supporters offered a structurally similar diagnosis of those who want to "stay" in the European Union. These diagnoses lead to the conclusion that populists' opponents are indeed cosmopolitan "anywheres" in a descriptive and non-pejorative sense, although as actually used in the debate the term was pejorative.[23] When populists try to explain the ground on which their opponents stand, they aren't *necessarily* treating opposition as disloyal.

But there's more. Sometimes the opposition is indeed disloyal. Rather than treating populist victors as winners in ordinary political battles, sometimes populists' opponents see the victors as illegitimate usurpers who have displaced those who should rightfully rule. Venezuela under Chávez and Bolivia under Morales are our examples. In both nations the traditional elites were baffled by the political successes of these leaders, who emerged from groups traditionally excluded from political power, and the elites were openly disdainful of those who had defeated them. Venezuela's opposition tried to mount a traditional military coup against Chávez; Bolivia's did oust Morales from office through a military coup.[24] These weren't acts of a loyal opposition.

So, our theme again. Specifics matter. Sometimes populists treat all opposition as illegitimate; when they do, they are anti-constitutional. Sometimes they face a disloyal opposition; when they do, their actions in self-defense aren't necessarily anti-constitutional (though sometimes specific self-defense measures are). And sometimes populists treat opposition as ordinary political disagreement; when they do, they are constitutionalists too.

[23] For a discussion of "anywheres" versus "somewheres," *see* DAVID GOODHART, THE ROAD TO SOMEWHERE: THE POPULIST REVOLT AND THE FUTURE OF POLITICS (2017).
[24] We note here that that characterization is controversial. We defend it in our case study of Bolivia in Chapter 8.

IV. The Role of Leaders (and Movements)

"I am your voice," and "I alone can fix [the rigged system]," Donald Trump said in his speech accepting the 2016 Republican Party nomination. Such expressions are said to be typical of populist leaders. They—and they alone—know what the people want. Once they are chosen, they have no need to find out what the majority wants, because they already know it. Or, to put it in terms of our idea of thin constitutionalism, these populist leaders don't need any mechanisms for reliably determining what the majority wants—other than consulting their own political instincts.[25]

No doubt some political leaders take the view that they know better than what the institutions for determining majority views seem to show. To take an example from someone few would describe as a populist, Richard Nixon said that he represented a Silent Majority—that is, a majority whose views weren't accurately revealed by elections. And no doubt, some political leaders get important political benefits from their personal charisma.

But, we think, it's important to treat a political leader's charisma as something separate from his or her approach to determining what the people want.[26] Many populist leaders, even charismatic ones, emerge from social movements of long standing. They take the movement's positions to reflect majority preferences. Or, again in our terms, populist leaders treat the movement as the mechanism for determining majority preferences. Their initial successes in reasonably free and fair elections confirm that judgment, and they continue to rely upon the movement as a source of policy throughout their terms in office. Of course, sometimes the charismatic leader can come to dominate the movement from which he or she emerged, but quite often—and perhaps always, over a sufficiently long term—the leader sustains his or her position through a complex interaction with others in the movement. The movement, that is, can constrain the leader in ways that make it misleading to describe even acknowledged populist movements as committed to "leader-ism."

Here are three brief examples.

- Bolivia's political system was dominated in the twentieth century by an elite consisting largely of descendants of European settlers (or invaders, on some views). Movements among the nation's indigenous peoples bubbled up,

---

[25] They might formally consult their acolytes, but only to obtain confirmation of their own insights into the people's wishes.

[26] We note that what counts as charisma is relative to political culture: Evo Morales's flamboyant political style would almost certainly have played badly in a Western European setting, and we think the case could be made that Barack Obama's cool self-presentation was charismatic (for his supporters) in the United States—and, as his reception in other nations suggests, elsewhere.

and eventually coalesced around Evo Morales. Morales developed a political style that resonated strongly with indigenous traditions, as was clear in
his television presentations, widely derided by Bolivian elites but compelling among Bolivia's indigenous population. Morales was a representative
of that social movement, and operated within the limits imposed on him
by his supporters. As our case study will show, eventually a significant seg-
ment of his supporters came to believe that it was time for him to go. These
defections forced him to retreat from his effort to obtain a third consecutive
term as president. (As our case study will show, the story continued in interesting and revealing ways, but for now we use it to show only that the movement that Morales came to lead also constrained him.)

- India's political system was dominated for generations by a secular, socialist-
  leaning elite for which the Congress Party was the vehicle. A Hindu nationalist
  social and political movement played a small but increasing role throughout the
  period of Congress Party dominance. The Bharatiya Janata Party (BJP) is the
  latest in a line of political parties associated with Hindu nationalism and that
  nationalism's long-standing civil-society vehicle, the Rashtriya Swayamsevak
  Sangh (RSS). The Congress Party attempted to limit the BJP's political power
  by invoking a statutory ban on parties that appealed to religious sentiments.
  The BJP survived, assisted by modestly helpful Supreme Court interpretations
  of the statute. The BJP entered government in 1999 as part of a coalition government. In 2014 the BJP won a majority of parliamentary seats, and its leader
  Narendra Modi became prime minister. Modi and the BJP won re-election
  in a landslide in 2019. Modi started his career as a staff member of the RSS.
  Eventually the RSS assigned him to work with the BJP, where he worked his
  way up the party hierarchy, ending as its general secretary. In 2001 he became
  chief minister in one of India's states, and then leader of the national party.

  Modi's government is often described as populist. He himself is rarely
  described as charismatic. Were we to use Max Weber's full set of categories, we
  would say that for most of Modi's career he was basically a party worker whose
  authority was founded in his bureaucratic position, and today draws legitimacy
  from the law that makes him prime minister. We've sketched the history of the
  BJP to show that far from being a leader who determines on his own what the
  government's policy will be, Modi is a more or less ordinary politician who has
  risen to his position because he reflects what the BJP (and the RSS) stand for.

- Pablo Iglesias Turrión leads Spain's Podemos, whose commitment to
  "power" and "democracy" is embedded in its name.[27] According to one

---

[27] We draw here on the account provided in JORGE TAMAMES, FOR THE PEOPLE: POPULISM IN
SPAIN AND THE US (2020), at pp. 244–46.

author, Iglesias is a "talented orator" with a "firebrand style," and his skills at mobilizing opposition to Spain's governing elites led to surprise victories in the 2015 national elections. Podemos's role in Spanish politics has been a complicated one. It began as an opposition party, then joined a coalition government based upon an agreement that did not fully reflect Podemos's full agenda. For present purposes the important point about Podemos and Iglesias is that despite his personal qualities Iglesias was unable to impose his will even on Podemos itself, much less on the government of which Podemos was a member. We needn't go into the internal maneuverings within Podemos except to note that they involved the terms on which Podemos would cooperate with the government, and that Iglesias didn't win every point.

We could go on. We doubt that anyone would describe Jarosław Kaczyński of Poland's Law and Justice Party as a leader who speaks for his party because of his personal qualities. In all these cases the "host ideology" associated with the populist party appears to do far more work than the leader's qualities.[28]

Of course, some parties commonly described as populist are the vehicles for a charismatic leader; Jair Bolsonaro in Brazil heads a party that he created and dominates. Yet, equally of course some leaders who no one would describe as either populist or charismatic dominate their parties; Lyndon Baines Johnson in the United States famously imposed his will on the Democratic Party for several years—until he couldn't.

In sum: "leader-ism" is neither always associated with populism, nor unique to it. More often than popular and scholarly writing acknowledges populist political leaders are associated with and are constrained by social movements. Sometimes but not always the leader is the people's voice who alone can fix things.

V. Populists and Constitutionally Entrenched Institutions

In September 2020 voters in Italy overwhelmingly supported a referendum that amended their constitution to reduce the size of the nation's parliament. Before the amendment, the lower house had 630 members, the upper house 315—by far the largest in the world (aside from China's People's Congress and the United

---

[28] Using a somewhat idiosyncratic definition of charismatic leadership, Takis Pappas concludes from an examination of European populism that the "linkage between populism . . . and charismatic leadership is, at best, a weak one," and that "when it exists, charismatic leadership is an important causal factor for the *success* of populist parties or movements." Takis S. Pappas, *Are Populist Leaders "Charismatic?"—The Evidence from Europe*, 23 CONSTELLATIONS 378 (2016), at p. 386.

Kingdom if one adds in the mostly ceremonial House of Lords). Nearly all Italian constitutional specialists thought that the parliament was too large to govern effectively. Yet, remarkably, three leading scholars posted blog comments indicating that, though they supported reducing parliament's size on the merits, they opposed the referendum. Why? In part because they thought that the change should be accomplished by an amendment that went through a different process, though the Italian constitution clearly allowed amendment by referendum. And in part because the referendum was sponsored by the Five Star Movement, a populist party that had become part of a coalition government and insisted upon a referendum on one of its favored programs. They opposed what they acknowledged to be a "good government" reform because its primary backers were populists—"the wrong means to the right end," as one post had it.[29]

This is, we think, worth thinking about in more detail. What could be wrong with a "good government" reform adopted through a constitutionally permissible process? The proposal's sponsorship taints it, seemingly because its success might strengthen a populist political party not by rigging the rules in its favor but by showing that the party can actually do things—here, good things, but perhaps not so good if the party became stronger as a result. A stopped watch can be right twice a day, as the saying goes, but you shouldn't buy it if you happen to see it at the precise moment that it's correct. That's perhaps a reasonable political analysis: Five Star put advocates of good government in an awkward position by sponsoring a good government reform as part of a "bad government" agenda. What matters here, as we construct the best version of the law professors' concerns, is Five Star's use of the referendum as a clever political tactic, a sort of Trojan Horse for its other, more troublesome policies. So, in fact, what really matters are those other policies— again, not the populist use of the referendum but Five Star's "host ideology."

The Italian scholars' reaction to the referendum highlights the "anti-institutionalism" or "impatience with institutions" that characterizes populisms. Notice that here we're *endorsing* the view that populists are impatient with institutions rather than saying that others describe it in those terms. And, one might think, anti-institutionalism must be in some tension with constitutionalism's commitment to entrenched institutions for decision-making. Such institutions place veto gates in the way of enacting new policies (and sometimes of repealing old ones). And the need to pass through those gates or figure out lawful ways around them does generate impatience.

---

[29] These are the blog posts: Francesca Rosa, Symposium | Part II | *Reducing the Size of the Italian Parliament: Why I Will Be Voting No*, INTERNATIONAL JOURNAL OF CONSTITUTIONAL LAW Blog, Sept. 17, 2020, available at: http://www.iconnectblog.com/2020/09/symposium-part-ii-reducing-the-size-of-the-italian-parliament-why-i-will-be-voting-no/; Francesco Palermo, Symposium | Part III | *Reducing the Size of the Italian Parliament: The Wrong Means to the Right End*, INTERNATIONAL JOURNAL OF CONSTITUTIONAL LAW Blog, Sept. 18, 2020, at: http://www.iconnectblog.com/2020/09/symposium-part-iii-reducing-the-size-of-the-italian-parliament-the-wrong-means-to-the-right-end/.

That impatience is reflected in the widely noted fact that populists around the world amend their constitutions a lot. The Italian referendum is simply an example. Hugo Chávez and Rafael Correa were behind total revisions of Venezuelan and Ecuadorian constitutions; the BJP majority in India led a push to amend the constitution's provisions for appointing judges. Indeed, we're hard-pressed to identify a populist movement or party that hasn't favored *some* constitutional revisions.

So what? Recall that all constitutions sensibly provide for their own revision or replacement. Ecuador's constitutional revision was adopted by means expressly authorized by the constitution. Venezuela's process was more controversial, but it was held constitutionally permissible by the nation's constitutional court, which at the time was composed of judges not affiliated with the Chavista political movement. India's judicial-nomination amendment was adopted by a near unanimous vote in parliament, well in excess of what the constitution required for an amendment. India's Supreme Court then held the amendment unconstitutional as inconsistent with the principle of judicial independence as embedded in the constitution's "basic structure"—which shows, perhaps, no more than that eternity clauses and their equivalents are not always well-designed.[30]

We think that populist impatience with institutions that impede the adoption of their policies needs to be unpacked. We start with the two most obvious points.

- It's not anti-institutional or inconsistent with constitutionalism to use the constitution's own provisions for amendment or replacement. Indeed, depending on one's theory of constitutional revolutions, it's not always inconsistent with constitutionalism to bypass those provisions.
- Not every veto gate or speed bump nor every entrenched provision is well-designed for contemporary circumstances. Perhaps we should have a mild presumption that what's in place is good enough to keep on the books. Constitutional provisions for amendment are the mechanism by which that presumption is overcome.

These points together mean that we can't automatically condemn populist proposals for constitutional change to be accomplished by using the constitution's amendment procedures. Constitutions accommodate impatience with institutions. To revert to our general framework: enthusiasm for constitutional amendment isn't inconsistent with constitutionalism.[31]

---

[30] For a discussion of the Indian amendment, see Chapter 8.

[31] The Austrian constitution has been amended 128 times since 1930, and no one thinks that the frequency of amendment tells us anything significant about Austria's commitment to constitutionalism.

So, once again, the merits matter. Of course constitutional revisions that directly impede good government are bad. Sometimes, for example, increasing a president's power to rule by decree will simply be bad (though one lesson of the 2020 pandemic is that suspicion of rule by decree may have become excessive). Suppose, though, that the reforms are, like the reduction in the size of Italy's parliament, defensible on good government grounds. When they are, we should ask the questions raised in our earlier discussion of the opposition between the people and the elites. Veto gates and speed bumps give elites a tool to use to stop populists from achieving their goals. If the goals are worthy (or, as we have emphasized, merely within the range of reasonable policy disagreement), removing a veto gate or a speed bump isn't itself inconsistent with constitutionalism.

One supporter of the Italian referendum said after it succeeded, this "opens up a season of reforms," alluding to other constitutional revisions in prospect. But, again, the merits matter. For decades constitutionalists in Italy have argued that its constitution isn't well-suited to modern conditions. The idea of substantially revising the Italian constitution has been rattling around for a long time—and the proposals come from "good government" constitutionalists. Their efforts at large-scale, all-at-once revisions have failed. Adopting reforms one by one—opening up "a season of reforms"—might be a reasonable alternative strategy.

Perhaps not, though. Removing one or two veto gates or speed bumps might not be inconsistent with constitutionalism, but removing all or nearly all of them might be. The new season might not be a rosy summer but a bleak winter. True enough, but once again this raises several questions: How many veto gates and speed bumps are actually to be destroyed? Will new ones be created? And, most important, are the constitutional revisions—deletions and additions—going to promote good government?

Though our evidence is anecdotal, we think that many populist movements support only limited institutional changes; The Bernie Sanders movement in the United States is an example. Some populist parties do support extensive changes that indeed threaten good government, as our case studies of Hungary and Poland show.[32] Some support extensive changes that in principle might promote good government, but that under the actual conditions in which they were implemented worked badly; our case study of Venezuela shows that, as does, more ambiguously, the case study of Ecuador. And a handful so far support extensive changes that if implemented might promote good government; we sketched some such possibilities in Chapter 1.

---

[32] Our statement of the problem here is truncated. We go into the problem in more detail in our discussion of the "Frankenstate," in Chapter 5.

Our message about populism's anti-institutionalism is a bit different from our message about other themes in populisms. As to the others our message is, "Sometimes yes, sometimes no." Here our message is, "Probably yes." Populism of any color—populism no matter what its host ideology—is quite likely to have some element of anti-institutionalism because entrenched veto gates and speed bumps are likely to be used by elites to prevent a populist government from implementing what the majority actually wants. Independent of the merits of a particular substantive populist agenda, anti-institutionalism is only worrisome when (a) the reforms are bad ideas in themselves, or (b) the reforms are so extensive that in combination they threaten good government.

VI. Anti-Institutionalism and Legal Theory

We conclude our discussion of populism and constitutionalism by addressing some broad but, we think, puzzling claims about the incompatibility of populism's asserted anti-institutionalism with some fundamental propositions about legal theory.

Some who write about populism criticize it for having an "instrumental" view of law.[33] We think this is designed to draw a contrast between liberals and populists. Suppose a liberal and a populist agree that adopting some policy would be good for the country. They examine the existing legal terrain and discover that some legal rule or principle stands in the way of the policy. The liberal says, "We can't adopt the policy until the law is changed according to the rules we have about changing the law—which might mean amending the constitution." The populist with an instrumentalist view says, "Come on, the Law in its grandest sense serves human well-being. We both agree that this policy would do that, and so we can simply disregard the legal rule you're worried about."

Note that this is a sort of anti-institutionalism, applied not to veto gates and speed bumps but at a more granular level to specific legal rules that are said to stand in the way of adopting policies the populist thinks are good ones—and our response is basically the same one we gave about anti-institutionalism: populists are typically willing to use the rules about changing other rules, and it's generally pretty easy for a sophisticated lawyer to show that the rule that seemingly

---

[33] See, e.g., Paul Blokker, Populism as a Constitutional Project, 17 INTERNATIONAL JOURNAL OF CONSTITUTIONAL LAW 536 (2019). Drawing on a report by the Venice Commission, Blokker uses the term "pejorative[ly]," and defines it as having "several aspects," including some themes in populism we've already discussed such as "the lack of respect for oppositional forces" and, most important here, "the neglect of existing rules and procedures, and . . . a goal-oriented, political use of the law." Id. at 545, note 42.

stands in the way, actually doesn't. Critics of populism rarely—to our knowledge, almost never—try to engage with arguments that the policy in question can be implemented without violating the legal rule that its opponents say bars the policy's adoption.

Here's an example. In the United States Senator Elizabeth Warren proposed to tax people based upon their wealth. Some constitutional lawyers objected that a wealth tax was what the U.S. Constitution referred to as a "direct" tax, and that direct taxes had to be collected from each state based upon its population. Treating a wealth tax as a direct tax to be "apportioned" by state population would make it a stupid policy. So, the argument would go, you have to amend the Constitution if you want to adopt a wealth tax.

A pure instrumentalist would treat that argument is completely irrelevant: if a wealth tax is a good idea, who cares whether it's a direct tax? And some populists do sometimes take that position, with respect to some of their policies. It's not the only stance they can and do take, though.

Faced with the argument that a wealth tax is a direct tax, Senator Warren's lawyers responded, "No it isn't." And they supported that response with legal arguments. We don't want to go into the weeds about this specific example.[34] Our point is that Senator Warren's lawyers didn't ignore the law; they worked within its bounds.

The point generalizes. Faced with an argument that the law rules out some policy, lawyers who support that policy look into their toolkit of arguments to see what they can use. They can focus on the purposes of the rule that's said to block them, and argue that those purposes aren't thwarted by the policy. They use cases allowing similar policies to go forward to generate distinctions between the things the rule bars and those it allows, and then argue that the policy they support is distinguishable in exactly the same way. And there are many more argumentative tools available.

We could end here with two assertions: As an empirical matter it's quite likely that decent legal arguments are available to work around the obstructive rule. When they are, implementing the policy doesn't show instrumentalism at work. And, those who describe populists as instrumentalists need to do more than identify a rule that in their view blocks some populist policy; they need to show that no reasonable arguments are available to support the policy.

---

[34] For the argument in detail, *see* Bruce Ackerman, *Taxation and the Constitution*, 99 COLUMBIA LAW REVIEW 1 (1999). For the application of the argument to Senator Warren's plan, see Bruce Ackerman, *The Constitutional Critiques of Elizabeth Warren's Wealth Tax Plan Are Absurd*, SLATE, Feb. 19, 2019, available at https://slate.com/news-and-politics/2019/02/elizabeth-warren-2020-wealth-tax-constitutional.html, archived at https://perma.cc/PJM2-LMVH.

We think we need to say a bit more, though. Sometimes the argument against instrumentalism is that, though distinctions and other legal moves can indeed often be made, there's a limit. And the limit is something like "the law's integrity." That is, once you start developing distinctions and exceptions, you're going to convert a sensible and relatively simple structure of law into a Rube Goldberg machine that might work (instrumentally) but that doesn't deserve the label "law."

In legal theory that account, or something like it, is often called "formalism." It sees "the law" as a well-integrated system whose numerous parts interlock to create something that holds together quite tightly, with rules so well-defined that they sharply limit the opportunities lawyers and judges have for implementing "mere" policies that might be instrumentally good but are legally indefensible.[35] This sort of formalism is more attractive to lawyers schooled in European continental legal systems than to those trained in common law jurisdictions, but it has a foothold everywhere. This isn't a book about deep legal theory, and we're not going to try to refute formalism. We note only two things. A legal theory called American Legal Realism offers a powerful challenge to formalism.[36] We think that it's correct. If it is, no populist has to be a legal instrumentalist though some might be (we think that not many are). And correct or not, American Legal Realism is a respectable account of the law and its fundamental structure. Describing populist instrumentalism as a mistake about legal theory gets into quite deep waters of legal theory. We don't think that treating that description as criticism goes far without a much more extensive defense of formalism than we've seen populism's critics offer.

**

We end with a boring restatement of our central points. Not all populisms have the same relation to constitutionalism, thick but especially thin. We don't want our treatment of specific actions by populist governments that, we've argued, are consistent with thin constitutionalism to leave the impression that populist governance is always like that. The cases of Hungary, Poland, and Turkey, among others, make it clear that populism can be anti-constitutional. It isn't always, though. Each theme associated with populism can and does come in constitutionalist and anti-constitutionalist versions. Specifics and details matter. The next part provides some.

---

[35] Sometimes formalism is described is "deductive," that is, as a method of legal reasoning that starts with general principles and deduces more specific ones. We think that this is a bit misleading: what is presented as a "deduction" is often an attempt by the lawyer to work out the meaning of the words used in the rules at issue in a way that preserves the coherence of the rule system as a whole.

[36] American Legal Realism has many components, and here we refer only to a strong version of what's known as "rule skepticism," the claim that legal rules constrain decision-makers in ways that are sometimes impossible to work around. The fundamental source on rule skepticism of this sort is KARL LLEWELLYN, THE COMMON LAW TRADITION: DECIDING APPEALS (1961). A more recent presentation is Duncan Kennedy, *Freedom and Constraint in Adjudication: A Critical Phenomenology*, 36 JOURNAL OF LEGAL EDUCATION 518 (1986).

PART TWO
POPULISM IN PRACTICE

4

Populist Authoritarianism: Hungary and Poland

Populists came to power in Hungary and Poland less than two decades after accession to the European Union. The global financial crisis in 2008 served as a catalyst for change. Alternative economic and political ideas emerged and spread through the region. Populists began to develop a compelling response to the grievances of citizens disappointed with neoliberalism: a nationalist, authoritarian populism, combined with a welfare chauvinist social policy, promised to protect ordinary people from liberal elites and to grow the economy based on "economic self-rule" and a conservative developmental state.[1] These programs thickened populism in Central and Eastern Europe with an economic dimension that fueled populist election victories. Populists protested against the "consensus at the center" between the center-right and center-left, rejected the idea that there is no alternative to globalization, and opposed IMF and EU influence.[2] At the same time, political liberalism has been challenged by open flirtation with illiberal and authoritarian forms of government.[3]

I. Populist Economic Policy Reform Agendas

We begin our examination of authoritarian populism in Hungary and Poland by looking at their economic programs because, we believe, those programs were at least as important in producing populist election victories as were thematic oppositions drawn between "the people" and "the elites" or "us" and "them."[4]

---

[1] Juliet Johnson & Andrew Barnes, *Financial Nationalism and Its International Enablers: The Hungarian Experience*, 22 REVIEW OF INTERNATIONAL POLITICAL ECONOMY 535 (2014); Katharina Bluhm & Mihai Varga, *Conservative Developmental Statism in East Central Europe and Asia*, 25 NEW POLITICAL ECONOMY 642 (2020).

[2] Johnson & Barnes, note 1 above.

[3] Jan-Werner Müller, *Eastern Europe Goes South: Disappearing Democracy in the EU's Newest Member States*, FOREIGN AFFAIRS 93:2 (March/April 2014), at p. 14.

[4] Parts of this section draw on Mitchell A. Orenstein & Bojan Bugarič, *Work, Family, Fatherland: The Political Economy of Populism in Central and Eastern Europe*, JOURNAL OF EUROPEAN PUBLIC POLICY (2020, forthcoming).

Power to the People. Mark Tushnet and Bojan Bugarič, Oxford University Press. © Mark Tushnet and Bojan Bugarič 2021. DOI: 10.1093/oso/9780197606711.003.0005

In 2010, Viktor Orbán's Fidesz Party won a supermajority in parliamentary elections on the heels of the global financial crisis and after years of economic mismanagement by the Socialist Party, exemplified by a leaked tape in which the Socialist prime minister admitted lying about the state of the economy. Orbán called his economic policy the "Eastern winds" approach to distinguish it from Western liberalism.[5] The key pillars of the policy were renationalization of certain private companies, mostly in what he considered to be strategic sectors like oil, gas, utilities, and banks; new taxes on foreign banks, insurance companies, and international supermarket chains; and domestic labor force activation.[6] Orbán forced foreign banks to convert foreign currency mortgage loans into Hungarian forints. During his first (pre-populist) term as prime minister, Orbán had created a compulsory private pension fund; now he nationalized that fund and used account balances to pay off Hungary's foreign debt.

In other areas, Orbán worked to develop a national capitalist class connected to his party, creating many "near-to-Fidesz compan[ies]," often by displacing prior owners while diminishing the power of international organizations and foreign banks in the Hungarian economy.[7] Magyar describes the creation of a "post-communist mafia state," a pyramid that encompasses state and economy with Orbán at the top.[8]

Orbán denounced the West as decadent and obsessed with money and outlined a future "work based society," moving toward it by creating a massive jobs program for the unemployed.[9] In 2019, Orbán sought to connect his conservative nationalist message to generous social policies by providing financial incentives to encourage Hungarian women and families to have more children. Orbán sought to address Hungary's low fertility rate of 1.45 children per female, well below replacement rate (2.1), with natalist policies that would create new Hungarians, rather than importing immigrant labor. The plan offered a lifetime exemption from personal income tax for women who bear and raise four or more children—Orbán and his wife have five. Women under forty who marry for the first time and have worked for at least three years are eligible for a €31,700 "childbearing" loan at a discounted rate, and the loan is forgiven as they have children. Larger families can apply for a €7,900 government grant toward the purchase of a seven-seat automobile. Grandparents taking care of children were made eligible

---

[5] The Economist, "Orbán and the Wind from the East," Nov.14, 2011.

[6] László György, Creating Balance: The Mission of Economic Policy (2020). György was a minister dealing with economic matters in Orbán's government.

[7] János Kornai, *Hungary's U-Turn: Retreating from Democracy* 26:3 Journal of Democracy 34 (July 2015), at p. 38; Johnson & Barnes, note 1 above.

[8] Bálint Magyar, Post Communist Mafia State: The Case of Hungary (2016).

[9] Andrea L.P. Pirro, The Populist Radical Right in Central and Eastern Europe: Ideology, Impact, and Electoral Performance (2015), at p. 149.

for benefits and leave from work and the government announced the creation of 21,000 new subsidized childcare places.

Critics took aim at the expense and conservative vision implicit in Orbán's policies, which encourage women to marry, work, buy houses, bear more children, and stay in Hungary.[10] As public policy scholars Noemi Lendvai-Bainton and Dorota Szelewa argue, Orbán's policies rewrote "the previous 'social contract.' . . . replac[ing] a welfarist social contract with a nationalist one based on identity politics."[11] Orbán's policies have consistently provided support for those who work and families described as deserving rather than merely very poor. Professor Agnes Batory finds that Orbán's policies reflect an authoritarian vision of Hungary rooted in self-responsibility as well as "a system of national cooperation," conveying communitarian values in opposition to transnational liberalism.[12]

While Orbán's combination of nationalism and populism has been "anathema to young, cosmopolitan Hungarians," other voters gave Orbán a comfortable plurality of votes (and a majority of seats) in the parliamentary elections of 2014 and 2018. Orbán secured his third successive election victory in 2018 on the back of record turnout, winning two-thirds of the seats. While Orbán deploys a range of cultural appeals, voters also rewarded him "for his clever harnessing of popular discontent with the neoliberal order and its acute side effects."[13] Orbán's policies succeeded in getting him re-elected, though the elections were less than entirely free and fair, his government having captured the Electoral Commission and gerrymandered districts to favor Fidesz over traditional left-wing parties.[14] There is no evidence his economic policies harmed Hungary's economy, as liberals claimed they would. They produced jobs, growth, and gains for the lower and middle classes. One study by a government-related think tank concluded that net real wages increased by 59 percent between 2010 and 2018, mainly because of changes in the tax structure that reduced income taxation, increased (foreign) capital taxation, and broadened the tax base, causing an additional 2.5–3.0 percent of GDP to flow to the household sector.[15]

---

[10] THE ECONOMIST, "Viktor Orbán's Plans to Boost Hungary's Birth Rate are Unlikely to Work," Feb. 16, 2019.

[11] Noemi Lendvai-Bainton & Dorota Szelewa, *Governing New Authoritarianism: Populism, Nationalism and Radical Welfare Reforms in Hungary and Poland*, SOCIAL POLICY & ADMINISTRATION, Aug. 2, 2020, at p. 564.

[12] Agnes Batory, *Populists in Government? Hungary's "System of National Cooperation,"* 23 DEMOCRATIZATION 283 (2015).

[13] PHILIPP THER, EUROPE SINCE 1989: A HISTORY (2016), at p. 234.

[14] Benjamin Novak, "Hungary's 2018 general election likely to be less fair than 2014's since Fidesz media takeover," available at https://budapestbeacon.com/hungarys-2018-general-election-likely-to-be-less-fair-than-2014s-after-fidesz-media-takeover/?_sf_s=electoral+rules, archived at https://perma.cc/VK4L-GN99.

[15] GYÖRGY, note 6 above, at pp. 216–18.

Critics argue that things are not as rosy as traditional macroeconomic measures suggest. Hungary has become the second most corrupt member of the European Union.[16] During Orbán's first six years in power, five of his closest friends were awarded roughly 5 percent of public procurement contracts, a total of $2.5 billion, according to an analysis by the Corruption Research Center Budapest.[17] Magyar argues that the post-communist mafia state "is not a mere deviation from liberal democracy, nor a transitional formation, but an independent subtype of autocracy."[18]

Orbán's economic policies are embedded in a broader project to create a semi-authoritarian "illiberal" state, as opposed to liberal democracy. After Orbán's well-known speech in Tusnádfürdö, it became obvious that he proposed creating an illiberal state, a different kind of constitutional order from liberal democracy.[19] Within ten years, Orbán transformed Hungary from one of the success stories of transition from socialism to democracy into a semi-autocratic regime, where the new constitutional structure vests so much power in the centralized executive that no real checks and balances exist to restrain this power.[20]

The story of economic policy in Poland is similar. After winning parliamentary elections in 2015, Poland's right-wing populist Law and Justice (PiS) government followed Hungary's mix of ethnic nationalism and redistributive economic policy. Its program was also tinged with an anti-liberalism reminiscent of the interwar period—when authoritarianism masquerading as democracy prevailed in Admiral Miklós Horthy's Hungary and Marshal Józef Piłsudski's Poland.[21] PiS's economic changes are part of a conservative political program founded on a set of moral values that purportedly serve to protect the Polish nation and its sovereignty from openness to foreign capital.[22]

PiS has consistently supported national populist politics at the level of ideology and rhetoric. PiS and its predecessors on the Catholic nationalist right have won around 30 percent of the vote in Polish elections since 1989 with consistently anti-Semitic, anti-EU, anti-immigrant, and anti-Russian appeals. A second group of PiS's base—secular anti-European conservative intellectuals—is also guided by ideology.[23] However, PiS's recent election victories added to this

---

[16] Transparency International, Corruption perception index 2019, available at https://www.transparency.org/en/cpi/2019, archived at https://perma.cc/PZ8J-7WCF.

[17] Patrick Kingsley & Benjamin Novak, "An Economic Miracle in Hungary, or Just a Mirage?," THE NEW YORK TIMES, Apr. 3, 2018, at p. A4.

[18] MAGYAR, note 8 above, at p. 73.

[19] Kester Edy, "EU Urged to Monitor Hungary as Orban Hits at 'Liberal Democracy,'" FINANCIAL TIMES, July 30, 2014.

[20] R. Daniel Kelemen, *The European Union's Authoritarian Equilibrium*, 27 JOURNAL OF EUROPEAN PUBLIC POLICY 481 (2020).

[21] THER, note 13 above, at p. 234.

[22] Bluhm & Varga, note 1 above.

[23] *Id.*; David Ost, *Workers and the Radical Right in Poland*, 93 INTERNATIONAL LABOR & WORKING-CLASS HISTORY 113 (2018), at p. 120.

traditional base by attracting voters using economic appeals. Some of these voters may have previously supported the post-communist left parties, which lost support precipitously as the PiS vote grew.[24]

PiS appealed to millions of Poles in the small towns and poorer regions of "Poland B" who "felt themselves to be marginalized and left behind by the bulldozer of economic liberalism. They were also, it's important to add, alienated by the social liberalism, on issues such as abortion, gender, and sexual orientation, which came with the opening to Western Europe."[25] PiS economic policy has focused on making life and work more secure. Under Prime Minister Mateusz Morawiecki's economic plan, "the government has vowed to stop the privatization agenda of previous governments and reindustrialize and 're-polonise' parts of the economy." The government imposed a levy on the banking and insurance sectors in 2016, increased state control of the domestic banking sector from 30 to over 50 percent and consolidated the domestic energy sector under state ownership to create a "national champion" to compete internationally.[26]

Despite robust economic performance, the previous governing party, the neoliberal Civic Platform (PO), had left many working people behind, with so-called junk employment contracts paying them less than $200 a month. PiS has also sought to stem the flow of youth out-migration by exempting all workers under age 26 from income tax.

PiS economic policy aimed to create a culture around family values, natalism, supporting those left behind by liberalism, and building up the Polish nation. As political theorist Leszek Koczanowicz argues, PiS "aims not only to transform certain external conditions, but also to accomplish a comprehensive re-invention of mentality and radically re-direct the trajectory of social thinking."[27] These features of the PiS program came together in its signature social program, Family 500+, launched in 2017. Family 500+ provided a generous family allowance of $144 a month per child, an amount equivalent to 40 percent of the minimum wage, for a family's second and each subsequent child. It was later expanded to cover a family's first child as well. Economically, Family 500+ was a major boon for Polish families, particularly those in Poland B, where wages were lower and residents more likely to emigrate. Family 500+ gave hundreds of thousands of working parents "a sudden untaxed pay raise of twenty or even forty percent. . . .

[24] Sheri Berman & Maria Snegovaya, *Populism and the Decline of Social Democracy*, JOURNAL OF DEMOCRACY 30:3 (July 2019), at p. 5; Gavin Rae, *In the Polish Mirror*, 124 NEW LEFT REVIEW 89 (July/August 2020).

[25] Timothy Garton Ash, *Is Europe Disintegrating?*, THE NEW YORK REVIEW OF BOOKS (Jan. 19, 2017), at pp. 22–26.

[26] Alen Toplišek, *The Political Economy of Populist Rule in Post-Crisis Europe: Hungary and Poland*, 25 NEW POLITICAL ECONOMY 388 (2020), at p. 393.

[27] Leszek Koczanowicz, *The Polish Case: Community and democracy under the PiS*, 102 NEW LEFT REVIEW 77 (Nov./Dec. 2016), at p. 94.

Single mothers found themselves able to quit overly exploitative jobs and seek other options."[28] Family 500+ dramatically reduced child poverty and enabled families to buy clothes, take a holiday, and pay for "school sets" at the start of each school year. As Rae reports, this policy had an immediate positive effect, with "child poverty falling from 23 to 11 per cent in just two years. The number of children with access to benefits nearly doubled, from 2 million to 3.8 million. This provided a new source of income for a wide range of social groups, including many from the middle class, thus cementing support for PiS across a broad spectrum of society."[29] According to political scientist Aleks Szczerbiak, "many Poles feel that, while politicians have often promised to help the less well-off, Law and Justice is the first party to actually deliver on these pledges on such a scale."[30] PiS funded Family 500+ through new taxes on banks and large businesses, following the Hungarian model, as well as through improved tax collection in a growing economy.

While Family 500+ was the most ambitious social policy reform undertaken in the region after 1989, it was not the only one. Ost notes, "Since winning power for the second time in 2015, PiS has taken real efforts to tame economic liberalism. It reversed the previous government's hiking of the retirement age, offered new drug benefits for the elderly, and has initiated a broad program for the construction of new affordable housing. It has limited employer use of insecure short-term 'junk contracts,' and raised the guaranteed hourly minimum to 13 złotys (nearly $4)."[31] PiS policies should be seen as a consistent effort to build a new Polish economy that taxes foreign investment more heavily and uses the revenues to support Polish families and workers, particularly in smaller towns and cities and rural areas, where PiS voters are concentrated.[32]

A. Populist Constitutional Reform Agendas

The economic policies we have described—which, we emphasize again, were important reasons for Fidesz and PiS electoral success—were embedded in a broader project to create a semi-authoritarian "illiberal" state, as opposed to liberal democracy. Orbán and Kaczyński have gone much further in subverting constitutional democracy than most of the other populists in Europe. Authoritarian

---

[28] Ost, note 23 above, at p. 115.

[29] Rae, note 24 above, at p. 99.

[30] Aleks Szczerbiak, *Why is Poland's law and justice government so popular?*, THE POLISH POLITICS Blog, Oct. 26, 2017, https://polishpoliticsblog.wordpress.com/2017/10/26/why-is-polands-law-and-justice-government-so-popular/, archived at https://perma.cc/8AQT-H4D8.

[31] Ost, note 23 above, at p. 115.

[32] Cyryl Ryzak, *The Law and Justice Party's Moral Pseudo-Revolution*, 67 (4) DISSENT 138 (Aug. 2020).

populists in Hungary and Poland have successfully institutionalized, through legal reforms, a new version of a semi-authoritarian regime, which is halfway between "diminished democracy" and "competitive authoritarianism."[33] Authoritarian populists in Hungary and Poland are explicitly anti-liberal but not necessarily anti-democratic. They embrace the form of democracy and claim to speak for the people themselves, a claim supported by their electoral successes, but, at the same time—by undermining its liberal constitutional foundations— they erode the substance of democracy and gradually transform it into a semi-authoritarian regime.[34]

Individually some of the constitutional reforms implemented in Hungary and Poland might be defensible, as we suggest later in this chapter, but as a whole they push toward authoritarianism. Sometimes that's because some changes interact with others to generate outcomes inconsistent with thin constitutionalism.[35] Sometimes it's because in the specific contexts of Hungary and Poland, the changes are symbolically important as indicators of a desire by Fidesz and PiS to repudiate liberalism even if the changes have no significant effects on the ground.[36] And sometimes it's because otherwise defensible changes are put in place with the specific intention of implementing them to strengthen the government's ability to secure re-election. We suggest that changes that fall into the second and third categories, while problematic in Hungary and Poland, might not be as troublesome when they are adopted in other populist regimes and so don't *in themselves* show that populists are anti-institutional.

We are driven to emphasize this point here because our discussion of specific constitutional changes is so detailed that we fear obscuring the forest by our attention to the trees. The core of our argument is this: we know from lots of things political leaders in Hungary and Poland have said that they are at least proto-authoritarians. You don't need to point to the constitutional changes they instituted to show that. And, because some of those changes are in principle defensible—that is, *might* be consistent with thin constitutionalism is some circumstances—it would be a mistake to generalize that all populists who

---

[33] On diminished democracy, *see* David Collier & Steven Levitsky, *Democracy with Adjectives: Conceptual Innovation in Comparative Research*, 49 WORLD POLITICS 430 (1997); on competitive authoritarianism, *see* Steven Levitsky & Lucian A. Way, COMPETITIVE AUTHORITARIANISM: HYBRID REGIMES AFTER THE COLD WAR (2010).

[34] Jan Zielonka & Jacques Rupnik, *From Revolution to "Counter-Revolution": Democracy in Central and Eastern Europe 30 Years On*, 72 EUROPE-ASIA STUDIES 1073 (2020). In their recent comparative study, Steven Levitsky and Daniel Ziblatt rate Hungary and Poland 'mildly authoritarian,' Turkey 'authoritarian,' and Russia 'highly authoritarian.' STEVEN LEVITSKY & DANIEL ZIBLATT, HOW DEMOCRACIES DIE (2018), at p. 188.

[35] For a more extensive discussion of this possibility, see Chapter 5 (on the Frankenstate).

[36] The major constitutional reform in Hungary included the insertion into the constitution of a statement referring to "the crown of St. Stephen." This is the kind of culturally significant but practically trivial symbolic gesture we refer to here.

propose similar changes are proto-authoritarians. As we proceed, we make this point by saying that some of the constitutional changes, though perhaps defensible in principle, were indefensible in these instances because they were adopted with the very intent of advancing the regimes' proto-authoritarian goals. Where such an intent is lacking, the constitutional changes—even (!) when advanced by populists—might be consistent with thin constitutionalism.

Both the Hungarian and Polish governments dismantled many key elements of constitutional democracy in a relatively short time. Though they focused on similar institutions—the courts, electoral rules, and the media—they followed slightly different paths to semi-authoritarian rule. The Orbán government implemented its constitutional reform agenda by using the constitutional amendment rules in place when it took office. The amendment route was not available to Kaczyński because the PiS majority wasn't large enough to amend the constitution on its own. The PiS invented a new form of constitutional revision, using ordinary statutes to significantly alter the practical functioning of the constitutional order.

These changes produced nominally democratic constitutions, which, as professors Miklós Bánkuti, Gábor Halmai, and Kim Lane Scheppele argue, "can no longer be described substantively as [those of] a republican state governed by the rule of law," certainly in a thick sense and in some aspects not in a thin sense either.[37] The major deficiency of the new constitutional structure is that it vests so much power in the centralized executive that no real checks and balances exist to restrain it.[38] In parliamentary systems like Hungary's and Poland's (both with weak but not impotent presidents), checks on the government's power sometimes flow from the courts, more often from opposition parties that are well-positioned to take over if the public turns against the governing party. The governments in both nations weakened or took over the courts and kneecapped the opposition.

Consider Hungary first. When Fidesz came to power the Hungarian Constitution of 1949 was formally still in force, with substantial amendments in 1989. The amendment rule was simple: a two-thirds majority of a single parliament could amend the constitution. The easy amendment rule, though a legacy of the Communist regime, made some sense even after 1989. Hungary was undergoing a transition and rules put in place early on might turn out to be unsuitable as democracy deepened. An easy amendment rule would smooth the way to adaptation under democracy. A seemingly important amendment was

---

[37] Miklós Bánkuti, Gábor Halmai, & Kim Lane Scheppele, "From Separation of Powers to a Government without Checks: Hungary's Old and New Constitution," in CONSTITUTION FOR A DISUNITED NATION: ON HUNGARY'S 2011 FUNDAMENTAL LAW (Gábor Attila Tóth ed. 2012), at p. 268.
[38] Id.

added in 1995: a four-fifths vote of parliament was required to set the rules for writing a new constitution. This made it almost impossible to change the constitution dramatically without consulting the opposition parties, as the prior constitutional arrangements required in practice.[39] The general amendment rule wasn't changed, though, to protect the new four-fifths rule amendment by a two-thirds vote. The Fidesz parliament used its two-thirds majority to eliminate the four-fifths rule from the constitution. With that rule out of the way, Fidesz could write a new constitution on its own.[40]

What followed was a series of constitutional amendments that changed the rules regulating the constitutional court, the referendum process, and the authority in charge of media control.[41] First, the parliament changed the rules for nominating constitutional judges so that Fidesz could use its two-thirds majority without needing multiparty backing—contrary to the requirements of the old constitution—to nominate candidates for the court. The second step was a restriction of the court's jurisdiction over budget and tax measures, prompted by the previous ruling of the court finding that a 98 percent retroactive tax on state employee compensation was unconstitutional. After the amendment the court could only review fiscal matters if those matters violated certain listed rights. With budget and tax matters removed from the court's jurisdiction, the Fidesz government could act in the financial arena "without having to pay attention to [prior] constitutional constraints. . . . Finally, a constitutional amendment increased the number of judges . . . from 11 to 15, giving the Fidesz government the chance to name four additional judges and thereby ensure a majority of its own candidates on the Court." [42] The once powerful and highly respected court disappeared from the political scene.[43]

In its next move, the Fidesz government brought the Election Commission under its political control, enabling Fidesz to block referendums offered

---

[39] Under the 1989 Constitution, Hungary had a constitutional framework that ensured checks on power, multiparty participation, and a substantial role for minority parties.

[40] More precisely, Fidesz could adopt discrete constitutional amendments by a two-thirds majority without having to worry about the possibility that a court would hold that one or more of them, or all of them together, amounted to creating a new constitution that could only be put in place with a four-fifths majority.

[41] For a summary of the process, see Gabriel L. Negretto & Sinlongo Wandan, "Democratic Constitutional Replacements and Majoritarian Politics: The Cases of Poland (1993–1997) and Hungary (2010–2011)," in REDRAFTING CONSTITUTIONS IN DEMOCRATIC REGIMES: THEORETICAL AND COMPARATIVE PERSPECTIVES (Gabriel l. Negretto ed. 2020), at pp. 160–61.

[42] Bánkuti, Halmai, & Scheppele, note 37 above, at p. 255.

[43] One of the few empirical studies has found that "most constitutional judges' votes coincided to a great extent with the political views of their nominators, regardless of the particular constitutional problem or the subject matter of the case under investigation by the Court. There were only three judges of the seventeen, who voted alternately for and against the constitutionality of laws adopted by the new government majority after the spring of 2010." Zoltán Szente, The Political Orientation of the Members of the Hungarian Constitutional Court Between 2010 and 2014, 1 CONSTITUTIONAL STUDIES 123 (2016), at p. 146.

by opposition parties. The new electoral law ended the terms of sitting commissioners and introduced a new rule according to which the members of the Electoral Commission were to be elected after each general election by a majority vote of the parliament. Previously the ten-member commission was divided so that half of its seats were filled by party delegates (one from each parliamentary party), while the other five were filled by mutual agreement between the governing and opposition parties. Fidesz immediately filled all the non-delegate seats on the commission with its own members, giving the ruling party a dominant majority on the commission.

The government was well aware of the importance of a free media environment. It reorganized the Media Authority, the state regulatory agency, supplementing it with the Media Council, a five-member "independent" body charged with ensuring "media balance." Soon the new chair of the Media Authority, with a nine-year term, was a former Fidesz MP, while the Media Council was filled with five Fidesz candidates.[44] The chair of the Media Council is nominated by the prime minister also for a nine-year term. However, the Media Act's provisions meant that the only possible candidate for council chair was the president of the National Media and Info-communications Authority, an administrative agency created by the Media Act, who is named directly by the prime minister.

And, finally, without changing the law, the Fidesz government elected former Fidesz vice chair Pál Schmitt as the new president of Hungary.[45] The Hungarian Constitution gives some checking powers to the president. The president can exercise a suspensive veto by sending laws back to parliament for revision, and can initiate constitutional review before the constitutional court. With "their" president in power, Fidesz no longer faced these additional checks on its executive power. As Bánkuti, Halmai, and Scheppele argue, these actions "effectively created an opening through which the Fidesz government could then push a new constitution without challenge."[46]

Then, less than a year later, the parliament adopted a new constitution, entitled the Fundamental Law of Hungary, which became valid on January 1, 2012. The new Szájer constitution, named after a Fidesz member of the European Parliament who headed the committee that proposed the new constitution,[47] contains several provisions that undermined previous checking mechanisms.[48]

---

[44] Miklós Bánkuti, Gábor Halmai, & Kim Lane Scheppele, *Hungary's Illiberal Turn: Disabling the Constitution*, 23 JOURNAL OF DEMOCRACY 138 (2012), at p. 139.

[45] Because of serious charges of plagiarism, Schmitt was forced to resign in 2012 and János Áder, a cofounder of Fidesz, was elected to replace Schmitt.

[46] Bánkuti, Halmai, & Scheppele, note 44 above, at p. 140.

[47] Jozsef Szájer, a member of the European Parliament and a top member of Prime Minister Viktor Orban's Fidesz Party, which is hostile to LGBT rights, resigned after he attended what Belgian media describe as a gay sex party in Brussels.

[48] László Sólyom, the former president of both the constitutional court and the Republic of Hungary, publicly stated that the "Fourth Amendment" removes the last traces of the separation of

Access to the constitutional court became modeled on Germany's constitutional complaint, limiting the access to the court only to those individuals whose constitutional rights have been violated by public authority. This eliminated the *actio popularis*, which allowed anyone to bring a case to the court, and which had provided the vehicle for many of the constitutional court's most admired—and liberal—decisions in the pre-Fidesz era.

By lowering the retirement age for ordinary judges from seventy to sixty-two, the government managed to remove almost all of the courts' presidents.[49] Legislation concerning the judiciary established a new National Judicial Office with the power to replace the retiring judges and to name new judges. The government appointed Szájer's wife, a close friend of Orbán, to the position of president of this body. The president of the National Judicial Office has unusually broad power to reassign specific cases from one court to another and, after a new constitutional amendment to the new constitution, even to choose, together with the public prosecutor, which judge will hear the case.[50]

In its next step, the government weakened the independence and autonomy of other important "fourth-branch" bodies with controlling functions. The prior system of four separate and independent ombuds offices was replaced with a "parliamentary commissioner for human rights" and the old data protection ombuds office was transformed into a quasi-governmental office.

Another striking example of using legal/constitutional tools to undermine checks and balances is the establishment of various new bodies, such as the Budget Council, the State Audit Office, and the Public Prosecutor, which are currently staffed with Fidesz loyalists with long terms of office (from six to twelve years) and strong powers to veto important decisions of Parliament, to investigate the government, and to assign cases in judicial proceedings. The Fundamental Law creates the Budget Council, which can veto any budget adopted by parliament that even minimally increases the national debt.[51] Two members of the

---

powers from the Hungarian constitutional system. Under the amended constitution, no institution has the legal right to check many key government actions.

[49] This change forced around 274 judges into early retirement. Those judges included six of the twenty court presidents at the county level, four of the five appeals court presidents, and twenty of the seventy-four Supreme Court judges. In November 2012, the European Court of Justice (ECJ) in Commission v. Hungary found this provision in violation of EU law. But, as Gabor Halmai argues, "none of these decisions were really able to reinstate the fired judges into their original position and stop the Hungarian government from seriously undermining further the independence of the judiciary and weakening other checks and balances with its constitutional reform." Gabor Halmai, "The Early Retirement Age of the Hungarian Judges," in EU LAW STORIES: CONTEXTUAL AND CRITICAL HISTORIES OF EUROPEAN JURISPRUDENCE (Fernanda Nicola & Bill Davies eds. 2017), at p. 471.

[50] See Articles 14 and 15 of the Fourth Amendment to the Constitution.

[51] The Budget Council's role in enforcing fiscal discipline is based on the provision of Fundamental Law that forbids Parliament to increase government spending as long as the debt/GDP ratio exceeds 50 percent. This is a more onerous threshold than those provided in the EU Stability and Growth Pact (SGP) rules, which allow 60 percent government debt.

Budget Council are elected by a two-thirds vote in Parliament and one is appointed by the president. Two members have a six-year term of office and one a twelve-year term. Moreover, if Parliament does not adopt a budget by March 31 of each year, the president has the power to dissolve parliament and call new elections. Assume that the opposition wins an election in the coming years. The Budget Council, still controlled by Fidesz loyalists, could veto the budget near the deadline, thus almost immediately triggering the constitutional provision allowing the president to call for new elections—in effect, making the opposition win at least two elections rather than one.

The state audit office, once known for its independent expertise, is now headed by a former Fidesz MP with a twelve-year term of office. Interestingly, the new head has no professional auditing experience. Similarly, the new public prosecutor, elected by a two-thirds parliamentary majority for a nine-year term, also has increased powers such as assigning any criminal case to a court of his choosing.

We've recited the long terms these officials have because they show how Fidesz has managed to entrench party loyalists "in every corner of the state."[52] For any future government not enjoying a two-thirds majority in the Parliament, it will be extremely difficult if not impossible to replace the Fidesz power-holders with new candidates. Imagine then, how difficult it would be for a new government to change the course and substance of politics as it is now entrenched by the new "partisan" constitution.

Last but not least, on March 11, 2013, the Hungarian Parliament adopted the so-called "Fourth Amendment," an amalgam of various constitutional provisions seeking to limit the independence of the judiciary, bringing universities under even more governmental control, opening the door to politically motivated prosecutions,[53] criminalizing homelessness, making the recognition of religious groups dependent on their cooperation with the government, and weakening human rights guarantees across the board. The most problematic, at least with our concerns in mind, are amendments that drastically limit the jurisdiction of the constitutional court. The amendments deny legal effect to all decisions made by the court before 1 January 2012 (when the new Hungarian Constitution entered into force). The precise legal effect of this provision is unclear, but it has accurately been described as "constitutional revenge" by the Orbán government against the court, reversing several government "losses" in previous decisions

---

[52] Bánkuti, Halmai, & Scheppele, *Disabling the Constitution*, note 44 above, at p. 145.

[53] Article 13/1 gives the president of the National Judicial Office exclusive power to manage the central administrative affairs of the courts. Article 6 passes financial management of the universities to the government. In combination with Article 9 (4) of the new constitution giving the president of the Republic the power to appoint both university presidents and professors, Article 6 thus represents a direct threat to the independence of universities. Article 14 entrenched the right of the head of the National Judicial Office to take any legal case and move it to a new court for decision.

and foreclosing the risk of future losses.[54] In addition, the court is banned from reviewing constitutional amendments for substantive conflicts with constitutional principles.

As we've noted, Poland's path to constitutional transformation was different from Hungary's. After winning a parliamentary majority in 2015, the PiS government in Poland quickly identified the Constitutional Tribunal as a target. Jaroslav Kaczyński, the party's leader, observed that "the reforms of the constitutional court were needed to ensure there are no legal blocks on government policies aimed at creating a fairer economy." In the early years of the post-communist transition period, the Constitutional Tribunal emerged as a "strong protector of democratic processes and of limits upon legislative and executive powers."[55] Because of the distrust of ordinary judges, many tainted by their service in the communist regime, constitutional courts became the centerpiece of the protection of the rule of law. But, in a centralized model of judicial review, only constitutional courts had the power of judicial review of legislation. That made the constitutional courts an easy target for populists determined to dismantle the "undemocratic" rule of elite, liberal judges. The first time the PiS was in power, from 2005 to 2007, the tribunal blocked a number of the government's plans. In May 2007, the tribunal invalidated several key sections of Poland's lustration law, the signature piece of legislation of that time, which governed the participation of former communists in government and the civil service.[56] Angered by the ruling, then–prime minister Kaczyński threatened to charge the judges with having acted "improperly."

Eight years later, Kaczyński, PiS's de facto leader, whose ultimate goal has been described as "a systematic and relentless annihilation of all independent powers which may check the will of the ultimate leader," turned the Constitutional Tribunal into an almost harmless judicial body.[57] The government managed with relative ease to render the constitutional court toothless by using ordinary procedures to pack it with loyalists as the terms of sitting judges expired. It took only one year for PiS-appointed judges to become a majority in the Tribunal. After the election of the new president of Tribunal, Julia Przyłębska, the process of creating a PiS majority on the tribunal was completed. As law professor Wojciech Sadurski (himself a target of PiS efforts to stifle opposition) shows in his

---

[54] Kim Lane Scheppele, "Constitutional Revenge," THE CONSCIENCE OF A LIBERAL blog, Mar. 1, 2103, available at http://krugman.blogs.nytimes.com/2013/03/01/guest-post-constitutional-revenge/. For additional discussion of this provision, see Chapter 8.

[55] WOJCIECH SADURSKI, POLAND'S CONSTITUTIONAL BREAKDOWN (2019), at p. 58.

[56] The Law of 18 October 2006, amended 14 February 2007, invalidated in part by the Constitutional Tribunal judgement K2/7 of 11 May 2007.

[57] Wojciech Sadurski, "What Makes Kaczyinski Tick," INTERNATIONAL JOURNAL OF CONSTITUTIONAL LAW BLOG, Jan. 14, 2016, available at: http://www.iconnectblog.com/2016/01/what-makes-kaczynski-tick, archived at https://perma.cc/88BG-AKJQ.

study of this transformation, the PiS-appointed judges "effectively paralysed the CT, rendering it unable to subject new laws to effective constitutional scrutiny."[58]

Court-packing was not the only process that PiS used to render the Tribunal subservient to its political will. The second strategy, a "legislative bombardment," involved a series of legislative proposals clearly aiming at curtailing the Tribunal's independence and paralyzing its work. In one year, from 2015 to 2016, the PiS-controlled Parliament adopted six new statutes on the Constitutional Tribunal, aimed at transforming it into "a positive aide" to the government.[59] The so-called Repair Act on the Constitutional Tribunal seemed to be custom-made to paralyze the Tribunal.[60] One key provision raised the bar for finding unconstitutionality: such rulings would have to be approved by a two-thirds majority, making it almost impossible to annul PiS-backed legislation. In the same act the quorum required for judgments initiated by abstract review increased from nine to thirteen out of fifteen judges. A combination of the two new voting rules virtually "ensured that a new judicial team on CT could veto any decision invalidating a new statute."[61] And cases must wait on the docket for at least six months before they can be decided.

Another group of changes aimed at enhancing the powers of the executive and legislature with respect to the Constitutional Tribunal. The president and minister of justice were given the right to start a motion for disciplinary process against a judge of the Tribunal and the Sejm could decide on disciplinary removal of a judge.[62]

"Most of these provisions were eventually found unconstitutional," but the Constitutional Tribunal was "effectively paralyzed by having to mainly consider laws on itself ('existential jurisprudence')."[63] This process continued only up to the moment when PiS acquired a majority on the Tribunal. The current law is based on two statutes adopted in 2016, which in many ways restored the situation that existed before the avalanche of new statutes in 2015 and 2016: "The earlier rules that seemed so defective to PiS when it did not have a majority on the CT turned out the be perfectly satisfactory once it had captured the majority."[64]

After neutralizing the constitutional courts, the PiS government continued its legal revolution with attacks on lower (regular) courts, the last bastion of judicial

---

[58]   SADURSKI, note 55 above, at p. 62.

[59]   Wojciech Sadurski, "How Democracy Dies (in Poland): A Case Study of AntiConstitutional Populist Backsliding in Poland," Sydney Law School Research Paper no.18/1 (2018).

[60]   The statute contained several other provisions exempting recent PiS legislation from constitutional scrutiny. The most interesting rule required to strictly respect the sequence of judgments according to the time the motion reached the CT. With a backlog of over hundred cases, this rule would effectively delay consideration of new laws (adopted by PiS) by many months.

[61]   SADURSKI, note 55 above, at p. 73.

[62]   Id. at pp. 73–74.

[63]   Id. at p. 74.

[64]   Id. at p. 75.

independence. The government prepared three bills, which aim to control and capture the Supreme Court (the highest court for non-constitutional matters) and the vast majority of other regular courts. By lowering the judicial retirement age (to age sixty-five), the government removed most of the presidents of the courts and replaced them with judges more to its liking.

At the same time that they mounted their attack on the judiciary, the governments in both countries engineered a radical transformation of the public media into a government mouthpiece. First, they changed the structure and per-sonnel of key regulatory agencies, and then they presided over an influx of party loyalists into public mass media outlets. In Hungary pro-government media dominates the market, with the second-largest private TV channel and several online and print outlets (including at least eight regional newspapers) in the hands of government allies. In the course of these acquisitions Hungary's leading critical daily newspaper was shut down.[65] Around 80 percent of the media in Hungary is financed by sources controlled by the ruling party or its friends. The Hungarian pattern is now being replicated in Poland as well. As Timothy Garton Ash puts it, Polish national TV, widely known as "TVPiS," "makes Fox News look like Canadian Broadcasting Corporation."[66] Independent journalism has been eliminated not by brute censorship but through the purchase of outlets by the government or friendly businessmen, A state-owned oil company "purchased two dozen regional daily newspapers . . . from their German owner."[67]

Rather than attacking civil rights and liberties directly, both governments use an indirect approach, adopting problematic measures concealed "under the mask of law"[68] to advance their versions of "autocratic legalism."[69] As Kim Lane Scheppele argues, the Fidesz government does not jail its opponents, it does not ban free travel, but it punishes political dissent by firing members of the polit-ical opposition from state sector jobs and by intimidating families of critical journalists.[70]

Some laws undermine civil rights and liberties indirectly, some directly. A typical example of the first group is the so-called Lex CEU, which on its face is a neutral piece of legislation requiring universities operating in Hungary to have substantial educational programs in the nations where they are incorporated. In

---

[65]   Freedom House, Hungary, 2017.

[66]   Timothy Garton Ash, "For a Bitter Taste of Polish Populism, Just Watch the Evening News," THE GUARDIAN, June 25, 2020.

[67]   "Poland Steps up an Assault on Free Expression. The U.S. Response will be Crucial," THE WASHINGTON POST, Feb. 16, 2021.

[68]   Ozan O. Varol, *Stealth Authoritarianism*, 100 IOWA LAW REVIEW 1673 (2015), at p. 1677; *see also* David Landau, *Abusive Constitutionalism*, 47 UNIVERSITY OF CALIFORNIA DAVIS LAW REVIEW 189 (2013).

[69]   Javier Corrales, *Autocratic Legalism in Venezuela*, 26 JOURNAL OF DEMOCRACY 37 (2015).

[70]   Kim Lane Scheppele, *Goulash Post-Communism*, 52(3) NEWSNET, NEWS OF THE ASSOCIATION FOR SLAVIC, EAST EUROPEAN & EURASIAN STUDIES 1 (2012), at pp. 3–4.

fact, its sole target was the Central European University.[71] Other laws attack civil rights directly. One of the most notorious examples is the "lex Gross" in Poland, which tried to make it a crime, punishable by three years in jail, to accuse "the Polish nation" of complicity in the Holocaust or any "Nazi crimes committed by the Third Reich."[72] The law was amended after extensive American and Israeli pressure to eliminate the criminal punishment as the main sanction, but it still retains civil sanctions for statements violating the reputation of Poland.[73] Though no prosecutions were initiated before the criminal sanction was repealed, the new law did chill public debate about the darker sides of the Polish history. The second example is the so-called Stop Soros laws in Hungary, which criminalize any individual or group that offers to help an illegal immigrant claim asylum and include a punishment of up to a year in prison for anyone assisting people to enter Hungary illegally. The legislation restricts the ability of non-governmental organizations to act in asylum cases. Parliament also passed a constitutional amendment stating that an "alien population" cannot be settled in Hungary.[74]

B. "Defending" the Constitutional Reform Agendas

We could hardly deny that the current Hungarian and Polish governments are at least semi-authoritarian, and perhaps worse, and we are wholly unsympathetic to their constitutional reform programs. Still, we think that we can get a better handle on thinking about the relation between populism and constitutionalism by doing our best to see what those governments' supporters might say in their defense.

We start with the observation that both governments had ambitious *substantive* reform agendas, as our discussion of their economic policies showed. Important parts of those agendas, such as the family support programs, might have been ill-advised because they couldn't be sustained. They were not, though, inconsistent with thin constitutionalism and indeed not inconsistent with some

[71] Gabor Halmai, "Legally Sophisticated Authoritarians: The Hungarian Lex CEU," VERFASSUNGSBLOG, 2017/3/31, https://verfassungsblog.de/legally-sophisticated-authoritarians-the-hungarian-lex-ceu/, archived at https://perma.cc/7XDJ-HVC9. The CJEU found the Lex CEU law in breach of EU law, but the ruling didn't really help the CEU, which had already relocated to Vienna.

[72] The name refers to professor Jan Gross of Princeton, whose books on Polish crimes against Jews provoked heated public debates in Poland.

[73] Marta Bucholc & Maciej Komornik, "The Polish 'Holocaust Law' Revisited: The Devastating Effects of Prejudice-Mongering," CULTURES OF HISTORY FORUM, Feb. 2, 2019, available at https://digital.herder-institut.de/publications/frontdoor/deliver/index/docId/175/file/Bucholc_Komornik_The_Polish_Holocaust_Law_2019.pdf, archived at https://perma.cc/VAP8-XW6R; SADURSKI, note 55 above, at pp. 154–56.

[74] Two laws in the Stop Soros package were found in breach of EU law by the Court of Justice in Luxemburg.

versions of thick constitutionalism. Suppose the governments' leaders believed not unreasonably that the institutions in place, including the constitutional and ordinary courts, might interfere with their ability to implement those substantive programs. As we've seen, Kaczyński expressly built this into his justification for constitutional changes in the judicial system.

These goals might have been reached by using regular methods of influencing those institutions, such as filling vacancies as they occurred (as indeed was the general course taken in Poland in connection with the Constitutional Tribunal). Suppose, though, that the leaders believed that implementing the programs was a matter of real urgency, whether for economic reasons (people desperately needed relief) or for political ones (the full program couldn't be implemented within a single parliamentary term, making it important to improve the government's re-election prospects to enable full implementation). They might then use existing amendment procedures to reduce the threat to their substantive programs. If that's what underlies the constitutional changes, the governments' defenders would argue that you can't point to the mere fact of constitutional amendment to demonstrate something like constitutional abuse; you have to show that the amendments' content is inconsistent with thin constitutionalism.

Of course, there's an alternative view: that the argument we've just outlined is just a sham. All that we've said *might* be true, but it wasn't in fact why Fidesz and PiS amended the constitutions. They did so simply to consolidate power. We agree with this alternative view, but explaining why requires us to explain first what's wrong with the regime defenders' imagined account.

The defenders' argument can't be dismissed out of hand because many—though not all—of the constitutional changes we've described aren't obviously inconsistent with thin constitutionalism. Some are arguably good-government reforms, others actually might remove obstacles to implementing the substantive reform agendas by adjusting the balance constitutions must strike between judicial independence and judicial accountability, still others are features common to many well-functioning constitutional democracies when a new party happens to win an election. Here's an annotated list of most of the constitutional changes that the regimes' critics have identified as problematic.

Judicial "reforms":

- Decreasing the requirement for nomination to the constitutional court to two-thirds. Constitutional systems vary enormously on this question. In Canada and Australia, the prime minister makes appointments with no formal role given to parliament. In the United States appointments require a simple majority in one house, and even some conventional requirements in recent decades—the need to overcome a filibuster—required only a 60 percent majority. We find it difficult to conclude that thin constitutionalism says much about the details of the judicial appointment process, and almost certainly doesn't bar a two-thirds majority rule.

- Imposing supermajority requirements for some constitutional rulings. Though such rules aren't common, they have been proposed as a formal mechanism for limiting the possibility that a court might come up with extravagant reasons for invalidating constitutionally permissible laws. Just as supermajority rules for legislation are thought to reduce the chance of overreaching, so with a judicial supermajority rule. Courts aren't exempt from the requirement that every important institution in a democracy should be subject to checks and balances. Put another way, judicial independence and judicial accountability go hand in hand.[75] A supermajority requirement can be a reasonable form of promoting accountability. Again, it isn't the content of the new laws regulating the Polish CT that's problematic; it's the intent with which they were adopted—not to promote accountability but to stop the CT from doing what the PiS government regarded as interfering with its ability to carry out its program.

- Limitations on access to the constitutional court. As initially conceived by Austro-German jurist Hans Kelsen only a select few—parliamentarians, some executive officials, some officials of local governments—could bring complaints to the constitutional court. Access to those courts gradually expanded, but many constitutional courts today—including the U.S. Supreme Court—limit access to those who have suffered specific and individualized harm. Some constitutional courts eliminated these so-called "standing" requirements. The older model, though, performed well enough in decently functioning democracies, and we doubt that reverting to it is inconsistent with thin constitutionalism.

- Limitations on the scope of constitutional review. Relatively few constitutional courts exercise jurisdiction over challenges to the substance of government budget decisions, and as with the reversion to the old model of access to the courts, so with abandonment of review of budgets: We think it difficult to connect such review to any component of thin constitutionalism.

Substantive review of constitutional amendments is a recent innovation that has perhaps become constitutional good practice.[76] But, as with so many good practices, constitutional democracies got along well without it for so long that we are again hard-pressed to see it as a requirement of thin constitutionalism.

---

[75] For additional discussion, see Chapter 8.
[76] For extensive recent examinations of the practice, *see* YANIV ROZNAI, UNCONSTITUTIONAL CONSTITUTIONAL AMENDMENTS: THE LIMITS OF AMENDMENT POWERS (2017); RICHARD ALBERT, CONSTITUTIONAL AMENDMENTS: MAKING, BREAKING, AND CHANGING CONSTITUTIONS (2019). For additional discussion, see Chapter 8.

- Court-packing, including reducing mandatory retirement ages. These are clearly the most problematic judicial reforms. We provide an extensive analysis of different kinds of court-packing in Chapter 8, and here simply summarize some concerns. It's important to distinguish between "irregular" court-packing, which occurred in Hungary, and court-packing that occurs in the ordinary course as judges serve out their terms, as occurred in Poland. In the latter case court-packing is simply a pejorative term attached to the simple fact that the government in power gets to fill vacancies when they occur.[77] Even irregular court-packing might be defensible if the judges in place were reasonably thought to be so hostile to a substantive reform agenda that they might interpose politically motivated constitutional objections to enacting or implementing the agenda. Irregular court-packing would then be a way of checking a wayward court.

The case for forcing judges into retirement by reducing the mandatory retirement age is similar. And indeed the governments in Hungary and Poland made it: they argued, though without offering much evidence, that too many older judges had served as willing tools of the Communist regime and might bring a repudiated cast of mind to thinking about contemporary legislation. True, one could use ordinary methods of judicial removal to get at individual judges who were biased against the populist governments. Proving such a bias might be difficult and, in some sense, trying to do so would be more intrusive on judicial independence than a categorical removal of all judges who had been on the courts too long. The pro-government argument here is fundamentally an empirical one, though one with a substantial predictive (and therefore unverifiable) component. For that reason, we note that the Hungarian and Polish governments never produced substantial evidence, a few anecdotes aside, supporting the argument. Not so incidentally, the general argument for constitutional reform to forestall obstruction of a substantive reform agenda has this same empirical/predictive character, and is similarly difficult to evaluate in the abstract.[78]

---

[77] Though not involving the courts, the appointment of a Fidesz loyalist as Hungarian president occurred in the usual course, and in our view for that reason isn't inconsistent with thin constitutionalism.

[78] A discussion of proposed judicial reforms in Slovakia concludes that "formal institutional arrangements and reforms cannot be viewed apart from their social and political settings." Peter Čuroš & Hans Petter Graver, "Dissimilar Similarities: Structural Reforms of the Courts in Norway and Slovakia," VERFASSUNGSBLOG, Nov. 26, 2020, available at https://verfassungsblog.de/dissimilar-similarities/, archived at https://perma.cc/JYU4-J48F. We agree with that conclusion. We lack sufficient information to confirm the authors' analysis of the specific reforms, but simply report their assertion that reforms aimed at reducing the number of judges and changing retirement ages were an effort to address problems created by the "highjack[ing]" of earlier efforts "to develop an independent judiciary" by "a group of corrupt judges," which takes the same form as the defense that the Hungarian and Polish regimes offered. We note as well that among the proposed reforms was the elimination of the possibility of judicial invalidation of a constitutional amendment, which another scholar characterized as "on collision course with the material core of the Slovak Constitution." Šimon Drugda,

Selected additional constitutional changes:

- Naming party loyalists to important positions on nominally independent democracy-monitoring bodies (the so-called fourth-branch institutions), to the point of gaining control of those bodies. This is a common practice, sometimes acknowledged in constitutional provisions that allocate seats on these bodies with the governing party getting a majority, the opposition a minority. Designs of fourth-branch institutions vary widely among democracies. Indeed, some democratic constitutions (the United States, Australia, and Japan most notably) don't provide for these institutions at all; some have statutory agencies whose composition can be changed by ordinary legislation. And, as a matter of practical politics, a party that controls the government for an extended period by repeatedly winning free and fair elections is eventually going to get control of these institutions.

- Dominating the media. Much the same can be said of public radio and broadcasting services. Even as famously independent an enterprise as the British Broadcasting Corporation has to operate with an eye over its shoulder to ensure that the prime minister and cabinet don't get too annoyed with what it airs. Still, converting public broadcasting into a propaganda arm of the government does seem inconsistent with some minimum requirements of thin constitutionalism because of the potential effects on how fair elections will be.

  More difficult to think about is the domination of *private* media by government allies. At the first cut one would think that newspapers and television stations that choose to support the government are exercising their own rights of free expression. Even buying a newspaper for the purpose of changing its editorial stance is an exercise of free expression, and that's so even if the purchaser is an oligarch whose wealth flows from a corrupt relationship to the government. That's happened in Hungary and perhaps in Poland, but it happens widely when there's corruption; that Fidesz and PiS are populist parties has little to do with this phenomenon. The problem, that is, is corruption not populism.

  One real problem would be government favoritism in dispensing its favors to private media operations that support it. This appears to have happened in Hungary, with some effects on the ability of newspapers opposed to Orbán to survive. With much advertising moving online, publishing public notices and the like might bring in enough revenue to matter

"On Collision Course with the Material Core of the Slovak Constitution," Verfassungsblog, Dec. 3, 2020, available at https://verfassungsblog.de/on-collision-course-with-the-material-core-of-the-slovak-constitution/, archived at https://perma.cc/QKF2-K95K.

even if the nominal amounts are small, but the revenues at stake—from publishing required government notices, for example—seem to us unlikely to be large enough to make much difference.[79]

- Giving quite long terms to members of fourth-branch institutions. As we've indicated, this practice does threaten thin constitutionalism, though the mechanism is more complicated than one might think. As our hypothetical example of the Hungarian Budget Council's power suggests, long terms for members of fourth-branch institutions make it possible for them to obstruct any government that manages to displace Fidesz—and the prospect of that happening makes it more difficult for the opposition to sell their alternative program to the public: "If we elect you," the public can say, "you won't be able to get anything done anyway, so why bother?"

- The attack on the CEU. The facial neutrality of the anti-CEU law plays a central part in its defense. The statute required universities with campuses in Hungary to have substantial educational operations in their "home" nations. On its face this might be defended as a consumer protection measure: Hungarian students might be attracted to a "university" with a good brochure and nice promises about the courses it offers, but which is a fly-by-night scam like Trump University in the United States. Such scams are harder to pull off if you actually have to run a university someplace else. Because every general rule is overly broad, the mere fact that this rationale clearly doesn't apply to the CEU isn't enough to show that it's indefensible; again, what matters is that the statute was adopted for the very purpose of shutting the CEU down.

- "Memory" laws. Several European nations have laws against "Holocaust denial," and some go a bit further to prohibit a few other "lies" about history. The Polish memory law differs from these laws, if it does, only because few serious people dispute the proposition that Holocaust denial is a lie whereas more people contest the proposition that the assertions targeted by the Polish statute are lies. Maybe we should say that Holocaust denial laws are inconsistent with thin constitutionalism and deprive the Polish memory law of its support in the laws of true democracies. The two of us disagree about the consequences if we don't. One finds advocating for "comparative victimology" quite uncomfortable, the other that the historical evidence on the two questions is strong enough to justify treating Holocaust denial laws as constitutionally permissible and the Polish memory law as unconstitutional.

---

[79] Attilá Batorfy & Agnes Urbán, *State Advertising as an Instrument of Transformation of the Media Market in Hungary*, 36 EAST EUROPEAN POLITICS 44 (2020), show that the Orbán government intensified the practice of directing government advertising to newspapers taking editorial positions the government favored, with at least one newspaper receiving such a high proportion of its revenue from such advertising that it probably should be regarded as an organ of the state.

What do we make of this list?[80] First, some of the constitutional changes are pretty clearly inconsistent with thin constitutionalism because they have the effect of entrenching the regimes in place: they tilt the electoral playing field quite substantially in the governments' favor—and the tilt is significantly greater than occurs when a government adopts a substantive reform agenda (family allowance programs, for example) whose popularity enhances its chance of re-election. Gerrymandering is the most obvious example, media domination another though more difficult one, but gaining control of the electoral commission and, in Hungary, giving Fidesz loyalists quite long terms in the various supervisory institutions have the same effect.

Further, we haven't yet mentioned other laws not involving structural changes in the constitutional system that are inconsistent with thin constitutionalism. These include restrictions on the constitutional rights and freedoms of ethnic minorities, Roma communities, Jews, homosexuals, and all those critical citizens who are not seen as "real" Poles or Hungarians. And patently fake justifications like the "consumer protection" argument for the anti-CEU law surely indicate that something else might be going on—and not merely with respect to that statute alone.

Our argument has been complicated and has gone into a lot of detail about *possible* justifications for the constitutional reforms adopted in Hungary and Poland even though we don't think for a moment that those actually were the justifications. We think that refuting the posited defenses of constitutional changes in Hungary and Poland by pointing to *other* indications of the desire to retain power—direct evidence of the authoritarian ideologies of Fidesz and PiS—is important for the comparative analysis of populism and constitutionalism. We don't think it's a conclusive charge against populists elsewhere that they've introduced constitutional reforms that look a lot like those in Hungary and Poland—that such changes show they are using a common playbook, to use a metaphor that's settled into the literature, to reach the common goal of anti-constitutionalism.[81] Many of the changes are defensible from the perspective of thin constitutionalism when examined in isolation from the entire package. That's important when we turn from Hungary and Poland to other countries, where only some of the changes have been made or proposed. We've argued that we might reasonably use some of the more troubling proposals as hints that something else is going on—that the changes are being made or proposed for

---

[80] We haven't included every constitutional change in the list, only enough—perhaps too many—to give readers a sense of how one might defend various changes as consistent with thin constitutionalism.

[81] For the metaphor, *see, e.g.,* ERIC A. POSNER, THE DEMAGOGUE'S PLAYBOOK: THE BATTLE FOR AMERICAN DEMOCRACY FROM THE FOUNDERS TO TRUMP (2020); Greg Rienzi, "The Authoritarian Playbook," JHU HUB, Oct. 30, 2020, available at https://hub.jhu.edu/2020/10/30/democracy-project-lisel-hintz/, archived at https://perma.cc/S9BC-CX9W.

the very purpose of allowing the government to adopt *other* policies that are indeed inconsistent with thin constitutionalism. We have to look carefully at specific cases to figure out whether the constitutional reforms are aimed at removing obstructions to an ambitious reform agenda without repudiating thin constitutionalism or whether, in contrast, they are aimed at entrenching for the indefinite future those currently holding power.

Still, we ourselves have a nagging feeling, which we think many readers will have as well, that picking apart the constitutional reforms—disaggregating them—might miss something important. We call what's missing a fallacy of disaggregation.[82] The fallacy is the assumption that as long as every piece in a constitution is consistent with thin constitutionalism, putting them all together must be similarly consistent. In some ways the fallacy is obvious: Suppose a constitution contains five different ways to keep the executive under control. Thin constitutionalism might require some checks on executive power, but it might well be that no single one of the five is necessary. The fallacy of disaggregation is that you can take away one of the five without violating thin constitutionalism's requirements, and maybe you can take away two or even three. When you take away all five, though, you're in trouble. Something like that can happen even when the provisions deal with seemingly disparate constitutional matters.

Kim Lane Scheppele argues that some constitutions consisting of individually acceptable pieces turn out to be Frankenstates. How that happens is the subject of the next chapter. It turns out that analyzing the Frankenstate problem is itself a complicated endeavor.

C. Conclusion: Democracy's Future in Hungary and Poland

Hungary and Poland may not yet be fully authoritarian regimes, but the combined effects of the described attacks on the key pillars of constitutional democracy show strong signs of a slide into authoritarianism. Despite the fact that the PiS government almost perfectly mimics the script used by Orbán, Poland is not yet Hungary. Orbán has been successful in capturing all the key governing institutions in Hungary. The Polish populists, in contrast, have made extensive progress in capturing some but not all rule of law institutions and the media, while most civil rights and liberties and the basic fairness of the electoral system

---

[82] We draw inspiration for the term from ADRIAN VERMEULE, THE SYSTEM OF THE CONSTITUTION (2011), chapter abstract (describing "the fallacy of composition," which is "to assume that if the components of an aggregate . . . have a certain property, the aggregate . . . must also have that property"). *See also* Wojeiech Sadurski, *Constitutional Democracy in the Time of Elected Authoritarians*, 18 INTERNATIONAL JOURNAL OF CONSTITUTIONAL LAW 324 (2020), at p. 326 (discussing this problem by describing the changes in Poland and Hungary as incremental).

still remain in place. Moreover, PiS has only a small parliamentary majority and not the supermajority needed for a Hungarian-style constitutional rewrite. And, while Orbán has been in power for two and a half consecutive four-year terms, Kaczyński's reign started only in 2015.

Recent elections suggest that the slide toward authoritarianism might be halted. Fidesz was able to take advantage of divisions among the opposition to win elections: conservatives and liberals ran separate slates that divided the anti-Fidesz vote. The opposition parties were sometimes successful when they managed to coordinate their efforts by choosing a single candidate. In 2019, for example, the opposition won mayoral elections in ten out of twenty-three of Hungary's major cities, including Budapest, the nation's capital.[83] And, late in 2020 the opposition parties announced that they had reached an agreement to run a single slate across the country in the parliamentary elections scheduled for 2022.[84] In Poland, PiS President Andrzej Duda was re-elected in 2020, but with a narrower margin than might have been expected.

The Polish case, where the opposition to the new populist government is stronger than in Hungary, and where the new government has not fully yet dismantled all the bulwarks of the rule of law, thus represents only an unfinished version of authoritarian populism.[85] While heading in the direction of the Hungarian model, Poland is not yet a non-democratic regime. While the battle for democracy in Hungary appears to have been largely lost, the Polish opposition parties and civil society groups still have a functional capacity to fight for democratic values and institutions.

---

[83] The Fidesz government responded by stripping city governments of important powers. For additional discussion, see Chapter 9.

[84] Péter Cseresnyés, *Main Opposition Parties to Run on Joint List in 2020*, HUNGARY TODAY, Dec. 21, 2020, available at https://hungarytoday.hu/hungary-main-opposition-parties-joint-list-2022/, archived at https://perma.cc/X69C-LHWU.

[85] Grzegorz Ekiert, "How to Deal with Poland and Hungary," Social Europe Occasional Paper, No.13, August 2017, available at https://scholar.harvard.edu/files/ekiert/files/ekiert_ocassional_paper_social_europe_2017.pdf. As Ekiert shows, Polish civil society has traditionally been the strongest in the region. *See* Roberto Stefan Foa & Grzegorz Ekiert, *The Weakness of Postcommunist Civil Society Reassessed*, 56 EUROPEAN JOURNAL OF POLITICAL RESEARCH 419 (2017).

5

The Problem of the Frankenstate

I. What Is a Frankenstate?

In April 2011 the Hungarian parliament controlled by Viktor Orbán's Fidesz Party adopted a new constitution. Over the next year, the parliament passed a number of laws that the constitutional court held unconstitutional. In March 2012 the Fidesz government responded by bundling those laws with other constitutional changes into the Fourth Amendment to the 2011 constitution. The aim of course was to insulate them from invalidation.

The government had to worry about audiences outside Hungary too. Many Europeans worried about the government. They understood that "Europe" had to put up with some diversity in its members' constitutional arrangements but were concerned that Fidesz had gone so far that it no longer could be treated as an ordinary member of the European family.[1] Responding to these worries, the Hungarian foreign minister commissioned three distinguished senior constitutional lawyers from Belgium, France, and Norway to write a report on the Fourth Amendment. They were charged with determining whether the amendment complied with "European norms and standards."[2] Two were retired law professors. Pierre Delvolvé, who had taught at the University of Paris-Panthéon-Assas, was clearly the most conservative. He had represented the quasi-military "security" arm of the Le Pens' extreme right-wing party and in 2013 was an active member of the opposition to the adoption of a marriage equality law. Francis Delpérée had taught at the Catholic University of Leuven and had been president of an international association of Francophone constitutional law scholars, and was a member of a "Christian humanist" political party with a center-left economic agenda. Eivind Smith, the third member, was a Norwegian law professor, well-known in the field of comparative constitutional law. Going into the exercise the group of experts probably tilted somewhat to the right. The Orbán

---

[1] Article 4 (2) of the Treaty on European Union protects the national "constitutional identity" of the Member States: "The Union shall respect the equality of Member States before the Treaties as well as their national identities, inherent in their fundamental structures, political and constitutional, inclusive of regional and local self-government. . . ."

[2] The report is available at http://vienna.io.gov.hu/download/1/ec/60000/alaptorveny_modositas_szakvelemeny_angol.pdf, archived at https://perma.cc/CRT8-DEJH.

Power to the People. Mark Tushnet and Bojan Bugarič, Oxford University Press. © Mark Tushnet and Bojan Bugarič 2021. DOI: 10.1093/oso/9780197606711.003.0006

government probably expected to get a mostly sympathetic hearing from the experts.

And indeed, it did. The experts' report concluded that the amendment's provisions did mostly satisfy European norms. Its ten substantive sections marched through the Fourth Amendment provision by provision—the disaggregation approach we worried about at the end of the preceding chapter. We describe only some of the report's analyses to give readers a flavor of the experts' approach.

One section discussed a provision regulating political advertising. As interpreted by the experts the provision required that publicly owned media operations—state television and radio, mostly—had to provide free access to political advertising, defined as "propaganda setting out political ideas, positions and projects of some groups, in particular those of political parties, and praising the virtues of the candidates." It also limited such advertising to those media during active political campaigns. So: free political advertising in the publicly owned media at any time, political advertising only in those media during campaigns. And no limitation on the publication of "political information" that aims at "inform[ing] the public about political events; [and] neutral analysis and observations" as long as they did not take "a stand in favor of candidates."

The experts began by observing that the provision appeared to be modeled on French law, but that French law limiting political advertising during campaigns to publicly owned media dealt only with "commercial advertising," defined as paid-for political advertising. In France, the experts said, you could publish political advertising in the privately owned media if they were willing to let you do so without charge. After directing attention to "the variety of solutions" available for the problem of political advertising, the experts turned to international human rights law. They cited a recommendation of the Committee of Ministers of the Council of Europe saying that media coverage of campaigns should be "fair, well balanced and independent."

The experts concluded that the Hungarian solution for political advertising outside of the campaign period (free on the public media, free or paid on private ones) "can be justified by the purpose to avoid the promotion of parties, groups and persons with large financial means and thus avoiding inequality between candidates" and the solution for the campaign period (no private media, free on the public media) could be justified "to ensure equal conditions for the competing candidates."

Several sections dealt with changes in court jurisdiction and operation. The most important, at least for our purpose, declared that "Constitutional Court rulings given prior to [January 1, 2012] are hereby repealed." Such rulings were to have no force as precedents, though they might have continuing "legal effect" on the rights and duties of the parties involved in the rulings. The date is significant.

From 1991 to 2012 Hungary's fundamental law took the form of a series of additions to a constitution dating from the communist era. A new constitution went into effect on January 1, 2012. The new constitution had many provisions that tracked those in the prior document, and the constitutional court had often interpreted those provisions to create liberal individualist constitutional rights. The point of the amendment was to wipe those interpretations off the books so that the new constitutional court could create its own jurisprudence.

This provision excited substantial opposition from liberal constitutionalists who admired the jurisprudence the Hungarian constitutional court had developed in the 1990s. A comment by the Venice Commission gives a taste of the concern: The provision "may . . . be used as an argument for ignoring the rich case law of the Hungarian Constitutional Court which, although based on this 'invalid' constitution, has played an important role in Hungary's development towards a democratic state governed by the rule of law."[3] Hungary's Helsinki Watch Committee wrote, "it is hard to see what the aim of the governing majority was . . apart from 'punishing' the CC for its unfavourable decisions. The vice-president of the governing party Fidesz stated in this regard degradingly that the CC may not 'crib by taking an old decision, Ctrl+C, Ctrl+V, and say that it is ready.' "[4]

The experts found the provision unobjectionable because after 2012 the constitutional court was interpreting a document that hadn't existed before. Their explanation was, "It is in the best interest of the constitutional judges to ground their decisions on the constitutional provisions which are in force as opposed to prior decisions of the Court, which were rendered in a particular political era and in a constitutional order with a fuzzy framework." The phrasing is telling. Some of the prior interpretations dealt with provisions adopted during the communist era. Was that the "particular political era," and was the fuzziness a result of the troubled normative foundations of communist rule? That, or something like it, was indeed Fidesz's formal constitutional theory.

The problem, though, was that the amendment wiped out jurisprudence from the post-communist era as well. So, to the extent that the experts had an account, it must have been something like this: the interpretations' origins in words adopted during the communist era somehow taint interpretations offered after communism's collapse. And that, we believe, was Fidesz's unstated constitutional theory: the "particular political era" was the post-communist period in

[3] Adopted by the Venice Commission at its 87th Plenary Session (Venice, June 17–18, 2011), CDL-AD(2011)016, ¶35, available at https://www.venice.coe.int/webforms/documents/CDL-AD(2011)016-E.aspx.

[4] Hungarian Helsinki Committee, "Main Concerns Regarding the Fourth Amendment to the Fundamental Law of Hungary," Mar. 13, 2012, available at http://helsinki.hu/wp-content/uploads/Main_concerns_regarding_the_4th_Amendment_to_the_Fundamental_Law_of_Hungary_13032013.pdf, archived at https://perma.cc/TGG8-JJNA.

which liberal constitutionalism was the prevailing ideology, and liberal constitutionalism was the "fuzzy framework." Yet the experts didn't examine how the communist legacy affected decisions made by the constitutional court after 1991.

A weaker and less politically contentious conclusion might have been enough: it was acceptable to treat the new constitution as having been written on a blank slate even if it used the very same terms used in prior documents.[5] Banning reliance on "old" jurisprudence was undoubtedly intended to give a symbolic slap to the prior constitutional court, but how it "punished" or "degraded" the current constitutional court is unclear.

A year later Professor Kim Lane Scheppele published a short article taking on the approach used in the experts' report and, she argued, in other assessments of constitutional innovations offered by constitutionalists around the world. The title was "The Rule of Law and the Frankenstate: Why Governance Checklists Do Not Work."[6] Scheppele observed that many human rights observers assessed constitutional performance by asking whether a nation's constitution had one or another provision, a checklist of "isolated and independent parts." But, she argued, checklists were inadequate because they ignored the possibility that seemingly independent parts, each of which worked well on its own, might interact in ways that produce anti-constitutional outcomes.

Scheppele's leading example was the Weimar constitution's treatment of emergency powers. One provision allowed the president to dissolve the parliament, "a perfectly reasonable . . . power given the tendency of Weimar parliaments to fragment." Another provision allowed the president to declare an emergency subject to parliamentary rejection. In 1933 President Paul Hindenburg acted on then Chancellor Adolph Hitler's request and dissolved parliament, with elections scheduled for early March. In late February Hindenburg declared an emergency, granting Hitler broad powers that freed him to attack his opponents. The March elections gave Hitler and his coalition a slim majority; by the end of March Hitler had maneuvered his way to getting a two-thirds majority for a new statute (the Enabling Act) granting him essentially dictatorial power.

Examined in detail, the episode doesn't quite establish that the interaction itself produced "a perfect storm of constitutional catastrophe."[7] Elections were held, after all, and Hitler didn't win enough votes to push through the Enabling

---

[5] The experts discussed three other categories of decisions, presumably for comprehensiveness: the constitutional court couldn't rely upon interpretations of provisions that had been expressly repealed; it of course couldn't rely on interpretations of provisions that were created in the new constitution; and it could rely on interpretations of provisions that had been included in the new constitution on the express understanding that prior interpretations would govern. (At least, this is how we interpret the experts' less-than-transparent explanation.)

[6] 26 GOVERNANCE 559 (2013).

[7] We note as well that, as we argue in Chapter 9, devising constitutional provisions dealing with emergency powers might well be the most difficult part of the task of constitution design.

Act on his own.[8] Scheppele's example from Hungary works better, though the example might not identify all the problems associated with disaggregating Hungary's constitutional revisions. With its power to amend the constitution, Fidesz changed the constitution's provisions on the state budget. The new provisions created a budget council whose members—of course to be appointed initially by the Fidesz government—with terms extending up to twelve years. The council can veto budgets that increase the state's debt. The amendments also set a deadline for passing a budget, with parliamentary dissolution to follow if there isn't an approved budget. Scheppele then asks us to consider what would happen if the opposition defeated Fidesz. The new government would have to propose a budget. The budget council could veto it just before the deadline. Parliament would then be dissolved and Fidesz would have a chance to retake power.

The idea that constitutional provisions, perhaps sensible on their own, can interact to produce bad outcomes seems clearly correct.[9] In that light, the common populist willingness to change constitutions when they make it more difficult for the populist government to implement its political program might be troublesome. When they follow through with constitutional changes, they run the risk of creating a Frankenstate.

As we've noted, a Frankenstate is made from bits and pieces of constitutional arrangements rummaged from a bunch of constitutions everyone regards as satisfying the requirements not merely of thin constitutionalism but as consistent with one or another thicker constitutionalism. When the Frankenstate takes life, though, it rampages through the countryside of constitutionalism and the rule of law, leaving only devastation behind. Given that each of its parts was drawn from some existing constitutionalist system—and in light of the "constitutional identity" provision in the basic treaty—how then could that happen?[10]

---

[8] For a detailed account of this episode, *see* BENJAMIN CARTER HETT, THE DEATH OF DEMOCRACY: HITLER'S RISE TO POWER AND THE DOWNFALL OF THE WEIMAR REPUBLIC (2018); HENRY ASHBY TURNER, HITLER'S THIRTY DAYS TO POWER: JANUARY 1933 (1996). As Daniel Ziblatt has shown, "the willingness of a weak and declining conservative party to save itself by forming a coalition with an extremist party—despite its animosity to it—was a key facilitating condition." DANIEL ZIBLATT, CONSERVATIVE PARTIES AND THE BIRTH OF DEMOCRACY (2017), at p. 350.

[9] Giving the budget council veto power is unusual and the twelve-year terms are unusual, but both are arguably defensible as a way of creating the kind of independence constitution designers seek for monetary institutions like central banks. The same political irresponsibility that leads to designs that provide independence for monetary authorities might justify independence for the body controlling fiscal policy.

[10] We feel compelled to note that in Mary Shelley's novel, Frankenstein's monster is at least as much a sympathetic victim as he is a scourge on the countryside.

II. How to Think about Frankenstates

We don't think that a Frankenstate comes into being every time a new constitution contains five or ten or . . . innovations. It's not the accumulation of innovations that matters. What matters is that something bad happens as a result of putting two or more otherwise fine (or at least "okay") innovations into action at the same time.

Victor Frankenstein constructed an elaborate machine to animate the "monster" he created. What are the mechanisms for animating a Frankenstate? We identify several. One is what legal theorist Tarun Khaitan describes as death by a thousand cuts. Death by a thousand cuts occurs when one after another anti-constitutional actions add up to a fatal wound.[11] Death by a thousand cuts is a bit different from the Frankenstate problem, but it's in the same general family and often occurs in conjunction with building a Frankenstate. The key is that each action considered in isolation is a *cut*—that is, it is anti-constitutional on its own. The Frankenstate is different because each of its components considered in isolation is within constitutional bounds.

Another mechanism is what we call an *interaction* mechanism.[12] As Professor Scheppele pointed out, combining some constitutionally okay innovations with others might be like combining two medications with disastrous results because their effects interact poisonously. Interaction effects come in two variants. One deals solely with the formal properties of several provisions and asks whether on their face they mesh badly. The other examines the material or substantive effects of the provisions—how they will operate within the legal and social system in which they are inserted. The experts' report to the Hungarian government took a completely formal approach and found no troubling interactions. A more substantive approach would have.

Finally, the very fact that some constitutionally okay innovations are adopted at the same time (or nearly so) might be a signal that something constitutionally problematic is lurking in the shadows. Call this the signaling account. As with the interaction mechanism, this one too is sometimes coupled with death by a thousand cuts.

The interaction account identifies a mechanism by which combining two things generates a bad outcome. The signaling account makes us suspicious

---

[11] Tarunabh Khaitan, *Killing a Constitution with a Thousand Cuts: Executive Aggrandizement and Party-State Fusion in India*, 14 LAW & ETHICS OF HUMAN RIGHTS 49 (2020).

[12] Wojeiech Sadurski, *Constitutional Democracy in the Time of Elected Authoritarians*, 18 INTERNATIONAL JOURNAL OF CONSTITUTIONAL LAW 324 (2020), includes the interaction account among the "factors" that create problems for analysis of democratic backsliding in Poland and Hungary (and elsewhere). *Id.* at p. 326. Other factors Sadurski identifies are that change occurs incrementally, that institutions are preserved but transformed, and that change with respect to specific components of thin constitutionalism occurs with varying speed.

about the possibility that the government plans to do something bad.[13] That's the short summary. Working out the details takes a fair amount of time and space, and we're not going to be referring to populism directly in much of what follows. Populism lies in the background, though, because we're worried about bad things that might happen when several constitutional changes occur at once or in close proximity—and because populists are said to be enthusiastic about making such changes.

A. The Interaction Account Analyzed

In thinking about troubling interactions, we think about distinguishing between a constitution's structural provisions and its rights-guaranteeing ones. Although both types can create bad interactions, we think—as Scheppele's examples suggest—that such interactions are more likely in connection with structural provisions.

- *Individual-rights problems.* Consider first the campaign-advertising regulation the committee of experts found consistent with human rights law. On their own terms, they appear to have been correct: equalization of resources is a widely accepted justification for regulating campaign finance and, though less widely used, for regulating political advertising. And we haven't been able to identify any other constitutional provisions with which the regulation might interact to cause problems.

  That doesn't mean, though, that the regulations are unproblematic. Think about the period outside political campaigns. Well-financed parties get free access to the public media and can buy time on privately owned media; poor parties get the first but not the second. It's not hard to imagine that Fidesz knew that it would be well-financed, could produce political advertising with high production values, and would have allies in the privately owned media—and that opposition parties would be poor, unable to make slick political advertisements for the publicly owned media, and find few sympathizers among the owners of private media. A similar analysis suggests that the ban on advertising during the campaign period would have a similar "disparate effect," as equality law would put it, on opposition parties.

---

[13] Somewhere between these two accounts, but closer to the interaction account, is the idea that some innovations—on their own—might put the constitutional system on a slippery slope to disaster. Like the interaction account, a slippery slope account describes a mechanism leading to disaster. In our experience, many critics tend to use the term "slippery slope" when they really have the signaling account in mind.

So, the campaign-advertising provision does create a problem, but we're not sure that it should be discussed in "Frankenstate" terms: There's an interaction, but it's not with other constitutional provisions. Rather, the interaction is with the social and political conditions into which the provision is inserted. And that kind of problem can arise everywhere. To see why the campaign finance provisions are troubling requires that we take a substantive rather than a formal approach to identifying interactions.

Here's another individual-rights example, the law dealing with libelous statements about public officials. Such a statement must make a false assertion of some fact about a public official that injures the official's reputation—a false statement that the official took a bribe, for example, or spent two-thirds of his working time cavorting on the beach. Legal systems differ widely in how they work out the details of libel law. Does the defendant have to prove that the statement was false, or does the plaintiff have to prove that it was true? For much of the history of libel in common law systems, defendants had to prove the truth of a statement that on its face was likely to cause harm to reputation; the recent trend is to place the burden of proving falsity on the plaintiff. Can the plaintiff recover damages only by showing that his or her reputation was harmed, and to what extent, or can we presume that false statements do cause harm? The older rule was that harm could be presumed, the newer one requires some sort of proof of real harm. And, finally, can a plaintiff win simply by showing that the published statement was false (making libel a strict liability tort), or must he or she show that the defendant published the statement without investigating it to any serious extent (negligence) or without following the standards of professional journalism, or for the very purpose of harming reputation (maliciously, in the ordinary sense of the word)?[14]

All these things can be mixed and matched in a host of ways.[15] If you're simply trying to come up with the rule that works best in your legal system, you have to worry about a lot of things. Everyone knows that having your name dragged through the mud is unpleasant for most people, which is why we have a law of libel in the first place. Public officials can be targets of unfounded accusations because they do things that some people don't like. So, the prospect of being libeled is something you take into account when you decide to go into public life. The easier it is for someone to get away with smearing your name, the more reluctant you'll be to become a public servant.

[14] The U.S. Supreme Court has held that plaintiffs can prevail only if they show that the statements were published with "malice," but it defines that term in an unusual way: with knowledge of the statement's falsity or with willful disregard of the statement's truth or falsity. New York Times v. Sullivan, 376 U.S. 254 (1964). We include this note because readers may be familiar with the *Times v. Sullivan* rule but unaware of the court's special definition of malice.

[15] That fact explains why it makes sense to have a margin-of-appreciation doctrine, to accommodate different mixes of the several components.

Another thing to think about is the quality of the press in your nation. If you have a lot of yellow journalism—papers and now websites that are willing to publish anything that gets circulation up—you might want to make it easy for libel targets to win their cases; if the press is generally responsible you might end up thinking that the occasional false statement is just a cost of being a public servant. Now throw into the mix the question of whether the press in your nation is highly partisan, and your choice gets even more complicated.

And finally (for present purposes), suppose your nation has a history of high-level corruption that you've recently managed to overcome with tremendous effort. You're going to worry that the public will lose confidence in the government if it's exposed to false statements that public officials are still corrupt, throwing into the trash all your effort to install good government.

When you put everything together, you might end up with a libel rule that makes it relatively easy for public officials to win libel cases. That's what Singapore has chosen. It follows the traditional common law rules about libel rather closely: defendants have the burden of proving the truth of their statements once the plaintiff shows that the statement might have caused harm to his or her reputation. Expressly referring to the strong interest in assuring the public that its servants are totally honest, the Singapore courts have held that the higher up the plaintiff is, the greater the damages: make a false statement about a member of parliament and you'll have to pay; make a false statement about the prime minister and you'll have to pay a lot more.

Since its creation as an independent country in 1965, Singapore has been governed by the People's Action Party (PAP), which has always won extremely large majorities in regular elections. One reason for the PAP's enduring success is libel law. Instead of locking political opponents up, PAP officials sue them for libel. The most well-known case was a suit by Prime Minister Lee Kuan Yew against Joshua Benjamin Jeyaretnam, a flamboyant opposition figure. Eventually Jeyaretnam had to declare bankruptcy to get out from under repeated libel judgments. That in turn had the perhaps not incidental effect of making him ineligible for election to parliament under a rule, sensible on its own terms, prohibiting people with bankruptcy hanging over them from serving in parliament because they would be serious targets for bribery attempts.

Here we see an interaction effect: maybe it's within bounds to make it fairly easy for public officials to win libel cases, and it's clearly defensible to prevent undischarged bankrupts from serving in the legislature (Singapore's rule on this isn't a dramatic departure from practice elsewhere). Put the two together, though, and government officials have a powerful weapon to turn on their political enemies.[16]

We've given one example of an interaction effect involving individual rights (libel, bankruptcy, qualification for office) and another that seems to us not best characterized in interaction terms (campaign-advertising regulation). As before, disaggregating constitutional provisions and examining their formal interactions doesn't capture how Frankenstates come about: what makes the provisions problematic lies outside the purview of the checklist of constitutional provisions.

- *Structural problems.* Our sense is that the case is quite different for structural provisions. We preview a more detailed argument we develop in Chapter 9 about the political logic of presidential term limits: a president unbound by term limits gets to appoint the members of a large number of the institutions created to check presidential power—audit bureaus, anticorruption prosecutors, the regulators of the career civil service. Having done so, the president can bend those other institutions to his or her will.[17] Scheppele's example of the Hungarian system for controlling a budget even if Fidesz lost a parliamentary majority is another example.

Why might structural provisions generate more problems—and present the Frankenstate risk—more often than rights provisions? We're unaware of much helpful scholarship bearing on this question directly, although some work in political science and public administration illuminates it. We offer three speculations based mostly on our experience in constitutional law.

Institutions are complicated, with many moving parts inside them even before they start interacting with other institutions. It's really hard to know how those internal parts actually work without putting them in motion.[18] That means that drafters are going to have to make some guesses about what's likely to happen—and some of those guesses are going to be wrong. Sometimes the mistakes can be remedied easily, but occasionally the errors, once they manifest themselves, will be disastrous quite quickly.

---

[16] Even fairly stringent liability rules can be used by political leaders to harass opponents by forcing them to spend time and money defending against them—and, of course, if the suits succeed, they drain the opponent's pocketbook. For example, the Supreme Court of Venezuela held in 2019 that a news site had to pay $5 million in damages to Diosdado Cabello, a political ally of Nicolás Maduro, for alleging that Cabello was "connected to a drug trafficking ring." Committee to Protect Journalists, "Venezuela's Supreme Court order La Patilla to Pay US$5m in Damages to Cabella," June 7, 2019, available at https://cpj.org/2019/06/venezuelas-supreme-court-orders-la-patilla-to-pay/, archived at https://perma.cc/S4VR-7NRY. This phenomenon can and does generate criticism of substantive libel rules, but the target is the liability rule standing alone, not its interaction with other rules.

[17] Scheppele's example of the Weimar Constitution, though as we argued imperfect, also involves structural provisions about who gets to control the parliament that is supposed to oversee declarations of emergency.

[18] The formal term for this is that institutions have emergent properties.

Rights provisions, in contrast, might have pretty complicated doctrinal structures, but repairing mistakes while the rights provisions remain operating seems to us easier: mistakes about rights provisions are like small problems with a seam on a large ocean liner; they can be patched up while the ship moves ahead. Not always, of course. The ship might hit an individual-rights iceberg and go to the bottom quickly. Badly designed rights provisions about the right to demonstrate against the government can lead to destabilizing armed clashes between street thugs associated with political parties (think again of Weimar). But our sense is that there aren't as many rights icebergs as structural ones.

A second consideration is that structures necessarily interact with each other. We know that these interactions can sometimes be pathological. In separation-of-powers and semi-presidential systems, for example, gridlock can occur when different structures are controlled by different political parties. Sometimes gridlock is itself destabilizing. Even more, gridlock leads the institutions to search for creative ways to get things done. Presidents claim strong power to rule by decree, for example. Anticorruption prosecutors target officials who might indeed be corrupt, but are chosen for prosecution because the prosecutor believes that getting rid of them will break the gridlock. In short, interaction effects among institutions are inevitable, and some of them can be pathological in ways that drafters can't always anticipate.

Rights provisions do interact, of course. A right to personal autonomy lets you decide whether to stay at home or join a protest on the street. An important line of argument holds that the right of choice with respect to abortion lets women make choices about their careers. Here too we have to be tentative, but our sense is that these interactions are more easily cabined than the interactions among governance structures, which suggests that disastrous interactions among rights are less likely.

Not impossible, though. Here our example is uniquely U.S.-based. It's the scenario of clashes among armed protestors exercising their free expression right to demonstrate on the streets. The demonstrations are protected by the right to free expression—and in the United States so is the right to be armed in public (on some interpretations of the Second Amendment to the U.S. Constitution). Put the two together and you might have created an iceberg (or a Frankenstate).

Finally, structures are inevitably operated by politicians either directly, as in legislatures, or indirectly, as when audit bureaus and similar "independent" bodies are staffed so as to make them somewhat accountable to politicians. Whether out of a desire for personal power or a desire to get things done for the public good, politicians will look around for opportunities to do stuff. They are like taxpayers looking for loopholes (with lawyers good enough to help their clients find the loopholes).

That's fine, or at least might be tolerable, if we think about one institution at a time: the legislature finds a loophole to enhance its power, but the president figures out how to close it. We can't think about institutions one at a time, though. Each institution is operated by politicians and everyone is looking for loopholes. Maybe, to deploy another of the metaphors we've invoked, this is how a death by a thousand cuts occurs: Each loophole lets some of the blood seep out of the constitutional system. Maybe one institution's constitutional creativity provokes an equally creative response by another institution, in the end depriving the constitution of any normative force and even operating effectiveness.

Here too we suspect that rights provisions are different. Rights holders do have incentives to be creative about their claims, and there's a whole literature about "rights escalation" dealing with that. But, as that literature suggests, rights escalate only when others agree with the claims. In the case of structures, disagreement is built in. Or at least you can try to build it in by using the technique identified by James Madison of setting the ambitions of the politicians in one institution against the ambitions of those in another.

Madison's technique failed when well-organized political parties on a national scale emerged in the United States.[19] Which is to say, it fails everywhere.

What happens when one party controls all the structures of government? You might get really efficient government advancing the public good—if that's what the governing party wants to do. You also might get a Frankenstate if the governing party doesn't care much about constitutionalism, thin or thick. That leads us to the signaling account.

B. The Signaling Account Analyzed

We've gotten a long way from populism, but now we're ready to return to it. Sometimes populist parties are the leading members of a governing coalition, but sometimes a populist party is also a dominant party. Yet, having a dominant party, populist or otherwise, doesn't mean that you automatically have a Frankenstate. We adapt a term introduced by John Rawls to suggest that there can be "decent" dominant party states—not great, not liberal constitutional

---

[19] The classic article, Daryl J. Levinson & Richard H. Pildes, *Separation of Parties Not Powers*, 119 HARVARD LAW REVIEW 2311 (2006), works out the argument to which we allude.

states, but not Frankenstates either. A constitutional monarchy like Bhutan today might be an example, but the premier one appears to be Singapore.[20]

Decent dominant party states differ from Frankenstates because of what the dominant party wants to do—in the former, govern in the public interest; in the latter, exercise power for its own sake or to make a small section of the nation much better off at the expense of the rest of the nation. The difference, that is, lies in the intentions of those at the head of the state.

The components of the Frankenstate are fine on their own. They could even be "good government" amendments in the abstract. One provision in Hungary's Fourth Amendment authorized parliament to require university students who received public financial support—basically, of course, scholarships—to work in Hungary "for a definite period" (or repay the aid). The experts pointed out that this provision addressed the problem of "brain drain"—a nation subsidizing the education of people who took what they learned and emigrated, depriving Hungary of the benefit of its investment in their human capital. It also might be seen as a version of a public-service obligation to build community within Hungary. Either way, it's pretty clearly unobjectionable.

What the signaling account tells us to worry about, then, are provisions with two characteristics: they don't interact with other provisions to cause problems (if they do, the interaction account is all we need), and they could be good-government reforms. But, why worry about good-government reforms?

Because, though these provisions *might* be good-government reforms, we have strong suspicions that they're not, although we can't quite pin down why if we look only at the reforms and other constitutional provisions. Consider here the Hungarian provision on the civic obligation of students who receive financial assistance. It could be a good-government reform. At the same time, it could be one of a series of anti-immigrant policies, aimed at increasing the domestic workforce so that immigrants wouldn't be able to "take jobs away from Hungarians"—Hungarians would be treated by doctors trained in Hungary, not in Syria. Similarly with the Polish family programs: they are in part components of a social-welfare reform to strengthen a social safety net. As with the interaction analysis, but in a different way, here too we have to pay attention to social context and ideology. The Hungarian and Polish programs *also* express conservative ideologies—ethnonationalism and pro-natalism.

The signaling account says that a government that adopts a specific provision that both on its own and in interaction with others might be fine signals its willingness to adopt other provisions that are inconsistent with constitutionalism.

[20] For a discussion, *see* Mark Tushnet, *Authoritarian Constitutionalism*, 100 CORNELL LAW REVIEW 391 (2015).

This might be especially true if the government adopts several of these provisions at almost the same time: although it might do so because it has an ambitious reform agenda that it believes would be blocked by existing institutions, it might also do so because it has anti-constitutionalist goals in mind. The government's willingness to amend the constitution in many ways signals that it might intend to modify it in more troublesome ones.

We confess our puzzlement about this. Unless we can find something intrinsic to the provision we're looking at that itself signals trouble—which we can't once we've reached this point in the analysis—we can't infer nefarious intent from the provision's adoption. Of course, we'll sometimes have other reasons to suspect the government of bad intentions, but then those other reasons are doing all the work: they are what signal anti-constitutional intent, not the specific provision at hand.[21]

The critical reaction we've reported to the provision of the Fourth Amendment wiping out pre-2012 precedents provides a decent example of the problem we've described. The critics said that the provision "punished" or "degraded" the constitutional court for its liberal rights jurisprudence. How the provision does that is hardly clear—except that the Fidesz government's account of constitutional history and theory leads us to believe that it intends to pursue an agenda inconsistent with a liberal rights jurisprudence. The provision doesn't do anything to bolster that belief.

Here's a more complicated example. The PiS government in Poland ran into trouble with European courts when it reduced the age at which judges were required to leave the bench, and applied the reduction to sitting judges. It also gave the nation's president a completely discretionary power to extend the term of an age-limited judge. The European courts concluded that these reforms interfered with judicial independence. There's something like an interaction account available. We can imagine that the cadre of senior judges forced into earlier retirement than they expected might have disproportionately favored a jurisprudence inconsistent with the one PiS favored. Getting rid of them, then replacing them with "neutral" judges or (better, from PiS's point of view) judges sympathetic to the PiS program would create a bench that overall would shift in the direction of rulings upholding PiS's program. This would not interfere with judicial independence with respect to any of the judges forced into early retirement (they've already made all the decisions they could). It might interfere with judicial independence understood as meaning that judges should develop their best view of the law—they should be accountable to law—without worrying about

---

[21] Cf. Sadurski, note 12 above, at p. 330 (discussing the "relative irrelevance of formal constitutional design" and concluding, with respect to the manner of judicial appointment, "what matters is political will and commitment on the part of the political elite").

the possibility that a new government will do something to make jurisprudence excessively politically accountable. And it might interfere with judicial independence by giving the targeted judges an incentive to shade their decisions to enhance the prospects that their terms would be extended.

Maybe so, but here's an alternative view. The new government can get away with this maneuver only if it's willing to get rid of all judges above the new retirement age. And that creates a collective action opportunity to preserve judicial independence. Any single judge can say, "Well, I can go on developing my own best view of the law, because if they want to do something to me they're going to have to do something to a whole bunch of other judges who might, for all I know, think that the PiS program is just fine." Maybe this is excessively rationalistic: the younger judges who retain their positions might irrationally overestimate the chance that the government, having reduced the retirement age once, will do it again even at the cost of getting rid of a bunch of judges who they thought— when they reduced the retirement age initially—weren't developing an inappropriate jurisprudence.

Another possibility, though, gets us to the signaling account. The starting point is that the reduction in retirement age isn't strictly speaking inconsistent with the rule-of-law requirement that laws generally not be retroactive. It isn't inconsistent with that principle because the non-retroactivity principle is justified on the ground that giving laws only going-forward effect allows people to plan their lives in light of the laws in place when they have to make decisions. Where the retroactive law is triggered by something over which you have no control, like your age, it can't affect your planning though it might defeat some of your expectations. Expectations, though, aren't protected by the non-retroactivity principle. People make investment decisions all the time based on the tax laws in place when they decide to invest, only to find that a later change in tax law wipes out the profits they expected to make. (Suppose PiS reduced the retirement age to sixty but said that sitting judges over that age could continue as judges for one more year before retiring. That law wouldn't be retroactive in a rule-of-law sense.)[22]

The next step in the signaling account is to note that reducing the retirement age might not be retroactive strictly speaking, but it's not great on the "expectations" dimension. And—finally—a government that's willing to push the idea of retroactivity this hard now (without actually violating the rule of law) might be willing to break the rule of law at some point in the future: Instead of using a generic characteristic over which you have no control to get rid of a cadre of judges

---

[22] There are some doctrines holding unconstitutional disruptions of expectations that are too sudden or excessive. In connection with retirement programs, the pensions available after retirement have some bearing on the analysis of whether disrupted expectations are unconstitutional.

who aren't helping the government enough, next time they'll simply fire individual judges who aren't doing with the government wants. And, indeed, the provision allowing the discretionary extension of terms has pretty much the same effect. That conclusion might be correct, but you have to have evidence beyond the reduction in the retirement age to support it. And, once again, if you do, that other evidence is what's doing the work.

We conclude with a few observations about the signaling account. People do grasp the signaling account, but we think they prefer an account like the interaction one that identifies a mechanism by which the Frankenstate is brought into existence. The reason, we believe, is that mechanism-based accounts explain the Frankenstate mechanically, so to speak—that is, without requiring that we say anything about why the Victor Frankensteins of constitutional design put together their monster: They could be evil or, like the character in the novel, well-intentioned, aiming to improve humanity's lot.

The signaling account, in contrast, requires us to say that the people we're talking about were badly motivated from the start. In the setting of constitutional design, though, saying that someone is badly motivated comes down to saying that they want to implement bad policies and are using constitutionally okay mechanisms to do so. To say that the policies are bad, though, is to make an expressly political judgment. This ties our analysis of the Frankenstate to our general theme: we don't actually care much about populists' willingness to innovate constitutionally so that they can implement their policies. What we care about is whether the policies are good or bad ones—that is, we care about the politics underlying populists' constitutional innovations.

We think that critics would be better off if they simply dropped from the discussion of Frankenstates provisions about which they can't identify troubling interaction effects. Concretely: the experts' judgments that some parts of the Fourth Amendment were reasonable specifications of components of constitutionalism were well-founded; some provisions may have been anti-constitutional but the experts gave them their stamp of approval because they ignored interaction effects. Also concretely: going through a rule-of-law checklist can be done badly when you ignore interaction effects; it can be done acceptably when the item checked off doesn't interact with others in a troublesome way.

III. What to Do about Frankenstates

We've suggested—we can't say that we've shown—that the interaction account requires some quite tricky analytic moves. We do think that we've shown that the interaction account doesn't describe many of the things people worry about when thinking about Frankenstates.

Professor Scheppele suggests that constitution designers can deal with the interaction problem by what she calls "forensic legal analysis." Examining a constitution, we should ask "a series of targeted 'what if?' questions to run legal problems through the legal system to see how they come out."[23] Other terms for the exercise are "stress tests" and "nightmare scenarios."

We offer two comments on this prescription. Both start out rather close to the ground but rapidly get us into large questions of constitutional and political theory.

- *The inevitability of failure under stress.* One problem with this prescription is that, whatever might be said about stress tests for financial institutions, we can always come up with nightmare scenarios for constitutions—stress tests that constitutions will inevitably fail.[24] Close observers of U.S. politics in 2020 obsessed over a host of nightmare scenarios that might have led to deep constitutional crisis. Another way to think of the difficulty returns us to an earlier metaphor: think of the constitution in the way a tax lawyer would think about the tax code, searching for loopholes that would let a client avoid taxes in an entirely lawful manner. Tax lawyers and scholars know that the tax law always has loopholes, and know as well that the only way to deal with them is to patch them up after they're discovered: You just can't write a tax code—or a constitution—without loopholes or vulnerability to nightmare scenarios.

What then might we do to avoid creating Frankenstates? Addressing issues of constitutional design in Central and Eastern Europe after the collapse of the Soviet empire, Professors Cass Sunstein and Stephen Holmes suggested that the best course was to write constitutions that would avoid the problems constitution drafters thought most likely to arise once the new constitution was up and running (and, of course, include a provision for amendment if new problems arose).[25] That seems to us good advice, but it's not going to help much with the Frankenstate problem. The drafters of the initial Hungarian Constitution

[23] Scheppele, note 6 above, at p. 562.

[24] We described a mundane version of this point in our explanation for including amendment procedures in constitutions in Chapter 1: you want to be able to amend the constitution after you discover some unexpected interactions that caused failure or near-failure. The usual example offered here is the initial design of the U.S. system for electing a president and vice president, which led to a deadlocked election in 1800 because the initial constitution's design worked badly once nationally organized political parties came on the scene.

[25] Stephen Holmes & Cass Sunstein, "The Politics of Constitutional Revision in Eastern Europe," in RESPONDING TO IMPERFECTION: THE THEORY AND PRACTICE OF CONSTITUTIONAL AMENDMENTS (Sanford Levinson ed. 1995), at p. 275. We note another possibility: a government of such limited power that it couldn't "fail" because it couldn't do much at all. Of course that could also be described as a strongly libertarian constitution, which means that it imports quite strong—"thick"—ideas

thought correctly that the most likely problem under the new constitution was a fragmented party system leading to unstable coalition governments that wouldn't be able to get anything significant done—thereby, they worried, perpetuating the cynicism about government that communist rule had fostered. As we discuss later in this chapter, their solution to that likely problem had dramatically bad effects when party fragmentation disappeared.

The prescription to worry about the most likely problems you can anticipate seems to us a good one. It has one massive difficulty, though. With a qualification we'll get to, we think it clear that no design for a constitutional democracy can prevent the nation's people from making disastrously bad decisions.[26] The people can elect authoritarians, and they can do so with large enough margins to allow the winners of a free and fair election to eliminate veto points or speed bumps aimed at impeding the transition from democracy to authoritarianism. If you're going to have elections, you have to run the risk of the "one person, one vote, one time" problem familiar to scholars of the post-1989 era.[27]

What's the qualification? The problem we're discussing arises when a majority of a nation's people vote for an authoritarian. Maybe we should think about designing institutions that would reduce the probability that people would *want* an authoritarian to govern them. Classical theorists of democracy did think about such institutions: the family, religion, civil society, even (in some versions) small-scale commerce and farming.[28] They didn't think that constitutions could do much to ensure that these institutions generated attachments to democracy or opposition to authoritarians. Perhaps constitutions could give them space within which the appropriate attachment would develop without also giving them space for authoritarian preferences to develop.

We think that experience has shown that this hope was misplaced. But, in our concluding discussion of democratic innovation, we explore the possibility

---

about constitutionalism into the design. (And even that sort of design can't rule out the possibility of a popular revolution that would displace the libertarian constitution with something else.)

[26] Cf. Stephen Gardbaum, *The Counter-Playbook: Resisting the Populist Assault on Separation of Powers*, 59 COLUMBIA JOURNAL OF TRANSNATIONAL L. 1 (2020) (arguing for constitutional revisions that would make it difficult for popularly elected executives to undermine the separation of powers).

[27] In 2020 Professor Joseph Weiler wrote that those who criticized the Orbán government should augment their criticisms by adding the Hungarian people as an object of concern. Joseph H. H. Weiler, *Editorial: Orbán and the Self-Asphyxiation of Democracy*, 18 INTERNATIONAL JOURNAL OF CONSTITUTIONAL LAW 415 (2020). Some responses to Weiler argued that the presidential election wasn't reasonably free and fair, which we believe is less accurate in connection with PiS election victories. (Bertolt Brecht's sardonic poem "Die Lösung (The Solution)" comes to mind here: in our view people who think something is a Frankenstate most often think that the people who elected bad governments should be replaced by a better people.)

[28] On commerce, *see* ALBERT O. HIRSCHMAN, THE PASSIONS AND THE INTERESTS: ARGUMENTS FOR CAPITALISM BEFORE ITS TRIUMPH (1981); on farming, *see* THOMAS JEFFERSON, NOTES ON THE STATE OF VIRGINIA, Query XIX (1787).

that some kinds of democratic governance quite different from traditional ones might be self-reinforcing. Notably these forms of governance tend to be associated with rather deep explanations for the populist attraction to majority rule.

- *The inevitability of political judgment.* Another difficulty with the prescription of stress tests is that most of the time we won't be able to figure out how to answer the "targeted what if" question in the abstract. Professor Scheppele discusses Hungary's election system. Like many, it used proportional representation based on national lists from political parties coupled with single-member districts. In that form PR systems typically produce multiple parties and coalition governments, and coalition governments can be unstable. To promote stability, the Italian system, which mirrored that in Hungary, gave a bonus to the party that wins the largest number of seats, thereby reducing the number of parties it needs to bring into a governing coalition. Hungary also had a single-house legislature, authorized to amend the constitution with a single two-thirds vote. For several years in the 1990s the system operated as expected, with a fairly large number of parties winning parliamentary seats. The number of parties gradually went down, weakening the case for the bonus seats. The constitution wasn't changed, though. And in 2010 Orbán's Fidesz Party won a 54 percent majority of the votes. When the bonus seats were added, Fidesz had a 68 percent majority—enough to amend the constitution at will.

  Applying an election bonus to a one-house parliament empowered to amend the constitution by a one-time vote of two-thirds of the members turned out to be a really bad idea when politics generated two stable party blocs—an obvious interaction problem. Note, though, the way we've attributed agency to "politics." The real actors, though, were voters. The design turned out to work badly when Hungarians decided that they preferred having a smaller rather than a larger number of parties.[29] As we've suggested, constitutional design can't do much if anything to prevent voters from making that decision.

  Reflecting on this case Scheppele asks, "What if an election law designed for a dozen parties suddenly regulates an election with only two?" The answer, we suppose, is that a victorious party might be able to amend the constitution with a free hand. Whether that's a good or bad thing depends upon what the party's policies are. To see the point, restate the answer as, "A party with an ambitious reform agenda that existing constitutional provisions

---

[29] The full story of why the party-system preferences of Hungarian voters changed is complicated and laying it out would get us deeper into the weeds of recent Hungarian political history than we think necessary for our purposes.

impede will be able to implement its program." Whether that's good or bad depends mostly on what you think of the substantive program.

We say "mostly," because we think there might be a couple of additional considerations. Maybe there's a principled argument that ambitious reforms should be adopted incrementally rather than suddenly. We're skeptical about that possibility, but are open to it. More important, maybe someone would take Judith Shklar's "liberalism of fear" as offering the best definition of liberal constitutionalism.[30] Return to our restated answer to the Hungarian election-bonus problem: the election bonus lets a party with an ambitious reform agenda implement its program. That program can be good or bad. If you worry a lot about downside risks—the possibility of a really bad outcome—and regard the upside benefits—the possibility of really good outcomes—as nice but not as important in the long run, you'll see the interaction effect as a real problem. That, we think, describes a liberalism of fear—downside risks are more important than upside potentials.

What do people base their choice or rejection of a liberalism of fear upon? Here we're well beyond our area of expertise, but we think it appropriate to offer some comments. Perhaps the choice is characterological: optimists will reject the liberalism of fear, pessimists will accept it. Or perhaps the choice is political: those who think things now are going reasonably well and need only modest adjustment to make them quite a bit better will see upside potentials as relatively small, and so might be attracted to a liberalism of fear that emphasizes downside risks. Those who think things now are really terrible and need major change might not. Those who are committed to the liberalism of fear worry about the people and democratic majorities. Populists are more optimistic. Those too are political positions.

---

[30] "The Liberalism of Fear," in JUDITH SHKLAR, POLITICAL THOUGHT AND POLITICAL THINKERS (Stanley Hoffman ed. 1998). In our view, Shklar's liberalism of fear was historicized, that is, offered as an account of the best version of liberalism appropriate to the Cold War circumstances of the 1950s and 1960s, rather than as a transhistorical normative version of liberalism.

6

Populism in Western Europe

The Hungarian and Polish cases show that proto-authoritarian populists enact laws that represent a threat to constitutional democracy; indeed, that's what makes them proto-authoritarian versions of populism. Other populist cases reveal a more complicated picture of populism's effects on constitutionalism and democracy. Benjamin Moffitt, for example, questions the received wisdom about populism's alleged illiberalism and even asks if populism is "actually synonymous with 'illiberal democracy'"?[1] In this chapter we argue that many cases of predominantly right-wing populism in Western Europe lack characteristics ascribed to them by those who point to a "built-in" anti-liberal and even anti-constitutional character in populism.

I. Italy and Austria

To examine whether populist commitment to liberal values is shallow or real, we have to look how this "liberal illiberalism" behaves once in power.[2] The Italian populist coalition between the League and the Five Star movement (M5S), which was in power only for fourteen months between 2018 and 2019,[3] is our first example of this different kind of populism. Its behavior in power illustrates the complexity and ambiguity we've alluded to. The League and the M5S governed together, but they represented "different kinds of populism and increasingly diverse constituencies." Their common target was national and international technocracy, the enemies of the people. Yet, their own visions of democracy couldn't

---

[1] BENJAMIN MOFFITT, POPULISM (2020), p. 71.

[2] Benjamin Moffitt, *Liberal Illiberalism? The Reshaping of the Contemporary Populist Radical Right in Northern Europe*, 5(4) POLITICS & GOVERNANCE 112 (2017). As the time of writing, populists are in power in the United Kingdom and Italy, where they are part of the ruling coalition (as a senior coalition partner). In other parts of Western Europe, populist parties remain in the opposition. For an exhaustive overview of a right-wing populism in Europe, *see* JEAN-YVES CAMUS & NICOLAS LEBOURG, FAR-RIGHT POLITICS IN EUROPE (2017); for a study of far right in the world, *see* CAS MUDDE. THE FAR RIGHT TODAY (2019). For comparison between right-wing and left-wing populism in Europe, *see* JOHN J. JUDIS, THE POPULIST EXPLOSION: HOW THE GREAT RECESSION TRANSFORMED AMERICAN AND EUROPEAN POLITICS (2016).

[3] In 2018, the populist parties together won almost 60 percent of the vote and made Italy the first country in Western Europe with a populist majority. While the Five Star Movement took 32 percent, becoming the largest party in parliament, the League emerged as the leading right-wing force, with 17 percent of the vote.

Power to the People. Mark Tushnet and Bojan Bugarič, Oxford University Press. © Mark Tushnet and Bojan Bugarič 2021. DOI: 10.1093/oso/9780197606711.003.0007

be more different. The M5S favors radical internet democracy, "to use the web to do away with elites altogether in favor of direct democracy."[4] The League, in contrast, is a nationalistic party promoting the idea of regaining control of national borders and national policies, and directly challenging the European integration project.

Matteo Salvini, the influential leader of the League and the coalition's interior minister, successfully pulled Italy to the far right. The main targets of Salvini's shift were immigrants and the EU.[5] His political behavior showed some strong signs of populist impatience with institutions, as in verbal attacks on the Italian judges who challenged his hardline anti-immigration policies. When Tito Boeri, the chief of the National Institute of Pension and Social Security (INPS) challenged those policies by saying that Italy needed more migrants to ensure the resilience of the country's pension system, Salvini told him to start looking for another job.[6]

In contrast, Lucia Corso's study of the M5S, the senior partner in the populist coalition, shows that the M5S largely supported constitutionalism and the rule of law.[7] One of its key electoral promises from the coalition contract stressed the importance of a depoliticized judiciary, proposing to bar sitting judges from running for elected office. As Corso argues, the mainstream emphasis on populist anti-constitutionalism "may lead us to overlook the oppositional aspect of populism and its anti-elitist stance, which persists even when populists take power."[8] She also argues that M5S "does not seem to display the features often ascribed to populist politics like decisiveness, disregard of formal law and a drive for a strong cabinet, thus threatening judicial independence. On the contrary, M5S has often relied on the power of the judiciary to carry out its moral battle against allegedly corrupt political power."[9] M5S often resorts to "legalism" to carry out its political program. Indeed, the coalition agreement with the League was drafted as a "legal contract" between the two parties, emphasizing the contractual obligation of the

---

[4] Roberto D'Alimonte, *How the Populists Won in Italy*, 30 JOURNAL OF DEMOCRACY 114 (2019), at p. 124.

[5] *Id.*

[6] "Italy's far right interior minister, Matteo Salvini, escalates attacks on judges," THE GUARDIAN, June 6, 2019; Alexander Stille, "How Matteo Salvini pulled Italy to the far right," THE GUARDIAN, Aug. 9, 2018.

[7] Lucia Corso, *When Anti-Politics Becomes Political: What Can the Italian Five Star Movement Tell Us about the Relationship between Populism and Legalism*, 15 EUROPEAN CONSTITUTIONAL LAW REVIEW 462 (2019). Unlike Corso, Nadia Urbinatti in her seminal study of populism and democracy argues that "popular democracy is fundamentally at odds with party-based representative democracy." NADIA URBINATI, ME THE PEOPLE: HOW POPULISM TRANSFORMS DEMOCRACY (2019), at p. 188 (quoting Ethan J.Leib & Christopher S. Elmendorf, *Why Party Democrats Need Popular Democracy*, 100 CALIFORNIA LAW REVIEW 70 (2012)). We believe that Corso's account better captures the reality of M5S's populism in practice.

[8] Corso, note 7 above, at p. 463.

[9] *Id.*

coalition partners to the foundational principles of the contract. The principal tool for the M5S's anti-corruption strategy has been an almost ritualistic adherence to public tenders and extensive audits, exemplary forms of legalism.

On the constitutional front, the populist government proposed a constitutional referendum to reduce the size of the Italian Parliament. To repeat some information we've already presented: before the amendment the lower house had 630 members, the upper house 315—by far the largest in the world. Nearly all Italian constitutional specialists thought that the parliament was too large to govern effectively. The amendment reduced the lower house to 400 members, the upper house to 200. The key argument for the amendment was that it would reduce costs and slash privileges for lawmakers; the latter point can fairly be described as an argument aimed at an elitist "political class."[10] The proposal was adopted in a referendum in September 2020, and got 70 percent of the votes. Remarkably, many leading Italian scholars opposed the referendum even though they supported reducing Parliament's size on the merits. As we observed in Chapter 3, they opposed what they acknowledged to be a "good government" reform because its primary backers were populists—"the wrong means to the right end," as one post had it.

In his overview of the populist engagement with constitutionalism, Matteo Bonelli argues that the Italian populist coalition "left no deep scars on the Italian constitutional system."[11] His analysis shows that the populist government had hardly undermined any of the key pillars of Italian constitutionalism. As reported by Bonelli, "there has simply been no structural undermining of institutional safeguards and democratic and rule of law institutions."[12]

[10] Those who opposed the referendum argued that a reduction in the number of MPs could adversely affect the quality of representative democracy. See "Matteo Garavoglia, Italy's constitutional referendum: The right solution to long standing problems?," LSE BLOG, Sept. 17, 2020, available at https://blogs.lse.ac.uk/europpblog/2020/09/17/italys-constitutional-referendum-the-right-solution-to-long-standing-problems/, archived at https://perma.cc/LA2N-5YSM. For an overview of these debates, *see* Giusepe Martinico, *Between Mimetism and Parasitism: Italian Populism in a Comparative Perspective*, 26 EUROPEAN PUBLIC LAW 921 (2020). We don't take any position on the question whether the referendum proposal was the best possible option for the Italian democracy. We simply note that it was perfectly compatible with our concept of thin constitutionalism.

[11] Matteo Bonelli, "The Italian Paradox: Is There Such a Thing as Too Strong Constitutional Safeguards?," in POPULISM AND DEMOCRACY (Sascha Hardt, Aalt Willem Heringa, & Hoai-Thu Nguyen eds. 2020), at pp. 240–41.For a more comprehensive overview of populism's relationship with constitutionalism in Italy, *see* ITALIAN POPULISM AND CONSTITUTIONAL LAW: STRATEGIES, CONFLICTS AND DILEMMAS (Giacomo Delledone, Giusepe Martinico, Matteo Monti, & Fabio Pacini eds., 2020). In his book review, Gabor Halmai emphasizes that "the authors . . convincingly argue that the constitutional developments in the last decades in Italy have been compatible with the ideals of constitutionalism despite the populist arguments and failed reforms." Gabor Halmai, *Book Review*, ZEITSCHRIFT FÜR ÖFFENTLICHES RECHT/AUSTRIAN JOURNAL OF PUBLIC & INTERNATIONAL LAW 1005 (2020).

[12] Bonelli, note 11 above, at p. 241.

II. Austria

After Brexit and Donald Trump's victory in the U.S. presidential elections, the march of populists seemed almost unstoppable. No longer limited only to a distant periphery of the EU, it has also spread to many Western European democracies. Austria had a populist coalition in power from 2017 to 2019. That government took office after the first in a series of elections that were thought to shed light on whether Trump's victory in the United States and the triumph of Euroskeptics in Britain were adding momentum to the populist surge in the West. While in office, the populist-influenced coalition undoubtedly moved some substantive policies sharply to the right (while maintaining and even expanding some aspects of the modern social welfare state, typically a leftist position). It did not, though, attack key pillars of liberal constitutionalism.

On December 18, 2017, a new Austrian government took office, consisting of a coalition between the conservative People's Party (ÖVP) led by populist Sebastian Kurz, and the right-wing populist Freedom Party (FPÖ).[13] Although it was the junior coalition partner, the anti-immigration Freedom Party secured several key posts in the new cabinet. The FPÖ, a descendant of the old Austrian Nazi party, is a right-wing party with a history of anti-Semitism and exclusive nationalism. It favors gun rights; stricter border controls; preventing gay couples from marrying or adopting children; opposes immigrants, particularly Muslims, globalization, the EU, and the euro. The FPÖ also favors protecting the welfare state for Austrian citizens, enabling it to tap a broad variety of different political constituencies and cultural values. Not unlike Trump, the FPÖ also shifts easily between different positions, if that is what it takes to capture more voters. Following the U.K. Brexit vote, the FPÖ hinted that it might call a referendum on Austrian membership. But after opinion polls showed that these remarks had upset voters, the FPÖ quickly backtracked.

In Austria, as in some other Western European democracies, the center-right party (ÖVP) adopted a new strategy in its struggle with at that time seemingly invincible populist right. To boost its own poll numbers, the ÖVP embraced the anti-immigration, anti-Islam, and tough law-and-order stance of the FPÖ in the run-up to the elections. A central pillar of these policies was a draconian and punitive approach to refugees from the Middle East. Kurz proposed to close the nation's borders to immigrants from Syria and elsewhere and to erect "legal walls," which would prevent immigrants from applying for asylum. The aim was straightforward: drain the FPÖ of its base of support. The tactic worked. The

---

[13] In the 2017 Austrian legislative election, the People's Party obtained 32 percent of votes, and the Freedom Party 26 percent of the votes, its best result since 1999, when it was also a junior partner in the conservative-populist government.

political price for this strategy was costly: by playing this game, the People's Party moved the political choices further to the right. The right-wing populists didn't dominate the government but they achieved much of their regressive policy agenda, because their major competitor adopted some of that agenda as its own. But not all of the agenda—and in particular not the parts of the agenda most incompatible with constitutionalism.

Apart from immigration, where both parties shared common language and policies, Kurz acted as a force of restraint, blocking several FPÖ's radical populist initiatives. For example, unlike FPÖ, he promised to promote economic liberalism and cultural pluralism.[14] He consistently pushed back against FPÖ's blatantly anti-Semitic, anti-immigrant, and sometimes even legally questionable activities.[15] After the FPÖ accused the Austrian national television ÖRF of a left-wing bias and pushed for its reform, "ÖVP pressure purportedly led Austrian Vice Chancellor and FPÖ leader Heinz-Christian Strache to apologize and pay damages to the country's top news anchor, Armin Wolf, after accusing him and the ORF of lying."[16]

As a result, there were no serious attacks on the independent judiciary or legislative branch of government. The government eventually collapsed in 2019, after the release of a video showing Heinz-Christian Strache, the far-right leader of the Freedom Party, trying to trade public contracts for party donations from a woman he believed to be the wealthy niece of a Russian oligarch. During the short populist reign, there was no need to use any of the many constitutional safeguards for liberal constitutionalism in the Austrian Constitution.[17]

How has the FPÖ's nationalistic and openly xenophobic rhetoric achieved such popularity in Austria, the twelfth richest country in the world with one of the highest per capita income levels in the EU with a more-than-generous welfare system? As John B. Judis explains, such "populism amid prosperity" has surfaced in the even more prosperous Denmark, which has the second-highest per capita income in the EU, and an unemployment rate of only 4.6 percent.[18]

---

[14] Franz-Stefan Gady, *Has Austria Found the Answer to Right-Wing Populism? Why Center-Right Parties Are the Establishment's Best Bet*, FOREIGN AFFAIRS, Sept. 11, 2018.

[15] In 2018, the Ministry of Interior, led by FPÖ politician Herbert Kickl, asked the Office for the Protection of the Constitution and Counterterrorism (BVT), Austria's domestic intelligence agency, to turn over the names of informants who had infiltrated the far-right scene, very likely including also FPÖ members. After the agency refused, armed police raided the agency's premises and took away years' worth of domestic files. The opposition accused FPÖ affiliates in Kickl's ministry of widely exceeding the intent of the investigation and attempting to purge political enemies. The regional court in Vienna ruled that the search of the BVT was illegal. The event also triggered the installation of a parliamentary inquiry committee, which since 2015 is a minority right. See Maria Bertel, "Austria-Protecting the Liberal Constitution," in POPULISM AND DEMOCRACY, note 11 above, at p. 140.

[16] Gady, note 14 above.

[17] See Bertel, note 15 above, at p. 133.

[18] JUDIS, note 2 above, at pp. 132–34.

Both the FPÖ in Austria and the People's Party in Denmark have undergone significant political "reorganizations" that downplay their allegiance to their extremist and xenophobic base, and rebranded themselves as parties of the "ordinary man" left behind by a corrupt system that caters to the elites. Both parties combine anti-immigrant rhetoric with strong support for the welfare state, which explains their increasing popularity among members of the working class.[19]

One possible take from the episode of populism-in-government in Austria is that when a more radical, right-wing populist party like the FPÖ is forced to cohabit in a coalition with a more moderate populist coalition partner, then the behavior of the senior, moderate partner matters a great deal. As Ziblatt and Levitsky show, when such mainstream parties entered into the "fateful alliances" with more authoritarian parties, their "gate-keeping" function and their resolve to resist the authoritarian impulse of their authoritarian political partners has so far been decisive for the fate of democracy.[20]

Both the Italian and Austrian populist governments were in power only briefly, and all we can say is that those populist governments didn't immediately go after liberal constitutionalism, much less our "thin" constitutionalism. Still, their behavior is a mark against the argument that populism is always and everywhere anti-constitutional. Coalition needs restrained populists-in-government. That means that we can't reject the possibility that the more extreme populist coalition party would be anti-constitutional were it able to govern on its own. Here electoral systems matter. Both Italy's and Austria's encourage the formation of coalition governments though one-party government has occurred in modern Austria.

III. The United Kingdom

Did the Brexit referendum and the U.K. Supreme Court's decision invalidating Boris Johnson's prorogation of Parliament in 2019 show that populism conflicts with constitutionalism? We argue that treating those episodes as illustrating a conflict between populism and constitutionalism obscures more than it illuminates, and that the more granular analysis suggested by our approach is better. More generally, we argue that Boris Johnson's version of

---

[19] The elections in 2017 marked the first occasion of the FPÖ receiving more working-class votes than the Social Democrats. Freedom Party leaders proudly pronounced themselves a "New Labor" party, signaling a proletarianization of the FPÖ electorate. The party's most effective message to capture voters who were once loyal supporters of the centrist ruling groups has been to warn that an influx of refugees will jeopardize the blessings of the welfare state—universal healthcare, child support, and free education for all.

[20] STEVEN LEVITSKY & DANIEL ZIBLATT, HOW DEMOCRACIES DIE (2018), at pp. 24–26.

"pluto-populism,"[21] often compared with Trump's more authoritarian version of plutocratic populism,[22] does not support the general claim that populists are always foes of liberal constitutionalism.

On June 23, 2016, the United Kingdom held a historic referendum on its continuing membership in the EU. On a high turnout of 72.2 percent of the registered voters, 51.89 percent voted to leave against 48.11 percent who voted to remain. The referendum was characterized as "the most significant development in the history of European integration"[23] and as "the most significant constitutional event in Britain since the Restoration in 1660."[24] The Brexit referendum was also a watershed event from the perspective of the rise of populism in the West. Together with Donald Trump's victory in the U.S. presidential elections a few months later, the Brexit referendum represented the most important victory for the populists in the West.

As Kenneth Armstrong explains, referendums "are not quite the constitutional novelty that they once were in the UK."[25] In the last four decades, there were three U.K.-wide referendums: two on independence of Scotland (1979 and 2014) and the Brexit referendum in 2016. Stephen Tierney identifies several reasons for this trend both in the United Kingdom and around the world.[26] One is "cognitive mobilisation," "the increasing sophistication of contemporary electorates through better education and access to information"; this increases popular pressure for a greater say in governmental decision-making. Another

---

[21] Martin Wolf, "The Fading Light of Liberal Democracy," THE FINANCIAL TIMES, Dec. 22, 2020. Wolf argues that Brexit Britain shares similar patterns with Trump's version of plutocratic populism. We note that it all looked different during the 2019 election campaign. Boris Johnson seemed to combine a socially conservative approach to culture and identity with promises to reduce the divide between a prosperous South and a declining North, increase spending on the NHS and infrastructure, increase the national living wage, address regional inequality, and provide state aid for failing U.K.-based businesses. These policies helped the Conservatives to capture many traditional Labour constituencies, dealing Labour a historic defeat. Yet since Boris Johnson's post-electoral promise not to abandon the former Red Wall voters, his words have not been backed by an economic nationalist agenda that would lift the majority of Britons who feel left behind. Boris Johnson's "levelling up" agenda does not appear to be accompanied by much that resembles an actual plan. See Laurence Whitehead, The Hard Truths of Brexit, 31 JOURNAL OF DEMOCRACY 81 (2020).

[22] Paul Pierson, American Hybrid: Donald Trump and the Strange Merger of Populism and Plutocracy, 68 BRITISH JOURNAL OF SOCIOLOGY S105 (2017); JACOB HACKER & PAUL PIERSON, LET THEM EAT TWEETS: HOW THE RIGHT RULES IN AN AGE OF EXTREME INEQUALITY (2020), at p. 5(defining plutocratic populism as a "bitter brew of reactionary economic priorities and right-wing cultural and racial appeals").

[23] IAN BACHE, SIMON BULMER, STEPHEN GEORGE, & OWEN PARKER, POLITICS IN THE EUROPEAN UNION (4th ed.): 2018 Supplement: Brexit 1 (20180.

[24] Vernon Bogdanor, Brexit, the Constitution and the Alternatives, 27 KING'S LAW JOURNAL 314 (2016), at p. 314.

[25] KENNETH ARMSTRONG, BREXIT TIME: LEAVING THE EU: WHY, HOW AND WHEN (2017), at p. 48.

[26] STEPHEN TIERNEY, CONSTITUTIONAL REFERENDUMS: THE THEORY AND PRACTICE OF REPUBLICAN DELIBERATION (2012), at pp. 8–9.

is the growth of voter dissatisfaction with conventional representative politics based on what those politics had produced.

With the referendum no longer a constitutional anomaly, the Political Parties, Elections and Referendums Act was passed in 2000 to provide basic legal rules regulating the conduct of future referendums. The Act established an Electoral Commission with oversight functions, including giving advice on referendum questions. The commission tests questions to determine their intelligibility to voters and whether the question's phrasing does not frame the matter in a way conducing voters to choose one side or the other.

In our view the Brexit referendum failed to satisfy a central element of thin constitutionalism—that the views of a current majority of citizens be reliably determined. The reason is that, though referendums are in principle one mechanism for obtaining a reliable determination, to perform that function they must avoid oversimplification of complex policy options.[27] The Brexit referendum failed in this regard. More precisely, the reason for the failure lies not in the complexity of the "leave or stay" choice itself, but rather lay in posing the choice badly. Perhaps the question of U.K. membership in the EU can be decided by the use of referendum. We agree with Richard Ekins and Graham Gee that "a convincing case can be made in representative democracies for occasional use of 'constitutional referendums' as a tool for resolving vital questions about the long-term identity of the state, such as the UK's membership of the EU."[28] The devil, though, is in the details.

In May 2015, the European Referendum Bill was introduced to the House of Commons. The bill proposed a Yes/No referendum question: "Should the United Kingdom remain a member of the European Union?" The Electoral Commission determined that the proposed question was misleading because it presupposed that voters knew that the United Kingdom was already an EU member state. The commission recommended a new formulation, which then became the accepted version in the final bill. The referendum question therefore was this: "Should the United Kingdom remain a member of the European Union or leave the European Union?"[29]

Framing the referendum question in a binary way failed to provide any guidance on what sort of future relationship with the EU the United Kingdom had in mind for itself. The implications of the Leave option were unclear because Brexit could occur in many ways. For example, four possibilities had been made clear

---

[27] For a more extensive discussion of this proposition, see Chapter 12.

[28] Richard Ekin & Graham Gee, "Miller, 'Constitutional Realism' and the Politics of Brexit," in THE UK CONSTITUTION AFTER MILLER: BREXIT AND BEYOND (Mark Elliott, Jack Williams, & Allison Young eds. 2018), at p. 252.

[29] TIM SHIPMAN, ALL OUT WAR: THE FULL STORY OF HOW BREXIT SANK BRITAIN'S POLITICAL CLASS (2017), at pp. 83–92.

by the European Union Committee of the House of Lords in a report entitled "Brexit: The Options for Trade": EEA (European Economic Area) membership or the "Norway deal"; an agreement to remain in the customs union, but not in the single market (the "Turkey deal"); an ad hoc trade agreement with the EU outside the single market (the "Canada deal"); and, finally, the hard Brexit—trade on the basis of WTO rules outside of the single market.[30] Only the last option ("hard Brexit") is more or less straightforward because it does not require any negotiations with the EU. As Pavlos Eleftheriadis correctly observes, "given the referendum question, voting 'Leave' was not a vote for choosing any particular of the four available options."[31] The referendum rejected the "Remain" option, but left all other future options indeterminate. As a result, it was not clear if the Leave supporters were voting for a "hard Brexit" or for one of many "soft Brexit" options, each entailing different policy options with serious economic and political implications for the future UK-EU relationship. As Liubomir Topaloff asks, "would voters have opted for Leave had they known that their vote would trigger a 'hard exit' option that would end the free movement of capital, goods, and services, along with that of people and would ultimately increase the cost to U.K. taxpayers?"[32]

The referendum provided a mandate for the ultimate goal—leaving the EU—but not for how that would be achieved. Kevin O'Rourke argues that the electoral logic of the referendum "seemed to imply that the government should pursue what soon became known as a 'soft Brexit,' that is to say a Brexit that involved the United Kingdom remaining inside the EU's Single Market, or a customs union with the EU, or both."[33] However, quite soon a number of other things were said to be mandated be the results of the referendum. When Theresa May became prime minister, she imposed her "red lines," which were understood to follow from the referendum result: the result was taken to mean that the United Kingdom would take control of its money, laws, and borders. These "red lines" meant that the United Kingdom could not be a member of the single market or the customs union, and entailed ending the jurisdiction of the Court of Justice of the European Union.[34]

---

[30] Michel Barnier, the chief EU Brexit negotiator, later presented his famous slide of "steps of doom," showing six different possible post-Brexit deal scenarios with the European Union, with the Switzerland and Ukraine deal added to the previous four. The slide is available at https://ec.europa.eu/commission/sites/beta-political/files/slide_presented_by_barnier_at_euco_15-12-2017.pdf, archived at https://perma.cc/2TKU-FY67.

[31] Pavlos Eleftheriadis, *Constitutional Legitimacy over Brexit*, 88 POLITICAL QUARTERLY 182 (2017), at p. 185.

[32] Liubomir Topaloff, *Elite Strategy or Populist Weapon?*, 28 JOURNAL OF DEMOCRACY 127 (2017), at p. 137.

[33] KEVIN O'ROURKE, A SHORT HISTORY OF BREXIT: FROM BRENTRY TO BACKSTOP (2018), at p. 206.

[34] BACHE ET AL., note 23 above, at p. 14.

The Brexit referendum led to a protracted period of political events that eventually ended the Brexit drama with the formal exit of the United Kingdom from the European Union on January 31, 2020. However, after Boris Johnson became prime minister in July 2019, the process of creative "reinterpretation" of the Brexit referendum was likely to continue. After Johnson declared that his government intended to "get Brexit done," it became clear that his understanding of Brexit referendum did not favor "soft Brexit," for many, the most logical preference of the British voters. The 1,200 page-long free trade deal with the EU reached on December 24, 2020, is closer to a "Canada-style" free trade deal than to "soft Brexit."

According to many British commentators, Johnson's decision to prorogue Parliament was the most dangerous assault on British constitutionalism in living memory. The critics claim that in stopping the House of Commons from deliberating about Brexit—or giving the growing number of his parliamentary opponents an opportunity to depose him—Johnson demonstrated that he considered himself a more legitimate spokesperson for the will of his countrymen than the institution that had been charged with this task for the past three centuries.

In its "historic" judgment in *Miller/Cherry* (*No 2*),[35] the U.K. Supreme Court unanimously held that the prorogation[36] of Parliament for a period of five weeks was unlawful, void, and without legal effect. The case concerned whether the advice given by Prime Minister Boris Johnson to Queen Elizabeth II that Parliament should be prorogued for five weeks during the closing stages of the Brexit process, thereby sharply limiting the time available to debate whether that process should continue, was lawful. As the Supreme Court explained in the key passage of its judgment:

> A decision to prorogue Parliament (or to advise the monarch to prorogue Parliament) will be unlawful if the prorogation has the effect of frustrating or preventing, without reasonable justification, the ability of Parliament to carry out its constitutional functions as a legislature and as the body responsible for the supervision of the executive. In such a situation, the court will intervene if the effect is sufficiently serious to justify an exceptional course.

The decision was celebrated by some as "the most significant judicial statement on the constitution in over 200 years," to be "discussed centuries from

---

[35] R (on the application of Miller) v. The Prime Minister; Cherry and Others v. Advocate General for Scotland [2019] UKSC 41 (Sept. 24, 2019).

[36] Prorogation is a political process in which the U.K. Parliament is suspended after the closure of one parliamentary session until a State Opening of Parliament several days later.

now,"[37] and criticized, by others, as "a historic mistake"[38] to be reversed by the next parliament.

Prorogation took effect at a delicate time in the Brexit political saga. While Johnson rejected claims that his decision was designed to block MPs from considering ways to thwart his Brexit plans after he was accused of mounting a "coup" against Parliament, it was quite clear from the outset that that was Johnson's covert aim behind the prorogation, despite the official justification by Johnson that it would allow him to "bring forward an ambitious new legislative programme for MPs' approval." For prorogation to last more than a month is unprecedented in recent times: since the 1980s prorogation has typically lasted less than a week. The length of the prorogation would clearly have narrowed rebel MPs' options—they would have several weeks fewer in parliament to pass any anti-no-deal legislation.

Taking prorogation to be an example of a populist action,[39] for present purposes we treat *Miller/Cherry* as posing two questions: (1) Was it appropriate for the Supreme Court to rule on the merits (or should the problem have been left to political constitutionalism)? (2) Was the Supreme Court correct on the merits?

The court spent most of its time asking whether prorogation is reviewable by the courts. Under British constitutional law, the executive branch of government enjoys a number of prerogative powers, such as declaring war and making treaties, which are sometimes but not always exempted from judicial review.[40] Many considered prorogation to be among the political matters so exempted. The court made it clear that the fact that a question before it "is political in tone or context" cannot render the matter non-justiciable.[41] As Mark Elliott explains,

[37] Thomas Poole, "Understanding what makes 'Miller & Cherry' the most significant judicial statement on the constitution in over 200 years," PROSPECT, Sept. 25, 2019, available at https://www.prospectmagazine.co.uk/politics/understanding-what-makes-miller-2-the-most-significant-judicial-statement-on-the-constitution-in-over-200-years, archived at https://perma.cc/BZ5M-DKXA.

[38] John Finnis, "The Unconsitutionality of the Supreme Court's Prorogation Judgement," Policy Exchange, Judicial Power Project, 2019.

[39] Nick Barber considers the prime minister's request for prorogation to fall within the realm of "constitutional hardball," as defined by one of us in his previous work. *See* Mark Tushnet, *Constitutional Hardball*, 37 JOHN MARSHALL LAW REVIEW 523 (2004). As Barber explains, prorogation belongs to examples of hardball "because though constitutionally obnoxious they might be legally sound." Nick Barber, *Playing Hardball with the Queen*," OXFORD HUMAN RIGHTS HUB, Aug. 31, 2019, available at https://ohrh.law.ox.ac.uk/playing-hardball-with-the-queen/, archived at https://perma.cc/3QSK-HMBG.

[40] As summarized by Mark Elliott and Robert Thomas, "there is no such a thing as a non-justiciable prerogative; rather, there are merely issues arising from the exercise of a prerogative—or any other kind power, including statutory power—upon which the courts may consider themselves unable to adjudicate." MARK ELLIOTT & ROBERT THOMAS, PUBLIC LAW (3rd ed. 2017), at pp. 561–62.

[41] The court offers two examples from the seventeenth and eighteenth centuries, the Case of Proclamations (1611) 12 Co Rep 74, and Entick v Carrington (1765) 19 State Tr 1029; 2 Wils KB 275, showing how the court limited the power of the crown to alter the law of the land by the use of the crown's prerogative powers.

the crucial issue for the court was "whether the scope of that power had been exceeded" and whether "the power had used for an improper purpose—such as avoiding accountability to Parliament—then this would render the issue justiciable."[42]

The court then explained the standard that determines the limits of the prerogative power. The court invoked two fundamental constitutional principles, parliamentary sovereignty and parliamentary accountability, to justify its ruling. The first principle prevents the executive from having "legally unfettered authority to prorogue Parliament." As Mark Elliott explains, "this does not mean that the Court could or should rule, at the level of detail, on what is and is not an acceptable period of prorogation. What it does mean, however, is that it would be incompatible with parliamentary sovereignty for the executive to have legally unfettered authority to prorogue Parliament."[43] The second principle, of parliamentary accountability, was, according to the court, "no less fundamental to our constitution than Parliamentary sovereignty." Citing Lord Bingham, the court gave the following definition to this principle: "the conduct of government by a Prime Minister and Cabinet collectively responsible and accountable to Parliament lies at the heart of Westminster democracy." The principle means that:

> Ministers are accountable to Parliament through such mechanisms as their duty to answer Parliamentary questions and to appear before Parliamentary committees, and through Parliamentary scrutiny of the delegated legislation which ministers make. By these means, the policies of the executive are subjected to consideration by the representatives of the electorate, the executive is required to report, explain and defend its actions, and citizens are protected from the arbitrary exercise of executive power.

Finally, applying the principle to the case, the court concluded:

> That principle is not placed in jeopardy if Parliament stands prorogued for the short period which is customary, and as we have explained, Parliament does not in any event expect to be in permanent session. But the longer that Parliament stands prorogued, the greater the risk that responsible government may be replaced by unaccountable government: the antithesis of the democratic mode.

---

[42] Mark Elliott, "A new approach to constitutional adjudication?: Miller II in the Supreme Court," PUBLIC LAW FOR EVERYONE, Sept. 24, 2019, available at https://publiclawforeveryone.com/2019/09/24/the-supreme-courts-judgment-in-cherry-miller-no-2-a-new-approach-to-constitutional-adjudication/, archived at https://perma.cc/MKW3-B94C.
[43] *Id.*

For some, the court's decision signals "the dissolution of the old political constitution."[44] John Finnis goes even further. Citing article 9 of the 1689 Bill of Rights ("Proceedings in Parliament ought not to be impeached or questioned in any Court or place out of Parliament"), he argues that "the Judgement itself undercuts the genuine sovereignty of Parliament by evading a statutory prohibition—art. 9 of the Bill of Rights 1689—on judicial questioning of proceedings in Parliament."[45] The court dismissed that argument, saying, "The prorogation itself takes place in the House of Lords and in the presence of Members of both Houses. But it cannot sensibly be described as a 'proceeding in Parliament.' It is not a decision of either House of Parliament. Quite the contrary: it is something which is imposed upon them from outside. It is not something upon which the Members of Parliament can speak or vote."

We agree with Elliott's argument that "the case amounts to a significant restatement of a range of key matters, but cannot justifiably be criticised as having cast aside established principle or as an instance of improper judicial overreach."[46] At the same time, as Richard Bellamy, a prominent proponent of political constitutionalism, argues, there is "nothing in the substance of the judgment with which a political constitutionalist could disagree."[47] The prorogation was undoubtedly an act of constitutional hardball, departing from prior practices but arguably within the scope of the prerogative power as previously understood. As such, it might have been a norm violation that foreshadows a larger transformation—or a false step to be retracted soon.[48] As we have shown, some scholars believe that the action was within constitutional bounds and that the U.K. Supreme Court was mistaken.[49] Others, including one of us, are inclined to think that the prorogation was an abuse of power.

What are we to make of a case where there appear to be plausible arguments supporting both sides when some seemingly detached observers find one or the other side's argument *more* plausible? Here too the idea that there can be reasonable alternative specifications of agreed-upon legal principles seems helpful. The U.K. Supreme Court chose one of several available reasonable specifications of

[44] Mike Gordon, "The Prorogation Case and the Political Constitution," U.K. Const. L. Blog (Sept. 30, 2019) (quoting Colm O'Cinneide), available at https://ukconstitutionallaw.org/2019/09/30/mike-gordon-the-prorogation-case-and-the-political-constitution/, archived at https://perma.cc/3LA9-EW5J.

[45] Finnis, note 38 above.

[46] Mark Elliott, "The Supreme Court's judgment in Cherry/Miller (No 2): A new approach to constitutional adjudication?," Public Law for Everyone, Sept. 24, 2019, available at https://publiclawforeveryone.com/2019/09/24/the-supreme-courts-judgment-in-cherry-miller-no-2-a-new-approach-to-constitutional-adjudication/, archived at https://perma.cc/NUM6-FW7E.

[47] Cited in Gordon, note 44 above.

[48] For additional discussion, see Chapter 10.

[49] For a powerful argument in this direction, see Martin Loughlin, The UK Constitutional Council's ruling on appeal from the judgement of the Supreme Court, *Policy Exchange* (2019).

the scope of the prerogative power. Were Parliament to respond by "reining in" the Supreme Court, thereby making it clear that it believes that a different specification was "more" reasonable, it would not thereby undermine constitutionalism as thinly defined. More generally, the populist-favoring positions—that the question should be left to political constitutionalism, and that the prorogation was constitutionally permissible—fall within the range of reasonable specifications of the content of British constitutionalism.

While Boris Johnson's rhetoric often resembles that of other proto-authoritarian populists, his words seldom materialize in actual changes going after liberal constitutionalism.[50] After winning the 2019 election, Johnson stressed the need to "look at the broader aspects of [the] constitution" by means of a new Constitution, Democracy, and Rights Commission, possibly including changes to the judicial appointment process. Many understood this statement as the announcement of Johnson's court-packing plan. In July 2020, the British government launched the Independent Review of Administrative Law, appointing a panel of legal experts to examine judicial review. The panel was to consider whether the current process strikes the right balance between "enabling citizens to challenge the lawfulness of government action" and "allowing the executive and local authorities to carry on the business of government." Many British constitutional scholars fear that the panel recommendations could lead to drastic changes of the scope of judicial review.[51]

Johnson's distaste for Channel 4's criticism of his actions in office led him to threaten to revoke its broadcasting license and announce plans to decriminalize nonpayment of the BBC license fee. These statements reveal his impatience with critical independent media. Apart from his continuing attacks on the BBC and installing a Tory Party donor as the new BBC Chair, Johnson's threats have not been followed yet by any legal or constitutional changes of the BBC's legal status.

While the United Kingdom's response to the pandemic has been more moderate than elsewhere, many academics have cautioned that the emergency powers contained in the Coronavirus Act 2020 confer a large concentration of power upon the executive branch of government and require close scrutiny.[52] In conclusion, we agree with Laurence Whitehead, who argues that Johnson "is a 'backslider,' but it remains to be seen he will prove a 'system-buster.'"[53]

---

[50] For more critical assessment of Boris Johnson actions, see James Grant, "Boris Johnson, Brexit and Britain's Constitutional Quagmire," THE ATLANTIC, Aug. 30, 2019.

[51] For a discussion of the relationship between populism and changes in judicial appointment processes, see Chapter 8.

[52] K. D. Ewing, Covid-19: Government by Decree, 31 KING's LAW JOURNAL 1 (2020).

[53] Whitehead, note 21 above, at p. 90.

IV. Right-Wing Populism in Power in Western Europe

Right-wing populism in Poland and Hungary has proven to be proto-authoritarian or, in the case of Hungary, very close to purely authoritarian. Right-wing populists who have been able to exercise a measure of governing power in Western Europe, in contrast, haven't yet made significant moves against core constitutionalist institutions. Occasional bluster, to be sure, and the adoption of policies inconsistent with human rights norms dealing with immigration. The latter, though, deal with noncitizens outside the nation's borders, either actually or metaphorically when they evade border controls and enter unlawfully. The relevant international human rights norms, which we endorse as such, can't plausibly be described as requirements of even a modestly thickened constitutionalism.

"Haven't yet" may be the operative words, though. We don't have to be enormously risk averse to be nervous in contemplating the possibility that right-wing populists in power, not bound by coalition constraints, for example, would send things off the rails. At the same time, though, keeping our risk aversion to an appropriate level would caution against adopting dramatic institutional responses, such as invoking the weapons of "militant democracy" (ballot disqualification, dismissal from public employment) against the rise of right-wing populism in Western Europe.

7

Southern Europe: Greece and Spain

As Pippa Norris and Ronald Inglehart argue, left-wing populism, though less common today than its right-wing variant, has grown in recent years.[1] While right-wing populism in Europe has been predominantly driven by "the fear that immigration will erode welfare state benefits" and related cultural issues,[2] left-wing populism's origins can be traced to adverse effects the great recession and the euro crisis had on the economies in Southern Europe. Although all countries in Europe were affected by the euro crisis, Greece and Spain were among the hardest hit. Greece has yet to recover, and unemployment remains high in both countries.[3]

In Greece and Spain, populist parties protested against the "consensus at the center"—between the center-right and center-left—around the idea that there is no alternative to neoliberal globalization. In the eyes of populists, the European project was the embodiment of a ruthless process of globalization responsible for intolerable levels of inequality, declining trust in democracy, and increasing fear of loss of one's "national" and "cultural" identity. On the left, populists in Greece and Spain supported both the euro and the European project. As political theorist Chantal Mouffe argues, populists in Greece and Spain are not against the European project as such, but only against the "neoliberal incarnation" of the European project.[4]

What is the empirical record for a democratic or left-liberal version of populism? Benjamin Moffitt argues that there are left-wing populists, "who often extend their conception of 'the people' to include various minority groups,

---

[1] PIPPA NORRIS & RONALD INGLEHART, CULTURAL BACKLASH: TRUMP, BREXIT, AND AUTHORITARIAN POPULISM (2019), at p. 11.

[2] Dani Rodrik, *Populism and the Economics of Globalization*, 1 JOURNAL OF INTERNATIONAL BUSINESS POLICY 12 (2018), at p. 25. *See also* JOHN B. JUDIS, THE POPULIST EXPLOSION: HOW THE GREAT RECESSION TRANSFORMED AMERICAN AND EUROPEAN POLITICS (2016), at p. 109.

[3] *See also* Peter A. Hall, *Anatomy of the Euro-Crisis*, HARVARD MAGAZINE, July–August 2013, available at https://harvardmagazine.com/2013/07/anatomy-of-the-euro-crisis, archived at https://perma.cc/7LLY-CYLY ("Across southern Europe, millions of families are living in misery, as rates of unemployment exceed 25 percent in Greece and Spain and approach 15 percent in Portugal (and, on the western periphery, in Ireland), while the salaries of teachers, nurses, and other public employees are slashed, and firms go bankrupt in unprecedented numbers. The suicide rate in Greece has doubled during the past three years.").

[4] Chantal Mouffe, *In Defence of Left-Wing Populism*, THE CONVERSATION, Apr. 29, 2016, available at http://theconversation.com/in-defence-of-left-wing-populism-55869.

Power to the People. Mark Tushnet and Bojan Bugarič, Oxford University Press. © Mark Tushnet and Bojan Bugarič 2021. DOI: 10.1093/oso/9780197606711.003.0008

which on the face of things seems to be in line with pluralism and liberalism."
Contrary to Mudde and Müller, Moffitt shows that left-wing populists "have put
forward characterisations of 'the people' that cannot seriously be considered either 'pure' or 'homogenous.'"[5] The European examples include Syriza in Greece,
Podemos in Spain, and Jean-Luc Melenchon's La France Insoumise. Similarly,
Mudde and Rovira Kaltwasser identify parties such as Podemos and Syriza and
movements such as Occupy Wall Street and the Indignados as cases of populism, noting that the latter "tried to develop a definition of the 'people' that was
inclusive to most marginalized minorities—including ethnic, religious and
sexual."[6] Moffitt argues that "the majority of left-wing populists in Europe and
North America—including leaders such as Bernie Sanders or Jeremy Corbyn,
parties such as Podemos, and the movements of the squares. . . .—cannot be seriously accused of authoritarianism either."[7] Carlos da la Torre is even clearer on
this issue, arguing that Syriza and Podemos are "are not a threat to democracy,
and Greece under Syriza has not experienced processes of democratic erosion."[8]
Moreover, in one of the first systemic studies of Syriza's politics, Cas Mudde
claims that "Compared to Chávez and Orbán, [Syriza leader Alex] Tsipras is a
committed liberal democrat. . . . So far, the ugly side of populism has mainly been
rhetorical, with accusing political opponents of betrayal and portraying them as
'enemies' of Greece."[9]

Syriza is the only left populist party that has entered government as the main
coalition partner in recent years. In January 2015 election, Syriza defeated the incumbent New Democracy and became the largest party in the Greek Parliament,
receiving 36.3 percent of the vote and 149 out of 300 seats. Syriza formed a coalition government with Independent Greeks (ANEL), a right-wing nationalist
party. It remained in power until 2018, when it was defeated by New Democracy.

As Judis observes, Syriza, as a populist party promising to fight the European
Union-imposed austerity regime, "appears to have failed."[10] Syriza's first term
in office (January 2015 to August 2015) was characterized by "defiant volun-
tarism," when "the Syriza-led administration tried to swiftly reverse a series of
unpopular neoliberal policies, articulating at the same time a defiant discourse
against the monitoring institutions of Greece's bailout programme."[11] In summer

---

[5] BENJAMIN MOFFITT, POPULISM (2020), at pp. 71–72, 84.

[6] CAS MUDDE & CRISTÓBAL ROVIRA KALTWASSER, POPULISM: A VERY SHORT INTRODUCTION
(2017), at p. 48.

[7] MOFFITT, note 5 above, at pp. 107–8. In asserting that populists "are no friends of independent
institutions," Moffitt uses only Latin American examples. Id. at p. 89.

[8] Carlos de la Torre, Is Left Populism the Radical Democratic Answer?, 27 IRISH JOURNAL OF
SOCIOLOGY 64 (2019), at p. 69.

[9] CAS MUDDE, SYRIZA: THE FAILURE OF THE POPULIST PROMISE (2017), at p. 51.

[10] JUDIS, note 2 above, at p. 119.

[11] Giorgios Katsambekis, "The Populist Radical Left in Greece: Syriza in Opposition and in Power,"
in THE POPULIST RADICAL LEFT IN EUROPE (Giorgios Katsambekis & Alexanderos Kioupkiolis eds.
2019), at p. 35.

2015, the EU imposed harsh loan terms on Greece even though they were previously rejected by popular referendum. As Greece's humiliating defeat by the German-led austerity coalition illustrated, only a concerted, Europe-wide initiative could help Greece to fight back.[12] With almost no allies and supporters in Brussels, Syriza was simply helpless in its attempted insurrection against the "Berlin consensus."[13] The defeat of Syriza by the German-led austerity coalition has had repercussions for other left-wing populist groups, particularly Podemos in Spain.

Although Syriza has been accused of "trying to undermine the independence of courts and free media," there is no solid evidence to confirm this argument, only anecdotal evidence of a few attempts by Syriza to criticize unfavorable judgments of the courts and to influence the media.[14] Syriza never tried to systematically undermine key rule-of-law institutions, as populists did in Hungary, Poland, and Venezuela.

In 2016, the government auctioned broadcast permits for only four private TV channels, leaving several existing TV stations facing closure. The Syriza government went ahead with the auction after failing to reach agreement with opposition parties over appointing new members to the media regulator's board. The government argued that the reform was needed to combat corruption and dismantle a network of vested interests among media "oligarchs," many of whom run TV stations, banks, and the political establishment.[15] The opposition responded that the government wanted to control information and create a media landscape more friendly to a party in power. The government also proposed a media law that would allow the government, not the independent broadcasting regulator, to oversee the licensing process. That statute was declared unconstitutional by Greece's highest administrative court, the Council of State. Under the constitution (article 15), private radio and TV channels are supervised by an independent authority, the National Council for Radio and Television (ESR) and its

[12] For a firsthand account of this story, *see* YANNIS VAROUFAKIS, ADULTS IN THE ROOM: MY BATTLE WITH EUROPE'S DEEP ESTABLISHMENT (2017). The American edition has a slightly different subtitle.

[13] Describing one of his first Eurogroup meetings, Varoufakis vividly presents the power of the Berlin consensus. Shortly after being elected by the Greek people, Varoufakis presented his arguments against the EU austerity regime to other EU finance ministers. He was swiftly rebuked by then German finance minister Wolfgang Schäuble, who said that "elections cannot be allowed to change economic policy." See VAROUFAKIS, note 12 above, at p. 237.

[14] Jan Werner Müller, *What's Left of the Populist Left*, PROJECT SYNDICATE, Feb. 21, 2019, available at https://www-project-syndicate-org.ezp-prod1.hul.harvard.edu/commentary/populist-left-wrong-political-strategy-by-jan-werner-mueller-2019-02, archived at https://perma.cc/QA4C-SXKH.

[15] The corrupt system known as *diaploki* has a long history in Greece. Previous Greek governments, both left and right, handed out television licenses to favored political clients, among them shipowners and large construction companies, in return for financial contributions for their parties and broadcasters' support for their policies.

members are appointed by parliament, by majority. This, the Council of State held, meant that the executive government could not take charge of the licensing process.[16] Prime Minister Tsipras criticized the court's ruling but at the same time also made clear that the government would comply with the Council of State's decision.

Moffitt mentions that the Syriza government was also accused of "tampering with the courts: the judiciary's highest body in the country, the Greek Union of Judges and Prosecutors, accused the government of 'systematically attempting to manipulate and fully control justice . . . so that it operates as a government mechanism.'"[17] We believe that these accusations are exaggerated. Syriza often criticized individual judicial decisions and appointed new presidents of the Supreme Court and Council of State from judges favorably inclined toward the government, who then initiated disciplinary proceedings against the judges and prosecutors who openly criticized the government, Syriza never attempted any legislative action directly aiming to undermine the independence of judiciary.[18]

The Syriza-Anel government announced proposals for constitutional reforms in July 2016. Tsipras proposed making constitutional referendums easier, increasing the role of the largely ceremonial presidency, limiting lawmaker's consecutive terms to eight years, and stripping lawmakers of immunity.[19] The key aim of the reforms was to strengthen direct democracy, particularly with two key changes: the obligation to ratify any treaty that transfers sovereign state power to others through a binding referendum; and making it possible to conduct a referendum after a public petition with a minimum of 500,000 signatures for national matters, and one million signatures for an existing law other than statutes on fiscal matters, and for any other legislative initiative by the citizens themselves. Constitutional lawyers opposed the proposals; they argued that constitutional changes had to originate in the parliament.[20] The electoral defeat of the Syriza-Anel coalition in 2019 prevented the realization of these plans. Putting to one side the procedural objections based upon Greek constitutional law, which we

[16] Katerina Serafeim, *The Greek State Council's Decision on the controversial television licensing law*, Feb.3, 2017, CST Online, available at https://cstonline.net/the-greek-state-councils-decision-on-the-controversial-television-licensing-law-by-katerina-serafeim/, archived at https://perma.cc/8RC7-8DUW.

[17] Moffitt, note 5 above, at p. 90.

[18] See also Chapter 8, discussing the difference between using regular and irregular mechanisms to modify the political accountability of courts.

[19] Maria Savel, *Tsipras Uses Constitutional Reform to Distract from Greece's Economic Woes*, World Politics Review, Aug. 5, 2016, available at https://www.worldpoliticsreview.com/trend-lines/19587/tsipras-uses-constitutional-reform-to-distract-from-greece-s-economic-woes, archived at https://perma.cc/D2NR-GPK5.

[20] One critic argued that the proposed constitutional reform "aimed at weakening check-and-balance mechanisms as well as the integrity of crucial institutions in the name of 'direct democracy.'" Ioannis N. Grigoriadis, *For the People, Against the Elites: Left versus Right-Wing Populism in Greece and Turkey*, 11 Journal of the Middle East & Africa 51 (2020), at p. 57.

are in no position to assess, we believe that on the merits the reforms look like a reasonable attempt to introduce more features of direct democracy and account-ability in the Greek model of representative democracy.

Against the common charge that populism is always is anti-pluralistic, Syriza's discourse is the party's effort "to defend a pluralistic version of 'the people,' one that transcends the boundaries of ethnic origin, religion or sexual orientation, but also an effort to highlight the party's left-wing identity and commitment to what is indeed a social-democratic agenda."[21] As one empirical analysis of Syriza's political rhetoric shows, it represents the case of "inclusionary populisms, reclaiming 'the people' from extreme right-wing associations and reactivating its potential not as an enemy but rather as an ally."[22] It is not surprising then that Moffitt strongly rejects Yascha Mounk's claim about Syriza's purported transition from populism to dictatorship.[23]

Podemos, like Syriza, "was an anti-austerity party contesting the EU rules and the Spanish government's capitulation to them."[24] Other key planks of its program called for ending evictions, creating a government-funded guaranteed annual income, making the Stability and Growth Pact "flexible" and making it include full employment in its objectives, democratization of the EU, repeal of Spanish balanced budget law, and a thirty-five-hour workweek. Another study argues that Podemos in Spain represents "a clear radical left-libertarian univer-salistic profile advocating minority rights, gender equality and civic liberties, pledging also to fight discriminations."[25]

After a series of impressive electoral results between 2014 and 2016 established Podemos as the second largest political party in Spain in terms of membership, Podemos faced a series of internal and external challenges that dramatically changed its political ideas. After Syriza lost its battle with Brussels, Podemos started backing away from its identification with Syriza. Podemos remained in the opposition until 2018, when it entered into a coalition with the Partido Socialista Obrero Espaol (PSOE) to get rid of the conservatives in power. Like

---

[21] Katsambekis, note 11 above, at p. 39.

[22] Yannis Stavrakakis & Giorgios Katsambekis, *Left-Wing Populism in the European Periphery: The Case of SYRIZA*, 19 JOURNAL OF POLITICAL IDEOLOGIES 119 (2014), at p. 138. *See also* Grigoris Markou, *The Rise of Inclusionary Populism in Europe: The Case of SYRIZA*, 4 CONTEMPORARY SOUTHEASTERN EUROPE 54 (2017).

[23] MOFFITT, note 5 above, at p. 107.

[24] JUDIS, note 2 above, at p. 124. *See also* JORGE TAMAMES, FOR THE PEOPLE: LEFT POPULISM IN SPAIN AND THE UNITED STATES (2020).

[25] Gilles Ivaldi, Maria Lanzone, & Dwayne Woods, *Varieties of Populism across a Left-Right Spectrum: The Case of the Front National, the Northern League, Podemos and Five Star Movement*, 23 SWISS POLITICAL SCIENCE REV. 354 (2017), at p. 364.

Syriza, Podemos "abandoned its populist stance for a center-left reformism and an appearance of just another political party."[26]

Indeed, that seems a fair characterization of the two parties more generally. They acted as "ordinary" parties, forming coalitions that required them to modify even a core position while advancing other parts of their agendas. And, notably, both are simultaneously universalist in the traditional liberal sense of acknowledging the moral and political equality of all people and pluralist in acknowledging and taking on claims by historically marginalized communities that they too are part of "the people."

In institutional terms, both parties advocate a hybrid model of participatory and representative democracy, Podemos even more so than Syriza. In its main manifesto, the Thessaloniki Programme, Syriza argued for strengthening democratic institutions and implementing forms of direct democracy. One of the key parts of Syriza's constitutional reform package was making constitutional referendums easier to boost direct democracy. A major innovation was the introduction of referendums by popular initiative.[27]

Though both parties have strong roots in protest movements—*aganaktismenoi* (outraged citizens) in Greece and "indignados" in Spain—the parties' social roots differ. Syriza was already an established political actor in 2011 when the Greek movements emerged. Podemos "almost organically emerged out of the squares."[28] Podemos developed a strong form of internal party democracy. It established local and sectorial "circles" of members and sympathizers, who debated politics and formulated policy proposals, it facilitated "on-line" forms of involvement accessible to all, and it undertook a collective construction of its program and electoral lists for the European Elections in May 2014.

In its early stage, Syriza managed to establish a powerful alliance and interaction with the squares movement: "This movement helped in unifying and symbolically representing several different struggles as one broader social/popular front. Syriza chose to first interact 'horizontally' with the protests, motivating its members and supporters to participate as individuals."[29] The political organization pursued identification with the mobilizations by becoming part of them in a concrete and often spontaneous way. The second step was to represent the movement within parliamentary politics, "taking a crucial step from identification

---

[26] Judis, note 2 above, at p. 130. *See also* Alexandros Kioupkiolis & Georgios Katsambekis, "New Left Populism Contesting and Taking Power: The Cases of SYRIZA and Podemos," in Left Radicalism and Populism in Europe (Giorgis Charalambous & Gregoris Ioannou eds., 2020).

[27] Under the existing constitution only parliament has the power to initiate referendums on "crucial national issues."

[28] Katsambekis, note 11 above, at p. 25.

[29] Costas Eleftheriou, "Greek Radical Left Responses to the Crisis," in Europe's Radical Left: From Marginality to the Mainstream? (Luke March & Daniel Keith eds. 2016), at p. 297.

to representation."[30] In its second term in office (2015–2018), Syriza's discourse retained certain populist characteristics, but became "less populist and more pragmatic/managerial than before." The party has become more "leader-centric."[31] The September 2015 electoral campaign was built mostly around Tsipras himself. Podemos, again in contrast, represents "an original fusion between 'participatory' and 'plebiscitary' politics, bringing together bottom-up deliberative processes with more traditional top-down mechanisms managed by dominant personalities such as Pablo Iglesias."[32] In the early stage, Podemos's strategy of mobilization rested primarily on a horizontal process of participatory assemblies and online voting, which originated in the 15M (Movimiento 15-M) and the "indignados" anti-austerity movement.

Over time, Podemos has transformed itself from a social movement into a more traditional party. In its 2016 election platform Podemos called for a reform in Spain's electoral system, advocating proportional representation, while endorsing a more institutionalized version of direct participation including a popular legislative veto, consultation initiatives, and the right to recall elected representatives. We believe that both examples of left-wing populism show that representative democracy can be combined with forms of direct participation and that use of referendums doesn't "disfigure" representative democracy, as argued by Nadia Urbinati, and how wrong is "the standard story" that "popular democracy is fundamentally at odds with party-based representative democracy."[33]

Moreover, Jan-Werner Müller's characterization of how populists conceive of the referendum is pretty much at odds with what actually happened in Spain and Greece. According to Müller, "the referendum serves to ratify what the populist leader has already discerned to be the genuine popular interest as matter of identity, not as matter of aggregating empirically verifiable interests."[34] As both cases show, populists in Greece and Spain used direct democracy precisely because they wanted to "deepen" sometimes too rigid and unresponsive channels of representative democracy.[35]

---

[30] Katsambekis, note 11 above, at p. 30. See also Alexis Tsipras, "Topical Question Addressed to the Prime Minister with the Subject 'Real Democracy,'" June 7, 2011 (Greek), available at http://www.syriza.gr/article/id/43646/-O-Proedros-thsKoinoboyleytikhs-Omadas-toy-Synaspismoy-Rizospastikhs-Aristeras-Alekshs-Tsipraskatethese-Epikairh-Erwthsh-ston-Prwthypoyrgo-me-thema:-%C2%ABPragmatikh-Dhmo%20kratia%C2%BB..html#.VS67w_msWAU, archived at https://perma.cc/DT9R-VT6V.

[31] Katsambekis, note 11 above, at p. 39.

[32] Ivaldi et al., note 25 above, at p. 369.

[33] NADIA URBINATI, ME THE PEOPLE: HOW POPULISM TRANSFORMS DEMOCRACY (2019), at p. 5; Ethan J. Leib & Christopher S. Elmendorf, *Why Party Democrats Need Popular Democracy and Popular Democrats Need Parties*, 100 CALIFORNIA LAW REVIEW 69 (2010), at p. 70.

[34] Jan-Werner Müller, *Real Citizens*, BOSTON REVIEW, Oct. 16 2016), available at http://bostonreview.net/politics/jan-werner-muller-populism, archived athttps://perma.cc/K45Q-XD7V.

[35] For additional discussion of populists and the removal of "veto points," see Chapter 8.

These examples of democratic, liberal, socially inclusive forms of populism show that authoritarianism and anti-pluralism are not necessarily elements of populism. Of course, some populist movements have the characteristics described by Müller, Mudde and Kaltwasser, Walker, and Blokker; so do some "ordinary" political movements. Once we expand our vision to include numerous populisms, not simply the usual suspects, we find that the relation between populism tout court and constitutionalism is far more complex than the common view has it. We might interrogate the process by which Hungary, Poland, and Turkey—the usual suspects—became the paradigmatic cases of contemporary populism rather than Podemos and Syriza. One possibility is that populists won more elections more decisively in the paradigmatic countries than Podemos and Syriza did. Another possibility is that scholars of constitutionalism are by inclination moderate progressives who are nonetheless committed to the view that, as apolitical constitutionalists, they must see conservative and progressive policies as equally permissible. By creating the category "populism" as a "thin" ideology, scholars can abjure direct political evaluation of the right-wing policies they dislike by attributing them to a populism that they can also find (symmetrically) on the other side of the political spectrum. Our argument, in contrast, is that such an approach breeds analytic confusion. Syriza, Podemos, and even the Five Star Movement simply aren't enough like Fidesz, PiS, and Erdoğan's AKP for us to learn much about constitutionalism by describing them all as populist parties.

The remainder of this part uses the case studies in this chapter as well as those in Chapters 4 and 6 as the basis for looking in more detail at some of the asserted relations between populisms and specific components of thin (and sometimes thicker) constitutionalism. To state once again our overall conclusion: sometimes we can see a tension between a specific populism and a specific component of constitutionalism, and sometimes we cannot. The analysis of specific populisms and their relation to constitutionalism must be highly sensitive to context.

8

Court-Packing or Court Reform?: Challenging Judicial Independence by Enhancing Accountability

I. Why Proto-Authoritarians (and Some Populists) Win Elections

We have to begin a discussion of populism, the courts, and executive power by thinking about why authoritarians or proto-authoritarians win elections in the first place—why voters give them the power to expand their own powers.

Opponents of authoritarian or proto-authoritarian candidates will tell voters, "Don't choose this person this time, because if you do it's going to be the last time you have a real choice among candidates."[1] Why do voters choose authoritarian or proto-authoritarian leaders if that's what they hear? Here are the two principal candidates we've found.[2]

- *The populist account.* "We don't believe what we're hearing because the people telling us how to vote have been discredited. They were running the government when bad things happened, and they bear some responsibility for the current situation. We relied on them before, and we can see how that turned out. We're not going to rely on them again, particularly when what they're saying has the obvious self-interest in staying in power behind it." Or—perhaps in addition, "You've got an interesting ambitious reform platform. The things you say you'll do to reverse what's led us into the current situation sound sensible, and we'd like to see you try."

---

[1] Again, the phrase "one person, one vote, one time" captures this idea.

[2] For a more analytic account, though one we believe consistent with our informal one, *see* Sheri Berman, *The Causes of Populism in the West*, 24 ANNUAL REVIEW OF POLITICAL SCIENCE 71 (2021). Berman identifies economic and sociocultural grievances as demand-side explanations, decreased responsiveness of governance institutions and technocracy as supply-side explanations (populism is "a symptom of institutional decay"), and voluntarist explanations focusing on choices politicians and their parties make.

Power to the People. Mark Tushnet and Bojan Bugarič, Oxford University Press. © Mark Tushnet and Bojan Bugarič 2021. DOI: 10.1093/oso/9780197606711.003.0009

- *The "authoritarian" account.* "We're in the current situation because the people we elected in the past weren't able to confront and overcome the forces that led us to our current situation. What we need now is strong leadership, so we're not going to worry when they tell us that the candidate we favor is going to be too strong. Strength is exactly what we're voting for."[3]

We agree that sometimes populists favor taking over the courts and expanding executive power, the topics of this and the next chapter, and that sometimes those populists are proto-authoritarians. Lurking in the background is the fact that non-populist authoritarians who win elections want to expand power too. That problem comes to the fore when we try to distinguish, as we think serious analysis requires, among candidates who win because the populist account describes their supporters, those who win because the authoritarian account does, and those who win because both accounts fit the case. Another problem is that sometimes we run across a populist leader who isn't even a proto-authoritarian but who is working in a political context that creates a political logic favoring expanding power nonetheless.

That political logic gets worked out in different ways depending on circumstances. The core idea, though, remains the same. When the populist account we've described explains the populist party's success, the party might come to office with an ambitious reform agenda. Typically, though, it will find people aligned with those the party defeated holding some of the reins of power: The populist party won a decisive victory in the lower and more important house of parliament, but the now-opposition has enough holdover members in the upper house to be able to block the reforms. Or, the topic of this chapter, judges on the constitutional court have terms that for good reasons extend beyond a single presidential or legislative term. When the populist government takes office, the constitutional court will typically have many members, and often a majority, appointed when the now-opposition was in power and more sympathetic to the opposition than to the new government. The new government can reasonably fear that the constitutional court will interpret the constitution—creatively perhaps but not wildly unreasonably—to make some of its most important platform planks unconstitutional.

As we've noted, from a political scientist's point of view, constitutionalism understood as a means of limiting power consists of a series of veto gates. You have to get through every one for your program to become law. Politicians with ambitious reform agendas see constitutionalism more expansively and more

---

[3] For evidence suggesting the cogency of the authoritarian account, *see* Roberto Stefan Foa & Yascha Mounk, *The Danger of Deconsolidation: The Democratic Disconnect*, 27 (3) JOURNAL OF DEMOCRACY 5 (2016); Roberto Stefan Foa & Yascha Mounk, *The Signs of Deconsolidation*, 28 (1) JOURNAL OF DEMOCRACY (2017) 5.

accurately. It's not merely about limiting government power; it's about enabling the exercise of government power to achieve the public good. And that's what politicians with ambitious reform agendas think their programs will do.

Facing a veto gate controlled by people who no longer have the people's confidence, an incoming party with such an agenda, whether the party is populist or otherwise, will think seriously about ways of evading the veto gate or, if the thing being blocked is truly important (as the party sees it) dismantling the veto gate either entirely or with respect to the program of concern.[4] Institutional reform might be necessary to carry out the party's agenda, and sometimes the reforms will be justified by that fact alone—that is, where the agenda is quite a good one and is being thwarted by an institution controlled by those the people have repudiated, changing the institution might be justified even if we acknowledge that there's a cost associated with dismantling *any* veto gate.

We develop the foregoing argument in this chapter by examining institutional reforms populists have proposed and on occasion adopted to limit judicial power—to attack the courts, as their opponents would have it. There's another way to frame the issues. Thin constitutionalism requires that courts be both independent and accountable to law. Some changes to courts strike a new balance between independence and accountability to law. Only if we assume unrealistically that the balance that's in place when the reform government takes office is perfect can we dismiss efforts to strike a new balance out of hand, as attacks on the courts and nothing more.

II. The Mechanisms of Independence and Accountability to Law (and Politics)

Thin constitutionalism requires that judges be independent and accountable to law. What does it *permit*?

- Announcing his nomination of Ruth Bader Ginsburg to the Supreme Court, President Bill Clinton said, "Throughout her life she has repeatedly stood for the individual, the person less well-off, the outsider in society, and has given those people greater hope by telling them that they have a place in our legal system, by giving them a sense that the Constitution and the laws protect all the American people, not simply the powerful." He referred to her "moral imagination" and her "values."

---

[4] Take constitutional courts: the first strategy might involve expanding ("packing") the constitutional court, the second limiting its jurisdiction. Similarly, an obstructive upper house can be packed—as was threatened for the House of Lords in the early twentieth century—or its power to veto specific matters (budget bills, for example) eliminated.

- Germany's parliament chooses judges for the nation's constitutional court.[5] Confirmation requires approval by two-thirds of the parliament. In practice, this has led to an agreement that the conservative and social democratic parties would alternate in choosing nominees, with an occasional hand-off to a third party such as the Greens and the Liberals.

These and many other examples we could provide show that thin constitutionalism allows processes for selecting judges that expressly take their values and even their political orientation into account. Judicial independence isn't compromised when some degree of political accountability is added to accountability to law.[6] That's because judges exercise a form of power that is both legal and to some degree political. Thin constitutionalism requires that those who make policy be accountable to the public. There's no strong reason to deny those who design constitutional systems the authority to include judges in that group—again, to some degree.

That point is driven home by referring to some well-known discussions of constitutional courts by political scientists. We discussed Ran Hirschl's work on the rise of "juristocracy" in Chapter 3. The suffix "ocracy" is telling: constitutional courts' exercise of form of political rule. To the same effect is the title of a work from the 1990s: "The Global Expansion of Judicial Power."[7] Writing in 1957, political scientist Robert Dahl observed of the U.S. Supreme Court that its holdings had never been out of line for long with the policy positions prevailing in the national governing coalition—a point to which we will return. When Austrian jurist Hans Kelsen came up with the idea of a constitutional court separate from the ordinary courts in civil law systems, he explained its composition by pointing out that it would resolve disputes about the allocation of power between the legislature and the executive government and between the center and federal states. Those disputes were political to the core,[8] and Kelsen described court decisions about them as "negative act[s] of legislation."[9]

---

[5] This is a simplified description, but accurate enough for our purposes. For details, *see* Uwe Kischel, *Party, Pope and Politics? The Election of German Constitutional Court Justices in Comparative Perspective*, 11 INTERNATIONAL JOURNAL OF CONSTITUTIONAL LAW 962 (2013).

[6] Again we stress that we're talking about what the judicial-independence element of thin constitutionalism permits: it allows but doesn't require some degree of political accountability.

[7] THE GLOBAL EXPANSION OF JUDICIAL POWER (C. Neal Tate & Thorbjorn Vallinder eds. 1997).

[8] Indeed, Kelsen argued that a constitutional court was essential because these disputes would often be political in a purely partisan sense. The constitutional court, that is, would be charged with resolving partisan disputes using legal criteria. Kelsen's adversary Carl Schmitt responded that doing so would necessarily remove the constitutional court from the domain of law. Kelsen replied in turn that the ordinary courts doing ordinary law disposed of cases by invoking policy concerns that were indistinguishable in principle (in this regard) from what the constitutional court would do. For the debates, *see* THE GUARDIAN OF THE CONSTITUTION: HANS KELSEN AND CARL SCHMITT ON THE LIMITS OF CONSTITUTIONAL LAW (Lars Vinx ed. 2015). We discuss this a bit more later in our treatment of the implications of modest American Legal Realism for constitutional adjudication.

[9] Hans Kelsen, *Judicial Review of Legislation: A Comparative Study of the Austrian and the American Constitution* 4 JOURNAL OF POLITICS 183 (1942), at p. 187.

We might be beating a dead horse here. Constitutional law inevitably has some political content, and thin constitutionalism accommodates that by including within it systems that impose some degree of political accountability on judges who decide constitutional cases.[10] Here's another, more "realistic" version of this point: the idea of "juristocracy" drives home the point that judges exercise power. It would be surprising to discover that other power-holders—that is, legislatures and executives—would put up with that without trying to build the judges into a comprehensive system of interactions among power-holders. They will try to check and balance the judges. That's just another way of saying that as a practical matter judges who exercise power are going to be held politically accountable no matter what, and the idea of constitutionalism risks irrelevance if it fails to acknowledge that fact.[11]

Does political accountability compromise the idea that judges should be accountable only to the law? As we pointed out in Chapter 1, some kinds of political accountability certainly do that. Thin constitutionalism doesn't generally allow what we might call case-specific accountability—deciding a specific case for the very purpose of satisfying demands from political actors, as occurs in "telephone justice."[12] The examples from the United States and Germany that opened this chapter involve political accountability in the form of taking political considerations into account when judges are appointed.[13] That does make judges political accountable (again, to some degree), but doesn't it reduce their accountability to law?[14]

Not when the law, fairly understood, itself has a policy or political component. Here we return to our discussion in Chapter 1 of American Legal Realism as a reasonable view of law. Legal Realists argued that purely doctrinal materials—"law" narrowly understood—sometimes run out, in

---

[10] On some reasonable views the application of ordinary, non-constitutional law similarly has policy content. Thin constitutionalism allows those views to be incorporated in system design by making ordinary judges politically accountable as well.

[11] Probably the most extreme form of political accountability of judges, typical for many states in the United States, is direct election of judges.

[12] We say "generally" because we think that there might be truly extraordinary and extremely rare cases where doing so might be necessary to avoid catastrophe. If such a case occurs, we would characterize it as posing a tragic choice between judicial independence and national survival, in which judicial independence and the rule of law truly must be sacrificed.

[13] Allowing them to be taken into account at the stage of removal is more problematic because of the risk that removal will occur for case-specific reasons, creating bad incentives for sitting judges. For an instructive example from Malaysia, see YVONNE TEW, CONSTITUTIONAL STATECRAFT IN ASIAN COURTS (2020), at pp. 57–59 (describing a judicial crisis in 1988 involving the removal of several judges because of a series of their rulings, leading to a decades-long "erosion of public confidence in the Malaysian judiciary's independence").

[14] The same question arises, as we discuss later, when political actors seek to enhance political accountability by changing the courts' jurisdiction or size.

the sense that they can be deployed by both sides in a dispute to support their positions. And, the Realists argued, the arguments on both sides were reasonable—fully compatible with law narrowly understood. Still, the dispute has to be resolved. How to do it? According to Realists, the judge in this situation makes a discretionary choice (they tended to call it a "policy" choice).[15] And, finally, if legislators are properly made accountable to their constituents for their discretionary choices, we can make judges similarly accountable—that is, politically accountable—for *their* discretionary choices. So, the Legal Realist argument goes, some degree of political accountability doesn't compromise judges' accountability to law when we understand "law" broadly.[16]

Some forms of political accountability are surely out of bounds even if they aren't "telephone justice" or other versions of case-specific accountability. That's why we've regularly said accountability "to some degree." Every political system strikes a balance between judicial independence and accountability to law on the one hand and political accountability on the other. How can we tell when the balance tips too far in favor of political accountability?

We approach this question from a perspective slightly different from the one we've been using so far. With the liberalism of the Warren Court in the background, two leading U.S. scholars of constitutionalism published major studies of the U.S. Supreme Court in 1957 and 1962. Law professor Alexander Bickel's book *The Least Dangerous Branch* argued that constitutional review in the United States posed a "countermajoritarian difficulty."[17] The Supreme Court, he observed, had the power to nullify legislation supported by legislative majorities. Perhaps it could do so when local legislatures were somehow out of tune with national majorities, although the court's assessment that that was so would always be uncertain. And, perhaps it could do so when public support for laws enacted years before had eroded without that erosion being reflected in the repeal of old or the enactment of new laws, though again how the court could know that was unclear. Setting aside recently enacted national laws, though, was pretty openly acting against a current national majority. Bickel asked the following: How could such a countermajoritarian institution be justified in a generally majoritarian democracy?

---

[15] For a major recent restatement and sophistication of the Legal Realist account, see Duncan Kennedy, A Critique of Adjudication (Fin de Siècle) (1998).

[16] As in Chapter 1, we note that, though we agree with the Legal Realist position, you don't have to do so to acknowledge that it is a reasonable one that, because of its reasonableness, is consistent with thin constitutionalism.

[17] Alexander Bickel, The Least Dangerous Branch: The Supreme Court at the Bar of Politics (1962). The core ideas of the book were first developed in Alexander M. Bickel, *The Supreme Court, 1960 Term—Foreword: The Passive Virtues*, 75 Harvard Law Review 40 (1961).

Political scientists provided an answer. We've already referred to Robert Dahl's article. Dahl's study led him to conclude, "the policy views dominant on the Court are never for long out of line with the policy views dominant among the lawmaking majorities of the United States." So, he wrote, "Except for short-lived transitional periods when the old alliance is disintegrating and the new one is struggling to take control of political institutions, the Supreme Court is inevitably a part of the dominant national alliance."[18] (As we'll see, the qualification for "transitional periods" is quite important in thinking about how populist governments have dealt with courts.)

How does this come about? Partly by the appointment process, which involves presidential nomination and Senate confirmation—political accountability. Partly by the influence in the background of social movements whose presence on the political scene can affect the way judges think about the cases they're deciding, another form of political accountability. Partly by picking judges from a pool whose understanding of what counts as law is strongly influenced by mainstream legal thinking. And partly by occasionally restructuring the courts, using techniques like depriving one court of jurisdiction and giving it to another and eliminating review of some categories of cases.

We stress that these are ordinary mechanisms, used everywhere though in different mixes, and not only by populists. The appointment process has been particularly important in the United States, less so in India. Politically motivated restructuring of the courts occurred in the United States in the period surrounding the Civil War; major statutes enacted in the mid-1990s sharply restricted the power of national courts to remedy bad prison conditions and to order the release of prisoners whose trials had been the occasion for constitutional violations.[19]

The question then becomes when does the use of these ordinary mechanisms become extraordinary? More precisely, are there criteria for identifying extraordinary uses of ordinary mechanisms that are independent of the purposes underlying decisions to employ them more often than other governments do, or with less justification?

---

[18] Robert Dahl, *Decision-Making in a Democracy: The Supreme Court as a National Policy-Maker,* 6 JOURNAL OF PUBLIC LAW 279 (1957), at pp. 285, 293. Decades later Terri Peretti amplified Dahl's argument: TERRI PERETTI, IN DEFENSE OF A POLITICAL COURT (2001).

[19] No one seems to make much of the fact, but most nations in the British Commonwealth changed their systems of final appellate review, making the last stop review in the nation's highest court and eliminating appeals to the Privy Council in London.

III.   The Political Logic of Political Accountability

We focus on appointments as a way of exposing the relevant political logic. No one seriously thinks that President Clinton's nomination of Justice Ginsburg was a form of "court-packing" or otherwise exceptional, even though he chose her in part to add a new liberal voice to the Supreme Court. The reason is obvious: the nomination occurred in the regular course. Justice Byron White retired, almost certainly timing his decision to ensure that a Democratic president could name his replacement, and Clinton filled the vacancy. In Poland PiS secured complete control of the constitutional court when the mandate (term) of the court's president expired, and the PiS government named his successor. In contrast, the Polish government's refusal to publish constitutional court decisions it lost was irregular, and Democrats in the United States claimed that the refusal to hold a hearing on the nomination of Merrick Garland to fill the seat opened by Justice Antonin Scalia's death was irregular, as (they claimed) was the confirmation of Justice Amy Coney Barrett to fill that opened up by Justice Ginsburg's death.

One criterion for distinguishing between actions that promote political accountability without damaging judicial independence and accountability to law and those that undermine independence and legal accountability thus appears to be whether the actions are regular or irregular.[20] Consider first *regular* appointments as the mechanism for achieving political accountability—and, in Dahl's terms, making the courts "part of the dominant national alliance." Using regular appointments to do so takes time. Analyzing U.S. presidential politics, political scientist Stephen Skowronek usefully distinguishes between calendar time and political time.[21] The former is obvious; the latter is the time politicians have to accomplish their goals—for U.S. presidents, presumptively four years, perhaps eight, conditioned by what happens according to the political clock determining when elections for the legislature occur.[22]

We add judicial time to the mix.[23] Judicial time has two components: the time it takes for constitutional issues to be framed and reach the constitutional court,

[20]   *See* David Kosar & Katarina Sipulova, *How to Fight Court-Packing?*, 6 CONSTITUTIONAL STUDIES 133 (2020), which includes irregularity as part of the definition of court-packing. We discuss the proposition that "regularity" is itself a politically contestable term later in this chapter.

[21]   STEPHEN SKOWRONEK, THE POLITICS PRESIDENTS MAKE: LEADERSHIP FROM JOHN ADAMS TO BILL CLINTON (1997).

[22]   Semi-presidential systems acknowledge the importance of political time when they coordinate elections for the president with those for the legislature. So, for example, France did so when it changed the timing of legislative elections to synchronize them with the presidential election to reduce the chance that the president would have to cohabit with a parliamentary majority from a different party than his or hers.

[23]   For an earlier presentation, *see* Mark Tushnet, "After the Heroes Have Left the Scene: Temporality in the Study of Constitutional Court Judges," in JUDICIAL POWER: HOW CONSTITUTIONAL COURTS AFFECT POLITICAL TRANSFORMATION (Christine Landfried ed. 2019).

and the pace at which vacancies on the court occur.[24] We continue to focus on the latter component.

Vacancies arise when a judge reaches retirement age, chooses to retire, passes away, or when the judge's mandate expires at the end of a stated term of years. Politicians know when some of these events will occur, but not all of them. They can coordinate political time with judicial time to some extent—counting on their ability to replace a judge who will reach retirement age in two years, for example. But—and this is our central point—sometimes, from a politician's point of view judicial time is much too slow compared to political time. These are the "transitional periods" to which Dahl referred. He called them "short-lived," but, again, whether they are momentary or extend for several years depends upon the relation between political and judicial time.

Think of yourself as the leader of a political party that has just won a reasonably free and fair election with an ambitious policy agenda. Maybe you won because you defeated a party that had run the government for several years and had made what turned out to be serious policy errors. Your agenda targets not only those errors but also what you think were their structural origins—political corruption, disregard of public views as they developed, the influence of rich people (and other elites) on political campaigns and outcomes. You might worry that the time you have to implement your policy agenda might be short relative to its ambition: important municipal or regional elections lie ahead in a year or two, some national elections in two years.

The party you defeated might be so stunned by its defeat that it's unable to mount continuing challenges to your program, even when in opposition. That appears to have happened in Venezuela, for example, after Hugo Chávez's first victory: perhaps a paralyzing dismay can explain the Venezuelan court's willingness to accept a contestable theory of constituent power to uphold the constitutionality of Chávez's proposed constituent assembly.[25]

We recount the Venezuelan story in some detail to show how initial steps toward constitutional reform can create a dynamic in which opposition turns out

---

[24] Both components can affect outcomes. In the United States it usually takes a fair amount of time for a case to be properly framed and litigated up to the Supreme Court; a great deal of good or bad can happen until the court decides. Constitutional courts that issue advisory opinions or that exercise ex ante constitutional review, issuing their judgments before a challenged law takes effect, move more quickly. Sometimes they hand down decisions when the heat of political controversy remains high, and they can exacerbate or calm the controversy (and in the process perhaps can be seared by the political heat).

[25] Divisions among Polish opposition parties after PiS's rise to power impeded their ability to halt PiS's moves toward authoritarian rule. We make these points in part to offset the all-too-common tendency in the literature on populism to attribute all agency to the populist party and none to its opponents.

to be futile, particularly if the opposition makes small strategic errors.[26] Hugo Chávez campaigned for the presidency in 1998 on a platform calling for a radical revision of the existing constitution. As Joshua Braver writes, that constitution was blamed for the nation's "economic woes" because it "divided political power between elitist parties to the exclusion and detriment of the common citizen"—a description cast in standard populist terms.

After winning a decisive victory Chávez moved ahead with the proposal. He didn't have a large enough majority in the legislature to use the methods prescribed in the constitution for its amendment or replacement. He therefore proposed to hold a referendum on the question of convening a constituent assembly, not provided for in the constitution, along with a question that would allow him to set the terms for conducting the election to the assembly. The Venezuelan Supreme Court—not yet captured by Chávez—invoked a theoretical position circulating in Latin American constitutional circles that the people had an "original constituent power" to write a new constitution, a power that couldn't be displaced by any constitution at all. The referendum on convening a constituent assembly would be an exercise of that original constituent power. A little more than a month later, though, it held that the second referendum question was badly posed. Chávez had to put to the people the choice of some specific plan for electing members of the constituent assembly.

Chávez was fine with the second decision. He revised the second question to propose an election with a national list and separate constituency-based elections, both governed by a first-past-the-post plurality winner system. Braver argues that this, rather than the convening of the constituent assembly itself, was the decisive choice. The reason was that Chávez's party was almost guaranteed to win first-past-the-post elections in the face of an opposition that hadn't figured out that it had to run a highly coordinated campaign, basically putting up only one candidate to oppose Chávez's candidate in each district. The result: Chávez's party won 65 percent of the vote and won more than 90 per cent of the seats in the constituent assembly.

When the constituent assembly met, it immediately convened itself as the nation's governing legislature, displacing the one in place when Chávez was elected. Then it systematically marched through the rest of the nation's governing bodies, firing everyone who exercised important power and replacing them with Chávez loyalists.[27] The institutions affected included the Supreme Court, which

---

[26] We draw on the description provided in Joshua Braver, *Hannah Arendt in Venezuela: The Supreme Court Battles Hugo Chávez over the Creation of the 1999 Constitutions*, 14 INTERNATIONAL JOURNAL OF CONSTITUTIONAL LAW 555 (2016), at pp. 565–69.

[27] Our description is rather informal. Braver provides a more precise one: the constituent assembly "effectively neutered Congress and the judiciary through a combination of limiting their powers, reorganizing their structure, shrinking their size, as well as asserting a right to veto their decisions, and fire individual members." The reorganized court then ruled that all this was a "valid . . . act[] of sovereign power." Braver, note 26 above, at p. 567.

not surprisingly issued decisions holding all this completely unconstitutional. It was too late, though. H.L.A. Hart, the famous jurisprude, described law as ultimately resting on a rule of recognition, which was essentially a sociological rule: you could tell what the rule of recognition was by seeing what officials actually did, and in Venezuela the relevant officials—in the end, probably the military being the most important—treated the decisions of the constituent assembly as creating the law they had to follow.

The next step occurred after a referendum approved the new constitution, with "a low turn-out of 30.4 percent" and a positive vote of 71.8 percent—the turnout resulting from an opposition boycott, so that (overstating the point) only Chávez's supporters voted in the referendum. With the new constitution in hand, the constituent assembly "removed a large number of judges, formally dissolved congress and state legislatures. . . ." It "replaced Congress with a national legislative commission whose members were chosen by the constituent assembly." It "also chose a new national ombudsman, chief prosecutor, and members of the National Electoral Council. It replaced many members of the Supreme Court with allies of the regime. . . ." All this froze the opposition out of any institutional source of legal power or even much influence in the nation's governing institutions.[28] Venezuela continued to hold elections in which votes were fairly counted, but the opposition had no leverage in those elections—and eventually the Chávez regime started to suppress opposition votes even more directly.

Chávez got away with a great deal because the Venezuelan Supreme Court gave him the path to transformation. Other politicians might not want to take the risk that their opponents will simply slink away. So, these politicians will look around to see whether the opponents continue to control veto gates that they can close to block the winners from actually implementing the program that was the basis for their electoral victory. We keep emphasizing that we're dealing with political leaders who have indeed received majority support for their policy agendas in reasonably free and fair elections because closing veto gates to those agendas can be understood as attempting to use existing constitutional forms to "overturn" the election's results.

These politicians might discover that the constitutional court is one of those veto gates still under their opponents' control because of the difference paces of political and judicial time. Indeed, Hirschl's story of "hegemonic self-preservation," which we introduced in Chapter 3, is one in which the opponents have deliberately created or expanded the court's powers precisely to thwart your ability to implement your program. Even if that's not why the constitutional court has the power to veto your actions, the fact that it consists of judges

---

[28] Braver, note 26 above, at p. 568.

appointed to make them sufficiently politically accountable to the now-departed regime might be worrisome.

As you think this through—that is, as you try to figure out how you're going to enact and implement the policy platform that you were elected on—you're also going to worry about the limited time you have to get things done, to show voters that they actually got what they were looking for. The longer it takes to implement the program, the more you're going to worry that voters will get disillusioned and start thinking that you're just another one of those politicians who promise anything to get elected and then forget about who put them there.

Putting all this together, you might conclude that your ability to succeed politically depends in part on making the constitutional court less politically accountable to the party out of power and more politically accountable to your party.[29] You ask your lawyers what you can do, and they offer some options, all of which they tell you are constitutionally permissible: you can amend the constitution to change the court's jurisdiction (if you have the votes to do that); you can create a new institution—a constitutional "quort"—that absorbs most of the existing court's jurisdiction; you can expand the court's size ("pack the court"); you can lower the retirement age with retrospective effect (if your lawyers can develop reasonable arguments that doing so is lawful); you can raise the retirement age to make sure that one or two judges who you think might sympathize with you stay on the court.

To conclude the story with our analytic point: you're doing all this in a constitutionally permissible manner to address the fact that the difference between political time and judicial time can put the balance between judicial independence and accountability to law and political accountability out of whack. Your actions might be a sort of fine-tuning of the constitutional mechanisms for setting that balance correctly.[30]

Now think about what's built into the story, and what we've left out. Notably, almost none of the elements of populism appear: charismatic leadership plays no role, nor does the fact that the winning political party says that it speaks for a unified people. And, indeed, we can see the story playing out in decidedly "non-populist" settings. The story we've told is a reconstruction of Franklin Delano Roosevelt's court-packing proposal in 1937. We might have used the response

---

[29] It is worth mentioning here that the constitutional courts were probably the key veto players in the post-war constitutional settlement, often described as "constrained democracy," intended to discipline, limit, and de-dramatize democracy. As Martin Conway argues, "the democracies of the post-war decades retained, at least until the upheavals of the 1960s, something of an anti-popular ethos." MARTIN CONWAY, WESTERN EUROPE'S DEMOCRATIC AGE: 1945–1968 (2020), at p. 115. *See also* JAN-WERNER MÜLLER, CONTESTING DEMOCRACY: POLITICAL IDEAS IN TWENTIETH CENTURY EUROPE (2011).

[30] Something similar might be said about responses to the control of other veto gates, or semi-veto gates, by the defeated regime. One such semi-veto gate might be the board controlling public broadcasting.

of the French Constitutional Council to François Mitterand's socialist agenda in the first years of socialist government there.[31] What's central to the story is that the winning political party has an ambitious legislative agenda that differs more than incrementally from existing policy. That might happen more often with populist parties than with non-populist ones, but it's the agenda—and political calculations that take into account the difference between political and judicial time—rather than the nature of the party that drives the story.

We've told the story to make its political logic clear. Before telling the story, we argued that judicial independence doesn't preclude making judges politically accountable to some degree. "To some degree" isn't a throwaway qualification. We ended the story by describing attempts to shift the balance as fine-tuning. Sometimes, though, the attempts will smash the watch—eliminate judicial independence entirely or (maybe the same thing) tilt the balance so substantially in favor of political accountability that thin constitutionalism's requirement of judicial independence and accountability to law is no longer satisfied.

Here as always details matter. Take Roosevelt's court-packing plan. As proposed it would have allowed Roosevelt to name six new justices to the nine already on the Supreme Court. In its immediate political context, the plan's intended effect would have been to create a reliable liberal majority of eight justices, eliminating the risk that the nine-member court would issue too many five-to-four conservative decisions.[32] Or take a change in the composition of a judicial nominating commission that adds one government minister and gives the government effective veto power over nominations.

Whether these are fine-tuning or smashing is a matter of judgment, but we would call them the former. Maybe there's a somewhat more objective standard. Maybe we should describe as fine-tuning any changes consistent with the constitution in place when they are made. If the constitution doesn't specify how many judges sit on the constitutional court and there are no embedded traditions about changing the court's size, expanding the court in response to the political logic we've described is fine-tuning.

Here the problem is that whether something is consistent with the constitution in place is often itself open to reasonable disagreement. Suppose the constitution doesn't specify the number of constitutional court judges. Is there nonetheless a

---

[31] The Constitutional Council effectively blocked the government's program of nationalizing the banks and of limiting the power of concentrated media ownership. For a discussion, see ALEC STONE, THE BIRTH OF JUDICIAL POLITICS IN FRANCE: THE CONSTITUTIONAL COUNCIL IN COMPARATIVE PERSPECTIVE (1992), at pp. 140–208.

[32] Why six new justices were needed rather than two (to change a five-to-four conservative majority into a six-to-five liberal one) depended on arcane details about Roosevelt's political calculations that we needn't go into here. For a discussion, see Barry Cushman, Court-Packing and Compromise, 29 CONSTITUTIONAL COMMENTARY 1 (2013).

non-textual constitutional principle limiting the reasons for changing the court's size? Once again, the details of domestic constitutional law will matter: in the nation's methods of interpreting the constitution, how important are arguments based upon non-textual fundamental principles?

Prior scholarship and case law suggests one overarching candidate to identify smashing rather than fine-tuning. Smashing occurs when the government takes an otherwise constitutionally permissible action for the very purpose of making the court politically accountable to it rather than to anyone else. The political logic we outlined means that this condition is always going to be satisfied in the cases we're interested in. The problem is that the condition is also going to be satisfied in the regular course—to revert to our argument about political accountability, when the president nominates someone who's expected to be politically "reliable" to fill a vacancy created by the expiration of a sitting justice's term, for example.

We suggest that those seeking some reasonably objective way of distinguishing between fine-tuning and smashing can find a way out by adding another condition: it's fine-tuning when there's a plausible (reasonable, defensible—the terminology doesn't matter, the underlying idea does) "good government" justification for the change, smashing otherwise. Roosevelt might have been acknowledging this condition when he initially defended his court-packing proposal. Its effect would have been to allow him to name six new justices to the court, but its form was different: he could name a new justice for every justice over the age of seventy-five. Roosevelt's defense of this form was good government. Elderly justices weren't able to keep up with the court's work. And, perhaps, the plan foundered both in practice and in principle because this good government justification simply wasn't plausible. Had the plan been presented as one designed to "rebalance" the court to bring political and judicial time into closer alignment, perhaps it would have been seen as a "good government" proposal.

Why, though, add this condition? The reason, we believe, lies in deeper concerns about smashing versus fine-tuning. A common argument against what looks like fine-tuning is this: "Sure, it looks as if this is merely fine-tuning, a small adjustment in the balance between independence and political accountability. But if we let the government do this, it could do a lot of other things that are much more problematic—it could smash rather than fine tune."

Here's an example. The Orbán government amended the provisions setting out the constitutional court's jurisdiction to eliminate its power to review constitutional challenges to budget provisions. It did so because, in its view, the constitutional court had inappropriately intervened in budget decisions by inventing constitutional objections. So far, an ordinary version of the political logic. And, no serious account of thin constitutionalism and only some serious accounts of thicker constitutionalisms require that constitutional courts have the power to set aside budget provisions as unconstitutional.[33] So far, still, so good. We know, and almost certainly knew when the Orbán government adopted that amendment, that it wanted to do more—in particular, to drastically limit the constitutional court's power to review claims that its laws violated fundamental human rights. And *that* would be smashing rather than fine-tuning.[34]

This is a classic "slippery slope" argument: if you allow this seemingly innocuous thing now, you're committed in principle to allowing a much more troublesome thing later on. Slippery slope arguments in law are widespread and famously problematic. Here we note two responses to this slippery slope argument, one sounding in legal theory and one in practical politics.

- *Legal theory*: Tell me what your concern is, and I'll design the principle to take it into account. If you're worried that allowing an amendment to prevent constitutional review of budget decisions will allow amendments to prevent such review in individual rights cases, I'll state a principle that defines fine-tuning as permissible with respect to government structures but not with respect to individual rights.
- *Practical politics*: Your concern isn't with what the government is doing now, but with what it might do later. This particular government, though, isn't planning to do the things you're worried about, and its overall political agenda doesn't include them. So, sufficient unto the day is the evil thereof.

Almost all the versions of the slippery slope concern we've seen reject the practical-politics response: "We are quite confident that this is a government that's willing to do bad things when it gets the chance." That was certainly true about the Orbán government's changes in the constitutional court's jurisdiction. Notice, though, that now we're talking about the government and its policy agenda, not about its court reforms alone. Or, to return to this book's general theme, we're talking about the merits, not about populism or anything similar.

The case studies that follow examine court reform, court-packing, and other modifications of judicial structure with these concerns in the background.

---

[33] It's almost impossible to imagine a case in which the U.S. Supreme Court would do so.

[34] Or maybe not. The Orbán government limited the constitutional court's jurisdiction over fundamental rights claims by eliminating its jurisdiction over claims filed by individuals, reverting to the Kelsenian model in which the constitutional court had jurisdiction only over complaints filed by parliamentarians (and some designated others). As we argued in Chapter 1, the Kelsenian model, though historically well-grounded, is no longer consistent with contemporary thin constitutionalism.

IV. India and Israel: Case Studies in Trying to Change How Judges Are Appointed

A. India—Creating a Judicial Nominating Commission

In April 2015 India's Parliament adopted the 99th Amendment to the nation's constitution. As the number of amendments indicates, it's easy for a parliamentary majority to amend the constitution; for most amendments simple majorities in both houses of parliament are enough. The 99th Amendment fell into a different category. It had to get support from at least half of the members of parliament and two-thirds of those present and voting, and it also had to be approved by half of the governments in the nation's states. That was no obstacle, though. The amendment was supported by both the Modi government, which had a majority, and the opposition parties; only one vote was recorded against the amendment. Sixteen of the nation's twenty-nine states signed on to the amendment.

The amendment created a judicial nominating commission to select candidates for appointment to high courts in India's states and to the national Supreme Court. Six months later the Supreme Court held the amendment unconstitutional, holding that it violated the principle of judicial independence that was an unchangeable part of the constitution's "basic structure."

The Modi government is often described as populist, and the Supreme Court's decision can easily be taken to show how a populist government undermines judicial independence. The overall story, though, is quite a bit more complicated. We describe the case for calling the amendment a "good government" change motivated only in part by concern that an unreformed court would obstruct the Modi government's legislative agenda. To be clear: We're not endorsing this alternative narrative; to do so would require a knowledge of the ins and outs of Indian politics that we lack. Rather, we treat the story of the 99th Amendment as a case study illuminating the claim that populist programs are anti-constitutional because, among other things, they undermine judicial independence.

The impetus for the 99th Amendment lay deep in India's fight for independence.[35] The movement for independence from British rule consisted of many social groupings. For our purposes the most important were secular and socialist-leaning nationalists centered in the Congress Party; Hindu nationalists associated with the Rashtriya Swayamsevak Singh (RSS) and later the Bharatiya Janata Party (BJP), in both of which Narendra Modi eventually played leading roles; and a number of parties representing India's large Muslim population,

---

[35] We provide a quite simplified version of an extremely long and complicated history. For additional details, *see* ARUN THIRUVENGADAM, THE CONSTITUTION OF INDIA: A CONTEXTUAL ANALYSIS (2017), ch. 1.

the most important of which was the Muslim League. The traumatic and violent partition of India in 1947 reduced the political power of Muslim organizations, but secularists defended the interests of the nation's Muslim population against sustained attacks by Hindu nationalists. These attacks meant that post-independence India continued to suffer from inter-communal violence, mostly provoked by Hindu nationalists.

The Congress Party tried to hold back Hindu nationalism in part by using the law and the Supreme Court. It enacted and did its best to enforce a statute, targeted at Hindu nationalism as a political movement, prohibiting political candidates from appealing for votes on the basis of religious affiliations. Some candidates were disqualified for violating the statute, and Hindu nationalist parties responded by changing the form though not really the substance of their message. Rather than seeking votes on the basis of Hinduism as such, they started to appeal to *Hindutva*, which they presented as a nonreligious cultural tradition consisting in the main of the values associated with Hinduism. Not surprisingly, their opponents sought to disqualify candidates whose programs invoked *Hindutva*. In a series of decisions in the 1980s and 1990s, the Supreme Court distinguished between prohibited appeals to religion and permissible appeals to values associated with specific religions.[36] These decisions placed the BJP on a reasonably firm legal footing. Still, RSS and BJP leaders resented being forced to defend an essentially religious program by misrepresenting it, and felt aggrieved by what they regarded as their repression by secularist elites.

With some but only modest accuracy, they saw the Supreme Court as an institution controlled by those elites. The Supreme Court currently has an authorized membership of 34, though there are almost always vacancies. It necessarily sits in panels, ranging in size from three to seven (and quite rarely somewhat larger). Panels of seven judges are required to decide constitutional claims, but some cases with constitution-like overtones involve, at the formal level, claims about how statutes should be interpreted or about unlawful administrative action. Such cases can be heard by smaller panels. The panel system has resulted in a chaotic and inconsistent body of precedent on nearly every important issue. What the law "is" at any point often depends upon who happened to sit on the most recent panel dealing with the issue.[37]

According to the constitution, judges are named to the court by the president after receiving advice from those already sitting as judges. In form that provision allows the president to take political considerations into account when making

---

[36] For an overview, *see* RONOJOY SEN, LEGALIZING RELIGION: THE INDIAN SUPREME COURT AND SECULARISM (2007), at pp. 29–35.

[37] *See* Nick Robinson, "Judicial Architecture and Capacity," in OXFORD HANDBOOK OF THE INDIAN CONSTITUTION (Sujit Choudry, Madhav Khosla, & Pratap Bhanu Mehta eds. 2016), at pp. 330, 337–40.

appointments. As practice evolved the president lost that ability. The reason appears to be rooted in India's political history. In 1975 Prime Minister Indira Gandhi declared a state of emergency, leading to a two-year period of harsh political repression. The emergency period ended in 1977 when Gandhi called a new election that she unexpectedly lost. Almost immediately thereafter the emergency worked its way into Indian political consciousness as a disaster.

That understanding in turn tarnished the Supreme Court because it had endorsed emergency rule. The conventional story is that the court's justices responded with a series of decisions aimed at rehabilitating the court in the public's eyes.[38] The court developed the field of public interest litigation, in which it actively sought out social problems to address—air pollution in Delhi, the prevalence of "street dwellers" (the homeless)—and offered judicial solutions. India's Constitution contained "directive principles" of policy dealing with social and economic rights, separate from constitutional provisions that were clearly enforceable by the courts. The constitution also contained a judicially enforceable right to life, and the supreme court read social and economic rights into that provision, transforming provisions that might have been merely hortatory into enforceable ones.[39] The court's public interest litigation cases and socioeconomic rights cases occasionally had real effects on the ground, though neither universally nor always large. The decisions did rehabilitate the court, though.

The court's decisions about how judges were to be appointed had similar roots. As the public and the judges saw the history of the emergency, the judges had been too subordinate to the government—too politically accountable. The solution was to reduce that accountability, and the mechanism was to convert the constitutionally required "advice" the judges gave the president into a rule that the president follow that advice to the letter.[40] In effect, the judges were able to choose their own successors.

By the early 2000s the system had reached this point: senior justices on the Supreme Court convened as what was known as the "collegium" and chose "nominees" to fill vacancies on the Supreme Court and state high courts. The collegium was completely opaque, providing no information to the public about who the judges considered or why they chose one rather than another nominee.

---

[38] We note that the conventional story attributes motivations to the court's justices without providing a great deal of evidence to that effect. The most that can be said, we think, is that the conventional story makes sense on its own terms, and that justices who made the relevant decisions haven't spoken out strongly against that story.

[39] These decisions stretched the boundaries of legality, though we believe that they are indeed consistent with the requirement of accountability to law.

[40] The court made this move in a series of cases, each of which placed increasingly stringent limits on the president's power to disregard the advice given, and ultimately made it clear that the president had to nominate the person the judges recommended. For a discussion of the cases, see the essays in APPOINTMENT OF JUDGES TO THE SUPREME COURT OF INDIA: TRANSPARENCY, ACCOUNTABILITY, AND INDEPENDENCE (Arghya Sengupta & Ritwika Sharma eds. 2018).

They did follow one guideline, though: to be named to the Supreme Court a candidate had to be a relatively senior judge on some other court. Coupled with a mandatory retirement age of sixty-five, this guideline meant that Supreme Court justices typically stayed on the court for only six or seven years. The stakes of any specific judicial nomination, then, are relatively low. Overall, though, the court's composition remains rather elitist: judges who serve long enough on state high courts to develop good reputations among legal elites, to the point where they are serious candidates for consideration by the collegium, tend to move in culturally elite and secular circles. This isn't universal, but the collegium's choices incline toward the elite and the secular. And, the collegium is completely unaccountable politically though its behavior—despite its lack of transparency—seems to suggest some degree of sensitivity to the surrounding political environment. That degree of unaccountability may be unique in the world; it certainly is unusual.

The 99th Amendment responded to that situation: a lack of political accountability in the not-terribly-high-stakes choices of mostly elite lawyers to sit on a Supreme Court whose decisions could more or less randomly impair the governing party's ability to carry out its programs. The 99th Amendment replaced the collegium with a judicial nominating commission modeled on those common elsewhere. The commission was to have six members: the chief justice of the Supreme Court and the next two most senior judges (reproducing part of the collegium), the government's minister for law and justice, and two "eminent persons." The latter were to be chosen by a committee consisting of the chief justice, the prime minister, and the leader of the parliamentary opposition. This is not dramatically out of line with practices elsewhere. Though bigger than the collegium, the commission would have been a bit small, especially given India's size. And it was almost guaranteed to have two representatives of the government in power on it, the minister for law and justice and at least one of the eminent persons. Perhaps two members of a six-member commission could dominate its deliberations, in way that they could not on a larger commission.

As we've said, the Supreme Court quickly held the 99th Amendment unconstitutional. It relied upon what's known as the "basic structure doctrine" for identifying unconstitutional constitutional amendments, that is, amendments adopted by procedures fully consistent with the constitution's requirements but are nonetheless impermissible for substantive reasons.[41] First articulated by the Indian Supreme Court in 1973, the basic structure doctrine has become reasonably well accepted around the world.[42]

---

[41] The already classic study of the idea of unconstitutional constitutional amendments is YANIV ROZNAI, UNCONSTITUTIONAL CONSTITUTIONAL AMENDMENTS: THE LIMITS OF AMENDMENT POWERS (2017).

[42] Some courts resist the doctrine, arguing that restricting a people's power to alter the constitution by which they are governed is anti- rather than pro-constitutional.

The doctrine seems quite useful to those who worry that populist or author-itarian governments will be able to amend their nations' constitutions in ways that are inconsistent with normative ideals of constitutionalism: the basic struc-ture consists of the core of those ideals (and occasionally some principles arising from a nation's specific constitutional history). The Indian Supreme Court iden-tifies secularism, federalism, and judicial independence as components of the basic structure. Worldwide the doctrine has been used most often to strike down constitutional amendments because they impair judicial independence.

Judicial independence was the reason the court invoked in holding the 99th Amendment unconstitutional. As with many judgments of the Indian Supreme Court, the precise rationale was unclear.[43] The core idea seems to have been that government appointees would have too much power—or, to put it in our terms, the role of government appointees on the commission would make the judges it chose too politically accountable. We find it hard to evaluate that claim in the abstract. Two out of six isn't a majority, but the dynamics of small committees might indeed give two people acting together too much power—though we're not clear on why that power wouldn't be offset by the coordinated power of the three judges on the commission.

Now we put this Indian case study into our larger story. Does it show how populist governments threaten judicial independence? We offer a firm "Maybe, maybe not" as our answer. Here are what we think are the most important components of the story, in no special order. The Modi government probably put forth the amendment because of a long-standing though not terribly well-founded sense of grievance at a court that had stood in its way; the amendment was probably badly motivated, at least to some degree. The collegium system was and is a terrible mechanism for choosing high court judges because it gives no structural guarantees that the appointment process will include attention to po-litical accountability; the amendment might have been a move in the direction of good government. The commission's size and the role of the two government appointees might be a bit worrisome, especially if there are India-specific factors of which we are unaware that make those two features particularly problematic. And, finally, the amendment had deep cross-party support; it wasn't a project of the Modi government pushing through a questionable policy that no one else thought a good idea.

Tarunabh Khaitan, an astute student of Indian constitutional law, describes the Modi government as inflicting death by a thousand cuts on liberal consti-tutionalism in India.[44] No individual cut is fatal, but taken together they doom

---

[43] For a collection of essays on the Amendment and the Supreme Court's decision, *see* APPOINTMENT OF JUDGES TO THE SUPREME COURT OF INDIA, note 40 above.

[44] Tarunabh Khaitan, *Killing a Constitution with A Thousand Cuts: Executive Aggrandizement and Party-State Fusion in India*, 14 LAW & ETHICS OF HUMAN RIGHTS 49 (2020).

liberal constitutionalism. And, for Khaitan, the 99th Amendment was one of those cuts. We're not quite as sure as he is that it was.[45] Even if he's right, though, we think it important to stress that the amendment matters only because it was part of a package of changes that, taken as a whole, threatens constitutionalism.

In that way the story of the 99th Amendment, even when told by an opponent, fits into the argument we developed in this chapter: you should worry about things like the 99th Amendment only because—and so only when—they are or soon will be accompanied by policies that are unequivocally anti-constitutional.

B. Israel—Changing a Judicial Appointments Commission

Israel provided Ran Hirschl with one of his examples of hegemonic self-preservation: a dominant cultural and political elite foresees the impending end of its political dominance and ramps up the power of constitutional review lodged in courts that it will continue to control because of the difference between political and judicial time. In Israel the contending forces were on one side Ashkenazi Jews of European heritage who were also either rather secular or only moderately observant Jews and on the other, Sephardic Jews of Middle Eastern heritage, highly observant Jews, and recent immigrants from Russia who were almost militantly secularists. For many decades after Israel's founding its politics was dominated by an Ashkenazi elite centered in the socialist-leaning Labor Party. As the nation changed demographically and in part as the result of Israel's control of the Occupied Territories/Judea and Samaria after the 1967 war, Labor was gradually and haltingly replaced by a more conservative and more observant coalition. Its appointees remained lodged in the Supreme Court, though.

Israel doesn't have a single document called its constitution. Instead, it has a number of "Basic Laws" enacted at different times to deal with specific topics that are embedded in other nations' constitutions: a Basic Law on the Knesset (Parliament), for example, adopted in 1958, another on the executive government adopted in 1968, and down through a list of fourteen separate topics. The ordinary parliament enacts Basic Laws, and it can repeal or amend them freely, though ordinarily only by a "qualified" majority—that is, by a majority of the parliament's membership rather than by a majority of a quorum or of those present and voting.

Controversies over how to protect religious freedom in a state whose Proclamation of Independence declared the nation to be Jewish and to observe

---

[45] For present purposes we don't dispute the proposition that the amendment might have some adverse effects on the way judges go about their work even after it has been held unconstitutional. They might treat the amendment's mere adoption as a signal that they should pull back from aggressively supporting liberal constitutionalism, for example.

the fundamental principles of democracy blocked the adoption of Basic Laws dealing with individual rights. Israel's Supreme Court managed to develop a body of quasi-constitutional law about rights anyway. Its most prominent technique was a quite robust version of the ultra vires doctrine. A staple of administrative law, that doctrine says that actions taken by executive officials are unlawful unless they are authorized by legislation.[46] When dealing with actions that in other systems might be treated as unconstitutional infringements on civil liberties, the Supreme Court required that the actions be authorized in quite specific terms by some clear statute.

With this doctrine in hand the Supreme Court came to play a significant role in Israel's overall system of government. The court has fifteen members. They are named to the court by the president, who is the formal head of state with mostly ceremonial functions—and not by the prime minister, who is the head of government. The president acts on nominations presented by a judicial selection committee. Judges serve until they reach the retirement age of seventy. One final part of the background: Aharon Barak. Barak was a brilliant legal scholar who won a major public honor in 1975, when he was thirty-eight years old—the nation's prize for academic excellence. He became attorney general in that year, and was appointed to the Supreme Court in 1978, meaning that he could and did serve for nearly thirty years. He was the court's dominating figure for almost all of that period, largely because he combined brilliance as a lawyer—even his deepest opponents conceded that he was unmatched as a legal thinker—with a powerfully assertive personality.

In 1992 the Basic Law: Human Dignity and Liberty was adopted. Within a few years Barak's Supreme Court declared that that statute worked a "constitutional revolution" by giving the Supreme Court the power to overturn legislation as violating the principles of human dignity and liberty stated in the Basic Law.

As Hirschl argued, this occurred just as the elite that Barak represented was losing political power. Barak was more than a mere lawyer, though; he was an astute politician, and he deployed the power he had in effect created in ways that protected the interests of the formerly dominant elite without openly confronting the new governing coalition on matters that would have torn the coalition apart by denying the government the power to do something an essential coalition member regarded as the thing that kept it in the government.

Barak's Court attempted to implement its vision of what constitutional democracy required in Israel while accommodating the interests of the parties

---

[46] We simplify here for expository purposes. Some executive actions, often associated with foreign policy, lie within a domain of "prerogative power," where executive actions need no legislative authorization. In Israel the domain of prerogative power in connection with national security and the governance of the Occupied Territories/Judea and Samaria is itself a seriously contested constitutional issue.

in the governing conservative coalition. Each decision that simultaneously advanced the old elite's vision while conceding something to the conservatives—whether on national security policy, the role of religious orthodoxy in public life, the status of Arabs who were Israeli citizens—managed incrementally to irritate one after another party in the governing coalition. No specific decision precipitated a crisis, but the new coalition's leaders came to fear that someday the court would thwart it on some policy objective it regarded as central to its program.

Those dissatisfied with the court searched for solutions to the problems they perceived. Repealing the Basic Law: Human Liberty and Dignity was out of the question, mostly for public relations reasons. In 2018 the coalition enacted a new Basic Law: Israel as the Nation State of the Jewish People, hoping that it could serve as a doctrinal counterweight to the Basic Law: Human Liberty and Dignity. The thought appears to have been that the earlier Basic Law was individualistic in orientation, the new one more communally oriented, and that the courts dealing with constitutional challenges would have to take both perspectives into account. Yet, even as the Basic Law: Nation State was being adopted, its supporters worried that the Supreme Court would invoke an Israeli version of the basic structure doctrine to hold it unconstitutional, or interpret it to render it ineffective.

Procedural options were placed on the table. Looking to Canada, the court's opponents proposed that the legislature be given an express power to override Supreme Court decisions (or interpretations of the Basic Law). That proposal didn't get enough political traction.

Proposals to tinker with the judicial selection mechanism did. When the politicians turned their attention to it, the Judicial Selection Committee had nine members: the president of the Supreme Court and two other justices, the minister of justice and another government minister, two members of parliament elected by the parliament (one of whom by tradition was from the political opposition), and two representatives from Israel's bar association. Appointments to the lower courts required a simple majority from the committee, appointments to the Supreme Court a majority of seven. The government had three reliable votes, and you might think that it could regularly pick up enough to get its preferred candidate named. In practice that was impossible. The three judges voted as a bloc. The bar association was controlled by cultural, mostly Ashkenazi, elites. Together with the opposition's representative, they had six votes. The government couldn't appoint its preferred candidates to the lower courts, and both sides could block appointment to the Supreme Court of judges they opposed.[47]

---

[47] In one well-known example, Justice Barak led a group that prevented the nomination of Professor Ruth Gavison, at the time perhaps the nation's most distinguished scholar of constitutional law, because she strongly opposed the direction that Barak had taken on the court. On another occasion the judges blocked the nomination of a candidate strongly favored by the Minister of Justice for what were reputed to be reasons personal to him.

You might think that over time that would lead to a gradual transformation of the Supreme Court—not into an ally of the government, but at least into a body that didn't systematically oppose it. Israeli scholars paint a different picture. Even after a process that seemed to screen out judges strongly allied with or strongly opposed to the traditional elites, the court seemed to maintain its course. While he was a member, Barak seemed able to persuade new arrivals to go along, whether by force of reason or force of personality. Even after he left in 2006, his heirs on the court remained; though they were neither as able nor as dominating as he, they were able to keep new arrivals in line.

Facing this difficulty, the court's opponents tried to change the judicial selection committee. Their core proposals would have increased the number of government representatives on the committee. None were adopted. Changes in the political environment, though, led to changes on the committee that favored the government. The opposition was a coalition and included some conservative parties who were unhappy with the court. The government used its parliamentary majority to choose as the opposition's representative on the committee a member of a conservative party. And the bar association gradually became more diverse, meaning in this context less secular and Askhenazi. Its leaders allied themselves with the minister of justice. This gave the government a majority on the committee, and with it the power to name lower court judges. The Supreme Court remained out of reach for either side. One telling indication is the appointment in 2018 of Alex Stein, a scholar of private law whose views on constitutional law were sufficiently opaque that both those who supported and those who opposed the court's constitutional jurisprudence could project their hopes onto him.

Mordechai Kremnitzer and Yuval Shany, two liberal Israeli scholars, offer this summary:

> The result of the "capture" of the judicial appointments committee by the governing coalition has been the appointment of a large number of judges who are acceptable to the ruling coalition in all judicial instances, including the Supreme Court. . . . [T]he vetting process . . . could result over time in a more compliant court system, less critical of the legislative and executive branches than before.[48]

Kremnitzer and Shany compare these developments, along with others, with those in Hungary and Poland: "All three countries appear to gravitate toward

---

[48] Mordechai Kremnitzer & Yuval Shany, *Illiberal Measures in Backsliding Democracies: Differences and Similarities between Recent Developments in Israel, Hungary, and Poland*, 14 LAW & ETHICS OF HUMAN RIGHTS 125 (2020), at pp. 141–42.

more nationalistic policies, and to adopt, at least in part, a populist discourse to justify specific illiberal measures, which . . . weaken traditional democratic checks and balances."[49] Noting that much less had actually been accomplished in Israel than in Hungary and Poland, Kremnitzer and Shany nonetheless conclude that "at least part of the story is the pursuit of an illiberal agenda, aimed against all independent gatekeepers, representing a rejection of traditionally liberal notions of checks and balances."[50] We emphasize here the form this concern takes. Kremnitzer and Shany acknowledge that "Israel[i] judges still enjoy full independence."[51] Changes in the judicial selection process might have been described as tweaks aimed at increasing slightly judges' political accountability at the appointment stage without affecting their independence when they decide cases. But, seeing these changes in the light cast by other policies, Kremnitzer and Shany worry. They see developments in Israel as Khaitan saw developments in India—the judicial reforms were one of a thousand cuts threatening constitutionalism. We think, as before, that the other policies—ones that are illiberal on the merits—are doing the work here, and that modest changes in judicial selection processes to increase political accountability aren't in themselves illiberal.

C. Coda—Packing or Rebalancing the Courts in the United States

U.S. Supreme Court Justice Ruth Bader Ginsburg died on September 18, 2020, in the middle of that year's presidential campaign. Having made appointments to the federal courts a central feature of the Donald Trump administration, Republicans rushed to fill the seat before the election. Nothing in the text of the Constitution barred them from doing so. Democrats pointed to what Republicans controlling the Senate had done in 2016, when Supreme Court Justice Antonin Scalia died in February: although President Barack Obama nominated Judge Merrick Garland to fill the vacant seat, Republicans held neither a hearing nor a vote on the nomination. They asserted that, with a new president taking office (and possibly a Republican one), the American people should be heard in November, when the election occurred, before the vacancy was filled. In 2020 Democrats called the Republicans hypocrites. Republicans responded that the cases differed in several ways: President Donald Trump was running for reelection and could be punished for making a bad choice; when the Senate and the presidency were controlled by different parties, the Senate had no constitutional

---

49 *Id.* at p. 149.
50 *Id.* at p. 152.
51 *Id.* at p. 141.

obligation to take up a nomination, but when they were controlled by the same party they could do so, no matter when the nomination occurred; and, probably most honestly, that the only thing that mattered was sheer political power—Republicans had the votes to confirm the appointment, and that was enough. They argued, in short, that what they had done occurred in the regular course because in the United States the Constitution's text alone determines what was regular.

As Republicans moved forward, Democrats began to propose Supreme Court reform. The most popular was placing limits on the terms justices could serve. Surveys showed that term limits had great popular support across party lines. The difficulty from a political point of view is that term limits couldn't be adopted without amending the Constitution—or, perhaps, by enacting a statute that wouldn't have any immediate payoff because only new justices, not the current ones, would have limited terms.

Other proposals floated to the surface. The one that attracted the most attention was expanding the number of justices on the Supreme Court—Court expansion to the mild-mannered, Court-packing to the more candid.[52] The politics were clear. From the Democrats' perspective, in 2021 the Court "should" have had five justices nominated by Democratic presidents—Garland and a replacement for Justice Ginsburg, as well as three already on the court—and four nominated by Republican ones, but it actually had six nominated by Republicans and three by Democrats. "Restoring" the one-vote margin required adding four new justices to create a seven-to-six division.

To support court expansion Democrats developed a counter-narrative: "We're not packing the Court. Republicans have done that through their actions on the two vacancies they filled recently. We're simply balancing the Court so that its composition more accurately reflects what's been happening in politics."[53] They pointed out, for example, that Republican presidents had nominated fifteen of the most recent nineteen justices named to the Court despite the fact that the presidency had more or less regularly rotated between Republicans and Democrats. And, from the Democrats' perspective, the Republican leader of the Senate gave the game away when he said, "A lot of what we've done over the last four years will be undone sooner or later by the next election. They won't be able

---

[52] Disclosure: Tushnet was the chair of the advisory committee of one of the leading lobbying groups favoring court expansion.

[53] For a version of this argument, *see* Duncan Kennedy, "Authoritarian Constitutionalism in Liberal Democracies," in AUTHORITARIAN CONSTITUTIONALISM (Helena Alviar & Günter Frankenburg eds. 2019), at p. 184: "When I agree with a frustrated majority, and when the consequences of the exercise of judicial review are plausibly very dire, and when the specific court packing plan is sufficiently careful to avoid collateral harm, then I am in favor of a dramatic intervention, at the expense of judicial independence and the separation of powers, to 'save the Republic'" (emphasis deleted).

to do much about this for a long time to come." Court expansion was something they could "do about this."

The lines were clearly drawn. Democrats charged Republicans with breaching norms about filling vacancies and asserted that Congress had the power to determine the Court's size. Republicans asserted that the president and Senate had the power to process nominations whenever they occurred and charged Democrats with breaching a norm that you shouldn't pack the Court merely to ensure that your side would win more cases.

The Republican argument about norms rested on the failure in 1937 of Franklin Roosevelt's proposal to expand the Supreme Court. According to one narrative that failure established or confirmed the existence of a norm against court-packing. The norm made sense, on this narrative, because court-packing invited increasing rounds of retaliation: "You name four; when we get a chance we'll see that and raise you two new justices," and on and on until the court had fifty-seven members (the number was drawn from an old advertising campaign about the varieties of catsup offered by a leading retailer). With members clearly chosen solely to advance partisan ends, the Court would lose the legitimacy it had gained by appearing to be above politics.[54]

Everyone knew that a fight over the Court's size would be difficult. Another lesson drawn by some from the 1937 fight was that it weakened Roosevelt permanently so that he couldn't get Congress to adopt much of his substantive agenda afterwards. Similarly, court expansion would take time and political energy that might better be devoted to enacting substantive statutes, even ones that the Republican-dominated Court might eventually strike down. To the extent that Democrats thought all this through, some might have said, "Well, they can't strike down everything we do."

This episode is interesting to us for several reasons. It illustrates how arguments over norms and guardrails develop. Democrats and Republicans offered competing characterizations of the applicable norms, and each characterization fit the facts. At the moment of controversy the choice between characterizations was made—and probably could only be made—on the basis of partisanship, what we have called a political judgment.[55] If we're correct, the thought that

---

[54] We note, for what it's worth, that a recent study of "curbing the Court" finds that the U.S. public is "weakly principled," that is, is committed to constitutional rights and institutions in the abstract but accepts "restrictions" at the level of specification. BRANDON L. BARTELS & CHRISTOPHER D. JOHNSON, CURBING THE COURT: WHY THE PUBLIC CONSTRAINS JUDICIAL INDEPENDENCE (2021), at pp. 36–43. This suggests that the "legitimacy risk" associated with changes in the court's structure may be smaller than is sometimes suggested.

[55] We include the qualification "at the moment of controversy" because we think it possible that over time participants in the political system might come to a reasonably stable agreement about what the correct characterization should have been—although we're reasonably confident that such an agreement could be easily destabilized were political circumstances such that one side found it politically useful to do so.

constitutionalism can be sustained against serious political challenges only be-cause of norms and guardrails would come under real pressure: the substantive political challenges would be accompanied by recharacterizations of the norms and guardrails that are supposed to hold the challengers in check.[56]

The episode also illustrates the disjuncture between political time and judi-cial time. Comparing the timing of judicial nominations with the alternation of Republican and Democratic presidencies gives a map of that disjuncture. It allows us to try to distinguish between fine-tuning and smashing in somewhat neutral terms, "When is judicial reform to align political and judicial time more closely a 'mere' rebalancing of judicial independence and accountability to law with political accountability, and when does it go so far as to threaten the former values by placing too much weight on the latter?"

As we write, the U.S. experience with court reform/expansion/packing remains inconclusive. We offer observations from two slightly different perspectives about how those interested in constitutionalism should think about the episode.

- Suppose you hold a thick version of constitutionalism, and you expect that the Supreme Court over the next period of judicial time—a few years, a decade, or more—will also hold a thick version. If you expect that you and the court will have the same thick version, everything's fine.

    If you think that your thick version is likely to differ from the court's, you have to ask yourself, "How serious will the bad effects on public policy be when the Court invokes its thick version to block the implementation of policies that, according to my thick version, should be allowed to go for-ward?" If you think the bad effects will be serious, you might want to con-sider doing something about the Court. This is what we've regularly called a political judgment on the merits.

    But, you should next ask yourself, "Does this reform threaten to do more than bring judicial time into closer alignment with political time? Would the new balance tilt too far against independence?" The answer to that second question will also have to take dynamic effects into account. As we've noted, sometimes we worry about judicial reforms because we think they're likely to ease the way to more substantive policy changes that are themselves normatively problematic. As the U.S. discussions show, we also have to worry about reforms if they're likely to generate subsequent court-oriented changes that overall will make the courts too politically accountable.

- The perspective from thin constitutionalism is simpler. Thick versions of constitutionalism, no matter what their content, are going to block the

---

[56] For additional discussion, see Chapter 10.

implementation of policies that thin constitutionalism says should be made according to majority rule. So, the only relevant question is about the new balance between judicial independence and political accountability, supplemented by the narrow question about the dynamic effect of this reform on later court-oriented reforms. These questions, we think, can generally be answered without referring to any matters of substantive policy.

***

So, once again: Context matters. Details matter. And, most important, intent matters. You can't tell whether a policy that affects what courts can do, or who the judges are, is an assault on judicial independence (smashing)—or, instead, is a minor adjustment in the balance between judicial independence and accountability to law, and political accountability (fine-tuning)—without making some judgment about what *else* the people proposing the policy want to do. Maybe it's easy to do that most of the time. These policies might regularly travel with others that are independently troublesome, and even if you don't immediately see the troublesome ones at hand, you might worry that the court-related policies are an early-warning signal about what's likely to come next. And, as we've suggested, the political logic underlying the proposals suggests that there's *something* down the line that would be easier to enact if the court-related changes were already in place. That might make it sensible to be suspicious of the proposals, at least if you don't know much else about what the people pushing them want to do.

Sometimes, though, you'll have a pretty good idea about what comes next. If you do, and it's innocuous, you shouldn't get up in arms about the court-related proposals. You might disagree with them, thinking for example that whatever's in place is working well enough. But, in the end, when you don't worry about what else is on the line, what's at stake are tweaks, not threats to even the thinnest of constitutionalisms.

Thin constitutionalism encompasses a rather wide range of arrangements to promote judicial independence, accountability to law, and accountability to politics. Changing from one arrangement within that range to another isn't a threat to thin constitutionalism in itself. What matters is whether the change is designed to make it easier for the government to adopt bad policies. And so, you can't escape making a political judgment—not about the value of judicial independence, but about the government's other policies.

9

Populism and Executive Power: Term Limits and Rule by Decree

Even thin constitutionalism stops governments from doing everything they might want right away; that's its point. Political leaders everywhere sometimes get impatient when they find themselves thwarted. As we saw in Chapter 8, sometimes they try to push aside whatever's standing in their way (there, the courts). Sometimes they say they need more time and ask voters to give them another term. And sometimes, if they can't run again because they've reached the limit the constitution puts on their terms, they'll try to amend the constitution. What's distinctive about recent times is that impatient chief executives seem to worry about the constitution.

Chief executives can get impatient with legislatures, too—sometimes, even legislatures that they control. Why take the time to get a new statute passed when you can simply rule by executive decree? Here too the constitution matters. These chief executives will look around for legal authority to do what they want. A constitutional provision might allow the executive to rule by decree in an emergency or a statute might delegate lawmaking authority to the chief executive in some field. Impatient chief executives will ask their lawyers to supply them with creative interpretations of such constitutional and statutory provisions.

Like every other government, populist governments advance their programs through a combination of legislation and executive action. And, as can be seen around the world, over the past decades, executive leaders, whether designated as president or prime ministers, have gradually accumulated lawmaking power.[1] Populist governments are no different. This chapter examines two aspects of how populists (and some others) deal with the power of the chief executive—how long he should serve, and how much lawmaking authority should he have. By this point our conclusion shouldn't be surprising: whether assertions of executive power by populists are troubling depends primarily upon the merits of the populist program, with the formalities of term length and rule by decree at most a matter of marginal concern.

---

[1] For an introduction to the literature on parliamentary systems, *see* Christian Elmelund-Præstekær & Ulrik Kjaer, *Presidentialisation of Parliamentary Systems? Frontrunner Concentration in Danish Local Elections*, 49 REPRESENTATION 155 (2013), at pp. 155–57.

Power to the People. Mark Tushnet and Bojan Bugarič, Oxford University Press. © Mark Tushnet and Bojan Bugarič 2021. DOI: 10.1093/oso/9780197606711.003.0010

I. How Executive Power Grows

We began this chapter by saying that authoritarians love expansive executive power. It's a commonplace, though, that *every* chief executive would like to have more power.[2] Take the United States. In a classic article, then-Professor Elena Kagan described the rise of "presidential administration" in the United States during the presidencies of George H.W. Bush and Bill Clinton, neither authoritarians nor populist leaders.[3] Presidential administration is the absorption of policymaking power in the White House even though it is formally lodged elsewhere in the government—in short, an expansion of executive power.

Political scientist Will Freeman usefully describes the "institutional strategies" by which chief executives can do so: colonization, duplication, and evasion.[4]

- They colonize other institutions by placing loyalists in them. Sometimes this occurs in the ordinary course: a judge's term expires, and a loyalist is appointed. Sometimes it occurs somewhat irregularly: a judge is encouraged to retire with an attractive retirement package—or by making continued service uncomfortable by reducing the staff the judge can use. And sometimes colonization occurs quite irregularly, as we discussed in connection with court-packing and court-trimming.

- They duplicate institutions by creating new ones that absorb the work done by institutions relegated to the sidelines. Freeman points to the displacement of local governments in Hungary. Fidesz faced its strongest opposition in the nation's largest cities, including the capital Budapest. Early Fidesz legislation transferred power to administer social services from cities to regional governments and the national government. After the opposition won the Budapest mayoral election in in 2019, the national government dramatically reduced its budget.[5]

- And they evade other institutions by taking advantage of gaps in statutes governing oversight and similar mechanisms designed to limit executive power. Where the statutes don't clearly specify which institution gets

---

[2] That proposition is at the heart of the standard public-choice analysis of executive power. *See, e.g.,* WILLIAM A. NISKANEN, BUREAUCRACY AND PUBLIC ECONOMICS (1971) (arguing that bureaucrats seek to increase their budgets and their power).

[3] Elena Kagan, *Presidential Administration*, 114 HARVARD LAW REVIEW 2245 (2001).

[4] Will Freeman, *Sidestepping the Constitution: Executive Aggrandizement in Latin America and East Central Europe*, 6 CONSTITUTIONAL STUDIES 35 (2020).

[5] See "Hungary's 2021 budget seen as bleeding opposition-led local governments," THE MAYOR. EU, July 4, 2020, available at https://www.themayor.eu/en/hungarys-2021-budget-seen-as-bleeding-opposition-led-local-governments, archived at https://perma.cc/2VTD-7G7P.

to audit the executive, for example, the government chooses to go to the one it thinks it already controls. Freeman points to the creation of "little Congresses" in Venezuela and Ecuador as new constitutions were in the process of being implemented. As many constitutions do, the new ones had provisions dealing with how to govern during the transition from old to new. These provisions were unclear on the breadth of the transitional legislatures' powers, and the legislatures exploited the ambiguity to put in place regulations that permanently enhanced executive power; in Ecuador, for example, the "little Congress" gave Correa the power to control the Central Bank.[6]

Freeman discusses these techniques in the context of democratic decline, with some references to populism specifically. We think it important to stress, though, that chief executives everywhere use the techniques. Franklin Roosevelt created a nationally administered public works program that bypassed local politicians, for example—a form of duplication because historically public works had been built by local authorities sometimes using money provided in part by the national government. Margaret Thatcher restructured the government of the Greater London Council because it was controlled by the Labour Party—another form of duplication.[7] And every U.S. president inserts party loyalists into the bureaucracy, sometimes using and sometimes bypassing regular civil service rules—a form of colonization. The connection between populism and authoritarianism and executive aggrandizement, to use another of Freeman's terms, requires, as we have regularly emphasized, attention to context and detail. This is especially true when contemplating mechanisms to limit the use of these techniques because such mechanisms might do some good where democratic decline looms and do some harm where it doesn't. Or, once again to repeat one of our themes, we can't analyze "executive aggrandizement" in the abstract; we have to analyze it with reference to the regime in which it occurs—which is to say, we have to make a political judgment about the merits of the regime's programs.

---

[6] Freeman, note 4 above, at pp. 46–48. Because the transitional provisions were obviously ambiguous, the actions taken under them were at least arguably lawful. Freeman notes that sometimes evasion by exploiting ambiguities in transitional provisions ends when the transition is completed, but that can take years. (He offers the example of an interim constitutional court in Ecuador, which lasted from 2008 to 2012.)

[7] The Thatcher government did the same for other county councils in major urban areas, for similar political reasons.

II. Presidential Term Limits, Populism, and Thin Constitutionalism

A. Preliminaries

We have to clear out a fair amount of underbrush before we can take up the central problems posed by presidential term limits for populist leaders. The first piece of underbrush is so obvious that we're almost embarrassed to make it explicit. The question of term limits applies only in presidential systems. Viktor Orbán, a populist prime minister, doesn't have to worry about term limits; he can be prime minister as long as he has the support of his party (and, of course, continues to win elections). Similarly with Jarosław Kaczyński, who isn't even prime minister. If even thick versions of constitutionalism can put up with prime ministers who can serve for a term that's not limited by the constitution, it's not clear why constitutionalism can't put up with presidents who do so.[8]

Examining presidential systems, we do see something like an international consensus, embedded in national constitutions, that presidents should be allowed to serve no more than two terms of no more than somewhere between four and six years. Should we treat that consensus as a component of thin constitutionalism? Doing so does bump up against an implication from the basic idea of majority rule. As Alexander Hamilton put it, term limits are inconsistent with the fundamental principle that "the people should choose whom they please to govern them."[9] We proceed on the assumption that a two-term limit on a presidency is required by thin constitutionalism. We also assume, though, that the requirement is a rather weak one because of Hamilton's principle,

---

[8] The obvious answer is that prime ministers' terms are limited in practice by the internal politics of their parties, whereas presidents can serve unlimited terms by appealing beyond their party to the public. We're not sure that that answer is entirely satisfactory. In South Africa, for example, the nation's president has to have the support of the dominant African National Congress, and Jacob Zuma was forced out of the presidency when he lost his position as party leader. But, for our purposes, we're willing to accept the proposition that thin constitutionalism *might* rule out a system in which presidents can serve for an unlimited number of terms but allow systems in which prime ministers can serve without facing any constitutionally prescribed time limit.

[9] Hamilton made the statement in the New York debates over ratifying the Constitution. *See* 2 DEBATES ON THE ADOPTION OF THE FEDERAL CONSTITUTION 257 (J. Elliot ed. 1863), quoted in U.S. Term Limits v. Thornton, 514 U.S. 779, 793 (1995). Constitutional courts in Costa Rica, Honduras, Nicaragua, and Bolivia accepted a version of this argument in holding presidential term limits unconstitutional. We discuss the Bolivian case below. For a general discussion, *see* David Landau, *Presidential Term Limits in Latin America: A Critical Analysis of the Migration of the Unconstitutional Constitutional Amendment Doctrine*, 12 LAW & ETHICS OF HUMAN RIGHTS 225 (2018), at pp. 239–44. In 2018 the Venice Commission, a body of experts associated with the Council of Europe issued a report saying that presidential re-election was not a fundamental human right of either the candidate or voters. Study No. 908/2017, Mar. 20, 2018, available at https://www.venice.coe.int/webforms/documents/default.aspx?pdffile=CDL-AD(2018)010-e, archived at https://perma.cc/4AUV-4TKM. As we write, the Interamerican Court of Human Rights is considering whether limitations on presidential re-election violate the Interamerican Convention on Human Rights.

meaning that it can be overridden for good reasons themselves grounded in thin constitutionalism.[10]

Another preliminary: Professor Mila Versteeg, with a number of co-authors, has shown that eliminating term limits is only one of several techniques that leaders can use to prolong their rule.[11] A term-limited president can step down, only to be replaced by his or her spouse or by someone the president expects to be a loyal successor/puppet. Term-limited presidents can get compliant constitutional courts to interpret the term-limits provision as inapplicable to their precise situation. (One version: the term limit was imposed during the president's current term, and that term shouldn't be counted against the term limit.) Of course, such presidents can try to get a constitutional amendment eliminating the term limit.[12] In the limit, they can invoke Hamilton's principle to obtain a holding that the term limit is unconstitutional.

None of these techniques is a guaranteed winner. Our case study of Ecuador, for example, shows that someone the president thinks of as a reliable puppet can turn out to be a politician with his own mind. We point out the existence of these techniques only to show that focusing on term limits alone might lead people to overlook the larger picture and, in particular, to pay attention only to efforts by populist leaders to eliminate term limits while ignoring functionally equivalent efforts by non-populist proto-authoritarians.

Finally, we connect the term-limit issue with one inessential but frequent component of populism. In Chapter 2 we discussed the proposition that populism typically involves a charismatic leader. We discounted that claim, but we acknowledged that sometimes populism did involve such a leader. Populisms with charismatic leaders are of course prime candidates for efforts to eliminate presidential term limits.[13]

B. The Political Logic of Eliminating Term Limits

Before we lay out the political logic underlying efforts to eliminate term limits, we sketch the political logic supporting such limits. The Colombian constitutional court explained that logic well. Colombia's 1991 constitution limited a

---

[10] The political logic we describe below provides an example—perhaps the only example—of what might count as a good reason of this sort.

[11] Mila Versteeg et al., *The Law and Politics of Presidential Term Limit Evasion*, 120 COLUMBIA LAW REVIEW 173 (2020).

[12] As we discuss later, doing so risks a holding by the constitutional court that the new provision is an unconstitutional amendment inconsistent with the constitution's basic structure.

[13] *See* David Landau, *Personalism and the Trajectories of Populist Constitutions*, 16 ANNUAL REVIEW OF LAW & SOCIAL SCIENCES 293 (2020) (analyzing this question with respect to the Latin American cases we discuss below).

president to a single four-year term. In 2004 President Álvaro Uribe succeeded in obtaining a constitutional amendment that would allow him to run for a second term. The constitutional court upheld the amendment. As his second term neared its conclusion Uribe proposed another constitutional amendment, this one to allow him to run for a third term. This time the constitutional court said no, preventing a referendum on Uribe's proposal.

The court's basic argument was that a president in office for twelve years could get control over essentially all the components of the government and use them to make it effectively impossible to throw him out of office in a fair election.[14] The easiest example involves control of the nation's election management office. The long-term president might come up with rules for running an election—defining district boundaries (gerrymandering), rules for getting candidates and parties on the ballot, procedures for counting disputed votes—that would prevent opposition candidates from winning elections. And the election commission with members the long-term president appointed would rubber-stamp these unfair rules.

The problem with a long-term presidency goes beyond government institutions and extends to voters as well. The concern about voters is what Professor Samuel Issacharoff calls "clientelism."[15] The idea is that a government in power can adopt policies that benefit many voters. That's a good thing from the voters' point of view. It leads them to support the president's re-election so that these good things continue to arrive. There's an underside, though. A president can control the distribution of these things, placing his or her flunkies in control of getting the goods to the voters. And those flunkies often have some discretion about how to distribute the good things. They can reward the president's supporters with good public housing units and punish opponents with bad ones; they can get food packages to supporters more quickly than to opponents. Voters become dependents upon the president's party and will vote to re-elect the president indefinitely out of fear that opposing the president will make the good things go away. Clientelism is another way of making elections less than fair.[16]

---

[14] See Miriam Kornblith, *Latin America's Authoritarian Drift: Chavismo After Chávez?*, 24 JOURNAL OF DEMOCRACY 47 (2013), at p. 49 (citing a source calling this a "hyper-incumbency advantage").

[15] SAMUEL ISSACHAROFF, UNMOORED: POPULISM AND THE CORRUPTION OF DEMOCRACY (forthcoming 2022).

[16] Issacharoff recognizes that it's not always easy to distinguish between programs that are simply good things for voters, who reward the government for doing good, and programs that create dependent clients. Consider here universal grants to the needy—family allowances, provision of specific goods such as milk or, in one of Issacharoff's examples, television sets. Issacharoff draws his examples from Brazil and Argentina, and treats some (the one dealing with televisions and another dealing with meat) as creating clientelism, while acknowledging that others are simply public policies that give recipients reasons to vote for the incumbent. We're not as sure as Issacharoff appears to be that this line can be drawn at all easily. Anthony Hall, *The Last Shall Be First: Political Dimensions of Conditional Cash Transfers in Brazil*, 11 JOURNAL OF POLICY PRACTICE 25 (2012), treats Brazil's family allowance, the *bolsa familia*, as creating a risk of clientelism (and as unsustainable in the long run).

So, there's reason to worry that presidential systems without term limits might end up with elections that aren't reasonably free and fair. Term limits might be required by thin constitutionalism.

There's a competing political logic, though.[17] It's quite similar to the one we described in discussing judicial changes in Chapter 8. Here as there it begins with a president taking office with an ambitious reform agenda. Term limits define political time for the president. Suppose the president has at most eight years in office. He or she wants to get as much of the policy agenda as possible adopted before leaving office. Now add to the political context the possibility that the president's policy agenda faces quite substantial opposition from those he or she defeated. At some point during the president's political time the president will assess how well or badly things are going. Maybe the president concludes that it's going to take more than eight years to get some really important part of the agenda adopted, given the strength of the opposition it faces.[18] The president might then think that lifting the term limit would be a useful, maybe even an essential tool to ensure that the agenda is implemented.

This political logic explains why lifting a presidential term limit might be a "good government" move—something that will allow a winning party do what it was elected to do. The story comes with a lot of conditions: an ambitious political agenda, concerted opposition that slows down the agenda's progress, and, notably, a president who isn't trying to enhance his or her personal power.

That final condition is obviously important. We can incorporate into the political logic, but doing so is like Euclid's parallel postulate: You can include it if you want, but it could be excluded without damage to the basic story. Here's how it goes: the final component of the political logic is that the president (or the president's party) concludes not only that the party needs to stay in office for more than eight years to carry out its program, but also that the specific individual who is president has to remain president for the entire period. Why not let the party choose a reliable successor? Maybe—and here the argument gets pretty thin—it's worried that any successor won't be as reliable as the person who led the party to victory, or it thinks that the president in place has special political skills in assembling and holding together a coalition, skills that others in the party lack. And, because you're writing something into the constitution, you have to think either that even after this particular president passes from the scene the next one will have the special bundle of skills (hard to believe, we suspect)

---

[17] John M. Carey, *The Reelection Debate in Latin America.* 45 LATIN AMERICAN POLITICS & SOCIETY 119 (2003), at p. 131, describes this logic as one about "lengthen[ing] the president's time horizon...."

[18] That opposition might be able to use veto gates or speed bumps to slow down the progress of the president's agenda, for example.

or—more likely—that you'll immediately amend the constitution to impose a term limit after the president leaves office.

We now provide case studies of Ecuador and Bolivia to illustrate when populist presidents might actually have been acting according to this political logic, and one (Venezuela) illustrating a president who probably was interested mostly in increasing his personal power. In each one we very briefly describe the economic and social background against which populism emerged, then turn to the constitutional developments that are our primary concern. As always, the details of the case studies show how complicated it is to associate populism as such with an unjustifiable attack on presidential term limits.

C. Case Studies

1. Ecuador

Ecuador in the late twentieth century was a democracy with enormous political instability. Presidents came and went without regard to the normal election calendar. Policy resulted from bargains struck by a small number of people who saw themselves as representing larger economic and social groupings without however actually having to do much to account to those groups for their actions.[19] Political instability mirrored economic instability. Ecuador's economy boomed and collapsed depending on the price of oil. High oil prices fueled economic growth but also inflation. Even when the economy as a whole was doing well, inequality persisted, with the nation's indigenous peoples in particular being left behind as their land was exploited. Some degree of economic stability was restored after austerity policies were adopted and the Ecuadorian currency tied to the U.S. dollar in 2000.

Left-leaning presidents had occasionally been elected in the 1990s, but they hadn't achieved much. An economist with a doctorate from the University of Illinois, Rafael Correa campaigned for the presidency in 2006 as a leftist, on a platform promising extensive new initiatives to deal with the economy, land reform, and ties with the United States (to be weakened) and other left-leaning Latin American countries (to be strengthened). Capitalizing on public concern about corruption, Correa also supported the idea that a constituent assembly should draft a new constitution. Acknowledging both the scope of his program and the resistance he thought it would face, after his election Correa said, "We won the elections, but not power," which remained with the banks and economic interests.[20]

---

[19] That is our informal description of what political scientists label Latin American corporatism.

[20] Quoted in Catherine M. Conaghan, *Ecuador: Correa's Plebiscitary Presidency*, 19 JOURNAL OF DEMOCRACY 46 (2008), at p. 47.

Correa made some progress with his agenda on all fronts, facing down a coup attempt in 2010 by the national police. His government "made important investments in education, health care, and infrastructure."[21] Correa pressured the opposition-controlled Congress into approving a referendum to convene a constituent assembly. That assembly produced a new constitution and, in the meantime, converted itself into a governing legislature along lines laid out in Venezuela in 1999.

Almost everything about the process was constitutionally messy. As the existing constitution required, the national legislature approved a proposal for a referendum on convening the constituent assembly. Before the referendum occurred, the proposal to be put on the ballot was changed so that the constituent assembly could act as an interim legislature if it chose. The election management body approved the change. In response, the legislature moved to impeach the election commission's chair. The commission, in turn, removed fifty-seven members of the legislature for attempting to interfere with an election. With new members replacing the "removed" members, the parliament then supported the referendum's revised scope. The constitutional court voted to reinstate most of the removed legislators, whereupon the reconstituted legislature voted to impeach the entire constitutional court for acting unconstitutionally.[22]

Meanwhile the referendum campaign was proceeding. In April 2007 voters approved holding a constituent assembly by a roughly 80 percent majority, and in September Correa's party won about 60 percent of the seats in the constituent assembly. A new constitution was put to the voters in September 2008, and received support from about two-thirds of the electorate.

The new constitution was innovative along many dimensions. It had an eloquent Preamble, including a commitment to "nature (Pacha Mama)," an extensive enumeration of social and economic rights characterized as "rights of the good way of living," rights for indigenous communities, a commitment to direct democracy, and a "transparency and social control branch" that in form at least built into the structure of government widespread participation by nongovernmental organizations and ordinary people.[23]

The new constitution limited the president to two four-year terms. Correa had taken office in 2007, but he took the position, ultimately validated by the

[21] John Polga-Hecimovich, "Constitutional Change in Ecuador Improving Democratic Accountability—and Constraining a Rival," CONSTITUTIONNET, Mar. 31, 2018, available at http://constitutionnet.org/news/constitutional-change-ecuador-improving-democratic-accountability-and-constraining-rival, archived at https://perma.cc/U5WW-VC6F.

[22] For the details, see Conaghan, note 20 above, at p. 52.

[23] Polga-Hecimovich, note 21 above, describes this branch somewhat tendentiously as "an unelected executive body that . . . usurped authority from the National Assembly." Article 207 of the 2008 Constitution provided for one of the components of this branch, "The selection of council persons shall be done from among candidates proposed by social organizations and the citizenry. The selection process shall be organized by the National Electoral Council, which will conduct the competitive

constitutional court, that the new constitution started the clock again. He ran for "re"-election under the new constitution in 2009, winning 52 percent of the vote. Symbolically, his inauguration was attended by other Latin American leftist leaders—Cristina Kirchner of Argentina; Evo Morales of Bolivia; Hugo Chávez of Venezuela; and, strikingly, Raúl Castro of Cuba. Correa ran again in 2013 (his third term by the calendar, his second under the 2009 constitution), increasing his victory margin to 57 percent.

After that Correa's popularity began to decline, although he remained the dominant figure in the nation's politics and also retained substantial popular support, which he both elicited and enhanced by routinely "going to the people" with referendums. His inability to disconnect Ecuador's currency from the U.S. dollar was a persistent problem, as were continuing conflicts over the exploitation of natural resources on indigenous lands.

In 2015 Correa proposed yet another change in the constitution—removing the limitation on presidential terms. Not surprisingly he invoked Hamilton's principle. Eventually the national legislature approved the amendment, but to obtain its passage Correa had to pledge not to run for a third term in 2017 while reserving his right to do so in 2021.[24]

Correa chose his vice president Lenin Moreno as his successor. Moreno narrowly won the presidency in 2017, and almost immediately turned upon his mentor. Moreno supported constitutional amendments, adopted in 2018, to undo many of Correa's constitutional revisions. The most important restored the two-term limit; another hollowed out the 2009 constitution's innovative "social control" mechanisms (the CCPSC), allowing Moreno to appoint new members.

The reconstituted social-control institution replaced Correa-appointed officials, including all the justices on the constitutional court. Elections followed in which Correa's supporters won seats on the CCPSC. They tried to reverse some of the removals, whereupon Moreno's allies in the legislature voted to remove the Correa supporters from the CCPSC.[25]

Correa campaigned against Moreno's proposals and then moved to Belgium, his wife's home nation, avoiding prosecution on corruption charges that were almost certainly politically motivated but that might have been well-founded

---

and merit-based public examination process, with submittal of candidacies, subject to citizen oversight and challenge in accordance with the law."

[24] For a useful analysis of these developments, see Carolina Silva-Portero, "Chronicle of an Amendment Foretold: Eliminating Presidential Term Limits in Ecuador," CONSTITUTIONNET, Jan. 20, 2016, available at http://constitutionnet.org/news/chronicle-amendment-foretold-eliminating-presidential-term-limits-ecuador, archived at https://perma.cc/L3XL-UH29.

[25] For the details, see Freeman, note 4 above, at pp. 51–53.

even so. The party that had once housed both Correa and Moreno split, with the former opposition parties now allied with the Moreno remnant.[26]

What does this story tell us about populism and presidential term limits? We've elided many details about the Ecuadorian constitutional processes, but even the sketch we provide shows a fair amount.

- Ecuador almost certainly had a more democratic system of governance during the Correa years than it had had before, but it probably had a somewhat less liberal system, without the Correa government limiting the opposition's ability to mobilize support, as shown by the fact that he was ultimately "forced" out of office because of popular opposition.[27] The government's policies produced significant economic growth, though the economy remained vulnerable to fluctuations in world oil prices. The policies also produced a significant decrease in economic inequality.

- Correa, who fits the description of charismatic populist leaders reasonably well,[28] did indeed try to transform the constitution in a way that would have allowed him to remain president indefinitely. He may have done so out of a quest for personal power, but neither we nor the sources we've consulted can rule out the possibility that he wanted to extend his term because of the political logic we've described: he did have an ambitious reform agenda, it seemed to remain politically popular as shown by Moreno's election on the same platform, it was only partly implemented when Correa faced the limits of political time, and Correa's promise not to run in 2017 suggests that he was concerned at least as much for the reform agenda as he was with personal political power.

- He didn't succeed notwithstanding his continuing popularity because he wasn't able to control his political coalition. He had to promise his own supporters in the legislature that he wouldn't run in 2017. He expected that Moreno would continue to push the reforms Correa favored, and that he could return to power in 2021 to continue pursuing the agenda.

---

[26] For these and related developments, *see* Jonas Wolff, *Ecuador after Correa: The Struggle over the "Citizens' Revolution,"* 39 REVISTA DE CIENCIA POLITICA 281 (2018).

[27] One can find in the literature the view that Correa's rule might lead to "the slow death of democracy," written as events were unfolding, but we believe that seeing the events as a whole leads to a different conclusion. *See, e.g.,* Carlos de la Torre & Andrés Ortiz Lemos, *Populist Polarization and the Slow Death of Democracy in Ecuador,* 23 DEMOCRATIZATION 221 (2016).

[28] Conaghan refers to him in the first years of his presidency as "charismatic and highly popular." Conaghan, note 20 above, at p. 46.

- He tried to work around his pledge by choosing Moreno as a "puppet" successor. That failed when Moreno decided to strike out on his own political path.[29]
- Takis Pappas describes Ecuador as a case where Moreno led a "transition[] from populist to liberal rule."[30] We think it worth at least entertaining the possibility that Correa's populism was not so deeply inconsistent with liberalism that we need to describe the events as a transition.

Freeman's judicious conclusion seems apt: "when new administrations take office after episodes of executive aggrandizement, they may find themselves incentivized to use legal strategies similar to those of their predecessors. As a result, it may be difficult to distinguish between the start of constitutional recovery and a new round of executive aggrandizement."[31] Looking solely at the term-limits issue, the story is as much about the limits of populist presidential leadership as it is about what populist leaders do with the power they have.

2. Bolivia

In its broadest outlines the Bolivian story about presidential term limits is quite similar to the Ecuadorian one. It features Evo Morales, the paradigm of a charismatic left-leaning populist. Through a series of quite messy—that word again—constitutional maneuvers, Morales found himself in a position to run for re-election indefinitely. In the end, though, he couldn't retain the presidency. Characterizing the end of the story (so far) is quite difficult, but we'll use the version Morales's supporters offer: He ran for re-election and won, quite narrowly, but was forced into exile by a right-wing coup. The new government reran the election, in which Morales's designated successor won by an extremely large margin. As we write it remains unclear what role if any Morales himself will have in Bolivian politics in the coming years.

Bolivia's economy has depended on extractive industries—natural gas and mining of tin and now lithium—and coca production. Historically the nation had extremely high levels of economic and social inequality. Workers in mines and on farms came from the nation's large Aymara and Quecha indigenous communities, and earned relatively little. As a practical matter they were excluded from national politics, which was dominated by elites who tended to regard the

---

[29] The strategy of appointing someone you believe will be a puppet succeeds more often than not. For an international survey, *see* Versteeg et al., note 11 above. That strategy is not confined to populists, though.

[30] Takis Pappas, Populism and Liberal Democracy: A Comparative and Theoretical Analysis (2019), at p. 257.

[31] Freeman, note 4 above, at p. 53.

indigenous population as subjects of government, not citizens entitled to shape political outcomes.

Not surprisingly this system of inequality and exclusion produced a reaction among the indigenous population. By the end of the twentieth century, miners and coca farmers had developed reasonably strong social movements and unions. Himself an Aymara, Evo Morales started his political career as an organizer for the union of coca growers, eventually becoming its leader. Along with other social movement activists, Morales formed and led the Movement Toward Socialism (MAS) as a coalition of urban workers and indigenous peoples, among others.[32] The party rather rapidly became a major player in national politics. Morales won the presidency in 2005 as the MAS candidate.

His political program was transformative. The government increased taxes on extractive industries without nationalizing them. Coupled with economic growth and the distribution of taxes imposed on profits, Morales's programs reduced radical inequality. As anthropologist Alice Postero puts it, though, Morales's policies tried to satisfy two demands, "indigenous activists pushing sustainable development based on native *cosmovisiones*, and leftists pushing industrialization."[33] If not strictly speaking irreconcilable, those demands were at the least difficult to satisfy simultaneously, and the Morales government's attempts to do so weakened its support from both sides.

The Morales government advocated for constitutional reform, and a new constitution for the "Plurinational State of Bolivia" took effect in 2009. It emphasized the role of the nation's indigenous peoples in its public life; as we said earlier, in traditional terms, we can describe it as transforming the indigenous population from subjects of rule to self-governing citizens. Committed to a list of ethical and moral principles, the constitution built popular participation into a range of its institutions. In a section on "participation and social control," the constitution provided that "Organized Civil Society shall exercise public monitoring of public management at all levels of the State, and of businesses, public enterprises, and private ventures that administer public fiscal resources." And it provided that the constitutional court would be elected by universal suffrage. When the election occurred the judges who won seats on the court were chosen by MAS.

The 2009 constitution limited the president to two five-year terms. As in Ecuador the MAS-dominated constitutional court held that the clock started with the constitution's adoption, which meant that Morales could run for election in 2009 and 2014. Political unrest increased after Morales's 2014 election, partly because his economic development policies clashed with environmental

---

[32] Technically the MAS as an organization predated Morales, but it was moribund. He negotiated an agreement with the organization that allowed him to take it over and transform it.

[33] Nancy Postero, The Indigenous State: Race, Politics, and Performance in Plurinational Bolivia 15 (2017).

protection and the interests of indigenous communities affected by development-related building and investment. Seeking to remain in office, Morales promoted a referendum to amend the constitution to allow a third term. Indicating how much Morales's political position had deteriorated, the referendum failed. In one analyst's words, "Evo's party suffered from political exhaustion. . . . Too many deals with too many interests had created machination, manipulation, and corruption within the government . . . [and an] exodus of committed pro-MAS militants."[34] Demonstrating his own lack of commitment to the populist idea that majority rule should prevail as widely as possible, Morales then turned to the MAS-dominated constitutional court, which invoked Hamilton's principle to hold the term limit unlawful.[35]

Morales then ran for a third term in 2019. Under the existing election rules, a candidate for the presidency could avoid a run off by receiving 40 percent of the votes with a margin of at least 10 percent over the candidate with the next highest number of votes. The nation's electoral commission had a tradition of announcing a "quick count" immediately after the polls closed. These quick counts had proven rather accurate in the past. The commission's quick count in 2019 was delayed for almost a day, leading Morales's opponents to suspect vote-tampering. When the report came in, it showed that Morales had won just a bit more than 40 percent of the votes with just more than a 10 percent margin—seemingly, re-elected without having to face a runoff. Election monitors from the Organization of American States immediately raised questions about the quick count's accuracy, asserting that there had been election irregularities and that vote returns from areas not fully included in the quick count might show that Morales had to go to a runoff election. Responding to demonstrations after the election, Bolivia's military supported Morales's opponents and demanded that he leave office. He resigned, as did his vice president. Morales was given political asylum in Mexico and, later, Argentina.

The Bolivian Constitution provided that in the absence of a president and vice president, the office would be filled by the Senate president, with a presidential election to be held within ninety days. In solidarity with Morales, the Senate president, a MAS member, resigned, and the MAS members of parliament boycotted the parliamentary session called to deal with the crisis. The extreme conservative Jeanine Añez was serving as second vice president, a position apparently reserved for the leader of the opposition. Without MAS members present to fill the position of Senate president, Añez became Senate president and, as a result, interim president.

As we've noted, describing these events is not easy. Morales's opponents argued that Morales had to depart because he had cheated, manipulating election

---

[34] Quoted in Postero, note 33 above, at p. 179.
[35] We use "unlawful" because we think it awkward to describe a provision in the comprehensive 2009 constitution as unconstitutional or, in the usage that's become common, an unconstitutional constitutional *amendment*.

results to avoid a runoff election that he thought he would lose. His supporters, in contrast, described the events as a right-wing military coup. We think that that description is a bit more accurate than the alternative. One later audit of the election results indicated that the quick count was basically accurate: Morales had indeed won enough votes to avoid a runoff, and there appear to have been no more than the usual number of election irregularities, not enough to change the result. When published, that audit was immediately challenged as itself flawed. The government that replaced Morales was hard to the right, had no indigenous people in the cabinet, and took quite repressive actions against MAS supporters.[36]

Meanwhile MAS retained a two-thirds majority in the legislature, sufficient to amend the constitution. Anticipating that it would fall below that level in 2020, the legislature amended the constitution to reduce the majorities required for some important actions from two-thirds to a simple majority. A MAS leader was quoted as saying that the changes will "speed up the legislative task."

The new government had to run an election within ninety days, which would have been in the spring of 2020. It delayed the election once because of the pandemic, and tried but failed to postpone it further. The election took place in October 2020. MAS candidate Luis Arce, who had been the minister of economics in Morales's cabinet, won a decisive victory with 52 percent of the votes. Whether Morales would return to political life in Bolivia is unclear as we write.[37]

As with Ecuador, we offer some observations about the Bolivian story.

- Evo Morales was a talented political leader who emerged from a significant social movement, and assembled a coalition from other such movements.
- He had an extremely ambitious reform agenda whose implementation would inevitably take a fair amount of time.
- He faced substantial opposition from the political elites he defeated, as shown by the events that forced him into temporary exile. The elites found it difficult to treat him and MAS as a legitimate political force in part because of its support from an indigenous population that they regarded as less than full citizens.
- The legislature's modification of amendment rules after Morales was forced out of the presidency, justified openly on the ground that it would make it easier to enact the MAS program, suggests that Morales's interest in extending his term resulted in part at least from the political logic we've described.

---

[36] The *New York Times* wrote that the government had "persecuted [Morales's] supporters, stifled dissent, and worked to cement its hold on power." Anatoly Kurmanaev & María Silvia Trigo, "A Bitter Election. Accusations of Fraud. And Now Second Thoughts," THE NEW YORK TIMES, June 7, 2020, p. A15.

[37] The constitutional court reversed its prior holding, concluding that the limit on presidential terms was lawful, thereby precluding Morales from running again for the presidency.

As with Ecuador, our conclusion is quite mixed: The events in Bolivia show that there's something to the story that charismatic populist politicians seek to extend their terms in office simply to retain power, but there's also something to the story that populists seek to extend presidential terms for long enough to allow them to carry out their reforms while winning elections that remain reasonably free and fair.[38]

3. Venezuela

And then there's Hugo Chávez, the first of twenty-first-century Latin America's Bolivarian leaders—charismatic to the extreme (to his supporters, of course), leftist, and perhaps proto-authoritarian but also perhaps acting according to the political logic we've emphasized. The story here is complicated by a confluence of factors: As happened later in Bolivia in connection with Evo Morales, Chávez's political opponents denied that he was a legitimate leader even though his first successful election occurred after a reasonably free and fair campaign; he almost immediately began to put in place processes that would make subsequent elections less than free and fair; his opposition was quite inept; he sometimes used authoritarian methods to counter his opponents; he died relatively young, preventing a fair assessment of the political arc he envisioned for himself and his political agenda; and his successor Nicolás Maduro was a straightforward authoritarian whose behavior casts a shadow backward on Chávez.[39]

In the last quarter of the twentieth century Venezuela was a reasonably stable democracy. Its elected leaders pursued neoliberal policies in an economy that depended heavily on oil, of which Venezuela had enormous reserves. Among the government's policies were lifting price controls and removing some of the subsidies on the price of gasoline, both of which led to unpopular price increases.

Chávez was a career military officer who seems to have been something of a rising star within the military. He helped organize a secretive group within the military, MBR-200, which apparently thought of itself as guarding Venezuela against the nation's own politicians. The MBR attempted a coup in 1992, during which Chávez, then a lieutenant colonel, made a dramatic appearance on national television. After the coup failed Chávez was imprisoned for two years.

Venezuela's economy deteriorated through the 1990s. By 1999 the nation "was governed by a corrupt two-party system that despite the wealth of the country was not able to address the material needs of the population or to recognize the

---

[38] As with Ecuador, assessments made while Morales was in office probably need to be modify to take account of the way the story seems to have ended. *See, e.g.*, Santiago Anria, *Delegative Democracy Revisited: More Inclusion, Less Liberalism in Bolivia*, 27 JOURNAL OF DEMOCRACY 99 (2016).

[39] Political scientist Javier Corrales used the term "autocratic legalism" in an analysis of Chávez's regime. Javier Corrales, *Autocratic Legalism in Venezuela*, 26 JOURNAL OF DEMOCRACY 37 (2015).

full rights of democratic citizens."[40] Chávez had been released from prison at least in part with the hope that he could help ease the political crisis of the early 1990s. When the crisis persisted, or took a new form, at the end of the decade, Chávez, who had previously foregone electoral office before, was elected president in 1999. As we've described in Chapter 7, he immediately proposed a referendum on convening a constituent assembly. The opposition made a serious strategic error in failing to participate in the referendum, which allowed Chávez and his allies to set the rules for the constituent assembly. The organized opposition parties also boycotted the elections for the constituent assembly, which therefore had a huge majority for Chávez.[41]

The Venezuelan Constitution of 1999 wasn't nearly as innovative as the later Bolivian and Ecuadorian ones. Presidential power, already rather large under prior constitutions, did increase. The constitution limited presidents to two six-year terms. Chávez was elected president under the new constitution in 2000, with 60 percent of the vote, and again in 2006, with 63 percent. In 2009 he sponsored a referendum to remove the term limit, which passed with 54 percent support. Chávez won his third six-year term in 2012, with 54 percent of the vote. These last two results showed that Chávez's popularity, while still high, had declined.

There's more to the story, though. Chávez began to lose political ground even though he had adopted policies aimed at severely disabling the opposition. Civil liberties deteriorated as Chávistas physically attacked their opponents. The government imprisoned some opponents on flimsy grounds and generally made life hard for opposition voters by, for example, denying them public services and firing them from their public sector jobs. The opposition wasn't entirely blameless for its plight. Objecting to the "Cubanization" of Venezuela's economy, the opposition organized a strike against price controls, basically withholding goods from the market to cause shortages and economic pain for Chávez's supporters. Chávez responded by increasing the pace of nationalizations, consistent with its general program but also with the effect of depriving the opposition of one of its sources of funding (contributions from owners of the expropriated businesses). And, most dramatically, the opposition tried the oust Chávez with a military coup, but failed embarrassingly.

Chávez was terminally ill with cancer when he was re-elected in 2012. He died in March 2013, and was replaced by his vice president Nicolás Maduro. The

---

[40] Cristóbal Rovira Kaltwasser, "Populism in Latin America and Beyond: Concept, Causes, and Consequences," in *Symposium: Populism in Comparative Perspective* (Matt Golder & Sona Golder eds.), CP: NEWSLETTER OF THE COMPARATIVE POLITICS ORGANIZED SECTION OF THE AMERICAN POLITICAL SCIENCE ASSOCIATION 26: 2 (2016), at p. 75.

[41] The boycotts are reflected in high levels of abstention—62 percent in the referendum on convening a constituent assembly, 54 percent in the elections for the assembly.

constitution required that a new election be held. Maduro won a bare majority. Under Chávez the nation's economy had weakened, partly due to fluctuations in the world oil market and partly due to the government's mismanagement of the nationalized petroleum industry. Things got even worse after Maduro's election, and Maduro responded by ratcheting repression up.

Maduro had a compliant Chávista legislature that endorsed his actions and gave him expanded power to rule by decree—until the regular parliamentary elections in 2015 brought the anti-Chávistas a substantial majority. Constitutional crisis followed constitutional crisis, though the details are not relevant for the story we're telling about presidential term limits except in one detail: Maduro's opponents managed to hang on to some degree of power despite his repression, but they weren't able to organize effectively against him, in part because they were inept. They developed an ingenious strategy that allowed them to claim that their leader Juan Guaidó was actually the lawful president but weren't able to make enough of that strategy. And they apparently sponsored a seriocomic attempted invasion led by a handful of U.S. mercenaries. As we've noted already, we bring the opposition's failures into the story to point out that political outcomes result from the interaction between populists and their opponents, and that bad outcomes shouldn't be attributed solely to populism's own dynamics when the opposition is politically inept.

Our bottom-line conclusion here is somewhat less qualified than our conclusions about Ecuador and Bolivia. Chávez is probably best seen as a proto-authoritarian left populist who faced extraordinary pressures that may have reinforced his own tendencies, and that absent those pressures his authoritarian tendencies might not have emerged nearly as forcefully. Maduro, Chávez's successor but not necessarily his designated political heir, is an authoritarian who appears to have abandoned any pretense of having a populist ideology. We're not sure that this tells us much about *Chávismo* as a form of populism.

***

What can we say about these case studies other than repeating our usual refrain about details? The international consensus that presidential terms should be limited seems sensible (when coupled with term lengths of four to six years). Hamilton provided a principled argument against term limits, but the counterargument about the risk of permanent entrenchment is quite strong.

We've identified a political logic against term limits under conditions that might come close to being met in the studies of Ecuador and Bolivia, but we ourselves aren't willing to say that the political logic justifies or even explains the removal of term limits there. Vladimir Putin relied upon precisely the same political logic to justify extending his term until 2036.[42] Perhaps Correa and Morales really wanted to be like Vladimir Putin, although at the times they sought to eliminate term limits, Correa and Morales's popularity had declined substantially and Putin's had not. Yet we also think it also important to point out that neither Correa nor Morales actually benefited from the removal of term limits—Correa because he was "betrayed" by Moreno and Morales because he was prevented from taking office for a third term.[43]

In short, removing term limits is probably a bad idea, but it's an idea that isn't distinctively associated with populism, and several of the most prominent examples of populists who tried to remove term limits didn't succeed (in the end).

III. Rule by Decree, Populism, and Thin Constitutionalism

Turkey's Recep Tayyip Erdoğan called a failed coup against him in July 2016 a "gift from God." Relying on the Turkish Constitution's provision allowing the executive government to declare an emergency in the face of "serious indications of widespread acts of violence aimed at the destruction of the free democratic order established by the Constitution or of fundamental rights and freedoms, or serious deterioration of public order because of acts of violence," Erdoğan issued an emergency declaration lasting three months, which was repeatedly extended. Decrees allowed Erdoğan to dissolve more than 2,200 educational institutions,[44] close 73 radio and TV stations and many other news outlets. A quarter-million people were detained, almost 130,00 public employees were fired. Many local governments were suspended, and about 1,000 private companies were taken over by the government.[45]

Erdoğan saw the failed coup as an opportunity to push through his long-desired program to transform Turkey's constitution from a semi-presidential system (though he had already effectively neutered the presidency) to a completely presidential one. A referendum on constitutional reform, held on April 16, 2017, while the emergency decrees were still in place, approved the changes by a narrow 51 percent to 49 percent margin, with credible allegations that

---

[42] See Emma Anderson & Zoya Sheftalovich, "Putin wins right to extend his rule until 2036 in landslide vote," POLITICO, July 1, 2020, available at https://www.politico.eu/article/vladimir-putin-wins-right-to-extend-his-russia-rule-until-2036-in-landslide-vote/, archived at https://perma.cc/UN2B-6665.

[43] We have no idea whether Chávez knew he was terminally ill when he sponsored the amendment to remove term limits, but he surely did when he ran for the third term.

[44] Fetullah Gülen, who coup organizers followed, operated a number of private schools in Turkey.

[45] See Zafer Yilmaz, *Erdoğan's Presidential Regime and Strategic Legalism: Turkish Democracy in the Twilight Zone*, 20 SOUTH EUROPEAN & BLACK SEA STUDIES 265 (2020), at pp. 268–69.

Erdoğan's party had suppressed "no" votes. Erdoğan waited until July 2018 to lift the emergency decrees.

Erdoğan didn't have to invent an emergency; there really was a coup attempt. He didn't have to create an emergency; the coup attempt wasn't a Reichstag fire that he himself orchestrated. What's the story about, though: proto- authoritarianism, populism, executive authority, the nature of emergency powers? Sorting through the possibilities, we conclude that there's no particularly interesting association between populism and exercises of or advocacy for ambitious versions of executive power.

A. Preliminaries

As with term limits, so with rule by decree and emergency powers: We have to clear away quite a bit of underbrush before we can see the fundamental issues clearly. And, we suggest, once the underbrush is cleared away, we'll see that there's nothing particularly inconsistent with constitutionalism about the way in which populists rule by decree (when they do).

We have to begin with the observation that executive governments *always* rule by decree to some extent. When they do so in the United States, we call their instruments administrative rules or regulations. When they do so in the United Kingdom, we call the instruments secondary legislation. And when they do so in civil law nations, the term is decree laws.

What do these differently named things have in common? They are all rules that have "the force of law," as it's put in U.S. law. In this they are just like statutes except that they don't come directly from the legislature the way statutes do. Instead, they come from the legislature indirectly.

The laws legislatures pass sometimes are quite specific—"the sale of a chemical pesticide with the following composition is banned"—but sometimes they aren't: "The sale of pesticides that endanger human health is banned." How can a pesticide seller know whether selling a specific brand is prohibited? Typically, the statute continues along these lines: "The Environmental Protection Agency is directed to compile and publicize a list of pesticides that endanger human health." The list is an administrative regulation, secondary legislation, or a decree law.[46]

This is entirely unexceptionable and, indeed, almost inevitable in a modern and fully constitutional state whose government is charged with addressing a wide range of social, economic, and cultural issues. Legislatures aren't

---

[46] We omit some details, primarily about the processes by which decree laws are generated by the executive branch and about judicial review of decree laws. We return to the latter below.

well-equipped to investigate everything of concern, and aren't able to move fast enough to deal with rapidly emerging problems.[47]

Constitutions try to limit the use of decree laws, but the limits are typically, understandably, and—again—constitutionally rather weak. The forms of words used to describe the limits vary from one system to another, but they circle around a set of ideas that we describe using the formulations in U.S. law. The legislature enacts a general law, and the executive government can use decree laws to fill in the details. To be able to do that—that is, to be able to distinguish between a mere detail and a fundamental policy choice—the statute has to give the executive government an "intelligible principle" to use. ("Endanger human health" is the principle in the statute we made up.) Sometimes constitutional law says that the statute has to be somewhat more specific when it deals with constitutionally sensitive matters: authorizing the agency that regulates radio and television to make rules about broadcasting hate speech might require a more precise definition of "hate speech" than you'd require when authorizing it to make rules to avoid electronic interference caused by having too many stations too close together in the radio spectrum.

These verbal formulations aren't terribly precise. That's because it's really difficult to figure out how to do two things at once: authorize, as you must, decree laws; and limit the executive government's power so that it can issue only "good" or "appropriate" decrees.

Our description has to be tweaked a bit before we move to more important general points about decree laws. So far we've described executive decrees authorized by general statutes. Some constitutional systems identify a domain of "prerogative" power in the executive. The heart of that domain tends to deal with foreign relations and national security, with executives trying to give broad definitions to those terms and legislatures sometimes insisting upon narrower ones.[48]

When operating within the prerogative domain the executive doesn't need to point to a statute authorizing its decrees. Not all constitutional systems say that executive prerogative exists, though most do—and that fact alone suggests that even a thicker idea of constitutionalism than ours has to put up with decrees based upon executive prerogative. Of course, when the executive purports to

---

[47] For a classic study highlighting some of the paradoxes of delegation in a specific comparative context, *see* Peter Lindseth, *The Paradox of Parliamentary Supremacy: Delegation, Democracy, and Dictatorship in Germany and France, 1920s-1950s*, 113 YALE LAW JOURNAL 1341 (2004).

[48] U.S. presidents have favored arguments that legislation within the domain of prerogative powers is constitutionally prohibited. (This is an especially strong version of what's known as the "unitary executive" theory of the U.S. Constitution.) As we discuss below, one plausible though not necessary version of Carl Schmitt's account of emergency power supports that position, but most constitutional theorists reject it as a general account (which doesn't imply anything about its accuracy as an account of any specific constitution).

issue a prerogative-based decree, all good lawyers will know how to generate arguments that the specific action isn't really within the prerogative domain; in some ways that's what the U.K. Supreme Court's decision on prorogation was about. The boundaries of the prerogative domain will be contestable in any specific case. As before, that fact of legal and political life suggests that constitutionalism has to tolerate a fairly large set of possible definitions of the boundary line.

No matter how thick your understanding of constitutionalism, it's got to allow the executive government to issue decrees with the force of law. Still, the idea that the executive's actions (outside the prerogative domain) have to be rooted somehow in a statute might have some real effects. To see why it might not, we have to direct our attention to party politics, which will also move us toward a discussion of populism and government by executive decree.

Consider an executive government that has solid control of a legislative majority.[49] Suppose, as in Modi's India, the governing party holds a majority of seats in the legislature. The distinction between governing through statutes and governing by executive decree will be quite thin, though not invisible. Suppose someone tells the prime minister, "You know, you just can't do this by executive decree; you'll need a statute to authorize it." The prime minister can respond, "Fine, let's go to the legislature tonight to enact this into law." And, because the prime minster has solid control of the legislature, the proposal becomes law.

In this scenario what might produce differences between governance by decree and governance by statute? One possibility is *transparency*. It might be easier for the executive government to sneak a policy into a decree—and start enforcing it—than it would be for the government to place the proposal on the legislative agenda for open debate even when the government has a firm legislative majority.[50] Another possibility is *review by the courts*. Some constitutional systems hold that courts should review decrees more closely than they review statutes. For example, they might require an especially clear authorization for particularly controversial proposals even if they would apply a single standard to all statutes. Or they can defer more to legislatures than they do to executive agencies.

To know whether government by decree is more closely constrained than government by statute, you'll have to look at the nation's constitutional system more broadly. And, we note, none of the descriptions of populism operate at a level of detail that would tell us whether "populism"—or indeed even specific populisms—occurs in constitutional systems that deploy the transparency and

---

[49] We lay out the argument mostly in connection with parliamentary systems, but we'll occasionally indicate in our notes how the argument changes for presidential systems.

[50] Sometimes we do observe governments railroading controversial laws through a legislature it controls with extremely truncated opportunities for debate, showing that the transparency advantage is itself subject to manipulation.

judicial-review advantages of rule by statute. And, when analysts provide specific examples of populists moving to rule by decree, they almost never situate those examples by describing as well the overall constitutional system. Put directly: where populist governments move to rule by decree *and* have solid legislative majorities, we'd need a lot more information about the underlying rules governing judicial review of statutes and decrees to know whether the distinction between rule by decree and rule by statute matters.

The picture changes when the prime minister's government is a coalition. The prime minister or an executive ministry might issue a decree that wouldn't get through the legislature because some coalition members might deprive the government of its majority on that issue but wouldn't be able to join with the opposition to overturn the decree by legislation.[51] At this point we can add presidential systems to the picture. Suppose the opposition controls a house of the legislature whose support is required for a proposal to become law, the president has the power to veto bills adopted by the legislature, and the opposition doesn't have enough votes to override a veto. In these variants rule by decree really is different from rule by statute.

Once again, populism has nothing to do with this argument. Some populist governments will have a free hand in choosing between rule by decree and rule by statute if they have a solid majority in the legislature. So will any other government with such a majority. Some populist governments may find themselves able to rule by decree more readily than they can rule by statute because of the way party power is configured in the legislature. So will any other government facing the same configuration of power.

There is one final piece of underbrush to clear away, and it's a huge one. The basic argument for allowing decree laws is that in some circumstances executive ministries can process information better than can legislatures and their committees and that executive ministries can respond more quickly to novel problems than can legislatures. "Emergencies" have these characteristics in spades, which is why prime ministers and presidents relish the opportunities emergencies give them and indeed sometimes strive to invent emergencies precisely so that they can shift power from the legislature to their governments.

Modern constitution-drafters know this and typically try to build limits on the power to declare an emergency into the constitution. They put in the constitution a list of things that can justify declaring an emergency: a natural disaster, an invasion by a foreign power, widespread civil disorder, financial collapse—although often the list ends with a catch-all to the effect "and anything else that

---

[51] As we've pointed out before, even dominant parties have the quality of a coalition made up of different factions or interests. The problem we discuss in the text would arise when some faction within the dominant party coalition objected to a proposed decree.

threatens the life of the nation" (that's an adapted version of the formulation in the International Convention on Civil and Political Rights). They also include requirements that the executive government consult with the legislature before and during a state of emergency, and sometimes include time limits on how long the executive can govern by decree before it has to go to the legislature to get a statute enacting its policies or extending the emergency.

Here are some examples.

- The 1958 French Constitution: the substantive standard is, "when the institutions of the Republic, the independence of the Nation, the integrity of its territory or the fulfillment of its international commitments are under serious and immediate threat, and where the proper functioning of the constitutional public authorities is interrupted." Procedurally, the president can "take the measures required" and then inform the nation.
- The 1947 Italian Constitution: the substantive standard is, "in case of necessity and urgency." Procedurally, the government must convert decree laws into statutory ones within thirty days.
- The 1978 Spanish Constitution: the substantive standard is, "cases of extraordinary and urgent need." Procedurally, decree laws "must be submitted forthwith" to parliament. If they aren't ratified within thirty days, they lose the force of law unless they are expressly extended for another thirty days.

These provisions actually don't do much to constrain the power of the executive government to rule by decree during what it decides is an emergency. Sometimes courts try to enforce the substantive and procedural limits, and occasionally they succeed, mostly with respect to the required procedures. Generally, though, attempts to limit the executive government's power in emergencies fail.

Carl Schmitt, the Nazi constitutional theorist, explained why in one of his most famous sentences: "Sovereign is he who decides on the exception." Schmitt eventually came to believe that that observation or definition justified dictatorial rule, but he initially offered it as part of a rather technical discussion of how the Weimar Constitution in Germany attempted to limit executive power in emergencies.

What did Schmitt mean? Look at the constitutional provisions we've quoted. Schmitt believed, we think correctly, that the terms used in constitutions to define the occasions when emergency powers could be exercised simply couldn't capture all the varieties of emergencies that might arise—or, if they did, it was only by using catch-all terms that didn't limit executive powers to declare an emergency and rule by decree. The Italian and Spanish provisions fall into the second category: *anything* serious can be "a case of necessity and urgency." And the French provision is either unsuitable for problems we can readily identify, or has to be given a distorted interpretation to cover them. Take the example of the novel coronavirus. ("Novel" is the scientific term, but it conveniently meshes with the constitutional issues.) Maybe you can say that the conditions created by the pandemic interrupt the functioning of the public authorities. Unfortunately, as a matter of ordinary constitutional interpretation, that's only one of two requirements. The interruption has to occur because of one of the previously listed conditions has occurred. The second refers to national independence, the third to territorial integrity, and the fourth to France's international obligations. These capture ideas about traditional national security—war, terrorism, and the like—and standard approaches to constitutional interpretation would lead you to think that the first condition, a threat to "the institutions of the Republic," had to fall into the same rough category.[52]

Well, you might say, too bad. If the constitution doesn't let the executive rule by decree when some unanticipated problem creates an emergency, no big deal. All the executive has to do is go to the legislature to get authorization for what it wants to do. That turns out to be a truly terrible way of governing. The dramatic version has terrorists blowing up the parliament building and killing half of its members; the less dramatic version is that the problem arises while parliament is out of session and something needs to be done before it can come back to meet. Again, urgency makes speed necessary, and only the executive can act quickly enough. You don't want to design your constitution with a really bad system of dealing with emergencies. Or, to revert to our terms, only something like thin constitutionalism can get you the kind of government you want when emergencies arise.

Schmitt's conclusion? Constitutions couldn't limit the executive power to rule by decree by identifying substantive criteria purporting to impose such limits.

What about the procedural limits? We've already hinted at the answer. They are likely to be pointless. An executive government with solid support in the parliament can push through a statute ratifying decree laws issued before parliament met.[53] If the executive can persuade parliament that the emergency lasts longer than thirty days, it can get its decree laws extended repeatedly. Sometimes the time limits will have some effect. Some elements in the government's coalition might get nervous as the emergency period goes on; the opposition might

---

[52] The interpretive principle has the Latin name *noscitur a sociis*, which is usually translated as something like, "A word is known by the company it keeps." Another interpretive principle, that terms should be given interpretations that make them redundant or surplus, generates a variant on the same argument: the second condition, "interruption of the functioning of the institutions," would automatically be satisfied if you treated any threat to the institutions as a condition that triggered the power to rule by decree.

[53] As we show in the next section, that's what happened in Hungary in response to the Covid-19 pandemic: the Orbán government quickly obtained parliamentary ratification of what it had done and authorization to do more.

have acquiesced in the early days but might reassert itself over time. Extensions of decree laws or regular re-ratification might not be possible if political support erodes.[54] We note two difficulties: First, a government seeing political support decline might well decide to cut the emergency period short. And second and more important, sometimes the draconian steps taken in the first days of the emergency can make it exceedingly difficult to organize political opposition. For reasons that seem good enough to parliament when first presented with early decree laws, such laws might authorize preventive detention of the government's critics, or prevent public gatherings, including political demonstrations.

Professors Adrian Vermeule and Eric Posner summarize the tame version of Schmitt's argument.[55] Before some unexpected event occurs, constitutional law distributes the power to make law between the legislature and the executive: some things have to be done through statutes, others can be done through decree laws. Call this the status quo distribution of lawmaking power. Then the unexpected happens: a new type of terrorist attack (Vermeule and Posner's example), the Covid-19 pandemic (ours, in the next section). The executive government thinks about the new problems of governance the event presents and decides that it would be helpful to issue a decree law that the status quo rule seems to say it can't. It offers the usual justifications for decree laws: it has better information than the legislature and the courts, and it can move more quickly to deal with the problem than they can. Posner and Vermeule argue that there's no reason to think that the status quo distribution of lawmaking power, having been developed without the information provided by the unexpected events, is best for the nation. We think they're basically right.

B. Populism and the COVID-19 Pandemic

Our case study here deals with government responses to the Covid-19 pandemic. The bottom line is clearer here than earlier: populist governments didn't stand out as especially power-grabbing when given the chance by the Covid-19 pandemic. As we write, the consensus appears to be that the pandemic actually did require rather severe restrictions on the basic civil liberties of personal mobility and choice about how to go about your life: lockdowns and mask mandates. The consensus also appears to be that New Zealand's left-liberal constitutionalist

---

[54] For a brief discussion of this argument, made in connection with Professor Bruce Ackerman's suggestion that reauthorization or re-ratification of decree laws should be allowed only with increasing margins in the legislature, *see* Mark Tushnet, *Review*, 122 POLITICAL SCIENCE QUARTERLY 316 (2007).

[55] ADRIAN VERMEULE & ERIC POSNER, TERROR IN THE BALANCE: SECURITY, LIBERTY, AND THE COURTS (2007).

government did the best job in the world in controlling the pandemic within its border.[56]

What did populist governments do? The Hungarian government adopted an extensive emergency law authorizing the executive government to issue many new more decree laws of an authoritarian sort. It also repealed that law after a short while and replaced it with one that constitutional experts who opposed the government described as doing pretty much the same things.[57] As we've suggested earlier, the Orbán government is an authoritarian government parading as a populist one. Its actions tell us more about how authoritarians behave than about how populist governments do.

Surveys of government actions taken in the first year of the pandemic don't suggest any strong differences between populist governments and others with respect to executives seizing the opportunity to expand their power to issue decree laws.[58] Some authoritarian governments did, some didn't—probably because their executives already could do pretty much whatever they wanted. Some standard liberal democracies also expanded executive power to rule by decree— and some didn't. And some populist governments did expand power.

In work in progress Professors Tom Ginsburg and Mila Versteeg compiled information about government responses to the Covid-19 pandemic.[59] Their data are not as clean as we would like because the information doesn't distinguish between parliamentary and presidential systems, and doesn't measure the strength of the government's control over the legislature. That said, Ginsburg and Versteeg's data show that legislatures were "directly involved" in crafting legal responses to the pandemic by declaring or extending a state of emergency or by passing new statutes in 64 percent of the nations in their data set; the data don't show how much of this was done at the executive government's initiative. They also find that "legislatures have an *ongoing* involvement" in 52 percent of the countries, extending emergency periods or passing and renewing temporary legislation or engaging in parliamentary oversight; again, particularly as to the first two forms of ongoing involvement the data don't break out actions the executive

---

[56] Daniel Ziblatt identifies state capacity, trust, polarization, and inequality, not the governing party's ideology, as the key factors influencing the quality of government responses to the pandemic. Daniel Ziblatt, "Covid-19 and the Resilience of Democracy," paper presented at a Council of European Studies speakers series, August 2020.

[57] For a description, *see* David E. Pozen & Kim Lane Scheppele, *Executive Underreach, in Pandemics and Otherwise*, 114 AMERICAN JOURNAL OF INTERNATIONAL LAW 608 (2020), at pp. 611–12.

[58] We are indebted to unpublished work in progress on government compliance with constitutional limits on emergency powers by Stefan Voight and Christian Bjørnskov. We interpret their data as showing a high degree of noncompliance with substantive and especially procedural restrictions on exercises of emergency power.

[59] Tom Ginsburg & Mila Versteeg, "The Bound Executive: Emergency Powers During the Pandemic" (July 28, 2020), available at SSRN: https://ssrn.com/abstract=3608974, archived at https://perma.cc/U4A3-GLCQ.

initiated. Ginsburg and Versteeg argue that their data show that executives are indeed bound by procedural requirements for exercising emergency powers. We think the evidence is more ambiguous and more likely shows that the procedural requirements mean in practice that legislatures rubber-stamp what the executive has done or wants to do.

The most interesting cases are two populist leaders who steadfastly refused to rule by decree during the pandemic—Donald Trump and Jair Bolsonaro. What are we to make of this executive "underreach," as Professors David Pozen and Kim Lane Scheppele call it?[60]

Trump minimized the health risks of the coronavirus, mocked people for wearing masks and encouraged those protesting local mask mandates, refused to use existing authorities that would have allowed him to order private companies to make protective devices quickly, and had his Department of Justice file briefs supporting churches that wanted to hold services with more people than local regulations allowed. Bolsonaro also minimized the threat and refused to wear a mask or encourage others to do so. Like Trump he refused to use existing decree powers to implement programs to contain the virus. He fired one health minister, and the replacement resigned in protest after less than a month.

Neither Trump nor Bolsonaro had an entirely free hand, of course. The opposition Democratic Party controlled the House of Representatives when the pandemic hit and would have negotiated hard to obtain policies that would at least operate even-handedly in Democratic as well as Republican states. At first glance, though, that seems to argue in favor of rule by decree, with executive actions that favored Republican areas.[61] The U.S. Constitution might have been interpreted to stand in the way of some of the most aggressive forms of mask mandates and lockdown orders. It might not have been interpreted that way, and in any event good lawyers could have come up with clearly constitutional versions of mask mandates and lockdown orders. (Without getting too deep into the weeds: such policies would be constitutional when cast as regulations of the operation of businesses that engaged in interstate commerce.) Trump's consistent reference to the virus as "the China virus" could have been used as the basis for even more aggressive uses of executive power against people who recently arrived in the United States.[62]

---

[60] Pozen & Scheppele, note 57 above.

[61] We can imagine the Trump administration thinking—against the advice it was getting from public health officials—that the pandemic would leave Republican areas untouched, and that underreach would therefore harm Democrats. Yet, this political calculation rests on rejecting the best advice it could get, and doesn't explain that foundational rejection.

[62] We draw this point from Tamar Hostovsky Brandes & Yaniv Roznai, "Can COVID-19 Save Democracy from Populism?," ROUNDTABLE, Nov. 11, 2020, available at https://www.iacl-democracy-2020.org/blog/2016/3/23/blog-post-sample-9wntn-6ye75-hwawc-47gsl, archived at https://perma.cc/2ZTC-W25Q.

Bolsonaro's underreach is even more puzzling because he was in a weak political position, scraping by with a tiny majority supporting him in the national legislature. Bolsonaro regularly favored appointments of military officers in other policy domains; in early 2020 seven out of twenty ministers came from the military, as did Bolsonaro's chief of staff, traditionally a quite powerful position. We can readily imagine a Bolsonaro administration with a military official as health minister governing by aggressive use of decree powers, deploying them to harass political opponents. What's more, the Brazilian constitutional court regularly pushed Bolsonaro to act more forcefully. It interpreted Brazil's federalism to allow state governors to go beyond what the national government ordered, insisting only that they rely upon science. It upheld local lockdown orders.[63] These decisions make it clear that Bolsonaro could have gone much further in the direction of overreach than he actually did.

So, why did Orbán overreach and Trump and Bolsonaro underreach? Pozen and Scheppele offer a laundry list of reasons why executives might underreach: "a desire to shift blame and avoid responsibility," "fear of alienating key supporters," a short political time horizon that leads them to ignore long-term effects, "a political program that disparages 'big government.'" Somehow, "international trends" of growing executive power and "the intensification of threats" demanding "a global response" also "increas[e] the risk of particularly pernicious forms of executive underreach."[64] The problems with this list are, we think, evident: other than opposition to big government, each item could just as readily be used to explain executive overreach. Overreach shifts blame to irresponsible people who refuse to take sensible precautions, for example.

In the end, the reasons for and objections to both executive overreach and underreach seem to be substantive and, importantly, not intrinsic to any ideological position no matter how thin. The terms "overreach" and "underreach" describe bad public policies. Executive officials make bad decisions, sometimes deliberately so, because they are bad at governing, not because they are authoritarians or proto-authoritarians or populists or left-leaning liberals.[65]

We can tell a story connecting the Trump-Bolsonaro position to their populism. Like all populists, the story goes, they are suspicious of technocratic elites

[63] The constitutional court published a "case compilation" of Covid-19-related cases in October 2020. In addition to noting the procedural innovations it had used to deal with the more than 6,000 applications for review it had received in such cases, of which 138 involved claims that the government had acted unconstitutionally, the compilation described 18 "important" decisions in the cases.

[64] Pozen & Scheppele, note 57 above, at p. 610.

[65] Pozen and Scheppele suggest in a footnote that Boris Johnson in the United Kingdom and Andrés Manuel López Obrador in Mexico, both of whom are sometimes described as populists, also engaged in underreach. They describe Sweden's response to the corona virus, which certainly looks to us like underreach, as "a good faith outlier" rather than "a willful underreacher, as its health authorities took a wide range of preventive measures—some of them mandatory, some advisory, all justified in a deliberative fashion...." Pozen & Scheppele, note 57 above, at p. 612 n. 21. For a contrary view of Johnson, *see* K.D. Ewing, *Covid-19 Government by Decree*, 31 KING'S LAW JOURNAL 1 (2020).

who invoke scientific expertise to impose burdens on ordinary people, who know from personal experience better ways of dealing with life's problems.[66] Public health scientists wanted to increase their power so they exaggerated the threat Covid-19 posed. Trump and Bolsonaro stood for common sense and ordinary people against these elitists.

We think that this story is a "just so" story dreamt up to drag populism into an explanation of Trump and Bolsonaro. Other populists didn't take the Trump-Bolsonaro line. As a member of the governing coalition, Podemos in Spain supported declaring and then extending a state of emergency.[67] Five Star in Italy also stood with its coalition partner in doing something—not terribly effectively, it turned out—about the pandemic.

Even more, imagine that Trump and Bolsonaro had supported an expansion of executive power. We're sure that we could come up with a story explaining why their populism led them to *that* position. Here's a sketch, necessarily thin because we're dealing with something that didn't happen. As populists Trump and Bolsonaro stood with ordinary people against social elites who, in the manner of numerous apocalyptic novels and films,[68] were able to isolate themselves in strongly protected fortresses while leaving everyone else exposed to the coronavirus. Mask mandates and lockdowns coupled with generous payments to ordinary people funded by taxes on the elites were true populist programs for the people.

In truth, we're pretty confident that Trump and Bolsonaro's populism isn't going to play a large role in whatever historians and political scientists end up saying about their response to the pandemic.

As we said at this section's outset, populism doesn't seem to have much to do with expanding executive power in times of emergency, either in general or in the specific case of the Covid-19 pandemic. As Levitsky and Ziblatt put it, "Autocrats Love Emergencies." But then there's Rahm Emanuel, Barack Obama's chief of staff, who said, "You never let a serious crisis go to waste."[69] We don't think there's enough evidence yet to say that populist chief executives are any fonder of rule by decree than chief executives guided by ideologies other than populism.

***

---

[66] As Pozen and Scheppele put it, "authoritarian and proto-authoritarian leaders . . . trade in falsehood and sneer at expertise." Pozen & Scheppele, note 57 above, at p. 610.

[67] Sam Jones, "No enemy but the virus? Why Spain's opposition is rounding on the government," THE GUARDIAN, June 20, 2020, available at https://www.theguardian.com/world/2020/jun/21/no-enemy-but-the-virus-why-spains-opposition-is-rounding-on-the-government, archived at https://perma.cc/U7E9-785R.

[68] The films "Snowpiercer" (2013) and "Elysium" (2013) are two recent versions.

[69] Steven Levitsky & Daniel Ziblatt, "Autocrats Love Emergencies," THE NEW YORK TIMES, Jan. 13, 2019, p. SR-4. Emanuel's statement comes in several variants.

The topics we've discussed here involve populists as chief executives. We've argued that their populism does lead many of them to bridle at presidential term limits, and that the political logic that might be thought to account for that position really can't do the required work. Here, to overstate a bit, populist chief executives do indeed seem to be power-hungry, and more so than many other chief executives. They aren't terribly successful at extending their terms, though. Only Chávez got away with it, and he died before he got a chance to do anything significant in his third term.[70] Further, we need to note once again that term limits matter only in presidential systems. Margaret Thatcher was prime minister for eleven years, and Angela Merkel will have served the equivalent of four four-year presidential terms by September 2021. They aren't populists, of course, but their examples do show that a system that allows the chief executive to serve for quite long times aren't always anti-constitutional.

With respect to rule by decree during the pandemic, populist parties and leaders seem basically indistinguishable from non-populist parties: parties in both categories sometimes expanded rule by decree, sometimes didn't, sometimes got legislatures to go along with them, sometimes didn't, sometimes were authoritarian, sometimes weren't. Our case studies are few in number and can't support broad conclusions. They do put on the table, though, the possibility that populism is pretty much a wash in connection with the threats executive power poses to constitutionalism: Some populists in power will threaten constitutionalism by expansively exercising executive power, some won't, and—maybe as important—some democratically elected chief executives who aren't populists by any stretch will threaten constitutionalism in this way.

---

[70] Turkey's Recep Tayyip Erdoğan kept himself in office by using the common strategy of resetting the clock by shifting from a parliamentary system to a presidential one. Versteeg et al., note 11 above, examine this strategy's use in non-populist settings, not all of which are authoritarian.

10

Guardrails and Institutions

Populists are fond of amending the constitutions they inherit, we're told. What do we know about the *general* prevalence of amendments? A systematic empirical study by Professors Tom Ginsburg and James Melton concludes that the best predictor of whether amendments are added to a constitution is what the authors call an "amendment culture."[1] They measure that culture by counting how often a constitution has been amended before.[2] The more your constitution has been amended, the more likely it is that it's going to be amended again.

Professors Ginsburg and Melton didn't include a measure of the political orientation of the government when an amendment happened, so their study doesn't tell us anything about populism. Still, their reference to "culture" is important. Almost everyone who examines whether liberal constitutionalism is strengthened, merely survives, or declines under pressure, ends up thinking that institutions—how easy or difficult the rule for amending the constitution is, for example—might matter on the margins but that the strength of the constitutional culture when the pressure starts to build matters much more.

An influential book by political scientists Steven Levitsky and Daniel Ziblatt captures a significant part of the idea of a pro-constitutional culture by describing it as providing "guardrails" that keep the vehicle of liberal constitutional from careening over the edge on a mountain road.[3] "Culture," though, is an elusive concept, and guardrails can be made of heavy steel or easily breakable wood. Levitsky and Ziblatt's work, and their idea of guardrails, is rightly seen as a major contribution. We supplement their analysis with closer attention to the relation between guardrails (constitutional culture) and institutions, including the institutions that constitutional scholars pay close attention to.

Introducing the idea that Ireland's practice of amending the constitution by using referendums has succeeded because Ireland has a "referendum culture," law professor David Kenny quotes Stanley Fish: a culture consists of "an ever-changing collection of rules of thumb, doctrines, proverbs, precedents, folk-tales,

---

[1] Tom Ginsburg & James Melton, *Does the Constitutional Amendment Rule Matter at All? Amendment Cultures and the Challenges of Measuring Amendment Difficulty*, 13 International Journal of Constitutional Law 686 (2015).

[2] That's a rough description, but good enough for our purposes.

[3] Steven Levitsky & Daniel Ziblatt, How Democracies Die (2018), at p. 9 (introducing the metaphor), ch. 5 (providing their analysis).

Power to the People. Mark Tushnet and Bojan Bugarič, Oxford University Press. © Mark Tushnet and Bojan Bugaric" 2021. DOI: 10.1093/oso/9780197606711.003.0011

prejudices, aspirations, goals, fears, and above all, beliefs."[4] That strikes us as about right, and we emphasize several points about the formulation: it doesn't include institutions on the list, written materials like a constitution or even statutes don't really appear on the list (the terms "doctrines" and "precedents" don't have to refer to written materials), and—very important—cultures are always in flux. That last fact certainly complicates the argument that a pro-constitutional culture serves as a guardrail against democratic decline: How can we be sure that important "rules of thumb" and "precedents" embodied in political practice won't change in the ordinary course when change is ever present? Or, put another way, maybe changes in constitutional culture cause democratic decline. If they do, we're going to have to look elsewhere—to institutions, we think—as the guardrails.

Another way of putting the point is this: more democracy can thwart democratic decline. Here's some evidence. In their book *Why Civil Resistance Works*, political scientists Erica Chenoweth and Maria Stephan use a large data set of major nonviolent and violent resistance campaigns from 1900 to 2006 to show that nonviolent resistance in the form of boycotts, strikes, and protests deters autocratic backsliding. Professor Sheri Berman argues that long-term democratic struggle should be credited for the development of liberal democracy in most of the European states. After reviewing two centuries of turmoil characterizing the development of liberal democracy in the United Kingdom, France, Germany, Italy, and Spain, she concludes that "fighting back against the populist tide and avoiding illiberal democracy . . . requires finding ways to remove the barriers that have weakened contemporary democracy and to encourage greater citizen participation."[5]

More democracy, though, occurs in and through institutions like political parties and civil society organizations—when people get together to do things for what they understand to be the public good. It's not merely an idea or a norm about how people should act. As Professors Tom Ginsburg, Aziz Huq, and Mila Versteeg put it, "crowds marching in the streets, and the people taking it upon themselves to enforce the social contract, . . . ultimately are the best protector of liberal democracy."[6]

---

4 David Kenny, "The Risks of Referendums: 'Referendum Culture' in Ireland as a Solution?," in CONSTITUTIONAL CHANGE AND POPULAR SOVEREIGNTY: POPULISM, POLITICS AND THE LAW IN IRELAND (Maria Cahill, Seán Ó Conaill, Colm O'Cinnéide, & Conor O'Mahony eds. 2021).

5 ERICA CHENOWETH & MARIA J. STEPHAN, WHY CIVIL RESISTANCE WORKS: THE STRATEGIC LOGIC OF NONVIOLENT CONFLICT (2013); Sheri Berman, *The Pipe Dream of Undemocratic Liberalism*, 28: 3 JOURNAL OF DEMOCRACY 29 (2017), at pp. 29, 38. Berman provides a more detailed account of the history on which she relies in SHERI BERMAN, DEMOCRACY AND DICTATORSHIP IN EUROPE: FROM THE ANCIEN RÉGIME TO THE PRESENT DAY (2019).

6 Tom Ginsburg, Aziz Z. Huq, & Mila Versteeg, *The Coming Demise of Liberal Constitutionalism*, 85 UNIVERSITY OF CHICAGO LAW REVIEW 239 (2018), at p. 253.

The general idea that constitutional culture matters a lot has been around for a long time—we can read it out of Montesquieu's focus on "The Spirit of the Laws," for example. Systematic examination of how guardrails actually work is more recent, and in our view more in the nature of gestures toward an analysis than explanations. Professors Levitsky and Ziblatt, for example, argue that "mutual tolerance," the practice of treating opponents as co-citizens rather than as enemies, and "institutional forbearance," refraining from pushing right up to the legal limits of your power, are the most important guardrails.[7] They make a good case for the proposition that constitutional democracy is in trouble when mutual tolerance and institutional forbearance wane, but they don't say much beyond exhortation to explain how mutual tolerance and institutional forbearance are sustained.

We don't offer any answers here. Instead, we explore why getting a handle on the idea of a pro-constitutional culture is so difficult once we understand that cultures are always changing.[8] From here on we'll refer to "guardrails" rather than constitutional culture, treating the guardrails taken as a whole to be the way we see the constitutional culture in action. And we apologize in advance to readers who think that on occasion we've forced the metaphor beyond its proper limits.

We introduce the issue by returning to Fidesz's electoral victory in 2010. It won 53 percent of the votes, which gave it 68 percent of the seats in parliament because of the boost the election laws gave to the party that won the most votes. The party hadn't made constitutional reform an important part of its platform during the election, but with more than two-thirds of the seats in parliament, the government could amend the constitution at will. And it did. The party basically retreated into its caucus, developed its constitutional reforms on its own without any public input or even exposure, and rammed the amendments through in a take-it-or-leave-it vote that gave the opposition no real opportunity to criticize the proposals or mobilize popular opposition outside the halls of parliament.

The government's critics leveled two charges against the constitutional reforms. The first was that they did bad things to the structure of Hungary's government. The second charge is the one that matters here. Critics said that the

---

[7] Levitsky & Ziblatt, note 3 above, at p. 102.

[8] Our examples are drawn almost exclusively from the United States, mostly because we're most familiar with the precise composition of the guardrails there. We are aware of course of a large body of scholarship dealing with the general topic of "constitutional culture." Some works describe the constitutional culture of one or more nations, and others sometimes offer a "comparative statics" account of changes in one nation's constitutional culture, but the latter works typically don't offer an account of how the nation got from one constitutional culture to a different one. Kenny, note 4 above, does offer an analysis of one aspect of Ireland's constitutional culture, identifying what he calls "four facets" of the referendum culture: "suspicion of vague referendum questions," the separation of your views about whether some issue should be decided by referendum or by the parliament from your views on the merits of the question once it's put to a referendum, informal controls by civil society on the dissemination of misinformation, and the broad role of civil society in referendum campaigns.

method by which the amendments were adopted was procedurally flawed. Good practices in constitutional amendment require, they said, several things that the Fidesz process lacked. Constitutional reform proposals should be part of a party's platform so that voters know what they're going to get if they vote for the party.[9] Specific proposals should be laid before the public and the parliament for a while before a vote is taken so that the public can weigh in with its views about the reforms, informed by whatever the parliamentary opposition has to say. And those who propose a constitutional amendment should be open to discussion and negotiation over details because outsiders might help improve the reforms.

These are indeed procedural flaws, but nothing Fidesz did was inconsistent with the procedures written in the constitution. The term "abusive constitutionalism" has come into wide use since law professor David Landau gave it its name. Fidesz may have abused constitutional*ism* but it didn't abuse the written Hungarian constitution as it then existed (or any unwritten rules that anyone regarded as legally binding). The good-practice norms of transparency provide examples of guardrails. They promote mutual respect by taking into account what opposition parties and the public through civil society organizations have to say. And they are norms saying that governments should forbear from using the sheer power they have.

It seems indisputable that there *are* guardrails, and that sometimes they get broken. How do the guardrails get built? How and why do they get broken? And, important for our argument, what happens when they do get broken? Breaking through the guardrails can have several possible effects, not just one. Most discussion of guardrails assumes that a vehicle that breaks though the guardrails will tumble down the mountainside and explode—breaching the guardrails leads to liberal constitutionalism's death. Sometimes, though, the vehicle tumbles down the side only to land upright on a different road—not pleasant while the vehicle's falling but not a disaster at the end and perhaps even a good thing if the new road that gets to the promised land of liberal constitutionalism more quickly than traveling on the initial road would have. And sometimes one guardrail breaks, the vehicle wobbles a bit, but then manages to stay on the road because another guardrail holds. Breaking the guardrails, we argue, may well be bad more often than not, but sometimes breaking the guardrails is good for a liberal constitutionalism that has settled into complacency in the face of real and urgent social needs (and sometimes breaking one or two guardrails turns out to have no effect on liberal constitutionalism).

---

[9] We note that Fidesz might not have included constitutional reform in its election platform because it didn't expect to be able to get reforms done. That it ended up with 68 percent of the seats was something of a surprise even to its leaders.

First, where do guardrails come from? One influential informal definition says this: they are pre-constitutional understandings that "go without saying" or are "taken for granted" in the daily working of a constitution.[10] An example: The U.S. Senate has rules that allow much of its work to go forward only if no senator objects. Most of these rules are trivial—without unanimous consent a committee can't hold a hearing if the Senate as a whole has been in session for two hours, for example. A single senator can bring the Senate's work to an end if she or he simply objects to waiving this or many other rules. It's taken for granted that senators won't actually exercise the power to withhold consent routinely. That's a guardrail against paralyzing the Senate—a practice of forbearing from exercising a power you unquestionably have.

These practices develop and change over time. American political scientists have a subfield known as "American political development." Those working in that field argue that U.S. political history reveals a series of what they call constitutional orders or regimes. Each one has its characteristic policies, ideologies, and ways of doing things. The "taken for granteds"—the unwritten guardrails—are among those ways of doing things. During the 1950s and 1960s, for example, the major U.S. parties were coalitions within themselves: Democrats had socially and economically liberal Northern members and socially conservative and economically liberal Southern ones, Republicans had socially liberal and economically conservative Northern members and economically and socially conservative western ones. This configuration produced a "taken for granted" assumption that you shouldn't adopt controversial legislation unless you had significant support from both parties.

Generalities like "mutual toleration" are brought to ground in more specific forms. In one nation, mutual toleration might be manifested by a practice of letting opposition parties propose as many amendments as they want to pending legislation (that is going to be enacted anyway), whereas in another the number of amendments might be limited but opposition parties might be given important roles on committees monitoring government behavior.[11]

In these concrete forms the "taken for granteds" are regime specific. The norm of bipartisanship produces legislative paralysis—the well-known "gridlock" in U.S. policymaking—if the parties become internally homogeneous and polarized. And regimes do rise, flourish, decay, and die, only to be replaced by another regime. The United States saw a New Deal/Great Society regime that began

[10] This definition is drawn from Mark Tushnet, *Constitutional Hardball*, 37 JOHN MARSHALL LAW REVIEW 523 (2004), at p. 523 n. 1.

[11] David Fontana, *Government In Opposition*, 119 YALE LAW JOURNAL 548 (2009), describes a number of practices in which opposition parties are given governing opportunities, few of which have ever been used in the United States even during periods when the norm of mutual toleration was widely honored.

sometime in the 1930s and decayed until its collapse sometime in the 1970s. It was replaced after a while by a Reagan regime that lasted from the1980s into the twenty-first century. Similar things happen around the world. India had a period of one-party dominance from independence into the 1970s, followed a period of coalition governments into the 2010s, followed—it now seems—by another period of one-party dominance. Populist governments took office in Latin America after the prior systems of governance by agreements among elites decayed because of corruption and poor performance.

Each constitutional order will have its own guardrails: things that are taken for granted that allow the order's institutions to get on with their daily work. Where parties are polarized and the nation closely divided, for example, party leaders will enforce party discipline more vigorously than when the parties are internal coalitions. Almost by definition coalition governments allow parties in the coalition to work for some policies inconsistent with those that hold the coalition together. "Confidence and supply" agreements (a weaker version of a coalition agreement) list a few items central to the government's fiscal program and let partners to the agreement do whatever they want on other issues.

If, as we've argued, guardrails are regime specific, no individual guardrail has any special justification as essential to preserving liberal constitutionalism. Forbearance from some behavior might be really important to preserve a specific version of liberal constitutionalism, and irrelevant or positively silly in another version. Canadians are incredulous about some of the things people in the United States take for granted—televised hearings on Supreme Court nominations, for example, even before recent debacles—but both are reasonably well-functioning liberal democracies (at least the United States was until 2017).

So far we've described regime-change as ordinary and not inevitably bad— indeed, sometimes actually good. On that description the fact that the guardrails keeping one regime on track have broken down isn't in itself a matter of concern. What matters is whether the *next* regime is just a new version of liberal constitutionalism or something more troubling—what we've repeatedly called the political merits, here of changing from one regime to another. When we see someone breaking through a guardrail—less metaphorically, breaching an unwritten but well-understood norm—we might be seeing a signal that something's afoot, and we can be pretty sure that things are going to get bumpy for a while, but we can't be sure that the ultimate result will be the demise of liberal constitutionalism. And even if we're quite risk averse and think that a small chance of that demise is something to worry about, at least we have to acknowledge the possibility that the new regime might be an improved version of liberal constitutionalism.[12]

---

[12] Here we refer once again to Hannah Arendt's discussion of revolutions whose outcome was the transformation of subjects into citizens.

Guardrails, then, are built in the course of constructing a constitutional order. They weaken as that order weakens. How, though, do we see the rot in or the rust on the guardrails? Sometimes, of course, it's right on the surface. Political actors say, "That old guardrail is keeping us from doing something we think is really important, so we're simply going to ignore it." When the Obama administration was pushing through its reforms in the provision of healthcare, some Republicans invoked one of the guardrails we've describe to object that the administration hadn't obtained bipartisan support for a change that would affect one-sixth of the U.S. economy. The administration went ahead anyway.[13]

Sometimes the norm is ignored on a one-shot basis. The politician says, "Right now the norm is standing in the way of something incredibly important, so I'll ignore it. But I agree that the norm is important too, and I'll follow it rigorously after this." The politician might be completely sincere at the time and her actions later on might confirm it. Sometimes, though, implicit in the norm's breach is the view that the norm doesn't fit well into a new or emerging constitutional order. The bipartisanship norm just didn't make sense anymore in light of changes in the U.S. party system, for example.

Another concern is that norm breaches occur when some political actor, a politically motivated norm-entrepreneur, as they're sometimes called, thinks that the prior regime has decayed far enough that a replacement is in prospect—but is wrong. The norm breach will occur and be disruptive for a while, but soon enough the old system, with all its rot, will return. The guardrail will get a jerry-rigged repair.

More interesting, though, are cases where politicians acknowledge that the norm exists and deny that they're violating it: "There's a guardrail here that keeps us from going right up to the constitutional limit on our power, so we're forbearing, just as we should, by staying away from the constitutional limit, but what we're doing is well inside the guardrail." At least in the United States that seems to be the most common way of dealing with the restraints that guardrails are supposed to place on political strategies and tactics. We'll begin with probably the most spectacular recent U.S. example, then proceed briefly with an examination of some of Donald Trump's norm violations; offer some generalizations about how guardrails decay; and end with some conclusions about the relation between guardrails, forbearance, and constitutionalism itself.

Supreme Court Justice Antonin Scalia died unexpectedly on February 16, 2016. After waiting a decent period, President Barack Obama nominated Merrick Garland to fill the vacancy. The nomination had to be confirmed by

---

[13] It had tried to get some support from Republicans, negotiating with a number of senators for several months before abandoning the effort. For an account, *see* JONATHAN COHN, THE TEN YEAR WAR: OBAMACARE AND THE UNFINISHED CRUSADE FOR UNIVERSAL COVERAGE (2021), at pp. 103–94.

the Senate before Garland could take his seat. The Senate had a Republican majority, and its leader Mitch McConnell announced almost immediately that the Senate would not hold hearings on Garland's nomination nor hold a vote on his confirmation—even a vote that would end with the nomination's defeat.[14] McConnell pointed to a norm he said emerged from considering the history of Supreme Court nominations: in modern times the Senate had never confirmed a Supreme Court nomination that was made in the calendar year of a presidential election. (If you define "modern times" carefully that was an accurate characterization of the history of nominations.)[15] Indeed, McConnell noted, in 1992 then-Senator Joe Biden had asserted that Republican President George H.W. Bush should not nominate anyone to fill any vacancy that might occur before the election. McConnell supported his action by invoking a principle: with an election soon to come, the American people would have an opportunity to express their opinion on the question of whether a Democrat or a Republican should fill the vacancy. McConnell's political strategy was vindicated in November, when Donald Trump won the election. Shortly after his inauguration, Trump nominated Neil Gorsuch to fill the vacancy.

Trump had the opportunity to fill two additional vacancies, and the third was a reprise of 2016. Justice Ruth Bader Ginsburg died on September 18, 2020, as the presidential campaign pitting Trump against Joe Biden was underway. Eight days later President Trump announced the nomination of Amy Coney Barrett to fill the vacancy. The Senate, still controlled by Republicans, held hearings starting on October 12, and the confirmation vote was held on October 26.

What had happened to the Garland precedent? After all, 2020 was a presidential election year as 2016 had been. In 2016 the parties hadn't even chosen their nominees when McConnell initially blocked Garland's confirmation, whereas in 2020 the campaign was coming to its conclusion; indeed, by October 26 some voters had already cast their ballots because their states allowed early voting before the official election day of November 3. Some Trump supporters gestured toward a distinction: in 2016, the president who nominated Garland was barred from running for re-election, while the president who nominated Barrett was on the ballot; voters could express their approval or disapproval of Trump's choice by their vote, while in 2020 all they could do was approve or disapprove of the nominating president's party. Or, perhaps, the history McConnell recited in 2016 showed that the Senate never confirmed a nomination made in an election year when the nomination was made by a president who lacked a majority in the

---

[14] McConnell feared that, though he could hold his Republican majority united on the question of holding a hearing, were the nomination actually to be voted on enough Republicans would vote for Garland that the nomination would be confirmed.

[15] Anthony Kennedy was confirmed in 1988, an election year, but he had been nominated at the end of November 1987.

Senate (again, an accurate description of the facts). These were fig leaves. Perhaps the Senate's treatment of the Garland nomination was consistent with a norm that hadn't been discerned previously because the facts triggering its application hadn't occurred. The Barrett nomination, though, was a simple exercise of the Senate's undoubted power with no forbearance whatever.

The Garland-Barrett nominations show us how politicians think about norms (and their metaphorical companion, guardrails). Norms of forbearance operate within the limits of constitutional power. Which is to say that the constitution's words don't tell us what the norms are. How then can you tell what the norms of forbearance and mutual respect counsel when specific political and policy issues arise?

There are of course an infinite number of ways you can refrain from exercising the power the constitution gives you. Sometimes, for example, a majority doesn't enact a statute because too many members disagree over the proposal's details. That's not forbearance. Forbearance occurs when you have some sort of principled reason for refraining from exercising your power. On the level of policy, you want to do something and you know that you have the constitutional power to do it. You forbear, though, because some norm overrides your policy preference.

The principle underlying the norm probably has to have some connection with democracy itself; it offsets the democratic loss that occurs when you don't do what you could do. Again, though, there are at least scores of democracy-related reasons for stopping short of doing what you're constitutionally allowed to do. Maybe, for example, really important legislation should have the kind of widespread support among the people that is evidenced by a bipartisan vote for the proposal.

McConnell's initial articulation of the rule about nominations during election years shows what you do when you don't have a text to rely on. You identify the applicable norm by examining past practice and inferring from it a principle that you can link to democracy. That is, you identify norms, the guardrails actually in place, by looking to precedents—not precedents in the sense of previously decided court cases, but precedents in the sense of prior actions taken by political actors.

Still, we've learned a lot about how to reason from precedents from long experience with lawyers' treatment of judicial precedents. This book isn't the place for a course on legal reasoning, but we can lay out some salient points that bear on our treatment of norms and guardrails.

- A prior decision—or, in our context, a prior political action—takes on its meaning from the case's facts.
- But not all the facts—only the relevant ones.

- You determine what the relevant facts are by looking at earlier cases that have some similarities to this one. You always find lots of cases similar to this one in some way, different in others. You compile a list of the ones you think are relevant, and doing that requires you to exercise good legal judgment.
- You look at your list and extract (tentatively, perhaps) a principle that explains as many of the cases on the list as possible.
- Sometimes you'll think that the principle you've generated from the list doesn't seem exactly right for this one—or, worse, seems to produce a wrong, unjust result.
- If that happens, you'll want to see if you can refine the principle so that the revised principle generates a result that seems to make more sense.
- You do that by looking again at the facts of the prior cases. You think about striking some of the cases off the list and bringing back some that you'd discarded earlier. Again, you have to exercise judgment here.
- At this point you're going to discover some cases that just don't fit within the principle. You have to "distinguish" those cases, and you do that by pointing to factual differences between them and the case you're dealing with (and, if you've done your work correctly, between them and the cases that *are* consistent with the principle you've extracted).
- At this point you have a principle, perhaps different from the one you started with, that makes sense of the precedents that count and that produces a sensible result to your problem.[16]
- Sometimes, though, you'll end up thinking that the current case is so different from everything that's gone before that prior decisions simply shed no light whatever on the problem. It's a "case of first impression," and you have to figure out what the best answer is on your own.

McConnell followed much of this outline when confronted with the Garland nomination. He examined prior practices and extracted the "no nominations during presidential election years" rule. To do so he had to define the "modern era" as the source of the precedents, treating nominations made before that—some of which had occurred in presidential election years—as irrelevant. Then, with the Barrett nomination he tried to refine the principle, though doing so was in such obvious bad faith that even he didn't make a serious effort.

A shorthand for this entire process is that norms are fact-specific—not of course limited to the facts of the case at hand, but generated by considering a

---

[16] Karl Llewellyn, a U.S. legal theorist in the mid-twentieth century, described this end state as "wisdom-in-result for the welfare of All-of-us." Karl Llewellyn, *Remarks on the Theory of Appellate Decision and the Rules or Canons about How Statutes Are to Be Construed*, 3 VANDERBILT LAW REVIEW 395 (1950), at p. 396.

wide range of facts that seem relevant. What seems relevant, though, almost always requires you to exercise judgment.

That's obvious when, early in the process, you've identified some prior actions and generated a tentative principle from them, and then have an inchoate feeling that that principle doesn't make sense for the present problem. To take a new example: The U.S. Constitution says that Congress has the power to declare war. Suppose U.S. armed forces are engaged in military action overseas. When is that a "war" that requires a congressional declaration? A rough statement of the official U.S. position is that a war in the constitutional sense occurs when, for a significant period of time, the lives of a significant number of U.S. military personnel are placed at risk overseas. This definition was generated by examining the large number of U.S. military actions overseas that had taken place without a congressional declaration of war (or its legal equivalent). The Obama administration invoked this definition to justify its 2011 bombing campaign in Libya. As U.S. military actions shifted from "boots on the ground" to drone warfare, though, some observers have begun to think that the "U.S. lives at stake" component doesn't make good policy sense today. New facts, perhaps a revised principle.

Now a longer list of examples, to bring populism directly into the discussion by treating Donald Trump as a "pluto-populist."[17] A week after the 2020 presidential election *The Washington Post* published a long article, "The Abnormal Presidency," that offered a list of the twenty most important norms Donald Trump had broken.[18] We won't reproduce the entire list, but here's a selection that gives a sense of what the writer believed to be acts that exhibited an anti- rather than a pro-constitutional attitude: not releasing tax returns, refusing oversight (the process that allows Congress to examine the executive branch's behavior in executing the law), interfering with Department of Justice investigations, abusing the appointment power, coarsening presidential discourse, undermining

---

[17] We have some difficulties in discussing Trump as a populist. Of course, he presented himself as one. Our primary difficulty is that, as was said early in his administration, he combined malevolence—the "bad intent" we've emphasized—with incompetence. (The first use of the phrase that we've found is Benjamin Wittes, "Malevolence Tempered by Incompetence," LAWFARE, Jan. 28, 2017, available at https://www.lawfareblog.com/malevolence-tempered-incompetence-trumps-horrifying-executive-order-refugees-and-visas, archived at https://perma.cc/JTS4-A2ZH). We find it difficult to offer an account that strikes the right balance (and in particular, one that doesn't give his malevolence too much weight). For near-polar positions on Trump's significance for U.S. democracy, *compare* Michael J. Klarman, *The Degradation of American Democracy—and the Court*, 134 HARVARD LAW REVIEW 1 (2020), *with* Samuel Moyn, "How Trump Won," THE NEW YORK REVIEW OF BOOKS, Nov. 9, 2020, available at https://www.nybooks.com/daily/2020/11/09/how-trump-won/, archived at https://perma.cc/5ECP-LWAN. We find ourselves somewhere between these two poles, with one closer to Klarman's "hair on fire" view and the other closer to Moyn's "nothing new to see here" view, but we're closer to each other than to either Klarman or Moyn.

[18] David Montgomery, "The Abnormal Presidency," WASHINGTON POST MAGAZINE, Nov. 15, 2020.

intelligence agencies, publicizing lists of potential Supreme Court nominees, abusing the pardon power, dividing the nation in times of crisis, contradicting scientists, derailing the tradition of presidential debates, and—last but not least—undermining faith in the 2020 election results.[19]

Some of these involve breaches of norms and norms only: there's a tradition of presidential debates and a tradition of releasing tax returns. No one contends that candidates or presidents are under any legal duty to participate in debates or release their tax returns—or that presidential discourse "has to be" elevated rather than coarse. Maybe refusing to take part in debates demonstrates a lack of mutual respect, though in the mode of "distinguishing" Trump's official story was that the form the debate was going to take, to deal with Covid-19 risks, involved a format that disadvantaged him (unlike the format of prior debates). Perhaps coarsening discourse also demonstrates a lack of mutual respect, though we're skeptical about that one. It's hard to see how refusing to release tax returns has much to do with forbearance or mutual respect, though.

Some of the listed items could and sometimes actually did involve breaking the law (abusing the appointment power), but the law violations occurred only because the Trump administration was famously inept at adhering to the procedural steps laid out in the laws such as those dealing with appointments. Better lawyers would have guided the administration through the hoops to the exact same end.

More commonly, the Trump administration argued either that the norm actually didn't exist or that it was complying with the norm properly understood: It wasn't "resisting oversight," it was ensuring that oversight occur within limits that respected the president's lawful range of discretion. It didn't interfere with Department of Justice investigations; it exercised supervision to ensure the faithful execution of the laws as the Constitution requires the president to do: some of the interferences with criminal investigations, while clearly inconsistent with a tradition of prosecutorial independence, were "merely" extraordinary but not unlawful departures from norms that are, we should note, in some tension with the obligation the Constitution imposes on the president to take care that the law be faithfully executed. One non-extreme view is that this clause imposes a duty on the president as an individual. The president can exercise that duty by delegating it to the Department of Justice and monitoring its actions. If the president decides that the department's lawyers are not executing

---

[19] Some of the items on the list involve actions that probably shouldn't be treated as implicating guardrails at all. Publicizing a list of potential Supreme Court nominees could well be regarded as making a bit more transparent processes that have traditionally been quite opaque. Including it on the list might have been a simple error. That the author thought it worth including does suggest, though, the fuzziness of the idea that guardrails can be identified more precisely than "mutual tolerance" and "forbearance." We discuss the problems associated with fuzziness later in this chapter.

the law faithfully—for example, by adopting an overly broad interpretation of a criminal statute—the president honors the "take care" duty by terminating the prosecution

The story's author uses disagreements about the response to the Covid-19 crisis to illustrate "contradicting scientists." The administration said that it didn't disagree with the scientists trying to figure out the virus's composition to develop a vaccine; it disagreed with scientists who offered policy recommendations based on guesses about how best to contain the virus (and some of those guesses turned out to be wrong). Indeed, one might say with some degree of accuracy that the administration was trying to maintain a norm that scientists should govern within their own domain but shouldn't cross the border into territory where scientific judgments have to be weighed against other considerations of public policy—real science for the scientists, decisions about public policy for politicians taking advice from scientists (acknowledging that the advice might be of varying quality and that the politicians might make good faith mistakes).[20]

The charge of undermining the intelligence agencies is more complicated. The administration's actions came in several forms, all directed at what Trump misleadingly called a single "Deep State." As all presidents do, he tried to staff the upper levels of the intelligence bureaucracies with adequately credentialed people who shared his overall world view—suspicion of China, admiration for Russia, and more. However misguided on the merits, these appointments were well within the boundaries of presidential power—not even coming close to the guardrails involving the intelligence community.

A second form involved rejecting the advice he received from career intelligence officers. Here there probably is a vague norm or weak guardrail counseling presidents to accept such advice as a general matter. Sometimes Trump appears to have rejected the advice because he thought it came from operatives of a "Deep State" intent on forcing him out of office.[21] That was delusional. Sometimes, though, he rejected the advice because it came from a weaker version of the Deep State. The intelligence bureaucracies are just that—bureaucracies staffed by career officers who, holding their positions for a long time, build up an institutional understanding of what works to advance the nation's interests. They are willing to change their minds when their political masters change, but actually getting

---

[20] Criticism of the administration for contradicting scientists might have been better illustrated by the administration's take on climate change, where it rejected a strong consensus among scientists. Even there, though, the administration's approach could be reconstructed as the following: accept that climate change is occurring, but reject the policy prescriptions scientists offer, because such prescription aren't within their distinctive scientific expertise. The problem with that reconstruction is that the administration didn't in fact accept that climate change was occurring.

[21] The term "Deep State" originated in analyses of the role military officers played in Egypt and Turkey in determining who could occupy their nations' presidency, mostly by preventing politicians they believed too sympathetic to Islamist rule from becoming or remaining president.

them to do so takes time, especially if, as with Trump, the new political master has a worldview quite different from that of his predecessors.[22] Rejecting advice given before the institutional culture changes is, on this view, consistent with the weak norm about respecting what the intelligence community tells the president.

We can see similar processes at work in European populisms. Good constitutional practice cautions against entrenching in a constitution detailed policy prescriptions, especially about the economic system, that might have to be changed when economic conditions change. Some of Hungary's constitutional amendments had that character, but Fidesz noted that the European Union had insisted on entrenching a hard budget constraint in the constitutions of EU member states. Fidesz reinterpreted the norm in light of those provisions to show that it actually hadn't breached a norm. Syriza in Greece breached the norm that you carry out your campaign promises, and justified its action on numerous grounds: It did so reluctantly, it faced enormous pressure from the European financial institutions, and overall Greece's economic circumstances changed significantly between the time it developed its platform and the time it took office.

Now put all this together with our earlier argument that norms are regime specific. Suppose we've identified a norm that guided forbearance during a prior constitutional regime or order—the "no significant legislation without bipartisan support" norm, for example, or the norm, "accept the intelligence community's advice." One obviously relevant fact about those norms is that they were generated during a prior constitutional regime (the era when internally the parties were coalitions in the first case, the Cold War era and the period of U.S. hegemony after the Soviet Union's collapse in the second). Put another way: we can distinguish our current situation from the prior one by pointing to the differences in party structure or international relations—by describing what made that regime different from the one we're living with now. When we don't follow that norm, we're not breaching a norm of forbearance that applies now.

That doesn't mean that forbearance and mutual respect aren't important in the new constitutional order, just that they'll take different forms. Or: the old regime had its distinctive guardrails, the new one will have different ones.

Of course it takes time to build new guardrails. As they're being put in place people may be nervous about the possibility that the vehicle will go over the mountainside. And it might. Still, one or two incidents of norm-breaching might not indicate that forbearance and mutual respect have disappeared. We should worry if we can see them disappearing across the board, or if the guardrail that's broken through is monumentally important because it's located at exactly the

---

[22] For an astute and generally sympathetic account of *this* form of Deep State, see JOHN A. DEARBORN, STEPHEN SKOWRONEK, & DESMOND KING, PHANTOMS OF A BELEAGUERED REPUBLIC (2021).

most dangerous point on the mountain road. Trump's persistent rejection of the 2020 election results is a good example.

Here our discussion of populism and its critics comes back into the story in full force: populisms with programs driven by a pervasive "we versus them" narrative that isn't justified by the facts are worrisome, and Trump's pluto-populism might fit that description. Not all populisms do.

There's one final matter before we conclude. So far we've used the passive voice in describing guardrails: They're in place, they are built up through practice, they rot or rust. Real guardrails are built and maintained by real people deployed by the Department of Public Works—by an institution. What institutions maintain the guardrails? With constitutional norms, the answer is, the courts, which keep political actors within bounds. The guardrails, though, keep politicians from pushing their power to its constitutional limits, so what the courts say doesn't help us identify the guardrails. The very definition of pre-constitutional norms or guardrails entails that there's no readily identifiable institution to keep the guardrails in good working order.

Here are three candidates.

- *Militant democracy.* Influenced in part by Germany's political turmoil in the 1920s and 1930s, some constitution-drafters tell constitutional courts that they can exclude "anti-constitutional" parties from the ballot and bar their members from being public servants in positions where they could exercise discretion in a politically biased way.[23] These are the big guns protecting against democratic erosion, and they can't be, and aren't, used that often. On the theoretical level, Jan-Werner Müller accurately calls them "prima facie illiberal measures" that a liberal democracy must deploy with great caution.[24] On the practical level, it's easy to disqualify a party with few adherents from the ballot, much more difficult to exclude a party that's grown to a politically significant size—but it's the latter, not the former, that pose the real threats to democracy.

- *Qualifications for office.* A list of populist leaders who have attained power will show that many were "outsiders" to the political system: Donald Trump, Silvio Berlusconi, the M5M's Beppe de Grillo. That's not surprising: at the heart of populist programs is opposition to entrenched political elites, and who better than an outsider to replace them? Maybe we can prevent outsiders

---

[23] For an overview, *see* Jan-Werner Müller, "Militant Democracy," in OXFORD HANDBOOK OF COMPARATIVE CONSTITUTIONAL LAW (Michael Rosenfeld & András Sajó eds. 2012), at p. 1253. Rivka Weill, *Secession and the Prevalence of Both Militant Democracy and Eternity Clauses Worldwide,* 40 CARDOZO LAW REVIEW 905 (2018), argues that eternity clauses that bar amendments to specified constitutional provisions can be a substitute for explicit "militant democracy" clauses.

[24] Müller, note 23 above, at p. 1253.

from breaking through guardrails by requiring that presidents or prime ministers have some degree of experience in political office before moving up to those positions. The difficulty here is that "prior experience" is only a proxy for "more likely to respect the guardrails," and at least anecdotally it's a terrible proxy. Jair Bolsonaro, Narendra Modi, and Rodrigo Duterte had decades of political experience. Many admirable political leaders have had no prior political experience: Corazon Aquino and Nelson Mandela, for example. (These might be thought special cases, but trying to write a provision exempting people "like them" from the prior-experience requirement is probably impossible.) In the United States such a provision would have prevented Dwight Eisenhower from becoming president and Wendell Willkie from running for the presidency. It would also sharply limit the number of third-party candidacies, converting third parties from vehicles for protest against the system into vehicles for politicians unable to win their party's nomination.

- *Electoral rules.* "Outsider" candidates are also typically protest candidates. You can design electoral rules that make it nearly impossible for protest candidates to win major offices. That comes at a cost, though. Knowing that the campaign is futile, few serious people will mount a protest campaign. Protest candidacies, though, provide information to the major parties about voter concerns.[25] So your election rules have to give them some realistic possibility of winning—and sometimes lightning will strike and they'll win.[26]

The weakness of the institutions maintaining the guardrails might actually be a good thing because, as we've repeatedly emphasized, breaching a norm or breaking a guardrail might not always be bad for democratic constitutionalism. Sometimes the constitutional order in place will have become so ossified that it no longer serves as a good example of democratic constitutionalism. To use another somewhat tired metaphor: if better replacements lie in the wings, they should have a chance to take the stage.

Writing in October 2020 as the U.S. presidential campaign was nearing its end, political scientist Corey Robin wrote a short essay on "The Gonzo Constitutionalism of the American Right." Robin described three institutional pillars supporting the Republican Party: the electoral college, whose bias in favor of small states tilted the presidential playing field toward Republicans; the malapportioned Senate; and a federal judiciary packed with recently appointed and

---

[25] At their start some Green parties were protest parties, as were all Pirate parties. Over time they worked their way into parliaments and eventually (for the Greens already, for the Pirates probably soon) into coalition governments.

[26] The usual examples involve coming close but not quite succeeding: Jörg Haider in Austria, who led his party into a coalition government but was too controversial to serve as Chancellor; and Jean-Marie and then Marie Le Pen in France, both of whom made it to the run-off round in French presidential elections.

young conservative judges with life tenure. He concluded his essay by observing that if the Democrats won the presidency and "hope[] to implement the merest plank of their platform" they would "have to engage in a major project of norm erosion"—packing the Supreme Court and eliminating the filibuster rule whose effect is to require sixty votes rather than fifty-one to enact a statute. If the Democrats did that, Robin concluded, "we will see that norm erosion is not how democracies die but how they are born."[27]

More precisely: norm erosion is how democracies die *and* how they are born. Something new is in prospect when the guardrails come off, but we can't know in advance whether what comes next will be authoritarianism or a revitalized or even enhanced democracy—or, indeed, and sometimes alas, the same old, same old.

---

[27] Corey Robin, "The Gonzo Constitutionalism of the American Right," NEW YORK REVIEW OF BOOKS, Oct. 21, 2020.

PART THREE

CONSTITUTIONALISM
AFTER POPULISM

11

Rejecting Democracy

We've argued that populism's contemporary critics fail to grapple with the populism's diversity. We believe that almost all versions of populism, the bad as well as the good, have directed attention to real problems with contemporary representative democracy. Now it's time to address what might be done about those problems. Without pretending to be comprehensive, we group the proposed solutions into two categories—in this chapter, challenges to democracy itself and in the next challenges to contemporary institutions of representation. In presenting the latter challenges, we try to present some institutional innovations that are, we believe, consistent with the best impulses underlying populism's rise.[1] And, in doing so we implicitly reject the argument that populism as such is anti-institutional and merely instrumental.

Writing after the suppression of a workers' uprising against the Communist regime in East Germany, Bertolt Brecht wrote a poem that referred to a statement by the governing Communist Party that "the people had forfeited the confidence of the government": "Would it not in that case be simpler for the government to dissolve the people and elect another?"[2]

Brecht used high irony to address one kind of disappointment with "the people." Different disappointments occasioned by some populisms have revived long-standing arguments against democracy. The arguments have a standard form: the people don't know enough about politics or policy for their views (reliably determined) to provide the basis for good and stable government. And the arguments generate a standard conclusion: government by the people should be replaced with government by someone else—technocrats, politicians relatively unencumbered by directives from their constituents, and (for libertarians) private entrepreneurs in a world where government's reach is dramatically limited.

---

[1] We emphasize that our discussion of these institutional innovations is both quite selective and not at all novel: we draw on a well-established and large literature on democratic innovation.

[2] Bertolt Brecht, "Die Lösung" (The Solution).

Power to the People. Mark Tushnet and Bojan Bugarič, Oxford University Press. © Mark Tushnet and Bojan Bugarič 2021. DOI: 10.1093/oso/9780197606711.003.0012

I. Technocracy Instead of Democracy

In 1878 Friedrich Engels wrote that in the aftermath of capitalism "the government of persons is replaced by the administration of things." A decade later Edward Bellamy published a best-selling novel *Looking Backward*, which described a future in which technology had solved all problems of material deprivation. A few decades later social theorists and lawyers associated with the American Progressive movement began to describe a new mode of governance—now known as the administrative state—where experts would determine major social policies including how to reduce the risks associated with modern life, what prices major industries could charge, and how to deal with criminals so that they wouldn't go back to a life of crime.

Technocratic government by experts often has been a left-liberal-progressive alternative to government by the people themselves. Technocracy made sense in contexts where everyone agreed on what the right social outcome should be—reduction of the risks of daily life to create a world in which people were prosperous, safe, and healthy, for example. Experts could figure out how to get from here to there by using science and mechanical (and sometimes social) engineering. Put another way: technocracy makes sense in domains where there are no fundamental political disagreements—and technocrats believe that those domains are quite large.

A common diagnosis of populism's rise in Europe points to the displacement of domestic policymaking by technocratic governance in the European Union—prescriptions about what could be placed on sale in grocery stores that seemed mindless to many but made sense to the technocrats in Brussels. What went wrong with the utopian hopes of technocrats on the left side of the political spectrum? In part, political opportunism. Some politicians misrepresented what the requirements were (Boris Johnson notoriously so). Many of the requirements made sense to technocrats concerned with ensuring that the goods sold weren't going to make consumers sick but were difficult to explain (every regulation inevitably covers something it shouldn't, and critics seized on this overbreadth to discredit the regulation for cases where it does make sense).[3]

We focus on one policy domain, the regulation of risks to health and safety, where the argument for technocratic governance has been particularly well-developed. The argument is basically that people don't know what's in their own best interests and experts do. We suggest that this disparagement of the people

---

[3] Left-wing populism was fueled by the commitment of Brussels technocrats to balanced budgets, which are sometimes but not always good policy. That commitment had a conservative spin, and we omit balanced budgets from our discussion because we're focused on the failure of the progressive technocratic vision.

has infected defenders of technocracy more generally, though we don't develop that extension of the argument in detail.

Air pollution makes it hard to breath and makes people sick. No one wants to work where they have to inhale hazardous fumes from chemicals or worry about being cut by flying pieces of metal. Too often, polluters don't care about the illnesses their factories cause as long as the factories are making money. And too often people can't demand hazard pay commensurate with the risks they face and can't quit the hazardous job because they need the money they earn. That's why governments regulate air pollution and workplace risks.[4]

People also know that reducing air pollution and workplace hazards costs money. We can protect ourselves from chemical fumes by wearing hazmat suits all the time and from flying pieces of metal by wearing a suit of armor. We don't do that because we think that we can protect ourselves enough by cheaper and less inconvenient methods. Instead of focusing on *our* behavior, we can change how much pollution factories put into the air and which chemicals the employer uses. But—key to the technocrats' arguments—we also know that changing what factories and employers do costs them money, and that as their costs go up, so do the costs we have to pay for the products they make. So, because we want health, safety, *and* prosperity, the regulations factories and employers have to comply with must balance reducing risks against increasing costs (not just to the factories and employers, but to us as consumers).

And here's where the technocratic displacement of democracy comes in. U.S. Supreme Court Justice Stephen Breyer is an exemplary liberal technocrat. In 1995 he published a short book, *Breaking the Vicious Circle*, criticizing the scope of regulation in the United States. Regulation went wrong for several reasons, according to Breyer. Among them were these: ordinary people, politicians, and some regulators picked out things to regulate almost randomly; and "the public's evaluation of risk problems differs radically from any consensus of experts in the field."[5] We regulate randomly because our attention is caught by events that happen to hit the front pages even if they aren't all that common (and more routine and more serious problems don't get equivalent publicity); we worry too much about low risks of getting cancer and not enough about having a persistent hacking cough.

A whole field of behavioral economics has grown up around these and similar observations. Behavioral economists identify what they call cognitive biases—defects in reasoning, which they sometimes argue are hardwired into our nerve

---

[4] Similar arguments support government regulation of risks associated with consumer purchases. We note that working out the arguments for regulation in detail is quite complicated, especially where people have full information about the risks they face from jobs and consumer products.

[5] Stephen G. Breyer, Breaking the Vicious Circle: Toward Effective Risk Regulation (1993), at p. 33.

system, that lead us to make mistakes in judgment.[6] We worry about things on the front page because of the "availability heuristic," for example.

Here's the payoff: ordinary people don't work out the right balance between improving health and safety on the one side and prosperity on the other. Sometimes they want too little regulation, subjecting themselves to risks that could be cut quite a bit without much effort—because they don't think that the risks are real or as large as they really are. Sometimes they want too much regulation, forcing prices up to pay for what companies have to do to reduce really small risks that people mistakenly believe are quite substantial.

The technocrats' solution is obvious: take the decisions away from the people and put them in the hands of experts who aren't (as) subject to these cognitive biases. Breyer's may be the most dramatic version of ideas that rattle around among technocrats. He proposed that the United States create a large cadre of civil servants, substantially insulated from political influence, with training and experience in fields associated with health and safety, and let them develop regulations that get the balance "right."

Cass Sunstein, himself a technocrat at heart, wrote in an admiring summary of Breyer's work as a Supreme Court justice, "there are multiple potential tensions between a belief in technocracy and a belief in democracy. . . . Technocrats are enthusiastic about a large role for insulated, independent experts, immersed in complex questions. Democrats are concerned that such experts lack accountability and may have an agenda of their own."[7] There are of course many critiques of the technocrats' diagnosis and prescription: if people worry about risks more than experts think they should, still their worries reduce their happiness and so, not matter how irrational the worries are, they should be taken into account; technocrats have their own biases; and more. For our purposes these critiques are less important than the fact that technocrats seek to displace politics by ordinary people—democracy—with something else.

These technocrats say that ordinary people aren't good at figuring out what's best for themselves in some areas.[8] We've focused on risk regulation because that covers an enormous range of contemporary policy: not only health and safety, but privacy in connection with new information technologies, employment in connection with artificial intelligence, and much more. The disparagement of

---

[6] Behavioral economics and cognitive biases have become part of the discourse among the well-informed public through such works as DANIEL KAHNEMANN, THINKING, FAST AND SLOW (2011); and RICHARD H. THALER & CASS R. SUNSTEIN, NUDGE: IMPROVING DECISIONS ABOUT HEALTH, WEALTH, AND HAPPINESS (2008). Note the subtitle of the latter work.

[7] Cass R. Sunstein, *From Technocrat to Democrat*, 114 HARVARD LAW REVIEW 488 (2014), at p. 489.

[8] Of course, some technocrats continue in the older tradition of seeing technocracy as a servant of popular will whatever it happens to be. Our concern here is with the newer, people-skeptical defenses of technocracy.

the ability of ordinary people to govern themselves can extend to many other domains. Many defenders of strong versions of constitutional review, for example, assert that that practice is required to prevent misguided majorities from restricting rights that the majority itself benefits from in the long run.

In Chapter 2 we argued that populism didn't necessarily take the form of pitting the people against the elites in a pejorative sense. When technocrats defend their role with the argument that they know better what's best for ordinary people than the people do, they come quite close to pitting themselves against the people. Not surprisingly and perhaps appropriately, ordinary people who sense that that's what happening sometimes become resentful.[9] We'd modify Cas Mudde's conclusion by omitting the word "illiberal," but otherwise we agree with his observation: "the populist surge is an illiberal democratic response to *decades of undemocratic liberal principles*."[10]

Those European populists who say that bureaucrats in Brussels are taking away their right to govern themselves are triggered by actions that go beyond any single intrusive EU regulation. They understand that "Brussels" is a metonym for how technocracy has shrunk the space for democratic decision-making. In many countries, populist parties are the only ones to argue that there exists a real alternative. They protest against the "consensus at the center" between the center-right and center-left, and so against the idea that there is no alternative to neoliberal globalization. In the eyes of populists, the European project is the embodiment of a ruthless process of globalization responsible for intolerable levels of inequality, declining trust in democracy, a rising danger of terrorism, and increasing fear of loss of one's "national" and "cultural" identity.[11] The populists do not seek to completely dismantle the European Union. As in the 1930s, populism appears in different political forms, but the common thread is that technocracy in Brussels has displaced politics at national capitals.

Some contemporary arguments for technocracy, particularly as instantiated in the European Union, no longer defend it as a purely technical exercise supporting democracy by ensuring that the people get what they want. These arguments have come to defend technocracy instead of democracy.

---

[9] We can't resist the obvious reference here to Hilary Clinton's misguided description of Donald Trump's supporters as a basket of deplorables.

[10] Cas Mudde, "Europe's Populist Surge: A Long Time in the Making," FOREIGN AFFAIRS, Nov.–Dec. 2016, p. 30. *See also* JAN ZIELONKA, COUNTER-REVOLUTION: LIBERAL EUROPE IN RETREAT (2018).

[11] Many major populist parties in Western Europe today are both anti-Eurozone and anti-European. On the left, only populists in Greece and Spain support both the euro and the European project. On the right, only two major populist parties (Germany's right-wing AfD and Italy's Five Star Movement) are not outright anti-European, but they are both against the euro. The populists in the East have gone even further in their confrontation with the European Union. They frontally assault core EU values, contest the legitimacy of EU institutions and policies, and, at home, dismantle constitutional democracy.

II. Representation Rather Than Direct Democracy

A prize-winning and provocative essay by law professor Ming-Sung Kuo argues "Against Instantaneous Democracy."[12] Professor Kuo frames his discussion by referring to the contemporary wave of populism and the Brexit referendum, and we take him to characterize contemporary populism as pointing in the direction of an as-yet-unachieved but thought-to-be-desirable practice of instantaneous democracy.[13]

For Professor Kuo, instantaneous democracy consists of a variety of mechanisms by which what he calls "unformed public opinion" can intervene at each stage. By "unformed public opinion," he appears to mean views of "the people" that are not sufficiently deliberated before their expression.[14] He contrasts this with the traditional view of public decision-making, where public opinion is mediated by such institutions as political parties and the mass media before it affects the policymaking stages.[15] Instantaneous democracy creates the "risk of merging [the stages] into a single, mixed stage, so to speak."[16]

Following an outline provided by Jeremy Waldron, Professor Kuo enumerates ten ("or so") stages that, he argues, are required for enactments and other forms of lawmaking such as constitutional amendment and the development of the common law. He links these to the standard Montesquiean tripartite structure of separated powers, though he does not contend that each set of grouped stages must be institutionalized in a U.S.-style separation of powers system. Professor Kuo argues that these stages are "articulated"—linked temporally, with some time spent at each stage. But, he argues, instantaneous democracy makes it possible to truncate the time spent at each stage.

Professor Kuo's account of how unformed public opinion is translated directly into public policy has several components, some described as much by allusion as by definition. Technology plays a role, for example: A populist leader's tweets can lead his or her supporters to place pressure on legislators, thereby truncating the deliberative legislative process.[17] Why this implicates *unformed* public opinion is

---

[12]   17 INTERNATIONAL JOURNAL OF CONSTITUTIONAL LAW 554 (2019).

[13]   Professor Kuo seems to waver between treating instantaneous democracy as a phenomenon in the real world of contemporary politics and a metaphor or a possibility. *See, e.g., id.*, at p. 568 ("The distinction between the incubation of opinions and the formation of policies is being *virtually* obliterated."); *id.* at p. 569 ("Instead, the exercise of political power is virtually turned into an endless careless reality show. . . .). We read the word *virtually* here to mean "nearly" or "almost," rather than "by use of the technologies of the virtual space," but concede the existence of an ambiguity.

[14]   *See id.* at pp. 567–68 (referring to "an instantaneous decision-making style, displacing the stepwise *and deliberative* political tempo that is critical to norm translation and internalization in constitutional governance.") (emphasis added).

[15]   *Id.* at p. 557.

[16]   *Id.* at p. 569.

[17]   *Id.*

puzzling: we would have thought that leaders' tweets help form public opinion.[18] And this suggests a broader concern. We wonder whether public opinion is *ever* unformed in any interesting sense. People don't wake up one morning and say to themselves, "Oh, we think a universal basic income would be a good idea!" They get their political ideas and form their opinions from somewhere—lived experience, conversations with family and friends, consuming what's produced by legacy media and new media, and much more. The forms and effects of mediation may vary depending upon what those sources are, but we think it misleading to describe the process of translating public opinions into public policy as instantaneous either at the stage of formation or, as we argue in a moment, at the stage of policymaking.

Professor Kuo offers another account of how unformed public opinion becomes public policy instantaneously. Populist leaders forge a "direct link" with the people whose effect is that populists take whatever the leader thinks as what policy should be. So, indeed, if the populist leader wakes up one morning thinking that a universal basic income would be a good idea, it becomes policy later that day. The leader "knows" what the people want because she or he almost literally embodies the people.[19]

Here the difficulty is selectivity and overstatement. As we argued in Chapter 2, some populisms have leaders like those Professor Kuo describes—but not all. Professor Kuo refers to the "vulgarity" of populist leaders, which is a fair description of Silvio Berlusconi but hardly of Narendra Modi.[20] And it's a fair description of non-populist leaders like Lyndon Baines Johnson. Similarly, Professor Kuo points to the "fad" of campaign biographies by populist leaders as support for the argument that the populist leader builds representativeness into his or her person.[21] This seems to us a simple mistake. In the United States today every presidential candidate writes a campaign biography. If such works are a fad, it's not one associated with populism—and for that reason it's not associated with the proposition that the politician embodies the people.

As to the articulated stages of policymaking: for Professor Kuo each stage requires "a certain period of time," not a "fleeting" or "transient" moment. Those periods "buy the democratic society time to reflect *and reconsider*."[22] Implicit

---

[18] At some points Professor Kuo appears to suggest that public opinion is formed (only?) by traditional intermediaries such as political parties and legacy media such as the press. *See, e.g., id.*, at p. 557 (referring to those institutions).

[19] As we understand his terminology, this is what Professor Kuo refers to as the leader's "authenticity." *Id.* at pp. 558–60.

[20] *Id.* at p. 560. Similarly with Professor Kuo's references to populist leaders' "showmanship" as distinct from charisma: some are showmen, some aren't (we revert to our usual examples here of Viktor Orbán and Jarosław Kaczyński).

[21] *Id.* at pp. 558–59.

[22] *Id.* at p. 572 (emphasis added) (referring specifically to the role that judicial review of legislation plays).

here is the thought that instantaneous decisions are more likely than deliberated ones to be mistaken and so should be more open to reconsideration. As before, we wonder whether any decisions by populist voters are instantaneous or non-deliberative in any interesting sense.

Consider, for example, a referendum. Here are Professor Kuo's first three stages, all related to initial adoption of a legal instrument: "the people must be able to envisage the desired political action (1), formulate the action plan as a policy in a legislative bill (2), and enact the policy into law through the legislative processes of deliberation and voting (3)."[23] Notably, referendums proceed through these stages. *Someone*—a political party or an NGO, for example—has to come up with an idea to be put forward as a referendum and then come up with a specific proposal that can be placed on the referendum ballot. There will inevitably be discussion—deliberation?—about whether the idea is worth pursuing and about whether the particular version is desirable.

For example, Switzerland held a referendum in 2016 on whether the nation should guarantee a basic income to all. That idea had been circulating in academic quarters for years, and ultimately gained support from two Swiss NGOs.[24] They circulated a petition that obtained the requisite number of signatures. None of this was "instantaneous," nor in any contemporary setting could it be. Professor Kuo's third stage of voting, then, seems to be the place where all the work is done, at least with respect to referendums. In some sense the referendum's result instantaneously sets policy. Of course, in parliamentary systems the vote at a third reading (or whatever the final stage is) also instantaneously sets policy in that same sense.

For that reason, the relevant question is comparative: Is the degree or quality of deliberation better in legislative forums than in referendum campaigns?[25] In Switzerland, the proposal as placed on the ballot would have provided a basic income to all Swiss residents. Among the issues discussed during the campaign was how the guaranteed income would be set, and whether it should be guaranteed only to Swiss citizens rather than all residents. As far as we can tell the quality of deliberation was no worse than it would have been in a legislative debate.

Neither a single example nor an accumulation of anecdotes can establish the general proposition that referendum campaigns are as deliberative as legislative debates. Today's populists do not contend that referendums should completely

---

[23] *Id.* at p. 563.

[24] For a collection of essays, *see* THE PALGRAVE INTERNATIONAL HANDBOOK OF BASIC INCOME (Malcolm Torry ed. 2019). Torry is the director of an NGO founded in 1984 that focuses on advocacy for a basic income.

[25] For a general observation, *see* JOHN G. MATSUSAKA, LET THE PEOPLE RULE: HOW DIRECT DEMOCRACY CAN MEET THE POPULIST CHALLENGE (2020), at p. 175 (questioning both the proposition that legislative debates are highly deliberative and the proposition that referendum campaign are not).

displace legislatures, or that referendums should resolve all contentious issues of public policy. So, the relevant question must be refined: With respect to the subset of policy issues that populists actually submit to referendums, is the quality of deliberation worse than in legislative debates on the same issues?[26] We are not clear on how the burden of proof should be allocated on the question: Should defenders of referendums or of legislation as it actually occurs have that burden?[27] That seems to us the real question.

Further, even the outcome of a referendum vote doesn't always determine policy. Consider again the Brexit example. Finding themselves bound by the vote,[28] politicians still had to do a lot of work to figure out the details of what "Brexit" actually meant—"strategies of enforcement," Professor Kuo calls them in describing the fifth stage of policymaking.[29]

We refrain from marching through the list of stages Professor Kuo provides to show that populist decision-making isn't instantaneous at all, but instead often also goes through those stages. We concede, of course, that sometimes individual policies become law under a populist government without going through each and every stage—but we also insist that that happens as well under non-populist governments: emergency legislation responding to the Covid-19 pandemic in several European nations, including France, Germany, and Italy (with a populist party as a distinctly secondary member of the governing coalition) went through quite truncated enactment processes.

Populist decision-making can have "the stepwise and deliberative political tempo that is critical to norm translation and internationalization in constitutional governance."[30] Whether or how often it does is of course an empirical question, not a conceptual one. We have provided an example or two that challenge Professor Kuo's account on empirical grounds. As we have said, a few examples and anecdotes can't resolve the empirical question. They can raise questions, though, about characterizing populism as an exercise in instantaneous democracy.

Professor Kuo's account is a defense of traditional elite-oriented accounts of how representation tempers the potential excesses of democracy. We don't

---

[26] Implicit in this question is the proposition, discussed in the next chapter, that the anti-institutionalism said to be associated with populism doesn't foreclose populists from using institutions to select those policy proposals that are to be submitted to referendums.

[27] Ron Levy, "Democratic Innovation in Constitutional Reform," in HANDBOOK OF DEMOCRATIC INNOVATION AND GOVERNANCE (Stephen Elstub & Oliver Escobar eds. 2019), at pp. 349–50, describes a "number of innovations—most as yet untried" that could improve the deliberative quality of referendums. In Chapter 12 we argue that populists can prescribe rules to regulate referendums, including the innovations that Levy describes, without relinquishing their anti-institutionalism.

[28] Though subject to the possibility of reconsideration through a later referendum, a question that was mooted during the Brexit process.

[29] Kuo, note 13 above, at p. 563.

[30] *Id.* at pp. 567–68.

contend that "representative democracy" is an oxymoron, as "technocratic democracy" might be. Rather, representative democracy is one form democracy can take—just not the only one. Populist democracy is another. Or so we argue in the next chapter.

Before that, we engage a final critique of democracy as a form of government that rests on a majority's judgments about what policies would be good for the polity.

III. No Government Rather Than Democratic Government

Philosopher Jason Brennan is admirably direct: *Against Democracy* (2016). So is economist Bryan Caplan: *The Myth of the Rational Voter* (2011). Democracy is a bad form of government, they argue, because ordinary voters don't know enough or care enough to cast their votes in favor of public policies that increase overall well-being. The solution? Some combination of "epistocracy"—rule by the knowledgeable—with a sharp reduction in the scope of government to lower the social damage irrational or ill-informed voters can inflict on the rest of us.

Professor Caplan purports to establish voters' irrationality by comparing what ordinary people think about a range of economic issues to what economists think. He begins his book with one such comparison, about tariffs and other forms of economic protectionism. "Economists across the political spectrum have pointed out its folly for centuries, but almost every democracy restricts imports." And they do so because ignorant voters cast their ballots for policies that comport with their "knee-jerk emotional and ideological reactions." So, he concludes, "democracy fails because it does what voters want." The "main alternative" to democracy is, for him, "markets."[31]

Professor Caplan relies upon a number of surveys and examines one in some detail. We suggest that the surveys don't show what he thinks they show, mostly because we think that ordinary people interpret the questions they're being asked differently from the way economists do—despite the fact that the words of the question are identical.

Take Professor Caplan's discussion of expert-public disagreement about tariffs. He reports that about three-quarters of economists agreed that "tariffs . . . usually reduce the general welfare of society." He then brings in a general public opinion survey juxtaposing the argument that without tariffs "the costs of goods would go down" to the argument that "tariffs are necessary to protect certain manufacturing jobs . . . from the competition of less expensive imports." The survey

---

[31] Bryan Caplan, The Myth of the Rational Voter (2011), at pp. 1–3 (emphasis omitted).

showed that about two-thirds of the public agreed with the second argument. Professor Caplan attributes this to "antiforeign bias."[32]

Professor Caplan acknowledges that the two questions are not precisely comparable, so he relies more heavily on a separate survey that asked large numbers of U.S. economists and ordinary people identical questions. Most asked whether specific policies were keeping the economy "from being as good as it might be," with the possible answers "not a reason at all," a "minor reason," or a "major reason."[33] For many policies the survey shows the public thinking that the policies at issue are more important than economists do. The survey had thirty-seven questions, and we focus on only a few of interest to the critique of democracy rather than going through the entire list.

- "Too many immigrants": The public thinks that immigration is a big reason for economic underperformance; economists think that immigration "increases the size of the pie . . ." and that "one more self-supporting worker is a net benefit, no matter where he was born."
- "Technology is displacing workers": The public thinks it is and causes economic underperformance. Economists think that "machines make us richer." Professor Caplan sees a "make-work bias" in the public's views.
- "Downsizing": "When a profitable company cuts its workforce, the typical person treats it as clearly bad for the economy," while economists disagree: "Doing more with less is the definition of progress." Again. this is said to show the make-work bias.
- "Trade agreements": It turns out that, according to the survey, a good-sized chunk of the public actually thinks that trade agreements are good for the economy, but to Professor Caplan that support is "half-hearted," because economists think that such agreements are almost always good for the economy. He finds that judgment confirmed by answers to another question, about whether trade agreements create more jobs in the United States, where the public thinks that such agreements cost jobs.[34]

Professor Caplan concludes that the survey "confirms the reality of large and systematic belief differences between economists and the public."[35] Now recall the reference in the book's title to the "myth" that voters are rational. Systematic disagreements with experts show irrationality or ignorance.

We are struck by something rather different. It seems clear to us that the economists and the ordinary people who were surveyed read the questions

---

[32] *Id.* at pp. 50–51.
[33] *Id.* at pp. 56–57.
[34] *Id.* at pp. 58–59, 65–67, 70 (describing answers to a slightly different question), 69.
[35] *Id.* at p. 81.

differently. Economists took the questions at face value: How important were these policies in generating economic problems for the country as a whole? The ordinary people, we think, read them as asking the following: Do these policies cause problems for a lot of people? That is, we think that the ordinary people were focusing on what they thought the policies' distributional effects were: how the fabled influx of Polish plumbers into Great Britain led lots of British plumbers to make less money (to shift to an international example), or so many ordinary citizens thought; how outsourcing automobile assembly costs U.S. autoworkers jobs.[36] Maybe they were wrong about distributional effects too, but the surveys Professor Caplan relies on don't show *that* (and, though we're not economists, we guess that the consensus among economists about distributional effects is weaker than the consensus about overall social welfare).

The economists say, "Sure these things happen, but the result is that the cost of plumbing and cars for everyone goes down." Ordinary people reply, "Maybe so, but the plumbers and autoworkers who lost their jobs can't buy things even at the lower prices." The economists do have an answer: "But we could develop 'trade adjustment assistance' policies using some of the money saved by lower product costs to retrain the workers who lost their jobs and make everybody better off— good new jobs and lower prices." And ordinary people are skeptical: "You say we *could* do that, and we agree that everything would be fine if we actually did it. But we've seen how trade adjustment assistance policies have worked in the past, and they do almost nothing for the displaced workers."

We're inclined to think that the ordinary people are "more correct" than the experts here—not irrationally motivated by an antiforeign bias or a make-work bias, but realistic about how politics won't deliver on the economists' promises that the policies in question, supplemented by laws to deal with the policies' distributional effects, will make everyone better off by "growing the pie." If we're right, Professor Caplan hasn't made out his case against democracy.

Professor Caplan is a libertarian or classical liberal, whose views about the relative ability of markets and governments to satisfy human needs even before he did his analysis counseled skepticism about government (whether democratic or

---

[36] We're not empirical social scientists, but we're confident that surveys that asked, "Do you think this and that policy is a good one?" (rather than "good for the economy"), and followed up by asking for the reasons people had for their views would show that those who thought the policies bad had distributional effects in mind. For some suggestive findings along these lines, *see* Richard K. Hermann, Philip E. Tetlock & Matthew N. Diascro, *How Americans Think about Trade: Reconciling Conflicts among Money, Power, and Principle*, 45 INTERNATIONAL STUDIES QUARTERLY 191 (2001), at p. 204 (finding that elite respondents favor free trade whether the benefits go to the poor or the rich whereas the general public "favor restricting trade when the benefits go to the rich" but support free trade when the benefits go to the poor); Xiaobao Lü, Kenneth Scheve & Matthew Slaughter, *Inequity Aversion and the international Distribution of Trade Protection*, 56 AMERICAN JOURNAL OF POLITICAL SCIENCE 638 (2012) (arguing that "inequity aversion" leads people to prefer trade policies that minimize inequality).

otherwise). We suggest somewhat snarkily that his interpretation of the evidence exemplifies the cognitive failing of "confirmation bias," the interpretation of possibly ambiguous evidence to confirm what you already believe.

Professor Brennan is also a classical liberal. He too starts with the premise that most ordinary citizens don't know much about policy-relevant questions, and he too uses Brexit, immigration policy, and protectionism as key examples.[37] He entertains and seems to endorse a solution different from Professor Caplan's. It is "epistocracy," or, as he puts it in one of his chapter titles, "The Rule of the Knowers." Professor Brennan offers several possible institutional forms of epistocracy, including limiting the franchise to voters who pass some sort of test and—interestingly for our purposes—delegating decision-making authority to a randomly selected group of people who will be given the information experts believe they need to make an informed decision (something like the deliberative polls we discuss in the next chapter).[38]

For Professor Brennan, some ordinary people are completely uninformed about policy; he calls them "hobbits." Others think they know something but what they know is highly skewed; he calls this group "hooligans." According to Professor Brennan, "[h]obbits generally have unstable or only weak ideological commitments," while "hooligans . . . have strong commitments to politics and to their political identity" but "are beset by cognitive biases."[39]

He also relies on the proposition that no individual can reasonably think that her vote will make a difference to an election's outcome to support the inference that neither hobbits nor hooligans have any reason to try to become better informed. The result? Policy is based on misinformation—the hobbits don't contribute anything to the discussion, and the hooligans distort it. And, Professor Brennan argues, democracy has no intrinsic value. It is a means to the end of good policy. Democracy might be instrumentally better than some other forms of government, generating good policy somewhat more frequently than arbitrary dictatorship, for example, but at least in principle it is inferior to epistocracy.

After setting out his case against rule by hobbits and hooligans, Professor Brennan turns to epistocracy itself. In a prefatory remark Professor Brennan observes that all of the institutions he described as potentially epistocratic will end up with "the rule of hooligans, but it would be a better batch of hooligans than we get in democracy."[40] He considers the possibility of restricting voting

---

[37] Brennan's book, Jason Brennan, Against Democracy (2017 paperback edition), liberally cites to Caplan's.

[38] Thomas Christiano provides a valuable review in the *Notre Dame Philosophical Reviews*, May 19, 2019, available at https://ndpr.nd.edu/news/against-democracy/, archived at https://perma.cc/TB8L-YGWT.

[39] Brennan, note 37 above, at p. x. We are compelled to note our discomfort with the condescension we think pretty close to the surface in Professor Brennan's use of these terms, though we suspect that he latched on to them mainly because they are eye-catchingly informal.

[40] *Id.* at p. xi.

to those who can "pass a voter qualification exam" that tests knowledge "about the election" and "basic social scientific knowledge." The exam would have to be "objective and nonideological," which for economics turns out to mean "closely match[ing] what economists of all ideological stripes believe."[41] An alternative is plural voting, in which some people who either demonstrate greater knowledge than others or who have some characteristics, such as advanced degrees, that are likely to correlate with policy-relevant knowledge get more votes than others.

A third is a version of Justice Breyer's technocracy. Here everyone gets to vote but a council of well-informed experts—chosen by passing a competency exam—has the power to veto anything that voters endorse. The council could have jurisdiction over everything or, in a way that moves toward technocracy, there might be a number of councils each with jurisdiction over some specific subject matter.[42]

Another possibility is an "enfranchisement lottery" devised by, among others, political theorist Claudio Lopez-Guerra, similar to deliberative polling.[43] Some authority conducts a lottery that chooses a number of people from the general voting rolls, and only those people will have a vote. The chosen few would convene in a "competence-building process carefully devised to optimize their knowledge about the alternatives on the ballot."[44] Professor Brennan finds "much to be said on behalf" of this proposal, as do we. He's a bit nervous about the possible downside of deliberation in small groups, and thinks that the difficulties of getting the chosen few up to speed might be quite substantial. He acknowledges that these are empirical questions, though, and is open to the possibility that the facts will come out in Lopez-Guerra's favor.[45]

We don't have much to say in criticism of Professor Brennan's work that we haven't said about Professor Caplan's, mostly because we think that their premises about ignorance and its consequences are flawed. As Thomas Christiano puts it, "the rather limited micro-theory on which Brennan relies is probably off course. . . ."[46] And, in what we regard as an important concession, Professor

---

[41] *Id.* at pp. 211–12.

[42] Professor Brennan offers some additional fanciful institutional designs. We suspect that he does so at least in part because he is a philosopher whose discipline invites people to consider fanciful hypothetical cases as a way of testing their ethical intuitions.

[43] CLAUDIO LOPEZ-GUERRA, DEMOCRACY AND DISENFRANCHISEMENT: THE MORALITY OF ELECTORAL EXCLUSIONS (2014), ch. 2. Lopez-Guerra notes the similarity to deliberative polling, *id.* at pp. 36–37.

[44] *Id.* at p. 24. Lopez-Guerra has an extremely brief discussion of the question, Who devises the competence-building process? *Id.* at p. 41 (dealing with the problem of manipulation and agenda control). As we discuss in the following text, perhaps the entire voting population has enough competence to identify an entity to do so.

[45] *See* BRENNAN, note 37 above, at pp. 214–15 (discussing Lopez-Guerra's proposal).

[46] Christiano, note 38 above, also points out that "Brennan tends systematically to overplay the negative evidence and underplay the more positive evidence." He also observes that Professor Brennan acknowledges polling data showing that people vote in part to advance what they believe to

Brennan acknowledges the possibility that ordinary voters have "reasonable concrete theor[ies] of competence" that they can deploy to allocate some decision-making authority to epistocrats.[47] Maybe, though, that is what ordinary people around the world have done: delegating decision-making authority to administrative agencies staffed by Justice Breyer's technocrats, for example; or to legislators who are better informed than voters, though perhaps only marginally so. And, more generally, we believe that deliberative polling is one of a suite of institutional forms that *democracy* can take, not a version of epistocracy unless it is offered as the sole version of what we would call empowered democracy.

The works we have examined here do not in our view show that democracy is bound to fail because voters don't know much about history, biology, geometry, or, as Sam Cooke memorably put it, "the French [they] took."[48] As we argue next, ordinary people actually know quite a lot about policy-relevant matters—and, as Professor Brennan suggests, we can develop institutions of direct popular governance that draw upon that knowledge.

be the common good, and that the presence of such motivations complicates the necessary analysis in ways that Professor Brennan does not "pursue[] or even broach[]."

[47] BRENNAN, note 37, above, at pp. 223–24 (discussing the problem of designing tests for competence).
[48] Sam Cooke, "Wonderful World" (lyrics by Sam Cooke, Lou Adler, & Herb Alpert, 1960).

12

Power to the People:
Empowered Democracy

I. Introduction: Populism and Institutions to Decide How to Decide

As with populism and constitutionalism, there is a large literature on what one handbook calls "democratic innovation and governance."[1] We make no effort to provide a comprehensive overview of these innovations. We do emphasize at the outset, though, that the innovations form a *suite* of institutional possibilities on which populists can draw as they choose. Populists need not be—and, as far as we can tell, aren't—committed in principle to using only one of the possibilities to address every policy question.[2] So, for example, populists might agree that a referendum might not be the best way to determine what a majority wants on a specific question but insist that a deliberative poll would be preferable to delegating the question to technocrats. And, nothing in the constitutional theory of populism forecloses them from choosing to use representative institutions to address some issues, perhaps the vast majority that a society faces at any one time. Populism, that is, is not a prescription for direct democracy on every issue at every moment.[3]

Seeing populism that way, though, raises an immediate question about what populism is—in particular, about the claim that populism is anti-institutional. After all, someone—some institution—has to decide whether some policy proposal should be put to a referendum or a deliberative poll or a representative legislature today, tomorrow, next week. . . . Call that institution "the Decider"—not deciding on the policy but deciding on how to go about deciding on the policy. Populists, it would seem, have to be committed to at least one institution, the Decider. And if one, why not more?

---

[1] HANDBOOK OF DEMOCRATIC INNOVATION AND GOVERNANCE (Stephen Elstub & Olive Escobar eds. 2019).

[2] We disagree with Nadia Urbinati, who argues that populism favors plebiscitarianiam and referenda and "wants weakly organized parties in order to deepen democracy." See NADIA URBINATI, ME THE PEOPLE: HOW POPULISM TRANSFORMS DEMOCRACY (2019), at p. 188.

[3] Contra URBINATI, note 2 above, who argues that populists' preference for direct democracy transforms (disfigures) representative democracy.

Power to the People. Mark Tushnet and Bojan Bugarič, Oxford University Press. © Mark Tushnet and Bojan Bugaric˝ 2021. DOI: 10.1093/oso/9780197606711.003.0013

We don't think this is a real problem for a principled populism. A populist government could create a Decider, whose choice of means to decide some issue will presumptively govern. The Decider could be a representative legislature, the chief executive, a "constituent assembly" that convenes at regularly specified intervals. The Decider says that employment policy will be decided by the legislature, marriage equality will be put to a referendum, and the like. The Decider's choice can be overridden, though, if a majority (reliably determined) disagrees. How can the majority do that without some other institutional mechanism for figuring out what it wants? Through a slew of informal political processes—public rallies ("Legislature, vote on marriage equality now!" and "Marriage equality referendum now!"), pamphleteering ("Why a Universal Basic Income Makes Sense" and "The UBI Would Be an Economic Disaster"), social media campaigns—that yield a social judgment that the people end up accepting, some enthusiastically, some grudgingly.

Now take the Decider out of the picture. Public agitation about marriage equality or the UBI begins to grow, supported by NGOs, rallies organized via social media, and the like. People go back and forth about the value of the policy *and* about how to decide what the policy should be. Over time things settle down: some general sense emerges either that it's not worth doing anything about the policy now or that we ought to decide it soon, and decide it by legislation or referendum or deliberative poll. Here a decision is made not by a well-defined institution but by an informal process of social judgment.[4]

How can this be? Suppose someone says, "We've spent enough time talking about how to decide marriage equality policy, we should hold a referendum now." Maybe there will be widespread enough agreement that that's right, and the legislature or an NGO organizes a referendum. Suppose, though, that a fair number of people say, "No, you're wrong; we don't agree that the time has come to decide, and we're speaking for a majority." The determination of the majority's view on how to proceed isn't reliable, they say. For populists, once again, informal politics resolves the conflict. If a referendum is held, its results won't be authoritative—won't become law on the ground—if those who objected turn out to have been correct. That's why people pay attention not simply to the "yes/no" division of votes in a referendum or election but to the participation rate as well.

There's a general point about populism lurking here. For populists, politics isn't fully captured in well-defined institutions, which is what we suspect lies behind the stronger and mistaken proposition that populism is anti-institutional. Populist politics occurs in many forms, with lots of back-and-forth iterations.[5]

---

[4] We think that this account is compatible with some jurisprudential views about "the nature of law," particularly H.L.A. Hart's, but don't think is valuable to defend that view here (largely because we don't think that it matters whether we're right or wrong in holding that view).

[5] For further discussion of the importance of iterative decision-making for populisms that empower democracy, see section II below.

And, importantly, institutions are only one of the ways we can arrive at a reliable determination of what the majority wants.

The enterprise in this chapter is to describe some mechanisms—institutions— populists have used to empower the people. That enterprise is part of, not inconsistent with, populism.

We begin our discussion with a thought experiment about how the policy questions that arose, and still arise, in the Covid-19 pandemic. That thought experiment leads us to outline the kinds of knowledge that ordinary people have and can (and would) bring to the innovative institutions of empowered democracy.[6] We then examine one such institution, the referendum, in some detail before offering a briefer look at other democratic innovations. With those materials in hand, we take a brief foray into political theory to see how the institutions of empowered democracy stack up against, not technocracy or epistocracy, but representative democracy. We end the chapter, and the book, with a case study of recent constitution-making exercises in Iceland, with a glance at Ireland, to show both the possibilities of and the limits to empowered democracy as the institutionalization of populism.

II. A Thought Experiment—Policymaking for the COVID-19 Pandemic

No government appears to have done a great job in figuring out how to deal with the Covid-19 pandemic. Some did a bit better than others, at least for a while, and others did a great deal worse. The most successful, at least initially, were island nations that were able to shut their borders earlier and prevent leakage, and even some of them suffered setbacks from time to time.[7]

These policy weaknesses, though, can't plausibly be attributed to voter ignorance. The governments in place when the pandemic came home hadn't been elected on platforms that said anything at all about Covid-19 or the possibility that the nation would face a pandemic. All that voters were asked about when those governments sought their votes was whether they thought the competing candidates were likely to be generally competent in dealing with policy matters.

---

[6] Our account of empowered democracy is in many ways informed by and symphathetic to work of Roberto Mangabeira Unger. ROBERTO MANGABEIRA UNGER, FALSE NECESSITY: ANTI-NECESSITARIAN SOCIAL THEORY IN THE SERVICE OF RADICAL DEMOCRACY (1987); ROBERTO MANGABEIRA UNGER, WHAT SHOULD LEGAL ANALYSIS BECOME? (1996); ROBERTO MANGABEIRA UNGER, DEMOCRACY REALIZED: THE PROGRESSIVE ALTERNATIVE (1998). For additional works that bring together questions of democratic theory and institutional design, see ARCHON FUNG, EMPOWERED PARTICIPATION: REINVENTING URBAN DEMOCRACY (2004), and DEEPENING DEMOCRACY: INSTITUTIONAL INNOVATIONS IN EMPOWERED PARTICIPATORY GOVERNANCE (Archon Fung & Erik Olin Wrights eds., 2003).

[7] We discuss aspects of government performance during the crisis in Chapter 8.

None of the surveys on which Professors Caplan and Brennan rely come close to providing information on voters' ability to do *that*, and indeed, as we have seen, Professor Brennan hints that he might agree that voters aren't bad at making generalized competence judgments.

Our thought experiment asks whether some other possible decision-making bodies could have done better than elected governments. The exercise is of course speculative, but we think that the answer is that ordinary people might have done a bit better than elected governments and technocrats, and that if they didn't do as well the differences would probably be small. Even if we're wrong, though, we believe that our fairytale lets us identify the kinds of knowledge ordinary people can bring to policymaking more effectively than their elected representatives and epistocrats can.

So, let's imagine that early in the pandemic the United Kingdom convened three groups. One would be composed of epidemiologists and public health specialists and another composed of economists. The third would have fifty randomly chosen ordinary people in fifty cities and towns. The groups' charge would be to come up with recommendations for policy responses to the pandemic: social distancing, restrictions on public gatherings, a total lockdown, closure of some businesses but not others, what to do about elementary and secondary schools, and indeed whatever other policies they might come up with, including doing nothing.[8]

Members of each group would bring their background knowledge to their discussion, and each group could ask for information its members thought of possible use. For example, someone in the third group might well say, "We have no idea about what this virus is and how it spreads; let's ask some scientists to tell us." And they could choose which scientists to ask, though of course they would have a slim evidentiary base for picking among the possibilities. Our guess is that someone within the group would say, "Let's look at the credentials of the scientists we could ask. This one's a neurosurgeon, that one studied the Ebola virus. The second one seems like a better bet." Focusing on credentials isn't a silly strategy. Similarly, the public health group could ask for input from economists about the economic consequences of different strategies. Time permitting, they could ask each other what they were thinking about and which strategies seemed best at the moment—and, especially, the citizens' groups could ask each other how things were going.[9]

---

[8] The U.K. policy decentralizes administration of Covid regulations to local governments; we're imagining an even deeper decentralization, and one that might go beyond administering centrally prescribed rules to developing locally distinctive rules.

[9] A trickier problem is that no one knew much about the virus and how it spread early in the pandemic, and that knowledge accumulated rapidly. Of course, when we say "no one knew much," we include the epidemiologists. It would be difficult to set things up so that the group of ordinary people could get regular updates as information came in, or to convene different groups of ordinary people and bring them up to speed on what was known when they convened. For purposes of our thought

Now comes the fairytale part of our thought experiment. What are the groups going to do? The technocrats are likely to act like technocrats. The epidemiologists will focus on policies to slow the virus's spread and keep deaths and serious illnesses low, and the public health experts will figure out ways to effectively communicate why the epidemiologists' policies make sense. Maybe this group will worry a bit about the economic effects of the policies they choose, and might ask the economists for help, but their professional commitments will incline them to rate health over economics. And we doubt that a group of epidemiologists would end up recommending that nothing be done to slow the virus's spread; doing so would probably feel like a betrayal of their core commitment to *acting* to preserve life and health.

The economists will do the opposite. They'll focus on the economic effects of various policies: How much economic activity will each policy suppress? What's the value of each life saved, maybe taking into account the number of years the policy will add to a person's life span? Maybe they'll worry a bit about how these economic burdens and benefits are distributed but as we've seen from the surveys that Professors Caplan and Brennan rely on, economists tend to leave distributional issues to one side.

We suspect as well that both groups will come up with "one size fits all" policies, to be applied everywhere in the United Kingdom, although maybe they'll come up with a handful of distinctions based upon population density and disease prevalence. And they'll probably figure out some way to build into their policy proposals a system for updating the regulations as new evidence comes in.

We're most interested in speculating about the kinds of things the groups of ordinary people will think about. They won't know much about the virus when they walk into the room (neither will the economists, of course), but they will certainly ask the scientists to give them some information. They won't understand it all, but they'll get a sense of the kinds of policies that might make sense. What they distinctively bring to the discussions, though, is local knowledge. One might point out that the pub owners in the area—unlike many—happen to be responsible people: if they're told to kick people out of the pub if they aren't wearing masks, they'll do so. Another might point out that there are a lot of real hooligans among their teen population, who are barely kept under control when they go to school. And, because this knowledge is local, most of the others in the group will agree with these observations. Each group will adopt a policy tailored to what the group members know about their local circumstances. They're going to make some mistakes, of course, but so will the scientists and economists.

---

experiment, then, we treat the group of ordinary people as convening for about a week early in the pandemic to set an initial course. How they thought about the problems then would of course be a source of information for the other groups, including the elected government.

The local knowledge we refer to is available to the scientists and economists, but at greater cost. Instead of starting out with that knowledge, they're going to have to learn it themselves. Or they can devise policies that allow for local deviations when someone brings them to their attention, again a costly process (and the public health specialists might tell the others that allowing for local variations might dilute the messages about how important complying with the regulations is).

We acknowledge that our speculation is pretty optimistic, and we're not contending that the groups of ordinary people would surely come up with better policies than the other groups would, or than their elected representatives actually did. We've used the thought experiment to bring out the fact that ordinary people know things—what we've called local knowledge—that technocrats and elected representatives can acquire only with more effort.[10]

Local knowledge can affect policy across the board, that is, beyond the imaginary world of pandemic regulation we've used. Consider education: teachers in the classroom know what the specific group of students in front of them know and what sorts of instructional techniques are likely to help them learn more. Rigid lesson plans dictated by the state or national education department are often ill-suited to many classrooms. Better to give teachers broad guidelines and illustrative lesson plans, and let them tinker with the materials to make them as effective as they can be for the students in their classes.

Similarly with the regulation of workplace safety. Scholars of production processes know that there's a lot of "shop floor" knowledge rattling around. Workers know what's going on in their workplaces. Occupational safety regulators might dictate that machine tools be spaced far apart and shielded by a guard that prevents little pieces of metal from flying off and injuring workers. Workers might know, though, that in their workspace the machine tools are located off to one side anyway, already reducing the risk of injury. And you might find someone in the shop who's an inveterate tinkerer, always on the lookout for ways to adjust existing equipment to make it work better or, important here, more safely.

Again, central regulators, whether technocrats or elected officials, can devise systems that capitalize on local or shop-floor knowledge. And, as we'll suggest, one promising model for empowered democracy involves letting small groups draw on local knowledge to devise policies suitable for them and having them transmit what they've done to some central body, which can consider whether they should adjust their general policies to allow everyone to use one or another of the locally devised policies. Again, though, the important point here is that

---

[10] For a now classic study defending the importance of local knowledge in devising good public policy (although not using that term), see James C. Scott, Seeing Like a State: How Certain Schemes to Improve the Human Condition Have Failed (1998).

ordinary people do know some policy-relevant things even if they don't know other things.

Finally, ordinary people know how regulations actually work out on the ground. Political scientist Katherine Cramer offers an instructive anecdote. The Wisconsin Department of Natural Resources developed rules about hunting deer, with different rules in different parts of the state depending on how many deer there were in the area. One hunter recounted an exchange at a meeting with DNR officials: "You tell them, 'There ain't no deer around.' But they keep telling ya, 'Well, there's twelve thousand deer in Unit 6.' Well, we hunt in Unit 6 . . . There ain't that many deer there. We tell them that. Oh no. 'Well, we're just gonna do what we wanna do.'"[11] Put aside for now the bureaucrats' resistance to local knowledge and focus on the fact that the hunters know that the experts' estimate of the deer population is wrong because the hunters are there. This is a good example of what John Dewey described: "The individuals of the submerged mass may not be very wise. But there is one thing they are wiser about than anybody else can be, and that is where the shoe pinches, the troubles they suffer from."[12]

As philosopher Derrick Darby points out in a recent contribution, in the early twentieth century Dewey and W.E.B. Du Bois relied on the fact that ordinary people were, as Du Bois called them, "sage souls" who brought a great deal of local knowledge to the ballot box.[13] There's an older tradition in political philosophy that has some bite here as well—the idea that ordinary people bring common sense to policymaking. In part, common sense expresses judgments ordinary people make based upon their daily experience. This form of common sense can be distorted by skewed experiences and cognitive biases, and it sometime can register a sort of conventional wisdom that is "in the air" rather than on the ground, so to speak. Common sense is more than that, though.

For the political philosophers of the Scottish enlightenment, common sense was a human capacity for judgment based on experience itself, without regard to what those experiences were. Political theorists Russell Muirhead and Nancy Rosenblum explicate this idea of common sense through a reading of Thomas Paine. For Paine, "Common sense belongs to the people generally. . . . It refers to shared experience as the basis for those things everyone can be expected to know. . . . Paine insisted that a true grasp of things is accessible to everyone."[14] For the Scottish philosophers, the capacity for common-sense judgment when

---

[11]   KATHERINE CRAMER, THE POLITICS OF RESENTMENT: RURAL CONSCIOUSNESS IN WISCONSIN AND THE RISE OF SCOTT WALKER (2016), at p. 128.

[12]   Quoted in Derrick Darby, "Du Bois's Defense of Democracy," in 53 NOMOS: DEMOCRATIC FAILURE (Melissa Schwartzberg & Daniel Viehoff eds. 2020), at p. 244 n. 55.

[13]   Id. at p. 207.

[14]   RUSSELL MUIRHEAD & NANCY L. ROSENBLUM, A LOT OF PEOPLE ARE SAYING: THE NEW CONSPIRACISM AND THE ASSAULT ON DEMOCRACY (2019), at pp. 135–38 (quotation from pp. 136–37).

used on matters of public policy yielded pretty good judgments generally—not always, and not always the best possible judgments, but often enough and good enough to justify rule by the people.

With the proposition in hand that ordinary people can productively bring local knowledge and common sense to bear on matters of public policy, we turn to the question: Can populists design institutions that capitalize on local knowledge more effectively than the standard institutions of representative democracy do while preserving the benefits that flow from specialized knowledge not widely held among ordinary people?[15] We argue that the answer is Yes.[16]

III. Referendums as a Populist Institution

We're about to launch into a somewhat extended discussion and defense of referendums as one means of reliably determining what a majority prefers.[17] Doing so runs a risk that we need to address at the outset. Focusing on referendums might misleadingly suggest that populists are committed in principle to a plebiscitary view of policymaking, in which policy is made on every issue at every moment by asking what the majority wants.

The proposition that populism is in principle plebiscitary can be found in the literature critical of populism, but it's wrong both in practice and in principle. Look around the world at populism in practice and you'll find some referendums, mostly (we think) about substantial constitutional revisions but sometimes about discrete policy proposals. You'll also find lots of other ways in which populists figure out what a majority wants, some attractive, some less so (as when a populist leader says that he knows what the people want because and only because he is one of them). More concretely, as far as we know, no populist leader or party—right-wing or left-wing, in power or out of power, proto-authoritarian or democratic—called for a referendum in the first half of 2020 to determine pandemic-related policy. Their populisms were satisfied by other modes of

---

[15] This formulation rejects the proposition that populists are anti-institutional as such.

[16] Our prior reference to Dewey shows that we aren't defending deep decentralization in principle. For a critique of advocates for a principle of deep decentralization, *see* Christopher Pollitt, "Decentralization: A Central Concept in Contemporary Public Management," in THE OXFORD HANDBOOK OF PUBLIC MANAGEMENT (Ewan Ferlie, Laurence E. Lynn Jr., & Christopher Pollitt eds. 2007). We believe that our views are compatible with ideas about combining centralization with a strong principle of subsidiarity, and with ideas of "democratic experimentalism" associated with Charles Sabel.

[17] We use the term "referendums" to refer to all forms of direct legislation by the people. In U.S. law direct legislation is sometimes done by means of what are known as initiatives, which—where they exist—have somewhat different prerequisites and consequences from referendums. For an overview of instruments of direct democracy in the same general class as referendums, *see* Maija Jäske & Majia Setälä, "Referendums and Citizens' Initiatives," in HANDBOOK OF DEMOCRATIC INNOVATION AND GOVERNANCE, note 1 above, at p. 90.

decision-making: new laws enacted by representative parliaments and emergency decrees issued by the executive. (We add, not incidentally, that we're not at all sure that calling for a referendum on pandemic-related policy in early 2021 would have been a bad idea, although we are, again, unaware of any such efforts.)

In practice, then, populists aren't plebiscitarians. What about in principle? Here we're going to sound a recursive note. Populists are committed in principle to the proposition that questions of public policy should be decided by the reliably determined preferences of the majority. One important question of public policy is this: What institution should decide which questions? Populists are committed in principle to the proposition that *that* question should be decided by the majority. So, for populists a majority can decide to put something up for a referendum, it can decide to use participatory budgeting, it can decide to create a technocratic agency to deal with some issues, and it can decide to leave a lot to decision by a representative legislature. And, in fact, that's what we observe in populist practice.

With the ground cleared of a misunderstanding, we turn to referendums. Concerned that readers' reactions to the issues we raise will be affected by the "availability" heuristic, leading them to think that all referendums are like the ones that come most readily to mind, we begin with a list of recent referendums. We've already mentioned Brexit, of course, and the Swiss referendum on a universal basic income. Ireland had quite a few referendums in the 2010s (and we note that no one says that Ireland is governed by populists).[18] In 2015 a 62 percent majority approved marriage equality. In 2018 a two-thirds majority eliminated a constitutional ban on abortions by authorizing the parliament to regulate them. The next year an 82 percent majority eliminated a constitutional requirement that divorces be preceded by a period of separation. In 2013 a narrow 51 percent majority voted against a proposal to eliminate the legislature's upper house.[19]

Legislation by the people themselves may be the cleanest example of populism.[20] We consider here what we believe to be the two most prominent concerns

---

[18] The Irish Constitution can be amended only by referendum.

[19] In 2017 Australia conduct a "postal survey" on marriage equality, which we regard as a quasi-referendum. Approximately four-fifths of Australia's voters returned the postcards, with 62 percent ticking the box, "Should the law be changed to allow same-sex couples to marry?" This is an example of a phenomenon we discuss later in this chapter, of politicians seeking shelter from political controversy by asking the people directly what they prefer.

[20] See JOHN G. MATSUSAKA, LET THE PEOPLE RULE: HOW DIRECT DEMOCRACY CAN MEET THE POPULIST CHALLENGE, at p. 154 (a referendum "allows the people to choose the policy they want"). As with populism, so with referendums: The literature is quite substantial, and we do not pretend to address every issue that scholars have raised. For a good relatively recent overview, see Xenophon Contiades & Alkmene Fotiadou, "The People as Amenders of the Constitution," in PARTICIPATORY CONSTITUTIONAL CHANGE: THE PEOPLE AS AMENDERS OF THE CONSTITUTION 9 (Xenophon Contiades & Alkmene Fotiadou eds. 2017). Rather than addressing the quite large number of policy issues associated with referendum design, we aim only to tone down claims about referendums sometimes made in connection with populism, to show how referendums within a barebones populism need not be too troubling. This section and the following one draw heavily upon Mark

about the compatibility of referendums with constitutionalism: (1) that referendums can oversimplify complex policy options in ways that sometimes produce outcomes that are indefensible in principle, incoherent, and inconsistent with what the people would prefer after the kind of deliberation that occurs in representative assemblies;[21] and (2) that referendums systematically, though not inevitably, threaten rights of minorities that liberal constitutionalism guarantees.[22] (We've already addressed the argument that referendums don't allow for enough deliberation, and will briefly return to that argument later in this chapter. For the moment, we'll note that treating deliberate-ness as a requirement of constitutionalism thickens the idea of constitutionalism quite a bit.)

The frame of the discussion is that populism leaves substantial room for policy choice through "ordinary" legislation pursuant to ordinary procedural rules. Populism might use referendums more frequently than non-populist constitutionalist systems and, perhaps more important, might use referendums in exactly the circumstances in which procedural regularity obstructs the determination of what the people prefer (with the referendum serving as the mechanism for reliably determining that preference).

A. Complexity

The Brexit referendum illustrates many aspects of the first concern. The implications of one of the options—Exit—were unclear because Exit could occur in many ways.[23] We can call this a problem of complexity: the people were asked

---

Tushnet, "Liberal Democracy without Representation: A Defense of Some Institutions of Popular Constitutionalism" (forthcoming 2022).

[21] For an overview of the problems associated with complexity, *see* Laurence Morel, "The Democratic Criticisms of Referendums: The Majority and True Will of the People," in THE ROUTLEDGE HANDBOOK TO REFERENDUMS AND DIRECT DEMOCRACY (Laurence Morel & Matt Qvortrup eds. 2018), at p. 149.

[22] For an overview of the problems associated with rights-related referendums, see Marthe Fatin-Rouge Stefanini, "Referendums, Minorities, and Individual Freedoms," in THE ROUTLEDGE HANDBOOK TO REFERENDUMS AND DIRECT DEMOCRACY, note 21 above, at p. 371. An additional feature—sometimes amounting to a "concern"—of referendums is that they can be the instruments of parties rather than the people directly, and more particularly can be the instruments of chief executives seeking a quasi-plebiscitary personal mandate. We put this issue to one side because our interest here is in the possibility of referendums as an institution for realizing populism, not in the conditions that increase the likelihood that such a possibility will be realized. MATT QVORTRUP, THE REFERENDUM AND OTHER ESSAYS ON CONSTITUTIONAL POLITICS (2019), collects a number of extremely valuable essays on these matters.

[23] *Cf.* MATSUSAKA, note 20 above, at pp. 148–49 (arguing that "things became . . . dysfunctional after the election" in part because the referendum did "not present[] voters with a concrete proposal."). Matsusaka writes that best practice in referendums is that the proposition "should ask a specific question, ideally whether to approve a specific law." *Id.* at p. 228.

to choose between a simple option and a complex one.[24] Even a referendum cast in "yes-no" terms can be complex. Consider for example a referendum on this question: "Should the following complicated tax law be adopted?" Complexity cannot be eliminated by offering the people several options: "Remain," "Exit on the following terms," and "Exit on these alternative terms," or the like. Formulating a complete set of options may be difficult or impossible. Even more, a referendum with more than two options makes the appearance of a Condorcet voting paradox possible, even likely if (as might well be) the complexity is not characterized by those features of policy choices that make preference rankings single-peaked.[25]

The idea of a voting paradox brings out one key problem with referendums on complex issues. Begin with the observation that complex policy proposals have numerous components. A person might prefer component A to component B only if the overall policy also contains component M. Some such preferences might be nonnegotiable, so to speak. The "only if" is quite strong. Other such preferences might be quite weak. The voter's view is that having components A and M is desirable, but a policy that contains component A but not M is tolerable if the policy contains a substantial number of other components unrelated to A and M. (And similarly for other people and other components.)[26]

Yet, the difficulty posed by complexity might not distinguish referendums strongly enough from ordinary legislative deliberation to count against the at least occasional use of referendums to determine public policy views. A voting paradox based on nonnegotiable demands can occur with respect to ordinary legislation considered by a representative assembly, that is, even within thin constitutionalism.

Sometimes it is said that a referendum presents people with a choice that cannot be amended or tinkered with to come up with a better option. In contrast, it is said, legislators can negotiate until they have before them a complex proposal that has a chance of being satisfactory to a majority. That contrast is overdrawn. Referendum proposers have an interest in allowing discussion and modifications that increase the proposal's chance of adoption once submitted. They can frame

---

[24] Constitutions that exclude financial, budgetary, and tax issues from referendums (Albania, Azerbaijan, Denmark, Estonia, Greece, Hungary, Italy, Malta, Poland on the initiative of the citizens, Portugal, and the Republic of North Macedonia) may reflect the concern that complex matters are unsuitable for submission to referendum.

[25] A voting paradox occurs when voters have to choose among three policies, and equal-sized groups of voters rank the policies as follows: Group One prefers A to B to C; Group Two prefers B to C to A; Group Three prefers C to A to B. Suppose a first vote asks for a choice between A and B. A wins. A second vote asks for a choice between A and C. Now C wins. Then voters are asked to choose between C and B. This time B wins. The result turns on the interaction between voter preferences and the order in which the questions are put.

[26] There is another sense of complexity that we explore below—issues that are complex because any simple resolution implicates competing policy and value concerns.

their referendum as a directive that the legislature adopt a general policy and work out the details in implementing statutes. A representative can refuse to vote in favor of a proposal that fails to satisfy a nonnegotiable requirement; a voter can vote "No" on any proposal that similarly fails to satisfy her nonnegotiable requirements. Representatives can make judgments that the proposal before them, while not perfect, is on balance better than the status quo; so can voters.

A related objection is that referendums can pose questions *too* simply, in the sense that voters might understand the proposal itself but not see that the proposal will have knock-on effects on other policies. After the referendum succeeds, of course, the legislature can address those other effects, but—if they can't change the policy adopted in the referendum—the adjustments they make might lead some of those who voted for the referendum to think that they had made a mistake (or, worse, to think that the legislature was trying to discredit the referendum-based policy by choosing bad adjustments when good ones were available). We could deal with this by allowing legislatures to give referendum-based policies the same treatment they give ordinary laws—subject to revision when problems arise.[27]

Knock-on effects that voters don't expect to occur are simply examples of a broader phenomenon. A clear policy can be a bad one, just as legislation can be bad. The solution to a bad statute is to repeal it. The solution to a referendum that generates bad policy is the same. We can allow the legislature to treat a policy adopted through referendum as it treats any other piece of legislation, subject to immediate revision or even repeal. Or, we can allow the legislature to modify a policy adopted through a referendum only after a prescribed period such as two years.[28] Or, we can allow modifications of referendum-adopted policy only by a second referendum.[29]

A related problem, or perhaps just a version of the "unanticipated knock-on effects" problem, is this: referendum-based policies have to be integrated

[27] You'd probably want to insist that the legislature give the referendum-based policy a fair shot by preventing its amendment or repeal within a few years of its adoption. For a discussion of complexity in connection with two referendums in New Zealand in 2020, which would have authorized legislation decriminalizing cannabis (the referendum failed), the other of which dealt (ambiguously) with either assisted suicide or withdrawal of support for continued life (which passed), see Janet McLean, "Referendums on Public Policy Questions: The Case of New Zealand," IACL-AIDC BLOG, Nov. 26, 2020, available at https://blog-iacl-aidc.org/2020-posts/2020/11/26/referendums-on-public-policy-questions-the-case-of-new-zealand, archived at https://perma.cc/W4HE-ZD6T.

[28] Morel, note 21 above, at p. 152, discusses the question of "reversibility," noting a Venice Commission recommendation that legislatures be barred for "a period of time" from amending a referendum-adopted provision, and mentions without describing several "well-known examples in Europe of referendums whose results have been within a short time, either overturned by Parliament or called into question by another referendum. . . ."

[29] Because referendum-adopted policies are not different in principle from representative-adopted legislation with respect to quality, we doubt that there could be a principled reason for barring successive referendums when (in the view of enough people) the referendum-adopted policy has turned out to be unwise. For a more complete discussion, see note 32 below.

into the existing corpus juris, and they might fit badly or cause unanticipated consequences. Here's a distinctively U.S. example. A referendum strictly limiting a legislature's ability to modify the existing property tax system may lead legislatures to increase sales taxes in ways that have troubling distributional effects, and it almost certainly will cause people to stay in the homes they own longer than is good for them. Again, in principle there is a simple solution to this problem when it arises. A referendum-adopted policy with these characteristics should impose an obligation on the legislature to adapt the corpus juris to this new feature.[30] And, if and when unanticipated consequences appear, the overall policymaking system should be allowed to address those consequences by mechanisms already described.

What about the facts that referendums are one-shot events, and that legislators have an opportunity to take successive votes? If a complex proposal is defeated on the floor because it is not on balance acceptable to a majority, representatives can retreat to the committee room and modify the proposal, then present the modification to see if it acceptable—and they can do so repeatedly.[31] Referendums have no opportunity for a do-over, and this does count against them as a decision-making device. We have noted, though, that there might be something like an "anticipatory" do-over, when those who oppose the referendum's substantive policy raise objections that make the proponents worry that they'll lose when the vote is taken—to induce proponents to tinker with the proposal, just as might occur in a legislature either before or after a proposal comes to the floor.[32]

Suppose we do say that referendums should be allowed only if they offer a choice between two clear policies. Where a complex policy is placed before the public, the alternative should be "No" rather than another complex policy,

---

[30] Here too referendum-adopted legislation is not all that different from representative-adopted legislation: Any significant piece of legislation can require changes in other laws, and good institutional design puts mechanisms for adaptation in place.

[31] This solution is unavailable when the proposal fails in the legislature because it contains some component or components that are nonnegotiably unacceptable to enough representatives or voters to defeat the proposal, and altering those components would make the proposal unacceptable to another group large enough to defeat it.

[32] In principle the people could be asked to vote repeatedly on variants of rejected proposals. In practice, though, successive referendums on variants are unlikely. This is different from the question of whether there should be in principle some limit on the ability to do over a referendum that accepts a complex proposal. In late 2019 the Scottish government issued a document supporting a second referendum on Scottish independence, in which a central argument was that there had been a "material change in circumstances" (relying on the concept of *rebus sic stantibus*, part of general international law and codified in Article 62 of the Vienna Convention on the Law of Treaties) since a prior referendum rejected independence. Scottish Government, "Scotland's Right to Choose: Putting Scotland's Future in Scotland's Hands," available at https://www.gov.scot/publications/scotlands-right-choose-putting-scotlands-future-scotlands-hands/, archived at https://perma.cc/5ZHF-WR7B. Whether such a change should be a necessary predicate for a second referendum is, we think, a question to be resolved politically, though we are reasonably sure that the argument against a second referendum will almost always be rather strong unless proponents can demonstrate something like materially changed circumstances.

because "forcing" a choice between two complex policies does not allow a voter to express a preference for the status quo or for another complex policy.

We might be concerned that clarity as a solution to the problem of complexity would create a different problem. In politics clear and accurate policy descriptions might be misleading. This might be particularly true of complex policies presented to the public as a list of clear components. Ordinary people might focus on one or two of the components on the list and not appreciate how those components might interact with other components in ways that alleviate (or exacerbate) the voters' concerns. Even more, political leaders might make one or two components the focus of their campaigns for or against the referendum, again with misleading effect.

One can imagine institutional responses to concern about misleading clarity. In the United States presumptively disinterested officials are sometimes charged with developing neutral and accurate descriptions of ballot propositions that are distributed to the public in advance (and that sometimes appear on the ballot as well). The British Electoral Commission did force a change in the Brexit referendum's wording to make it more neutral and clear, though of course the outcome suggests that attempting to purify the questions put to the voters might fail (though, we think, for reasons other than unclarity or bias in wording).

More significantly, though, the concern about misleading clarity rests on assumptions about voter incompetence. And populism rests on the contrary assumption, that ordinary people are at least as competent as the representatives they elect in making political decisions. Perhaps critics of referendums could develop more precise accounts of specific forms of voter competence that would be consistent with the assumptions of popular constitutionalism that would allow some but not all referendums on complex policy questions.[33] Such accounts would of course have to explain why *representatives* would not adopt the same sort of distorting clarity in their deliberations that critics cite in opposing referendums on clear questions over which popular discussion might be distorted.

---

[33] Consider here that constitutions sometimes prohibit referendums on specific matters. In addition to the exclusions for fiscal matters noted above, some constitutions prohibit referendums on amnesties and pardons (Albania, Azerbaijan, Georgia, Italy, Poland on the initiative of the citizens, and the Republic of North Macedonia) and restrictions on fundamental rights (Albania, Armenia, Georgia). Other less common exclusions are for territorial integrity (Albania), states of emergency (Albania, Estonia), the powers of parliament, judicial bodies and the constitutional court (Bulgaria), texts concerning the civil service, naturalization and expropriations (Denmark), the monarchy and the royal family (Netherlands under the temporary law applicable up to 2004 and Denmark to a certain extent), legislative acts that are submitted to a special procedure and whose content is imposed by the constitution or acts constitutionally necessary for the operation of the state (Italy, Portugal), and appointments and dismissals (Republic of North Macedonia). The implementation of international treaties cannot be submitted to the decision of the people in Denmark, Hungary, Malta and the Netherlands (temporary law), so as to avoid a breach of international law. Similarly, Swiss law allows for (but does not make compulsory) an international treaty and its implementing provisions (constitutional or legislative) to be put to a single vote.

Should simplicity be another criterion for referendums? Consider a referendum on the question, "Should the legislature guarantee a minimum income of at least X—adjusted for inflation—to every person residing in the nation?" This proposal is clear.[34] It is not simple, though. It implicates complicated policy questions: How much less (if at all) will people work if guaranteed a minimum income? What will the effects on economic growth be? It also implicates moral questions: What duties do we have to noncitizen residents, whether long-term or otherwise? Populism rests on the not-obviously incorrect judgment that ordinary people are not systematically worse than their representatives in assessing these policy and moral questions.[35]

We conclude our discussion of these issues by observing that we've identified a number of problems associated with designing referendums whose results can fairly be described as reliably revealing what a majority prefers. We've also suggested a number of techniques that referendum drafters can use to address those problems. How can those techniques, or others that might be devised, be adopted?

That question returns us to the discussion of populism and institutions in Section I. There we suggested the possibility of a Decider whose choices would be presumptively accepted. In the referendum context, the Venice Commission has provided "best practices" guidelines that might serve as such a Decider.[36] One guideline, for example, is that "[t]he question put . . . must be clear and comprehensible," and that "voters must be informed of the effects of the referendum" all to be supervised by "[a]n impartial body."[37] Populist referendums could take these in the spirit of guidelines, presumptions that might be overcome when the referendum's proposers thought appropriate.

---

[34] The example is adapted from a referendum in Switzerland. A similar example can be found in a 2015 Greek referendum. Syriza proposed a referendum asking the Greeks to support Syriza. In fact, the referendum endorsed an austerity program proposed (or imposed) by external financial agencies, or as some put it, whether Greece would remain in the European Union. For a discussion, see Alkmene Fotiadou, "The Role of the People in Constitutional Amendment in Greece: Between Narrative and Practice," in Contiades & Fotiadou, note 20 above, at p. 56.

[35] One might think, for example, that representatives would be better at evaluating the policy questions and worse at evaluating the moral ones, and that on balance the improved quality of the moral evaluation outweighs the weakened quality of the policy evaluation.

[36] The European Commission for Democracy Through Law (Venice Commission), "Revised Guidelines on the Holding of Referendums," Oct. 8, 2020, CDL-AD(2020)031, available at https://www.venice.coe.int/webforms/documents/?pdf=CDL-AD(2020)031-e, archived at https://perma.cc/D24V-QHJ9. This document is a revision of an earlier one issued in 2007.

[37] Id., Principles I-3.1.c, I.3.1.d, and II.4.1. (describing the "impartial body"). The principles also include the equivalent of a "single subject" requirement: "there must be an intrinsic connection between the various parts of each question put to the vote" except "in the case of a total revision of a text." Principle III.2.

B. Referendums on Rights

Concerns about relative voter competence animate the concerns about complexity and the like that we've discussed. Referendums that have moral dimensions, like one that would exclude long-term noncitizens from a basic income, are sometimes thought to raise additional concerns. The problem is not that some moral questions are complicated. Rather, the problem is something akin to self-interest: voters asked about the rights of noncitizens are, it is suggested, likely to undervalue those rights relative to their own rights or, more important, their own interests.

This concern is generalized in suggestions that it is inappropriate to subject questions about individual rights to referendums.[38] John G. Matsusaka's conclusion from his review of referendums in the United States is that "[i]nitiatives do pose a threat to minority rights, but . . . the threat is not immense."[39] The most common example from recent history is the Swiss referendum approving a limitation on the construction of minarets. Yet, we should keep in mind the equally recent Irish referendums on marriage equality and abortion (and the Australian quasi-referendum on marriage equality) in thinking about the "no referendums on individual rights" proposition.

These examples suggest that we could benefit from a more differentiated analysis. The distinction between rights and specifications developed in Chapter 3 can be helpful here. First, the government policies associated with specifications typically serve nontrivial public interests in a not entirely unreasonable way. Consider restrictions on tobacco advertising: in the language that prevails in comparative constitutional discourse, such restrictions impair the advertisers' free speech interests in the service of important public health goals. One might reasonably believe that specifying the content of a right of free expression so as to allow such restrictions is reasonable—though of course one could reasonably take the converse view.

In these and similar cases, we can see how reasonable people could disagree about whether the government policy does indeed violate the right. It is not

---

[38] For example, noncitizens of Athens were the main victims of plebiscitarian democracy in Athens. *See* JAMES MILLER, CAN DEMOCRACY WORK?: A SHORT HISTORY OF A RADICAL IDEA, FROM ANCIENT ATHENS TO OUR WORLD (2018), at pp. 32–39.

[39] MATSUSAKA, note 20 above, at p. 211. Drawing on a comprehensive data set of referendums in U.S. states, Matsusaka observes that referendum outcomes tended to favor women and be adverse to marriage equality and minorities disadvantaged by English-only laws. *Id.* at pp. 209–10. Stefanini, note 22 above, at p. 374, observes: "Swiss citizens, although notoriously conservative, seem more reasonable . . . [having, before 2004,] rejected virtually all of the referendums that could have infringed on rights and freedoms, including those of minorities." *See also id.* at p. 383 ("It is difficult to draw general conclusions about the effects of referendums on fundamental rights and freedoms. The procedure . . . [and] the subject matter, how the question is formulated, how the campaign is organized and funded, are all factors that must be taken into account. . . .").

clear that ordinary people are incompetent or likely to be biased in evaluating whether a referendum threatens rights in a case of specification. Or, more narrowly, perhaps we can make progress in figuring out the difference between the Swiss minaret referendum and the Irish referendums by thinking about why ordinary people might have been (more) biased in the first than in the second and third cases.[40]

Second, perhaps unreasonable specifications result at least as much from self-interested decisions by political leaders—from representative government—as from self-interest among the general population. This is clearest with respect to sedition law: political leaders who develop policy are likely to be especially sensitive about criticisms of their policies, perhaps more so than the voters they represent. For that reason, they may be more likely to adopt a sedition law than would the people through a referendum. Similarly, John Hart Ely's account of the proper bases for constitutional review refers to the fact that the "Ins" are sensitive to challenges from the "Outs." And here he rather clearly had legislators in mind, not the voters they represent. At least with respect to this set of issues voters aren't "Ins" in Ely's sense.[41]

This second thought might also lead to a more refined account of the circumstances under which referendums implicating questions of individual rights might be appropriate—roughly, in cases involving unreasonable specifications. We note one difficulty, though: political leaders might see political advantage in promoting a referendum on a specification even if ordinary people on their own would not put the referendum process in motion. This might suggest some sort of institutional response, through the development of some limits on the role political leaders can play in referendum campaigns. What such limits (consistent with ideas about freedom of expression) could be is unclear, though.[42]

Our discussion suggests that populists should think about the proper domain of referendums—and the fact that populists aren't in practice plebiscitarians suggests that they do. Referendums are only one of the tools available for

---

[40] The *why* question matters because it's circular to say that the Swiss referendum was bad and the Irish one was good because Swiss voters were more biased against Muslims than Irish voters were against gays and lesbians. We confess our inability to come up with decent answers to the *why* question, which for us suggests that there's no general problem with holding referendums on rights-specifications.

[41] JOHN HART ELY, DEMOCRACY AND DISTRUST: A THEORY OF JUDICIAL REVIEW (1980).

[42] The Irish High Court has repeatedly held that the elected government cannot use public funds to support or oppose the proposition put to a referendum. McKenna v. an Taoiseach (No. 2), [1995] 2 I.R. 10; McCrystal v. Minister for Children and Youth Affairs, [2012] I.E.S.C. 53. The Venice Commission's "best practices" guidelines say that "*administrative* authorities" must maintain "a neutral attitude," (Principle I.2.2.a (emphasis added), that the publicly-run media must give equal access to both sides (Principle I.2.2.b), and that "public resources" can't be used "for campaigning purposes," though political parties and elected representatives can "take active[] part in the campaign" (Principle I.3.1.b). Venice Commission, note 36 above.

populists seeking to determine what a majority prefers. Populism doesn't require the comprehensive substitution of policymaking by the people directly for policymaking by representative assemblies. Put more directly: referendums will deal with only some areas of public policy. In our view we are unlikely to develop substantive criteria for identifying those areas. Rather, the domain of referendums will be determined by the people's views about which policies are important enough to be put to the people (and perhaps secondarily, the people's views about which of *those* policies are tractable to adoption by referendum). With respect to the subset of policy issues that populists believe should be submitted to referendums, is the quality of deliberation worse than in legislative debates on the same issues? We are not clear on how the burden of proof should be allocated on the following question: Should defenders of referendums or of legislation as it actually occurs have that burden? We incline to thinking that the burden should be on legislation's defenders, but whatever the answer, the question isn't, "Referendums yes or no."[43]

IV. Other Tools for Reliably Determining Majority Preferences

Well-designed referendums reliably determine the majority's views—a requirement of thin constitutionalism—with direct popular participation in governance, which many populists find attractive. Other institutions can have similar features.[44] As we said at this chapter's start, many innovations in democratic governance are on offer these days—participatory budgeting, digital town halls, and more—and we don't propose to discuss them all.[45] We focus on deliberative polling and the citizen assembly, a close relative, that have been used in constitutional reform efforts.[46]

---

[43] Jäske & Setälä, note 17 above, at pp. 96–97, observe that different forms of referendums elicit varying degrees of deliberation before and after the vote.

[44] The institutions we describe sometimes are "merely" advisory or agenda setting. We don't regard those functions as unimportant, but we think it important to describe the institutions when they do make law themselves—or, as with some mechanisms for constitutional revision, when several mechanisms of direct popular participation are combined to make law.

[45] The literature on participatory budgeting is extensive. For discussions with references to the literature, *see* Ernesto Ganuza & Gianpaolo Baiocchi, "The Long Journey of Participatory Budgeting," in HANDBOOK OF DEMOCRATIC INNOVATION, note 1 above, at p. 77; HOLLIE RUSSON GILMAN, PARTICIPATORY BUDGETING AND CIVIC TECH: THE REVIVAL OF CITIZEN ENGAGEMENT (2016). On digital participation in general, *see* Hollie Russon Gilman & Tiago Carneiro Peixoto, "Digital Participation," in HANDBOOK OF DEMOCRATIC INNOVATION, note 1 above, at p. 105. On digital town halls, *see* MICHAEL A. NEBLO, KEVIN M. EASTERLING, & DAVID M. J. LAZAR, POLITICS WITH THE PEOPLE: BUILDING A DIRECTLY REPRESENTATIVE DEMOCRACY (2018).

[46] Ron Levy, "Democratic Innovation in Constitutional Reform," in HANDBOOK OF DEMOCRATIC INNOVATION, note 1 above, at p. 339, provides an overview of these and similar mechanisms. A task force created by the mainstream American Academy of Arts and Sciences recommended expanding the use of citizens' assemblies, participatory budgeting and other modes of participatory

One concern always comes up in discussing deliberative polling and other democratic innovations. The stories about them, including the ones we tell, almost always begin by describing gatherings of relatively small numbers of people—fifty or a hundred at most. Law professor Ron Levy accurately calls them "mini-publics."[47] Whatever might be said about the democratic characteristics of such gatherings and about their capacity to make good decisions, can they be scaled up for use in national governance? As we'll show, citizen assemblies are designed precisely so that they can be scaled up. Evidence on deliberative polling isn't as substantial because it's a recent innovation still undergoing development. What evidence there is does suggest that it can indeed scale to the national level.[48]

Political scientist James Fishkin developed a technology he calls deliberative polling. In ordinary polling the pollster asks a large number of randomly selected people a series of relatively short questions, sometimes preceded by a tiny bit of information to set the context. A typical question might be, "Do you think President Biden's policies are helping the nation's economy, hurting the nation's economy, or aren't making much of a difference?" Answering such questions does not take much time.

Deliberative polling brings together a smaller group of randomly selected people for a longer period.[49] A typical deliberative poll covers only a handful of issues, sometimes even just one issue. Deliberative pollsters give the respondents a packet of materials developed by experts describing the issues in some detail

decision-making, and virtual town halls as a means of "ensur[ing] the representativeness of political institutions." Commission on the Practice of Democratic Citizenship, "Our Common Purpose," pp. 41–47 (2020), available at https://www.amacad.org/ourcommonpurpose/report, archived at https://perma.cc/FT5B-UKJU.

[47] Levy, note 46 above, at p. 344.

[48] For perhaps the most prominent statement about inability to scale, *see* ADAM PRZEWORSKI, DEMOCRACY AND THE LIMITS OF SELF-GOVERNMENT (2010). Political scientist Christopher Achen stated, "In my view, the few careful empirical evaluations of citizen deliberation and deliberation assemblies have generally been depressing, and the more closely one looks at their evidence, the more depressing they become," *quoted in* Nathan Heller, "Politics without Politicians," THE NEW YORKER, Feb. 19, 2020, available at https://www.newyorker.com/news/the-future-of-democracy/politics-without-politicians, archived at https://perma.cc/YEM3-MYXG. (We note that Achen is primarily a methodologist, a subspeciality whose members in our experience require quite high levels of confidence before they are willing to say that something works—which may be appropriate for their disciplinary purposes but which may be a bit too stringent for policymakers trying out novel approaches.) For evidence about successful scaling, *see, e.g.,* Thamy Pogrebinschi, *The Squared Circle of Participatory Democracy: Scaling Up Deliberation to the National Level,* 7 CRITICAL POLICY STUDIES 219 (2013) (discussing Brazilian National Public Policy Conferences, which are advisory bodies that develop proposals for legislative adoption); HÉLÈNE LANDEMORE, OPEN DEMOCRACY: REINVENTING POPULAR RULE FOR THE TWENTY-FIRST CENTURY (2020), at pp. 182–87 (discussing several additional examples of institutions scaled up to the national level).

[49] A variant, similar to what occurred in Iceland, involves elections to citizen assemblies, where candidates are self-nominated and can't have strong affiliations with political parties (such as being a member of a party governing body or serving as a party representative in a legislature).

from a variety of political and policy perspectives. Then the respondents sit down to talk about the issues. Experience with deliberative polling strongly suggests that people who start out disagreeing with each other can hash out their differences and end up generally agreeing on how to deal with the policy questions they've been asked to consider.[50]

Deliberative polling has been used outside the United States to generate proposals on constitutional matters: Korean unification, schooling in Northern Ireland, whether Australia should become a republic. One well-known example is the British Columbia Citizens' Assembly on Electoral Reform.

> [The Assembly] met on weekends over a period of eleven months. In the in-
> itial 'Learning Phase', assorted political scientists instructed members on
> electoral models. Learning strategies included interactive participation, a
> dedicated web-site, assigned readings and structured group work overseen by
> graduate students. Early on, the body's 162 members settled on a set of 'shared
> values' for mutually cooperative engagement. 'Public Hearing', 'Deliberation',
> and 'Referendum' phases took place later. At the Deliberation phase members
> sifted information gained from both expert and lay sources, and spent over two
> months discussing and decided on an electoral reform recommendation ulti-
> mately put to voters in the referendum.[51]

The proposal received 57 percent of the votes cast, meaning that it failed because the government had specified that it would go into effect only if it received more than 60 percent of the votes cast.[52]

Perhaps because of the scope of the issues such polls have dealt with, and per-haps because almost all of their proposals have to be funneled through existing institutions before they become law, their immediate impact on policy has been relatively small, though the results may have had some modest effect in shaping public debates.[53]

---

[50] There is some evidence, though, that these deliberations can sometimes push people to polar-ized positions, apparently when there's a slight imbalance between those who support and oppose each other on issues that both sides care deeply about. CASS R. SUNSTEIN, GOING TO EXTREMES: HOW LIKE MINDS UNITE AND DIVIDE (2009).

[51] Levy, note 46 above, at p. 345. For a more detailed description of this and subsequent Citizens' Assemblies in Canada, see Lawrence LeDuc, Heather Bastedo & Catherine Baquero, "The Quiet Referendum: Why Electoral Reform Failed in Ontario," June 2008, available at https://www. democratienouvelle.ca/wp-content/uploads/2012/08/lawrence_leduc_heather_bastedo_catherine_ baquero-the_quiet_referendum_why_electoral_reform_failed_in_ontario_2008.pdf, archived at https://perma.cc/K8M5-T9ZX.

[52] Two subsequent referendums failed, with the proposal receiving far short of even a majority.

[53] See Center for Deliberative Polling, "What is Deliberative Polling?," available at https://cdd. stanford.edu/what-is-deliberative-polling/, archived at https://perma.cc/4RF5-LNQ8. It may be worth noting that juries consist of randomly selected people who make legally significant deter-minations of criminal and civil liability, and some theorists have suggested that random selection ("sortition") could be used more widely. For example, we might use a representative random sample

Deliberative polling has obvious drawbacks.[54] Critics have questioned the neutrality of the expert briefing material presented in deliberative polling,[55] and the possibility of getting a truly representative group of people to take the time to participate. Almost by definition they do not give special weight to those thought to be most knowledgeable about specific matters.[56] It might be thought undesirable for the institution that makes binding policy on matters requiring special knowledge to identify and elaborate good policy to lack guarantees of access to such knowledge.[57] And if a deliberative poll results not in advice to the government or to a requirement that the legislature consider a proposal but actually makes law, we might think that everyone other than those at the meetings can't be described as authors of the laws that govern them, which as we discuss later is a desirable, perhaps necessary, feature of legitimate government.

Some of these problems are more substantial than others. In addressing them, we have to be careful not to compare a realistic account of deliberative polling, with its virtues and flaws, to an idealized account of other modes of decision-making such as legislation and administrative rulemaking. The comparison has to be "realistic to realistic." And, we believe, when we do that the question of which mode is better is at least quite a bit closer than skeptics about deliberative polling think.

Here are some of the difficulties and some ways of dealing with them. The informational materials given to participants can be drawn from submissions by political parties and NGOs with different and sometimes opposing views. The materials might end up with some modest tilt, but informational bias occurs in every other decision-making institution—lobbyists feed information to

---

of the population as the electorate for a referendum rather than a jurisdiction's entire voting population. The Wikipedia entry on sortition has a useful compilation of proposals to use sortition to generate binding law. *See also* Hubertus Buchstein, *Diarchyal politics—Thinking with Urbinati beyond Urbinati*, 15 CONTEMPORARY POLITICAL THEORY 209 (2015). This article is part of a valuable symposium on NADIA URBINATI, DEMOCRACY DISFIGURED: OPINION, TRUTH, AND THE PEOPLE (2015), which is Urbinati's defense of representative democracy as better than technocracy and populism understood as plebiscitary democracy.

[54] Drawing on Irish experience, which is generally regarded as supporting arguments for innovative deliberative processes, Oran Doyle and Rachel Welsh provide a compendium of critical observations. Oran Doyle & Rachel Welsh, "Deliberative Mini-Publics as a Response to Populist Democratic Backsliding," in CONSTITUTIONAL CHANGE AND POPULAR SOVEREIGNTY: POPULISM, POLITICS AND THE LAW IN IRELAND (Maria Cahill, Colm O'Cinneide, Seán Ó Conaill, & Conor O'Mahony eds. 2020). Doyle and Welsh argue that features of Irish political culture account for much of the success of deliberative processes there. That argument is broadly consistent with our argument that discussions of populism and constitutionalism must be quite attentive to local circumstances.

[55] See Doyle & Walsh, note 54 above (identifying the problem of "artificial neutrality").

[56] Doyle & Walsh, note 54 above, describe efforts to incorporate technical expertise in deliberative processes but note that doing so might reproduce problems of technocratic governance that the processes aim at displacing.

[57] Doyle & Walsh, note 54 above, observe as well that political elites can use deliberative processes to delay and ultimately defeat proposals that actually have broad popular support.

legislators and the leaders and staffs of administrative agencies, and we know that on every specific issue that information is tilted toward one or the other side (mostly, the side favored by the relatively well-to-do).

Populists might decide—in the ad hoc way we've described—that they shouldn't use deliberative polling to decide highly technical questions. Even as to those questions, though, the information provided to participants can include enough technical information to allow them to make an informed, though not fully informed, decision. After some point the more technical experts know, the worse they become at making good decisions. The title of Thomas Dolby's song "She Blinded Me with Science" describes a real phenomenon about policymaking as well as personal relationships. Our discussion of the degree to which economists ignore distributional concerns that ordinary citizens worry about points to another problem with relying too heavily on experts.

Issues about participation are more significant. Not everyone has the time to take part in a deliberative poll, especially if it extends over several days or weeks: They have to go to work, take care of their children, do the shopping, go out with their friends—live their regular lives, in short. Relying on volunteers, as ordinary polls do, risks getting outcomes skewed by the volunteers' characteristics. There's good reason to think that the relatively well-off are more likely to volunteer than others, for example.

Economists have an easy solution: pay people to participate and make sure that their employers hold their positions open and don't penalize them for taking time off by slowing their advance up whatever job ladders they're on. That might be all right if the poll was organized by an NGO and ended up with something like a position paper that the NGO presented to lawmakers. Deliberative polling is an alternative to voting, and we don't know of any jurisdiction that pays people to vote. The reason, of course, is that we regard voting as a civic obligation. Populists devoted to deliberative polling could mount "put your name on the list" campaigns similar to "get out the vote" campaigns. More pertinently, in the United States and to a lesser extent elsewhere we do have an institution that relies on randomly chosen ordinary people to make legally binding decisions: juries. Jury service is a civic obligation, reinforced by efforts to educate the public about it. There's an even stronger version available. In Australia voting is mandatory.[58] You're fined if you don't vote. The fines are modest—around $20 Australian for a first offense. A "none of the above" option can be put on the ballot to accommodate true protest voting, which does reveal something about public views. These approaches could be adapted when deliberative polling becomes a significant mode of making law.

---

[58] A handful of other nations have mandatory voting as well.

Suppose, though, that your system of deliberative polling meant that a group of fifty randomly chosen people would actually make law for everyone else—to take a dramatic example, decide to institute capital punishment. Theorists of representative democracy argue that lawmaking by a body selected by voting open to all results in laws that legitimately bind because each person can and should regard himself or herself as an author of the rules that govern their lives.[59] An alternative and less metaphorical version: every person has to have the opportunity to take part in the processes that produce the laws that bind them. The problem then is this: when a legislature adopts capital punishment, defendants charged with capital crimes can and should regard themselves as authors of that law because they had the opportunity to vote for the legislators who enacted the law.[60] How can they do the same when the law was adopted by a group of fifty randomly chosen people?

One concern is that the particular group, though randomly chosen, might not be truly representative of the larger population. This is a phenomenon statisticians call "variance": The smaller the group selected out of a large population the greater the chance is that the small group will have more extreme views than the average in the large population. You can design deliberative polling to reduce the variance problem, not by making each group larger but by having more of them—as in our earlier example of small groups in fifty cities to develop Covid-19 policy. A policy would become enforceable law only if a good chunk of the groups settled on that policy after their deliberations.

A more serious concern is that the metaphor of authorship works, if it does, because everyone has the opportunity to vote. Yet, only fifty people had the opportunity to take part in the deliberative poll about capital punishment. Suppose, though, that we didn't have only a deliberative poll on capital punishment, but one on tax rates, another on policy for dealing with psychoactive drugs, and so on through the list of policies that a legislature can take up.[61] Everyone would have an equal opportunity to participate in a deliberative poll on *something*, and

---

[59] For a recent short discussion of this position, see Oliver Gerstenberg, *Radical Democracy and the Rule of Law: Reflections on J. Habermas' Legal Philosophy*, 17 INTERNATIONAL JOURNAL OF CONSTITUTIONAL LAW 1054 (2020).

[60] We put aside obvious objections associated with laws enacted by legislatures before the defendant was born, or before he or she moved into the jurisdiction. Theorists have developed answers to those objections, and it would take us too far from our main concerns to go through them here.

[61] For an account broadly similar to ours, see LANDEMORE, note 48 above. What distinguishes Landemore's ideal from other lottocratic models, such as Guerrero's, is the breadth of her funnel: the goal is to involve as much of the public organically in as many decisions as possible. Her open-democratic process also builds in crowdsourced feedback loops and occasional referendums (direct public votes on choices) so that people who aren't currently governing don't feel shut out. Landemore also offers an extensive account of the historical antecedents of models like hers and ours.

perhaps that would be enough to allow us to say that everyone is indeed an author of the laws overall.[62]

Maybe, though, the ad hoc nature of populist choices of institutions to determine majority views implies that we can't be sure that enough policies will be decided through deliberative polls to make everyone the author of the laws that govern them. If so, a deliberative poll making binding law on a single issue denies people the right to author the laws that govern them would indeed be a problem. That suggests that deliberative polls should ordinarily be advisory or agenda setting rather than binding. As with all the arguments about designing populist institutions of governance, though, this is a guideline, not a rigid rule.

As we've said, deliberative polls are typically about one or a few issues. Citizen's assemblies are a version of deliberative polls that have been used for constitutional reforms, partly because constitutional reforms tend to involve more issues and partly because citizens' assemblies can build from the small fifty- to one hundred-person local groups to groups (sometimes of roughly the same size, sometimes a bit larger) organized regionally and then nationally.[63]

As does nearly every other analyst, we use Ireland and Iceland as our examples.[64]

- *Ireland.* The Irish parliament created a "constitutional convention" consisting of a mix of randomly chosen citizens (66 of 100 members) and politicians (33 members), and a chair chosen by the government.[65] The chair was Tom Arnold, an economist who had spent a great deal of time as the chief administrator of a number of NGOs. The parliament charged the convention with considering eight issues. It met over ten weekends starting in early 2012. On each issue the members received a briefing paper prepared by experts, then listened to a debate between advocates for competing positions, then held a discussion among themselves, after which they voted

---

[62] This is only a sketch of the argument, of course. The full argument develops the implications of the fact that you're an author of the laws that govern you even when your favored candidate lost, or when you vote for some candidate (who wins) because you agree with her position on the issues most important to you but disagree with her position on other issues.

[63] For a proposal (simultaneously utopian in scope and pragmatic in detail) for widespread use of citizens' assemblies with mostly agenda-setting power, *see* CAMILA VERGARA, SYSTEMIC CORRUPTION: CONSTITUTIONAL IDEAS FOR AN ANTI-OLIGARCHIC REPUBLIC (2020), ch. 9 (with the details laid out at pp. 250–64).

[64] For discussions of a somewhat similar process in Oregon, see Jäske & Majia Setälä, note 17 above, at pp. 99–100. They describe the Citizen's Initiative Review as "essentially a citizens' jury, which evaluates ballot initiatives" before balloting occurs. The panels have around twenty randomly chosen members who meet over several days. The members hear witnesses and ultimately generate a short statement of "key findings." The statement is then included with the informational material on the referendum that all voters receive.

[65] For a description of the first convention, *see* Eoin Carolan, *Ireland's Constitutional Convention: Behind the Hype about Citizen-Led Constitutional Change*, 13 INTERNATIONAL JOURNAL OF CONSTITUTIONAL LAW 733 (2015).

on the proposal. The convention recommended that referendums be held on a range of issues, including some the convention added to the list it had received from the parliament. It also recommended that another convention be assembled to deal with additional matters. The parliament authorized referendums on only two of the proposals. One, on marriage equality, succeeded; the other, on reducing the eligibility age for the nation's president from 35 to 21, failed.

Another convention was held in 2016–18, this one called a Citizens' Assembly. It fulfilled the agreement that produced a government coalition in 2016, and it had the same 100-person structure at the prior convention. It was charged with considering five specific issues including abortion and climate change. To illustrate its processes: on the issue of abortion, the assembly first discussed whether to eliminate or modify the existing constitution's ban on abortions, and whether new regulations should be inserted into the constitution or left up to the parliament. Having chosen the final option, the members then discussed a range of possible regulations, recording its votes on each alternative, presumably to inform parliament's later deliberations. The government held a referendum on the assembly's constitutional proposal, which was adopted by a two-thirds margin, and then parliament enacted a statute allowing abortions for any reason up to the twelfth week of a pregnancy, and for fetal abnormality or serious health risks to the woman up to viability.

- *Iceland.* For about a decade, a "crowd-sourced" constitution has been on Iceland's political agenda.[66] The first step was a "National Forum" convened by a nongovernmental organization after consultation with the legislature. The assembly brought together 1,000 people chosen at random from the national census list to discuss national problems.[67] Ultimately the assembly recommended adoption of a new constitution. The national legislature

---

[66]   ICELANDIC CONSTITUTIONAL REFORM: PEOPLE, PROCESSES, POLITICS (Ágúst Þór Árnason & Catherine Dupré eds. 2020), provides a detailed overview of the quite complex process, which we simplify dramatically. See especially Björg Thorarensen, "The Role and Impact of the Constitutional Commission in Preparing the Constitutional Revision," in *id.* at p. 77 (Thorarensen was a member of the Constitutional Commission); Salvör Nordal, "The Work of the 2011 Constitutional Council: A Democratic Experiment in Constitution-Making," in *id.* at p. 103. See also Jón Ólafsson, "Experiment in Iceland: Crowdsourcing a Constitution," available at https://www.academia.edu/ 1517443/Experiment_in_Iceland_Crowdsourcing_a_Constitution, archived at https://perma.cc/ 9J4X-NAT3; Thorvaldur Gylfason, "The Anatomy of Constitution-Making: From Denmark in 1849 to Iceland in 2017," in REDRAFTING CONSTITUTIONS IN DEMOCRATIC REGIMES: THEORETICAL AND COMPARATIVE PERSPECTIVES (Gabriel L. Negretto ed. 2021); Björg Thorarensen, "The People's Contribution to Constitutional Changes: Writing, Advising or Approving?—Lessons from Iceland," in CONTIADES & FOTIADOU, note 20 above, at p. 103.

[67]   According to Thorarensen, note 66 above, at p. 85, "Eventually, 950 people . . . attended the National Forum, with an almost equal gender balance and representation of all parts of the country. Every participant was paid a low fee for his or her role, and full travel cost was paid for those who traveled to Reykjavik."

then set up elections for a "constitutional assembly." Anyone could nominate himself or herself to sit in the assembly, but people currently serving as political party officers or holding political office were disqualified from serving. More than five hundred people ran for the twenty-five seats.

The constitutional assembly operated as a standard constitutional convention, except that it was internet accessible. Everything it did was almost immediately available on the internet, and it accepted suggestions from the public for constitutional provisions—the crowdsourcing part of its design. Some of these suggestions were of course lunatic, and some bolstered ideas that were already on the agenda, but the assembly took some crowdsourced suggestions seriously.

The public endorsed the constitution the assembly came up with, in a referendum that was technically only advisory to the legislature.[68] The legislature in turn stifled the proposal, partly because Iceland had recovered well from the financial crisis and partly because the legislature's political parties had opposed rewriting the constitution from the beginning. Elections in 2017 revived the idea of adopting the new constitution, because of the new Pirate Party's electoral success. Though that party was ultimately left out of the coalition government, its advocacy of constitutional reform kept the issue alive.[69]

We know that populist parties often support referendums on constitutional revision, and not only when, as in Ireland, such revisions can only be done by referendum. What's the relation between populism and other forms of direct democracy? Participatory budgeting's first major success came in the city of Porto

---

[68] Jón Ólafsson, "Crowdsourcing the 2011 Proposal for a New Constitution: When Experts and the Crowd Disagree," in ICELANDIC CONSTITUTIONAL REFORM, note 66 above, at p. 136, observes, "Foreign visitors observed that there seemed to be much more enthusiasm about the constitutional experiment abroad than within Iceland."

[69] LANDEMORE, note 48 above, at pp. 180–91, discusses the objections that we shouldn't generalize from Iceland's experience because it is small and culturally rather homogeneous. On size, she points to similar institutional forms used (in her view successfully) in India, Brazil, and France. On homogeneity, she questions the assumption that Iceland is dramatically more homogeneous than many other nations, and argues as well that widespread democratic participation might cause a form of homogeneity within the domain of politics. Perhaps similar arguments could be made about Ireland (which has certainly become more heterogeneous over the past one or two generations). We are interested in citizen assemblies as examples of multistage processes of participatory governance. The conditions for using such processes well are an important question, but one upon which there is almost certainly too little evidence to draw even tentative conclusions. We think that the most one can reasonably offer are informed speculations about possible limitations, although we suspect that many commentators will offer more than that. For a positive view of the Icelandic constitutional reform, see Zachary Elkins, Tom Ginsburg & James Melton, *A Review of Iceland's Draft Constitution*, CONSTITUTIONMAKING.ORG, University of Chicago, Oct. 15, 2012, available at http://comparativeconstitutionsproject.org/wp-content/uploads/CCP-Iceland-Report.pdf?6c8912, archived at https://perma.cc/G42F-ABZF.

Allegre, Brazil, when its mayor was a leading figure in the Workers Party, so perhaps we can count it as an innovation linked to a populist party.[70] We don't know of populist parties in power that have used deliberative polling or citizens assemblies. Some of Podemos's internal decision-making processes look a lot like citizen assemblies, as do some of M5S's, though, so we might stretch things a bit and say that those parties used citizen assemblies where it did have power, that is, within the party.

The Icelandic constitutional process was set in motion by a populist movement, though not by a populist party. The 2008 fiscal crisis led to a near collapse of the Icelandic economy, which in turn produced what Icelanders called the "pots and pans revolution," a sustained series of demonstrations in front of the nation's parliament building with a clear "us versus the bankers" theme. Groups in civil society began to press for constitutional reform through some sort of direct democracy. When the protests led one government to resign and another to take office, the civil-society agenda moved into parliament, with the government endorsing and providing a modest bit of structure to the citizen assembly process.[71] Then, when the reform project stalled because of opposition from the major political parties, its banner was taken up by the Pirate Party, which at least in its origins had a populist tinge.

The first Irish constitutional convention was entirely the product of an interaction between civil society and the established political parties.[72] The second, though, resulted from a coalition agreement in which one party insisted upon constitutional reform via a citizen assembly (rather than reform generated entirely by the political parties themselves). Ireland did see a political party taking direct democracy as part of its program and to that extent saw an existing party become more populist.

There's some evidence, though not much, that populist parties and these institutional innovations aren't entirely strangers to each other. Yet, for us it's not at all clear why the analysis of populism and constitutionalism can't encompass populist *movements*, as in Iceland, as well as populist parties. If it can,

---

[70] The Workers Party is a long-established political party and probably never really became a "populist" party, even when it was led by Luís Inácio Lula da Silva, but certainly falls in a category we can call "populist lite."

[71] The government's role in creating the process was brought home when the nation's Supreme Court voided the initial election of the twenty-five-member Citizens Council because of procedurally irregularities. The government then named the same twenty-five people to the Citizens Council, which then went forward with its work. Ólafsson, note 68 above, at p. 136, suggests that the Supreme Court's decision "may have contributed to public apathy about the Proposal." As a theoretical matter, the shift from elected to appointed members (even though the individuals were the same) reduced the democratic warrant for the council's actions.

[72] Levy, note 46 above, at pp. 346–48, describes a variety of forms of public consultations, now widely used around the world, that are collaborative efforts involving governments and direct public participation. Participatory budgeting can be regarded as one form of public consultation.

then—acknowledging that the evidence is thin because the innovations are relatively recent—we think that we can fairly associate the innovations with populism.

The stories we've told also illustrate (again to a modest extent) that institutions of direct democracy can be combined with representative institutions without difficulty. That's something we already knew from our observation of the limited use populist parties make of referendums, but it's worth emphasizing that it occurs in connection with deliberative polling and constitutional reform through citizen assemblies. We're sure that it would occur in connection with every other form of direct democracy as well. In some sense the reason is clear: if populists are anti-institutional and instrumental, they're going to be against using any one institution for all purposes. They're going to ask, "Given the nature of the problem we're trying to deal with, what's the best institutional mechanism for coming up with the best—or at least a better—answer?" Their answers will emerge from a pragmatic assessment of the circumstances at hand.

None of this is to say that these democratic innovations are without their problems. Professor Gavin Barrett worries that the timeline for the Irish citizen assemblies was too compressed and that the interactions between traditional institutions and democratic innovations will bias the assembly's composition and its agenda. When ordinary people deal with issues about government organization, their "relative lack of attachment . . . to the political process may lead to dislocation from political reality"—they will propose changes that sound good in the abstract, and might actually be good in the abstract, but that will fit badly with parts of the political system they don't propose to change.[73]

Barrett offers an interesting version of the usual concern about the ignorance of ordinary people. Another example is the view taken by some experts that the constitution drafted in Iceland had some technical flaws.[74] Political scientists Christopher Achen and Larry Bartels ground their skepticism about the quality of referendum outcomes in their assessment of citizen competence.[75] We note, though, their conclusion:

---

[73] Gavin Barrett, "Some Reflections Concerning Referendums in Ireland," in CONSTITUTIONAL CHANGE AND POPULAR SOVEREIGNTY: POPULISM, POLITICS AND THE LAW IN IRELAND (Maria Cahill, Colm O'Cinneide, Seán Ó Conaill, & Conor O'Mahony eds., 2020).

[74] Ólafsson, note 68 above, describes expert criticisms of the Icelandic proposal emanating from domestic scholars, writing, "A central target of this criticism was the lay character of the Proposal and the Constitutional Council's failure to meet the expectations of the academic community," at p. 129. In addition, the Venice Commission of the Council of Europe issued an opinion on the draft that offered mostly technical criticisms of some provisions. Venice Commission, Opinion on the Draft New Constitution of Iceland, Mar. 11, 2013, available at https://www.venice.coe.int/webforms/documents/?pdf=CDL-AD(2013)010-e, archived at https://perma.cc/VZ4W-KENU.

[75] CHRISTOPHER H. ACHEN & LARRY M. BARTELS, DEMOCRACY FOR REALISTS (2017), at pp. 73–85.

The lesson we draw ... is not that some direct popular control of policy-making is always undesirable. Rather, it is often costly, sometimes frighteningly costly— and a political culture that uncritically equates "good government" with "more democracy" will be ill-equipped to sensibly weight the benefits of greater popular control against the costs.[76]

We're not sure that populists have to disagree with this. Having available a suite of mechanisms of direct popular control seems to be compatible with the view they indirectly state, that direct popular control can sometimes be desirable. And, with a bit of word play we return to the point that evaluation must always be comparative: Populists don't "uncritically equate[] 'good government' with 'more democracy,' " they equate it with "more democracy than we have now."

[76] *Id.* at p. 85.

Epilogue

A wave of populism washed over the world in the early twenty-first century. Constitutionalists worried about populism because some of its manifestations were truly worrisome: Hungary, Poland, the Philippines, and the United States.

Perhaps, though, the wave might be ebbing. The V-Dem Institute's "Democracy Report 2020" had the title, "Autocratization Surges—Resistance Grows," and concluded by highlighting the fact that "democratization continues to progress around the world."[1] January 2021 did after all see *the end* of Donald Trump's term. As we pointed out in Chapter 4, the opposition in Hungary seems to have gotten its act together and is now in a stronger position to challenge Fidesz's parliamentary dominance than it has been. The Polish presidential election in 2020 saw a closer PiS victory than scholars would have thought a year earlier. Jair Bolsonaro's popularity has fluctuated wildly, and he might be at a low point when elections roll around in 2022. Rafael Correa and Evo Morales no longer hold office and are unlikely to do so in the future. Only Rodrigo Duterte—who might well now be a traditional authoritarian who remains in office by force of arms rather than by reasonably fair elections—and Narendra Modi seem entrenched enough to support a confident projection of worries about their regimes five or so years into the future.[2]

Meanwhile, left-leaning populists in Europe struggle to work themselves into governing coalitions. Their leaders and members worry about the possibility that doing so will betray their populist commitments but that failing to do will render them politically irrelevant. The number of referendums has escalated, and we're learning more about the conditions under which they produce good-enough public policy. Experiments in direct democracy on a small scale proliferate, and we expect that some will be scaled up.

---

[1] Anna Lührmann, Seraphine F. Maerz, Sandra Grahn, Nazifa Alizada, Lisa Gastaldi, Sebastian Hellmeier, Garry Hindle, & Staffan I. Lindberg, "Autocratization Surges—Resistance Grows: Democracy Report 2020," V-DEM INSTITUTE (2020), available at https://www.v-dem.net/en/publications/democracy-reports/, archived at https://perma.cc/U599-S7SE.

[2] Recep Tayyip Erdoğan hovers on the border between proto- and true authoritarian, and the losses his party sustained in 2019 make us uncertain about his prospects for re-election in 2023.

By now readers will have figured out that we're relatively sanguine about contemporary populism.[3] Its worst versions seem to us less stable than the literature on populism suggests and its better versions seem both interesting and modestly promising. We certainly hope that a few years from now we'll be seen as following the path of Hegel's "Owl of Minerva."

---

[3] For a similarly sanguine view, *see* Kurt Weyland, *Populism's Threat to Democracy: Comparative Lessons for the United States*, 18 PERSPECTIVES ON POLITICS 389 (2020) concluding that "[p]opulist leaders manage to suffocate democracy only when two crucial conditions coincide. First, institutional weakness . . . [and] [s]econd, even in weaker institutional settings populist leaders can only succeed . . . if acute yet resolvable crises . . . give them overwhelming support. . . .").

Index

For the benefit of digital users, indexed terms that span two pages (e.g., 52–53) may, on occasion, appear on only one of those pages.